THE LORD'S TEST

Don Bradman, whose superlative 254 in 1930 remains the highest Test score at Lord's Cricket Ground

THE LORD'S TEST

1884–1989

Steven Lynch

Foreword by David Frith

SPELLMOUNT LTD
TUNBRIDGE WELLS, KENT

In the Spellmount/Nutshell Cricket list:
The Test Match Career of Geoffrey Boycott
by C D Clark
The Test Match Career of Sir Jack Hobbs
by Clive W Porter
Cricket Anthology
by Samuel J Looker
Cricket at Hastings
by Gerald Brodribb
The Test Match Career of Walter Hammond
by Derek Lodge
Kent Cricketing Greats
by Dean Hayes
The Test Match Career of Ted Dexter
by Derek Lodge
Gloucestershire Cricketing Greats
by Dean Hayes

First published in the UK in 1990 by
SPELLMOUNT LTD
12 Dene Way, Speldhurst
Tunbridge Wells, Kent TN3 0NX

© Steven Lynch 1990

British Library Cataloguing in Publication Data
Lynch, Steven R., 1957–
  The Lord's test
  1. England. Cricket. Test matches.
  I. Title
  796.35865

  ISBN 0-946771-22-7

Printed in Great Britain by
Biddles Ltd, Guildford, Surrey

For my mother

ACKNOWLEDGEMENTS

All photographs of matches from 1972 to 1989 were provided by Patrick Eager, who also supplied the jacket photograph. Illustrations accompanying the match reports prior to 1971 come from the Sport & General Photographic Agency, David Frith, or the author's private collection. Although efforts have been made to trace the present copyright-holders of photographs, the publishers apologise in advance for any unintentional omission or neglect and will be pleased to insert the appropriate acknowledgement to companies or individuals in any subsequent edition of this book.

Foreword

Most people remember with notable clarity their first visit to Lord's. While being neither the world's oldest nor largest Test match ground, it is unquestionably the arena most steeped in history, 'liquid history' as an earlier cricket-writer described it; and he was not referring to the gin-and-tonic in the committee-room or the flat English beer in the bars around the ground. The effect of the architecture – principally of the great Victorian pavilion – and of the general ambience of the place is usually, to pilgrims, emotionally spectacular, while even the most hardened and long-term spectators reserve an exceptional sense of importance and anticipation for the journey to the still-developing cricket venue founded, at the third attempt, in 1814 by the shrewd Yorkshireman, Thomas Lord.

All this is without taking into account the awe customarily felt by the players themselves, particularly those from other lands, who may never have had the benefit of an earlier, low-key introduction to Lord's in a county match or two before descending those hero-trodden, sprig-pitted stairs in a Test match and passing through the cathedral-like Long Room, where the clapping always seems somehow a trifle irreverent. That clapping was actually tinged with relief in 1975 when David Steele finally appeared, having overshot on the staircase and finished up in the gents' toilet in the basement as he tried to find his way out to bat against Australia for the first time.

Readers will be reminded, from incidents noted herein, of their own presence at the ground on days sunlit or soggy. The memories of some will stretch back to England's only victory over Australia at Lord's this century, in 1934, or even to 10 years earlier, when Hobbs and Sutcliffe scored 200 runs before lunch against South Africa, and England 503 in the day. More recently, who recalls Greg Chappell hitting his first ball for six, or the dark days when Springbok Geoff Griffin was repeatedly no-balled for throwing? Then there was the prolonged agony of the Watson-Bailey salvation of England in 1953, and the golden partnership of Compton and Edrich in 1947. So much of Lord's Test match history is celebrated and hallowed: Bradman's perfect and dominant double-century in 1930 and Hammond's in 1938 place them in a the forefront of a cavalcade of heroes such as Jessop and Trumper and Verity and Massie.

There are, too, the lesser-known features. Walter Hadlee sent 36 bottles of beer into the Press-box in 1949 when New Zealand took their first-ever lead over England on first innings. There was the absurdity of Australia's captain, in 1884 when Lord's was an unpretentious little ground, substituting for England and catching one of his own men. The 1888 Test was over by 4.25 pm on the second day, an even greater absurdity. If any doubts remain that the game was regarded somewhat differently a century ago, Stoddart preferred to play for Middlesex than for England in 1890, while in 1896 F.S. Jackson, seeing his outfield catch missed when spectators impeded the Australian fielder, immediately offered another, which was safely held. And how many are aware that Lord's was once the setting for an Australia v South Africa Test?

For sheer nervous drama it is hard to separate 'Jock' Cameron's removal on a stretcher, when Tate thought he was dead, after being felled by a Larwood bouncer in 1929, and the genteel pandemonium that followed the bomb alert in

1973. Or was the final day of the 1963 England-West Indies Test the highest point of all?

The 84 Test matches at Lord's between 1884 and 1989 are recreated by Steven Lynch with a meticulous touch that I've observed from close range for several years. He questions apparent truths, like a good sleuth, and ferrets out the more obscure, like a keen prospector. He actually worked at Lord's for 10 years before a hat-trick of triumphs in the tough annual *Wisden Cricket Monthly* quizzes won him a place in the magazine's editorial department. Since then his grasp of matters historical, statistical and journalistic has increased to the point where channelling the knowhow into a book of significance and unique worth became only a matter of time.

Steven, if he was unaware previously, now knows all about the blood, sweat and perhaps even a few tears which inevitably go into the construction of a book entailing extensive research, with accuracy as the sacred precept. His story of the Lord's Tests has been spun from a wide variety of sources, and has been written with evident affection for the ground where he himself once worked. That ground can only loom even larger in history as the summers tick by. So do enjoy the tales of past battles. They must enhance your future enjoyment of events at the metropolitan cricket ground which is a walled-in world insulated from the often coarse and disappointing world around it.

Guildford, 1990   DAVID FRITH

Introduction

'For cricket-lovers there is no place like Lord's during a Test match. Lord's must be a bit like Heaven. There are many mansions in it. It caters for all tastes, classes, colours, ages, points of view, degrees of skill, levels of knowledge'

For me, the above quotation says everything about the unique atmosphere which prevails at the Lord's Test. The quote comes from *Hit Hard and Enjoy It*, written by the former Essex opener T.C. 'Dickie' Dodds, who, although he never actually appeared *in* a Lord's Test, has obviously been present *at* several.

Even though The Oval and, by a few weeks, Old Trafford staged international cricket in England before Thomas Lord's third ground, it was not long until the Lord's Test assumed a prime position in the minds of the public and, more importantly, the players, particularly those from overseas. Australia's Don Bradman, whose 254 in 1930 was perhaps the greatest of his many marvellous innings, set down his initial impressions of the place in his first book: 'How we all itched to get there! I found Lord's different from what it had been represented to me. It is a magnificent ground.' One of Bradman's successors as Australia's captain, Ian Johnson, expanded: 'Winning the Lord's Test of 1956 . . . gave me a greater thrill than any other win I have known. You see, even to play at Lord's is a great experience.'

Not all visitors to the place Sir Neville Cardus described as the 'Valhalla of cricketers' are impressed at first, however. India's greatest batsman, Sunil Gavaskar, wrote of his first visit: 'The ground is most uninspiring. It slopes from one end to the other. I shuddered to think of it as the Headquarters of cricket!' Keith Miller was another whose first view of Lord's left him unmoved, but both grew to appreciate the place, Gavaskar even delaying the announcement of his impending retirement to be sure of playing in the MCC Bicentenary match in 1987, which afforded him his last chance of reaching a century at Lord's, where he had surprisingly never previously exceeded 59 in a first-class match: he top-scored with 188.

Among England Test players, Sir Pelham Warner wrote that he 'loved every stick and stone of Lord's', while Denis Compton, another now immortalised with his 'own' stand at the ground, reckoned it 'the best place in the world to play'. Basil D'Oliveira, whose journey there was more convoluted than most, wrote simply: 'Lord's meant everything to me.'

Part of the mystique of Lord's lies in the fact that it is the nerve centre of world cricket. Many momentous decisions have been taken behind the imposing doors that cut off the committee-room from the ordinary member; perhaps this explains Clyde Walcott's delight at West Indies' first-ever win in 1950: 'We had won, not at Lord's, but at Headquarters!'

Things change, but it is still true to say that every cricketer worth his salt aspires to play at Lord's, while those blessed with special talent hope to excel in what remains constant as cricket's greatest event: the Lord's Test. Long may it remain so.

It remains for me to thank those without whom this book would have remained on the 'good-ideas' spike. Prominent among them is David Frith, the Editor of

Wisden Cricket Monthly, who sowed the first seeds back in 1985 when he tempted MCC's Cricket Office manager away from Lord's after 10 years: his evidence that his new acquisition could write anything more than a standard letter was flimsy, to say the least, but over the years under his guidance the letter-writer became a cricket-writer, of sorts. More pertinently, he provided the generous foreword and helped with picture-selection for this book. Publisher Ian Morley-Clarke, of Spellmount Ltd, jumped at the general idea with more speed than I had thought possible in the publishing world, while an earlier 'mentor', Trefor Jones, gave assistance in compiling the elusive close-of-play scores.

A frightening number of books and magazines were consulted during the preparation of the match reports but, like many before me, I have good reason to be grateful for the consistency and accuracy of *Wisden Cricketers' Almanack*. Another from the *Wisden* stable, Bill Frindall's *Wisden Book of Test Cricket*, was the starting-point for the scorecards.

I have dedicated this book to my mother, Gillian Rideout, in gratitude for her patience and support over the years (she even read the proofs!). If the original idea of a series of books chronicling the Test 'careers' of the major grounds comes to fruition, others may qualify for the same honour, notably my father Brian Lynch, my stepfather Professor Roger Rideout, and the other members of my family both here and in Australia – and, last but never least, Julie, the fairest of them all.

Banstead, 1990   STEVEN LYNCH

1884

Although in some ways it was a mixed year for MCC – their president, the Hon. Robert Grimston, died in office, the only one of the club's incumbent presidents to do so – 1884 did at least see Test cricket played at Lord's for the first time.

The teams came to Lord's all square, the first Test at Old Trafford having been drawn after Manchester's scheduled first day of Test cricket was rained off. At this time the England side was chosen by the ground authority staging the match, which meant that Lancashire's A.N. Hornby skippered the side at Old Trafford, but, appropriately enough, Lord Harris led out the England team at Lord's. MCC's committee also included, for his only Test anywhere, Stanley Christopherson, who later rose to be president of the club for a record span of time during the Second World War.

Australia's touring side was weakened by the absence of prominent players in Edwin Evans (always a reluctant tourist), Tom Garrett, Tom Horan and Hugh Massie, but nonetheless their strong bowling attack, which included 'The Demon' Spofforth, 'Joey' Palmer (considered as Spofforth's equal by many in Australia) and champion allrounder George Giffen, had posed problems in the truncated Old Trafford Test, where England were bowled out for 95 in the first innings. Australia's side also contained an intriguing character in W.E. 'Billy' Midwinter, playing the only Lord's Test of a nomadic career which, improbably, saw him appear for Australia against England in the very first Test of all, then for England against Australia, and finally for Australia against England once more.

Some 13,456 spectators paid to watch on July 21, the first day of Test cricket at Lord's. They saw Australia's captain Murdoch win the toss, and must have been delighted when left-armer Peate removed McDonnell for a duck. Peate worked steadily through the early order, dismissing the top five and eventually finishing with 6 for 85. From 93 for 6, Australia were rescued by 63 from Giffen and a resolute innings from H.J.H. 'Tup' Scott, who acquired his nickname on this tour for his liking for twopenny bus rides around London.

After adding 69 for the last wicket with Boyle, Scott, who hit 10 fours, was finally out in unusual fashion for 75. W.G. Grace had left the field after injuring a finger, and his substitute was none other than the Australian captain, Murdoch, who took the catch off Steel's legspin that ended the innings at 229.

Despite his injury, Grace began England's reply, in company with Lucas, but both openers fell to Palmer, and Giffen removed Shrewsbury before the close.

The second day saw a magnificent innings from A.G. Steel, who compiled the first Test century at Lord's. Steel made the most of a let-off at short leg when he had made 48, and reached his century in 170 minutes with an on-driven four off Midwinter. After two early wickets had fallen, captain Harris reputedly told the incoming batsman 'For Heaven's sake, Barlow, stop this rot!' – and the tenacious Lancastrian certainly did his best, contributing 38 to a stand of 98 in even time with Steel.

Steel went on to 148 – the highest innings scored against the Australians on their 32-match tour – before he was yorked by Palmer, having been dropped the ball before. Apart from his two chances Steel's domination was threatened only by an objection by Murdoch to the width of his bat (it was found to be legal on

A.G. Steel, the first Lord's Test centurymaker of them all

examination). The Australian captain's action was in retaliation for W.G.'s similar query against the bats of Bannerman and McDonnell in the first match of the tour, a friendly at Sheffield Park. On that occasion, McDonnell's bat was found to be too wide, and had to be shaved down.

Allan Gibson Steel, the first Lord's Test centurymaker, was a slight figure around 5ft 8ins in height. He had been a member of the Cambridge University side that beat the 1878 Australians, and by 1884 he was rated an allrounder second only to the great W.G. A clever legspinner, his bowling in this 1884 Test was restricted by a back injury.

The persistent Palmer finished with 6 for 111 from 75 four-ball overs, but England's lead of 150 looked likely to be decisive, especially as Spofforth's spikes had cut the pitch about. Ulyett, pitching into the rough, took three quick wickets that evening, his return catch to dispose of McDonnell being an especially fine effort.

On the final day Ulyett proved almost unplayable, ending up with 7 for 36 as Australia crumbled to 145 all out. The Yorkshireman also caused the retirement with a damaged left hand of Blackham, who rather unwisely had chosen to bat without gloves. Only Scott, who made 106 runs for once out in the match, passed 30 in Australia's disappointing second innings, and England emerged victorious from the first Lord's Test by an innings and 5 runs.

ENGLAND v AUSTRALIA
July 21, 22, 23, 1884

AUSTRALIA

P.S. McDonnell	b Peate	0	b Steel	20
A.C. Bannerman	b Peate	12	c and b Ulyett	27
* W.L. Murdoch	lbw b Peate	10	c Shrewsbury b Ulyett	17
G. Giffen	b Peate	63	c Peate b Ulyett	5
W.E. Midwinter	b Peate	3	(7) b Ulyett	6
G.J. Bonnor	c Grace b Christopherson	25	(5) c and b Ulyett	4
† J.M. Blackham	run out	0	(8) retired hurt	0
H.J.H. Scott	c sub (W.L. Murdoch) b Steel	75	(6) not out	31
G.E. Palmer	c Grace b Peate	7	b Ulyett	13
F.R. Spofforth	c Barlow b Grace	0	c Shrewsbury b Barlow	11
H.F. Boyle	not out	26	b Ulyett	10
Extras	(b5, lb3)	8	(bl)	1
	(105.2 overs)	229	(94.1 overs)	145

Fall: 0,25,32,46,88,93,132,155,160.   33,60,65,73,84,90,118,133,145.

Bowling: Peate 40-14-85-6, Barlow 20-6-44-0, Ulyett 11-3-21-0,
Christopherson 26-10-52-1, Grace 7-4-13-1, Steel 1.2-0-6-1.
Second innings: Peate 16-4-34-0, Christopherson 8-3-17-0, Ulyett 39.1-23-36-7,
Steel 10-2-26-1, Barlow 21-8-31-1.

ENGLAND

W.G. Grace	c Bonnor b Palmer	14	Bowling:
A.P. Lucas	c Bonnor b Palmer	28	Spofforth 55.1-19-112-2,
A. Shrewsbury	st Blackham b Giffen	27	Palmer 75-26-111-6,
G. Ulyett	b Palmer	32	Giffen 22-4-68-1,
A.G. Steel	b Palmer	148	Boyle 11-3-16-0,
* Lord Harris	b Spofforth	4	Bonnor 8-1-23-1,
R.G. Barlow	c Palmer b Bonnor	38	Midwinter 13-2-29-0.
W.W. Read	b Palmer	12	
† Hon. A. Lyttelton	b Palmer	31	
E. Peate	not out	8	
S. Christopherson	c Bonnor b Spofforth	17	
Extras	(b15, lb5)	20	
	(184.1 overs)	379	

Fall: 37,56,90,120,135,233,272,348,351.

Toss: Australia   Umpires: F.H. Farrands and C.K. Pullin
Close of play: (1) E. 90 for 3 (Ulyett 18)
(2) A. 73 for 4 (Giffen 4)
Blackham retired hurt at 94 for 6

ENGLAND WON BY AN INNINGS AND 5 RUNS

*A draw in the final Test at The Oval was enough to give England the Ashes. It was
a high-scoring match, Murdoch scoring the first Test double-century, while
McDonnell and Scott of Australia and England's W.W. Read all made hundreds.*

3

1886

The 1886 Australians, led by 'Tup' Scott, were an unhappy side: *Wisden's* account referred to the tour as 'a feeble and spiritless thing'. Already lacking experienced players like Bannerman, Boyle, Horan, McDonnell and Murdoch (the captain for Australia's last three visits), the team suffered a grievous blow when Spofforth injured a finger on his bowling hand, which meant that the 'Demon Bowler' was able to play in only half of the tourists' matches, although he was fit to play at Lord's. The star performer of the tour was the South Australian allrounder Giffen, who achieved the 'double' with 1424 runs and 154 wickets in first-class matches.

England, now under the captaincy of Steel, the hero at Lord's in 1884, won the low-scoring first Test by four wickets, and came to Lord's confident of tying up the three-match series.

Steel won the toss and, in the almost unvarying fashion of the day, opted to bat, even though rain had affected the pitch. W.G. was soon caught by 'Affie' Jarvis, who had replaced Blackham behind the stumps, although the Victorian kept his place in the side. The new batsman, Shrewsbury, was missed at slip off Garrett when he had scored only 1, but he stayed to add 50 with Scotton, a noted stonewaller, who made 19 before he was bowled by Garrett.

Shrewsbury went on to fashion one of the greatest innings seen in a Lord's Test. Jarvis missed a stumping when Shrewsbury had made 35, and he offered a sharp chance to short leg as well, Giffen being the unlucky bowler both times. Read and Steel came and went, but Barnes took root, sharing a stand of 161.

Shrewsbury, exhibiting great defensive skill in fending off shooters and kickers alike, had reached 91 by the end of the first day, which was shortened by 85 minutes by a shower soon after the start, and early on Day 2 he progressed to his century. After Barnes fell he continued to defy the best that Spofforth and the rest could hurl at him, to be last out for 164, after surviving 411 minutes. He hit 16 fours in what was, at the time, England's highest Test score (Grace surpassed it in the next Test).

Replying to England's imposing total of 353, Australia had no answer to the canny bowling of Lancashire's Johnny Briggs, who, aided by good English fielding, soon reduced the tourists to 67 for 6. Brothers-in-law Palmer and Blackham led a late rally, but the eventual total of 121 (Briggs 5 for 29) meant that Australia had to follow on.

Palmer's stout first-innings effort resulted in his promotion to open second time around, and he resisted for 2½ hours in scoring 48, by some way Australia's highest score of the match. His team-mates, however, were once again unable to come to terms with the wiles of Briggs, whose slow-medium left-armers from the Nursery end accounted for six more wickets, none of them needing assistance from other players. Australia subsided to 126 all out, England completing their second innings victory in successive Lord's Tests by 3.15 on the third day.

Shortly before the end Evans became the first player to complete a 'pair' in a Lord's Test – it was a miserable match for him, as he also failed to take a wicket. A much happier man was Briggs, who finished with match figures of 11 for 74, the first time a bowler had taken 10 or more wickets in a Test at Lord's.

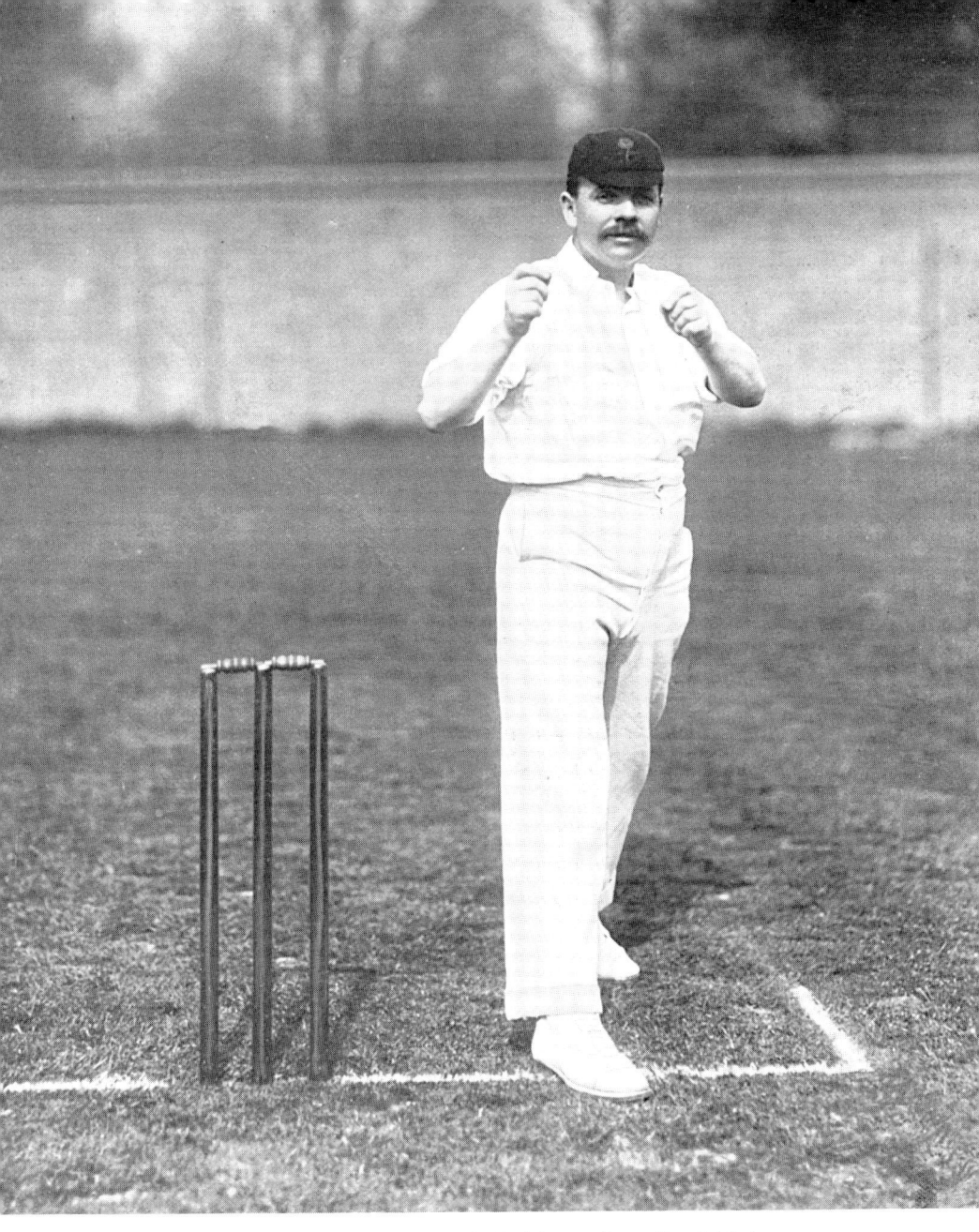

Lancashire's Johnny Briggs, who took 11 wickets as Australia subsided to an innings defeat in 1886

The overall paying attendance for the three days was 33,015, and the gate-money was distributed in a way which might bring a smile to the lips of the money-minded mandarins of today's Test & County Cricket Board: 80% of the gate went to the Australians, while the other 20%, which amounted to about £165, was presented to the Cricketers' Fund Friendly Society.

ENGLAND v AUSTRALIA
July 19, 20, 21, 1886

ENGLAND

W.G. Grace	c Jarvis b Palmer	18		Bowling:
W.H. Scotton	b Garrett	19		Garrett 72-40-77-2,
A. Shrewsbury	c Bonnor b Trumble	164		Evans 36-20-37-0,
W.W. Read	c Spofforth b Giffen	22		Palmer 38-15-45-1,
* A.G. Steel	lbw b Spofforth	5		Spofforth 56-26-73-4,
W. Barnes	c Palmer b Garrett	58		Trumble 14-4-27-2,
R.G. Barlow	c Palmer b Spofforth	12		Giffen 40-18-63-1,
G. Ulyett	b Spofforth	19		Jones 3-1-2-0.
† E.F.S. Tylecote	b Spofforth	0		
J. Briggs	c Jones b Trumble	0		
G.A. Lohmann	not out	7		
Extras	(b24, lb4, nb1)	29		
	(259 overs)	353		

Fall: 27,77,112,119,280,303,333,333,340.

AUSTRALIA

S.P. Jones	c Grace b Briggs	25	(4) b Briggs	17
* H.J.H. Scott	lbw b Briggs	30	(5) b Briggs	2
G. Giffen	b Steel	3	(6) b Barlow	1
A.H. Jarvis	b Briggs	3	(7) not out	13
G.J. Bonnor	c Grace b Steel	0	(8) b Briggs	3
J.W. Trumble	c Tylecote b Briggs	0	(3) c Tylecote b Barnes	20
G.E. Palmer	c Shrewsbury b Barnes	20	(1) c Lohmann b Barlow	48
† J.M. Blackham	b Briggs	23	(9) b Briggs	5
T.W. Garrett	not out	7	(2) b Briggs	4
F.R. Spofforth	b Barnes	5	(11) c and b Briggs	0
E. Evans	c Ulyett b Barnes	0	(10) run out	0
Extras	(b4, lb1)	5	(b13)	13
	(82.3 overs)	121	(111.1 overs)	126

Fall: 45,52,59,60,62,67,99,109,121. 6,56,91,95,98,105,120,126,126.

Bowling: Barnes 14.3-7-25-3, Lohmann 7-3-21-0, Briggs 34-22-29-5, Steel 21-8-34-2, Barlow 6-3-7-0.

Second innings: Briggs 38.1-17-45-6, Lohmann 14-9-11-0, Ulyett 8-3-13-0, Steel 16-9-14-0, Barnes 10-5-18-1, Barlow 25-20-12-2.

Toss: England   Umpires: F.H. Farrands and C.K. Pullin
Close of play: (1) E. 202 for 4 (Shrewsbury 91, Barnes 28)
                 (2) A. 12 for 1 (Palmer 2, Trumble 6)

ENGLAND WON BY AN INNINGS AND 106 RUNS

England wrapped up the series 3-0 with another innings victory at The Oval. As mentioned above, W.G. Grace broke Shrewsbury's new record with an innings of 170, and Surrey bowler George Lohmann took 12 wickets.

1888

The third Test at Lord's saw all 40 wickets fall for just 291 runs – easily the lowest match aggregate for a Lord's Test – with Australia's first-innings 116 being, by some way, the largest innings of the match.

Steel, captaining England for the last time, lost the toss in this, the first Test of a three-match series. The Australians, now captained by London-born Percy McDonnell, were without Spofforth and Palmer, their redoubtable bowlers of earlier tours, but had discovered an equally potent pairing in Turner – 'The Terror' – and Ferris, who were to take 18 of the 19 England wickets to fall to bowlers in this match and a combined total of 534 wickets in all matches on the tour.

The tourists' plans were also shaken by the absence of S.P. Jones, who contracted smallpox early on. Although he made a full recovery, managing to play in some of the later matches of the tour, the need to keep details of his illness private must have caused a strain.

In Jones's absence the Australians co-opted New South Wales-born allrounder Sammy Woods for the Tests. Woods was an undergraduate at Cambridge University at the time – in fact he never played State cricket in Australia – and his elevation was no doubt helped by his performances for the Gentlemen against the Players in the week immediately preceding the Lord's Test: he took five wickets in each of the three innings in which he bowled at Lord's and The Oval. His Test performances for Australia were disappointing, and he never played for them again – but he did make three further Test appearances for England, against South Africa (and he also played rugby for England).

Heavy overnight rain delayed the start of the match until three o'clock on the first day. Australia were soon in trouble, Alec Bannerman and Harry Trott both collecting ducks. The big-hitting Bonnor went for 6, but useful scores from McDonnell, Blackham, Woods and Edwards saw three figures onto the board. Yorkshire slow left-armer Peel took four wickets, Briggs three and Lohmann two.

Australia's 116 hardly seemed to be an imposing total, but England, 18 for 3 overnight, lost three more wickets with their score at 22, and were soon in danger of following on, their target being a meagre 36 (at the time the margin for a follow-on was only 80 runs), but a flourish from Briggs took the total to 53, England's lowest-ever at Lord's, Turner finishing with 5 for 27.

The mud pitch was now virtually unplayable, and Australia also struggled: Bannerman completed a 'pair', and only bowlers Turner and Ferris – probably inspired by the thought of bowling on such a spiteful pitch – made double figures as the visitors were all out for 60, their second-lowest total in a Lord's Test. Lohmann took four more wickets, as did Peel, who finished with match figures of 8 for 50.

England needed 124 to win, and 'The Champion', W.G. Grace, set off as if he meant business: Abel, making his Test debut in the most trying of circumstances, fell for 8, but the hammer blow fell when Grace was out for 24 (the highest score of the match) with England's total at 34. The last eight wickets gathered just 28 more runs as Turner (5 for 36) and Ferris (5 for 26) shared the spoils. The pair bowled unchanged throughout England's second innings, and brought the match

C.T.B. Turner – 'The Terror' – took 10 wickets in Australia's first win in a Lord's Test. Eight of his victims came during the sensational second day's play, where 27 wickets went down for 157 runs in little more than three hours

to a conclusion at 4.25 on the second day – a day which had seen a Test record 27 wickets go down, in just over three hours of actual playing time.

ENGLAND v AUSTRALIA
July 16, 17, 1888

AUSTRALIA

A.C. Bannerman	c Grace b Lohmann	0	b Peel	0
* P.S. McDonnell	c O'Brien b Peel	22	b Lohmann	1
G.H.S. Trott	c Lohmann b Peel	0	b Lohmann	3
G.J. Bonnor	b Lohmann	6	c Lohmann b Peel	8
† J.M. Blackham	b Briggs	22	run out	1
S.M.J. Woods	c Gunn b Briggs	18	c Grace b Peel	3
C.T.B. Turner	c Lohmann b Peel	3	c Grace b Briggs	12
J.D. Edwards	not out	21	c Sherwin b Lohmann	0
A.H. Jarvis	c Lohmann b Peel	3	(11) c Barnes b Peel	4
J. Worrall	c Abel b Briggs	2	b Lohmann	4
J.J. Ferris	c Sherwin b Steel	14	(9) not out	20
Extras	(b5)	5	(b3, lb1)	4
	(71.2 overs)	116	(29.2 overs)	60

Fall: 0,3,28,32,65,76,76,79,82. 1,1,13,15,18,18,18,42,49.

Bowling: Lohmann 20-9-28-2, Peel 21-7-36-4, Briggs 21-8-26-3, Barnes 6-0-17-0, Steel 3.2-2-4-1.

Second innings: Lohmann 14-4-33-4, Peel 10.2-3-14-4, Briggs 4-1-9-1, Steel 1-1-0-0.

ENGLAND

W.G. Grace	c Woods b Ferris	10	c Bannerman b Ferris	24
R. Abel	b Ferris	3	c Bonnor b Ferris	8
W. Barnes	c Jarvis b Turner	3	(9) st Blackham b Ferris	1
G.A. Lohmann	lbw b Turner	2	(10) st Blackham b Ferris	0
W.W. Read	st Blackham b Turner	4	(4) b Turner	3
T.C. O'Brien	b Turner	0	(5) b Turner	4
R. Peel	run out	8	(3) b Turner	4
* A.G. Steel	st Blackham b Turner	3	(6) not out	10
W. Gunn	c Blackham b Ferris	2	(7) b Ferris	8
J. Briggs	b Woods	17	(8) b Turner	0
† M. Sherwin	not out	0	c Ferris b Turner	0
Extras	(lb1)	1		0
	(50 overs)	53	(47 overs)	62

Fall: 5,14,18,22,22,22,26,35,49. 29,34,38,39,44,55,56,57,57.

Bowling: Turner 25-9-27-5, Ferris 21-13-19-3, Woods 4-2-6-1.
Second innings: Turner 24-8-36-5, Ferris 23-11-26-5.

Toss: Australia Umpires: F.H. Farrands and C.K. Pullin
Close of play: (1) E. 18 for 3 (Grace 10)

AUSTRALIA WON BY 61 RUNS

Following England's reverse at Lord's, Grace took over as captain, winning the other two Tests by an innings, Australia's highest total in the remaining four innings of the series being 100 at The Oval.

1890

By now, the Lord's Test was assuming its pre-eminent place in the minds of most cricketers and cricket-watchers: *Wisden*, for example, referred to the 1890 Lord's Test as 'emphatically the great match of the tour'. This sentiment was not quite all-pervasive, however. The amateur A.E. Stoddart declined to play for England at Lord's, preferring to play for Middlesex (things were worse for the second Test, though: Yorkshire refused to release Peel and Ulyett, and Stoddart again declined to play. Briggs was injured and missed both matches). By now, W.G. Grace had assumed what many saw as his rightful place as England's captain.

Despite the return of Murdoch as Australia's captain, the tourists once again had a disappointing time, losing more matches than they won. Alec Bannerman and Bonnor were late withdrawals from the selected side, as was George Giffen, who (as in 1888) refused to come as his brother was not chosen. As Walter Giffen's three-Test career resulted in innings of 2, 0, 1, 3, 3 and 2, one is bound to sympathise with the selectors, whose reputation, however, took rather a knock when they chose Ken Burn as reserve wicketkeeper – the Tasmanian had never kept wicket before in his life!

The Australians' bowling once again was carried by Turner and Ferris, who took 179 and 186 wickets respectively in first-class matches. The visitors were without Spofforth, who by now had settled in England. Playing for MCC against the tourists at Lord's, 'The Demon' curtailed a rumbustious knock of 99 (out of 117) in 75 minutes by Lyons, whom Sir Pelham Warner described as 'a man of granite strength . . . a great firm-footed hitter'.

The South Australian Lyons obviously had a liking for Lord's, for he led off the first Test in rousing fashion, reaching 50 out of 55 in 36 minutes. He was eventually yorked by Barnes for 55, made in 45 minutes and including eight fours.

Two quick wickets from Attewell, playing the only home Test of the 10 he was to play, pegged Australia back after their quick start, and when a wicket fell on the stroke of lunch the visitors were 109 for 4. After the interval, however, three quick wickets from Peel and more success for the persistent Attewell polished off the innings for the addition of another 23 runs.

England's reply began badly, with Grace offering a return catch to Turner from the second ball of the innings, and things went from bad to worse when Ferris removed Shrewsbury and Walter Read, the former to a smart piece of work by Blackham. Overall, the Australians' fielding was most impressive, with Syd Gregory, making the first of an eventual record nine Lord's Test appearances by an overseas player, being particularly outstanding.

The situation was rescued by Maurice Read and Ulyett, who shared a partnership of 72 in 90 minutes, then Ulyett, now in concert with Peel, saw out the day. On the second morning, the pair took England into the lead. Ulyett eventually fell for 74, and England were all out for 173, with occasional bowler Lyons (5 for 30) returning by far his best bowling figures in Test cricket.

By 1.40 on the second day Australia were batting again, and they made a poor start, losing Turner for 2 and Trott for a duck, Peel taking both wickets. Lyons, batting at No. 4 this time, made a quickfire 33 in 25 minutes, but wickets tumbled at regular intervals, Lohmann taking three and Grace two as Australia declined to 168 for 9, a lead of 127, by the close.

The sturdy Jack Lyons was Australia's star in 1890: he rushed to his first-innings half-century in just 36 minutes, and later took five wickets

The one bright spot for Australia was in the batting of Barrett, a dour left-hander playing in his first Test. A doctor from Melbourne, he batted throughout Australia's second innings, which ended early on the third morning, surviving for four hours 40 minutes and becoming the first player in all Tests to carry his bat through a completed innings. Only three batsmen (W. Bardsley, W.A. Brown and G.M. Turner) have since achieved the feat in a Lord's Test.

Despite Barrett's heroics, England needed only 137 to win, and a fine innings of 75 not out from Grace – surprisingly, 'The Champion's' highest score in a Lord's Test – saw them safely home by seven wickets.

ENGLAND v AUSTRALIA
July 21, 22, 23, 1890

AUSTRALIA

J.J. Lyons	b Barnes	55	(4) c Attewell b Peel	33
C.T.B. Turner	b Attewell	24	lbw b Peel	2
* W.L. Murdoch	c and b Attewell	9	(5) b Lohmann	19
J.E. Barrett	c Grace b Ulyett	9	(1) not out	67
G.H.S. Trott	run out	12	(3) b Peel	0
S.E. Gregory	b Attewell	0	c Lohmann b Barnes	9
P.C. Charlton	st MacGregor b Peel	6	lbw b Grace	2
† J.M. Blackham	b Peel	5	c Barnes b Grace	10
J.J. Ferris	b Attewell	8	lbw b Lohmann	8
E.J.K. Burn	st MacGregor b Peel	0	(11) c MacGregor b Attewell	19
H. Trumble	not out	1	(10) c Barnes b Lohmann	5
Extras	(lb3)	3	(lb2)	2
	(86 overs)	132	(140.2 overs)	176

Fall: 66,82,93,109,111,113,120,131,131. 6,8,48,84,106,109,119,136,142.

Bowling: Lohmann 21-10-43-0, Peel 24-11-28-3, Attewell 32-15-42-4,
Barnes 6-2-16-1, Ulyett 3-3-0-1.

Second innings: Attewell 42.2-22-54-1, Peel 43-23-59-3, Ulyett 6-2-11-0,
Lohmann 29-19-28-3, Grace 14-10-12-2, Barnes 6-3-10-1.

ENGLAND

* W.G. Grace	c and b Turner	0	not out	75
A. Shrewsbury	st Blackham b Ferris	4	lbw b Ferris	13
W. Gunn	run out	14	c and b Ferris	34
W.W. Read	c and b Ferris	1	b Trumble	13
J.M. Read	b Lyons	34	not out	2
G. Ulyett	b Lyons	74		
R. Peel	c and b Trumble	16		
W. Barnes	b Lyons	9		
G.A. Lohmann	c and b Lyons	19		
† G. MacGregor	b Lyons	0		
W. Attewell	not out	0		
Extras	(lb2)	2		0
	(110.1 overs)	173	(3 wkts) (75 overs)	137

Fall: 0,14,20,20,92,133,147,162,166. 27,101,135.

Bowling: Turner 35-17-53-1, Ferris 40-17-55-2, Trott 3-0-16-0, Lyons 20.1-7-30-5,
Trumble 12-7-17-1.

Second innings: Turner 22-12-31-0, Lyons 20-6-43-0, Ferris 25-11-42-2, Trumble 8-1-21-1.

Toss: Australia   Umpires: A. Hill and C.K. Pullin
Close of play: (1) E. 108 for 5 (Ulyett 45, Peel 8)
                (2) A. 168 for 9 (Barrett 63, Burn 15)

ENGLAND WON BY 7 WICKETS

*England retained the Ashes with a victory in a low-scoring match at The Oval; the
third Test, scheduled for Old Trafford, was abandoned without a ball being
bowled.*

1893

The familiar figure of W.G. Grace was missing from a Lord's Test for the first time in 1893. The good doctor had injured a finger, and A.E. Stoddart – who had declined the invitation to play at Lord's in 1890 – took over as captain. Flowers of Nottinghamshire replaced Grace, although Walter Read (unavailable) had been the original choice as replacement.

One interesting character who might have played in this Test but did not was C.J. Kortright, the Essex bowler rated as one of the fastest of all: he took 7 for 73 for the Gentlemen against the Players at Lord's the previous week, but was not selected (indeed, he was destined never to appear in a Test).

With Murdoch having appeared for England in a Test in South Africa, Blackham assumed the captaincy of Australia. The 'Prince of Wicketkeepers' was making his eighth and last tour of England, and in Grace's absence he became the only player to appear in each of the first five Lord's Tests. However, he was not an inspired choice as leader. The team's results were indifferent, and there were reports hinting at misbehaviour by some of the players. Australia were strengthened, though, by the return of George Giffen, who had missed the previous two visits. During the 1891-92 season, Giffen had achieved one of the greatest allround feats in cricket history: for South Australia against Victoria at Adelaide, he had scored 271, then took 16 wickets.

In the Lord's Test, the first of the series, new captain Stoddart won the toss, and batted first despite rain having gingered up the pitch. Another masterful display by Shrewsbury, who became the first player to amass 1000 runs in Tests when 7, offset the loss of two early wickets to the impressive Turner.

Shrewsbury took an hour to reach double figures, but slowly he took control. His partner, F.S. Jackson, was playing in his first Test, but seemed unaffected by nerves: he batted stylishly to reach his half-century, at which point he was dropped at mid-on. Jackson made the most of his let-off, and proceeded to 91, with 13 fours, before he was splendidly caught low down by wicketkeeper Blackham, whose remark to the departing batsman sounds unlikely today: 'Bad luck, young fellow. It was an awful fluke!' The young Yorkshireman and Shrewsbury had put on 137.

Meanwhile, Shrewsbury rolled on. Missed off Bruce by mid-off when 40 and again 30 runs later, this time at long-on off Giffen, he reached his second Lord's Test century with his ninth four: it took him four hours. Soon afterwards, he was out for 106, another victim for the persevering Turner, who finished with 6 for 67 as England totalled 334.

There was time remaining on the first day for Australia to reach 33 for the loss of two important wickets. Earlier in the tour Lyons had continued his love affair with Lord's with a barnstorming innings of 149 in 95 minutes against MCC (he reached his century in an hour and hit 22 fours in all). Now he fell to Lockwood, one of four England debutants, for 7, and the same bowler bowled Giffen for a duck.

Lockwood continued his good work on the second morning, taking all the wickets as Australia declined to 75 for 5. At this point Gregory, still scoreless after 25 minutes, was joined by Harry Graham, another player new to Test cricket. They set about the bowling to such good effect that in the 80 minutes

Arthur Shrewsbury, who scored his second Lord's Test century in 1893. Shrewsbury became the first batsman to amass 1000 Test runs during his innings

leading up to lunch 120 runs were scored, with Graham, who became known as 'The Little Dasher', reaching 50 in 55 minutes. Sir Pelham Warner later recalled the pair's 'brilliant strokeplay and fearless and rapid running'.

Gregory (57) fell to Lockwood soon after the interval, but Graham, who had made 82 at the time, soon reached his century, which had taken him 125 minutes in all. Shortly afterwards, Mold had Graham caught behind: he had offered three chances, but had hit 12 fours and a five (a single plus four overthrows). After Graham's demise the innings folded for 269, giving England a lead of 67.

Once more, Shrewsbury was to the fore when England batted again. Stoddart went for 13, but county colleagues Shrewsbury and William Gunn then added 152 for the second wicket, an England record which stood until 1932-33. Shrewsbury was unlucky to miss his second hundred of the match, becoming one of Giffen's five victims. At lunch on the third day, Stoddart became the first captain to declare an innings during a Test, setting the visitors a victory target of 300, but rain set in to wash out any further play.

ENGLAND v AUSTRALIA
July 17, 18, 19, 1893

ENGLAND

A. Shrewsbury	c Blackham b Turner	106	b Giffen		81
* A.E. Stoddart	b Turner	24	b Turner		13
W. Gunn	c Lyons b Turner	2	c Graham b Giffen		77
F.S. Jackson	c Blackham b Turner	91	c Bruce b Giffen		5
J.M. Read	b Bruce	6	c McLeod b Bruce		1
R. Peel	c Bruce b Trumble	12	(9) not out		0
W. Flowers	b McLeod	35	(6) b Turner		4
E. Wainwright	c Giffen b Turner	1	b Giffen		26
W.H. Lockwood	b Bruce	22	(7) b Giffen		0
† G. MacGregor	not out	5			
A.W. Mold	b Turner	0			
Extras	(b19, lb9, nb2)	30	(b16, lb9, w1, nb1)		27
	(125 overs)	334	(8 wkts dec) (116.4 overs)		234

Fall: 29,31,168,189,213,293,298,313,333.   27,179,195,198,198,198,234,234.

Bowling: Turner 36-16-67-6, Bruce 22-4-58-2, Trumble 19-7-42-1, Trott 9-2-38-0, McLeod 21-6-51-1, Giffen 18-3-48-0.

Second innings: Turner 32-15-64-2, McLeod 25-11-28-0, Giffen 26.4-6-43-5, Trumble 11-2-33-0, Bruce 20-10-34-1, Trott 2-0-5-0.

AUSTRALIA

J.J. Lyons	b Lockwood	7	Bowling:
A.C. Bannerman	c Shrewsbury b Lockwood	17	Peel 22-12-36-0,
G. Giffen	b Lockwood	0	Lockwood 45-11-101-6,
G.H.S. Trott	c MacGregor b Lockwood	33	Mold 20.1-7-44-3,
R.W. McLeod	b Lockwood	5	Jackson 5-1-10-0,
S.E. Gregory	c MacGregor b Lockwood	57	Wainwright 11-3-41-0,
H. Graham	c MacGregor b Mold	107	Flowers 11-3-21-1.
W. Bruce	c Peel b Mold	23	
C.T.B. Turner	b Flowers	0	
H. Trumble	not out	2	
*† J.M. Blackham	lbw b Mold	2	
Extras	(b15, lb1)	16	
	(114.1 overs)	269	

Fall: 7,7,50,60,75,217,264,265,265.

Toss: England   Umpires: W. Hearn and J. Phillips
Close of play: (1) A. 33 for 2 (Bannerman 9, Trott 4)
                (2) E. 113 for 1 (Shrewsbury 45, Gunn 43)

MATCH DRAWN

England won the second Test at The Oval, Jackson scoring 103 and Briggs taking 10 wickets, and the home side regained the Ashes (lost in 1891-92) when the third Test, at Old Trafford, was drawn.

1896

Few Test matches at Lord's have had such a remarkable start as the 1896 match. Harry Trott, in his first match as captain, won the toss and chose to bat on what appeared to be a perfect pitch: within minutes Australia had lost three wickets for four runs, and they were all out in 75 minutes for 53, their lowest-ever Test score at Headquarters. Earlier in the tour the Australians had been humbled for 18 by MCC at Lord's, Dick Pougher taking 5 for 0.

The architect of the startling Test collapse was Surrey's fast bowler Tom Richardson, who bowled all six of his victims, beating most of them for pace. He had the advantage of bowling from the pavilion end, where there was no sightscreen, and he was assisted by Lohmann, who took 3 for 13 in his last Test. Of the Australians, only Darling, Gregory and Eady reached double figures.

Much to their astonishment, England were batting before lunch, and a stout partnership of 105 ensued between Grace, captaining England in what turned out to be his last Lord's Test, and Abel: the Surrey man, let off in the slips when 9, hit 13 fours and was unlucky to miss his century by six runs. Grace weathered some fiery bowling from Jones to score 66, while Jackson contributed 44 as England made their way to 286 for 8 – a commanding lead of 233 – by the close.

A huge crowd estimated at 30,000 (25,514 paid, plus a substantial number of members) watched the exciting proceedings on that first day, but their conduct left something to be desired, showing that bad crowd behaviour is no recent innovation. *The Times* was quite indignant: 'Lord's has scarcely ever before been the scene of so much noisiness and rowdyism as was displayed yesterday when the crowds encroached on the ground.' Many of the spectators had little or no sight of the play, and quite frequently the crowd spilled over onto the playing area. During one such incursion, Darling in the deep field was obstructed as he attempted to catch Jackson: the batsman immediately gave his wicket away by repeating the stroke.

No such problems marred the second day's play. Many potential spectators stayed away, thinking that England had the match won. The absentees seemed to have chosen correctly when Australia were soon in trouble at 3 for 2 after Trott had finished off the England innings for 292. Giffen and his captain took the score to 62 before Richardson claimed his ninth wicket of the match, but his 10th was a long time coming.

Trott and Gregory set about them, adding 90 in 65 minutes before lunch, and continued in like vein after the interval, eventually adding 221 in 161 minutes, a record partnership for all Tests at the time. Gregory, becalmed on 93 for 20 minutes, eventually fell for 103, which included 13 fours. Trott was out five minutes later for 143 (24 fours), but he had been given not out after a confident appeal for a slip catch off Jackson when 61, and he had also had an adventurous trip through the 'nervous nineties': when 98, wicketkeeper Lilley had dropped him off Richardson, and one run later the Australian captain might well have been run out.

The fine stand between Trott and Gregory had put Australia back in front, but J.T. Hearne, plying his thoughtful medium-pacers on his home ground, took five wickets as the tourists slid to 347 all out. The final wicket to go was that of

The hardworking Surrey favourite Tom Richardson crossed the river to take 11 wickets in 1896: he and George Lohmann bowled unchanged through Australia's miserable first innings of 53

Donnan, who had sustained an injury and came in last after opening in the first innings. Batting virtually one-handed, he resisted for a while and added 29 valuable runs with Kelly.

England needed 109 to win, and scored 16 of them for the loss of Abel on the second evening (*note that England's first wicket fell at 6, not 16 as shown in most modern reference books*). A victory seemed a formality, but overnight rain affected the pitch, complicating the task. Grace and Hayward fell cheaply, and the speedy Jones was a fearsome prospect in indifferent light. Brown, with a patient 36, steadied the ship, and Stoddart saw England home with an undefeated 30, but it might have been a different story had Australia hung on to all their catches, with Kelly – who had taken over from the venerable Blackham behind the stumps – proving especially fallible.

England's celebrations might have been muted had they known that this was to be their last victory over Australia at Lord's until 1934 – and England have not managed to beat the 'Old Enemy' at HQ since then.

ENGLAND v AUSTRALIA
June 22, 23, 24, 1896

AUSTRALIA

H. Donnan	run out	1	(11) b Hearne	8
J. Darling	b Richardson	22	b Richardson	0
G. Giffen	c Lilley b Lohmann	0	b Richardson	32
* G.H.S. Trott	b Richardson	0	c Hayward b Richardson	143
S.E. Gregory	b Richardson	14	c Lohmann b Hearne	103
H. Graham	b Richardson	0	b Richardson	10
C. Hill	b Lohmann	1	b Hearne	5
C.J. Eady	not out	10	(1) c Lilley b Richardson	2
H. Trumble	b Richardson	0	(8) c Lilley b Hearne	4
† J.J. Kelly	c Lilley b Lohmann	0	(9) not out	24
E. Jones	b Richardson	4	(10) c Jackson b Hearne	4
Extras	(b1)	1	(b7, lb4, w1)	12
	(22.3 overs)	53	(133 overs)	347

Fall: 3,3,4,26,26,31,41,45,46.   0,3,62,283,289,300,304,308,318.

Bowling: Richardson 11.3-3-39-6, Lohmann 11-6-13-3.
Second innings: Richardson 47-15-134-5, Lohmann 22-6-39-0, Hayward 11-3-44-0, Hearne 36-14-76-5, Jackson 11-5-28-0, Grace 6-1-14-0.

ENGLAND

* W.G. Grace	c Trumble b Giffen	66	c Hill b Trumble	7
A.E. Stoddart	b Eady	17	(5) not out	30
R. Abel	b Eady	94	(2) c sub (F.A. Iredale) b Jones	4
J.T. Brown	b Jones	9	c Kelly b Eady	36
W. Gunn	c Kelly b Trumble	25	(6) not out	13
F.S. Jackson	c Darling b Giffen	44		
T.W. Hayward	not out	12	(3) b Jones	13
† A.F.A. Lilley	b Eady	0		
G.A. Lohmann	c sub (F.A. Iredale) b Giffen	1		
J.T. Hearne	c Giffen b Trott	11		
T. Richardson	c Hill b Trott	6		
Extras	(b5, lb2)	7	(b3, lb4, w1)	8
	(107.4 overs)	292	(4 wkts) (47.1 overs)	111

Fall: 38,143,152,197,256,266,266,267,286.   6,20,42,82.

Bowling: Jones 26-6-64-1, Giffen 26-5-95-3, Eady 29-12-58-3, Trott 7.4-2-13-2, Trumble 19-3-55-1.
Second innings: Jones 23-10-42-2, Trumble 20-10-37-1, Eady 3-0-11-1, Giffen 1-0-9-0, Trott 0.1-0-4-0.

Toss: Australia   Umpires: J. Phillips and W.A.J. West
Close of play: (1) E. 286 for 8 (Hayward 12, Hearne 11)
              (2) E. 16 for 1 (Grace 7, Hayward 4)

ENGLAND WON BY 6 WICKETS

Australia squared the 1896 series with a win at Old Trafford, despite the efforts of K.S. Ranjitsinhji, who scored 62 and 154 not out on his Test debut. The England side was still selected by the ground authority, and MCC had, after lengthy discussions, decided not to pick Ranji, but Lancashire had no such qualms. England took the three-match series with a win at The Oval, thereby retaining the Ashes, but overall the Australians – who toured without Bruce, Lyons and Turner, stalwarts of previous visits – could be satisfied with their tour; they won 19 and lost only six of their matches. The great allrounder Giffen, on his last tour, once again achieved the 'double', as he had in 1886 and 1893.

1899

The Test programme for 1899 established a pattern which remained largely unchanged for many years until the advent of 'twin tours' and six-Test summers in the 1960s. For the first time in England, five Tests were played, Lord's being allocated the second of them, a position and a time (mid-June) that, barring exceptional circumstances, still prevails.

A further improvement was the setting-up of a proper selection committee to choose the England side – this task had previously been the responsibility of the ground authority, an arrangement which occasionally led to some eccentric and parochial choices. England's first selectors were W.G. Grace, H.W. Bainbridge of Warwickshire and Lord Hawke. Following a drawn first Test at Old Trafford during which the bulky W.G., nearly 51, had found fielding difficult, the other members of the committee were spared a potentially embarrassing decision when 'The Champion' retired from Test cricket.

Lancashire's Archie MacLaren, who was destined to be captain in more Ashes Tests than anyone else, was the slightly surprising choice as Grace's replacement (Jackson was thought to have better credentials, and MacLaren was out of practice), and his bowling attack was particularly raw, Jessop, Mead and Townsend appearing in their first Tests and Rhodes in his second. Australia's side, capably led by the no-nonsense left-hander Joe Darling, looked strong, and in the first Test they had given a first cap to a 21-year-old from Sydney. He was Victor Trumper, destined to adorn and enliven the 'Golden Age' of cricket.

MacLaren won the toss but was soon the first victim of an extremely quick spell from Jones, who, operating from the Nursery end, finished up with Test-best figures of 7 for 88. Ranji, attempting his famous leg glance, sent a return catch to Jones, and in an hour England were deep in trouble at 66 for 6. Jackson, with 73, and the mighty hitter Jessop (51) counterattacked with a stand of 95 which took little more than an hour, but England's eventual total of 206 was disappointing.

Two quick wickets from Rhodes reduced Australia to 28 for 2, and when Jessop dismissed Gregory at 59 it seemed that honours were roughly equal. However, Hill and Noble now combined in a stand which saw out the first day and stretched to 130 on the second morning until Noble fell to Rhodes after making 54. Hill, who had survived a stumping chance when 82, was 92 when Trumper joined him, and soon reached his second Test century; he went on to 135 before being brilliantly caught in the deep by Fry, one of eight England players appearing in their first Test at Lord's. Hill hit 17 fours in his four-hour stay.

Trumper now took centre stage. H.S. Altham wrote, rather picturesquely, that 'before he had batted for half an hour it was obvious that a new star of unsurpassed brilliance and charm had joined the cluster of the Southern Cross'. Trumper swept to his first Test century in 145 minutes, and when he ran out of partners he had hit 20 fours in his chanceless 135.

Facing a deficit of 215, England were soon in trouble at 6 for 2, and despite a sterling 77 from Hayward and a masterly undefeated 88 from down the order by MacLaren, the final total of 240 left Australia needing only 26 to win. Jones had taken another three wickets, making 10 in the match, while Laver's tempting

The legendary hitter Gilbert Jessop faces Ernie Jones in this panoramic view of Lord's as it was at the end of the last century. The picture is taken from what is now the Warner Stand, looking towards the Mound

swingers had accounted for three important middle-order batsmen. Trumble, a great bowler who, strangely, never shone at Lord's, made an important breakthrough when he caught-and-bowled Jackson just before stumps on the second day.

Australia knocked off the required runs without difficulty, the openers being the captain, Darling, and Worrall, who was making his second (and last) Lord's Test appearance 11 years after his first.

ENGLAND v AUSTRALIA
June 15, 16, 17, 1899

ENGLAND

* A.C. MacLaren	b Jones	4	(6) not out		88
C.B. Fry	c Trumble b Jones	13	b Jones		4
K.S. Ranjitsinhji	c and b Jones	8	c Noble b Howell		0
C.L. Townsend	st Kelly b Howell	5	b Jones		8
F.S. Jackson	b Jones	73	c and b Trumble		37
T.W. Hayward	b Noble	1	(1) c Trumble b Laver		77
J.T. Tyldesley	c Darling b Jones	14	c Gregory b Laver		4
G.L. Jessop	c Trumper b Trumble	51	c Trumble b Laver		4
† A.F.A. Lilley	not out	19	b Jones		12
W. Mead	b Jones	7	(11) lbw b Noble		0
W. Rhodes	b Jones	2	(10) c and b Noble		2
Extras	(b2, lb6, w1)	9	(b2, lb2)		4
	(80.1 overs)	206	(117.4 overs)		240

Fall: 4,14,20,44,45,66,161,184,194.

5,6,23,94,160,166,170,212,240.

Bowling: Jones 36.1-11-88-7, Howell 14-4-43-1, Noble 15-7-39-1, Trumble 15-9-27-1.

Second innings: Jones 36-15-76-3, Howell 31-12-67-1, Noble 19.4-8-37-2, Trumble 15-6-20-1, Laver 16-4-36-3.

AUSTRALIA

J. Worrall	c Hayward b Rhodes	18	not out	11
* J. Darling	c Ranjitsinhji b Rhodes	9	not out	17
C. Hill	c Fry b Townsend	135		
S.E. Gregory	c Lilley b Jessop	15		
M.A. Noble	c Lilley b Rhodes	54		
V.T. Trumper	not out	135		
† J.J. Kelly	c Lilley b Mead	9		
H. Trumble	c Lilley b Jessop	24		
F. Laver	b Townsend	0		
E. Jones	c Mead b Townsend	17		
W.P. Howell	b Jessop	0		
Extras	(lb4, nb1)	5		0
	(170.1 overs)	421	(0 wkt) (11 overs)	28

Fall: 27,28,59,189,271,306,386,387,421.

Bowling: Jessop 37.1-10-105-3, Mead 53-24-91-1, Rhodes 39-10-108-3, Jackson 18-6-31-0, Townsend 15-1-50-3, Ranjitsinhji 2-0-6-0, Hayward 6-0-25-0.

Second innings: Jessop 6-0-19-0, Rhodes 5-1-9-0.

Toss: England   Umpires: T. Mycroft and W.A.J. West
Close of play: (1) A. 156 for 3 (Hill 72, Noble 42)
              (2) E. 94 for 4 (Hayward 42)

AUSTRALIA WON BY 10 WICKETS

The remaining three Tests were drawn, Australia thus retaining the Ashes (won in 1897-98) by virtue of their victory at Lord's. Rain robbed England of a probable victory in the third Test (Headingley's first), and the home side could not capitalise on their advantage after making Australia follow on at Old Trafford and The Oval.

1902

The first Lord's Test of the new century is remembered for all the wrong reasons. Only 105 minutes' play was possible on the first day, rain washed out play entirely on the second day, and the ground was so waterlogged that the match was abandoned before the scheduled start time on Day 3.

The watery match was thus a great disappointment to England followers, who had seen Australia bowled out for 36 (their alltime low) in the first Test at Edgbaston. There, again, rain had ruined any chance of an England victory, only 75 minutes' play being possible on the third day as the tourists followed on.

The abbreviated Lord's Test was not without incident. Australia had gone into the match with several injury problems, and were forced to field Saunders, who had tonsillitis, as well as Darling and Noble, who had recently recovered from influenza. Rain delayed the start until 2.45, and it was so cold that some of the Australians took the field with their blazers under their sweaters.

In miserable conditions Hopkins, opening the attack for the only time in his Test career after taking 7 for 10 against Cambridge University in the previous match, induced Fry to play what *Wisden* called 'a deplorable stroke' to be caught by Hill; he then bowled Ranjitsinhji. Both failed to score (Ranji's three Test innings at Lord's brought him scores of 8, 0 and 0), and England were 0 for 2. After breaking his duck, Jackson gave a chance at slip which would have made it 1 for 3, but he survived and, with MacLaren, exhibited some fine strokeplay in taking England to 102 for 2, at which point rain set in.

The great stylist Victor Trumper had sprung to prominence with a memorable
century in the 1899 Lord's Test – but rain prevented him from repeating his feat in 1902

ENGLAND v AUSTRALIA
June 12, 13 (no play), 14 (no play), 1902

ENGLAND

* A.C. MacLaren	not out	47	Bowling:
C.B. Fry	c Hill b Hopkins	0	Jones 11-4-31-0,
K.S. Ranjitsinhji	b Hopkins	0	Hopkins 9-3-18-2,
Hon.F.S. Jackson	not out	55	Saunders 3-0-15-0,
J.T. Tyldesley			Trumper 8-1-33-0,
† A.F.A. Lilley			Armstrong 5-0-5-0,
G.H. Hirst			Noble 2-2-0-0.
G.L. Jessop	did not bat		
L.C. Braund			
W.H. Lockwood			
W. Rhodes			
Extras		0	
	(2 wkts) (38 overs)	102	

Fall: 0,0.

AUSTRALIA
V.T. Trumper, R.A. Duff, A.J.Y. Hopkins, C. Hill, S.E. Gregory, *J. Darling, M.A. Noble, W.W. Armstrong, †J.J. Kelly, E. Jones, J.V. Saunders.

Toss: England   Umpires: C.E. Richardson and V.A. Titchmarsh
Close of play: (1) E. 102 for 2 (MacLaren 47, Jackson 55)

MATCH DRAWN

The remainder of the 1902 series included two of the most famous encounters in Test history. After Australia won Sheffield's one and only Test, they retained the Ashes with an agonisingly close 3-run win at Old Trafford. England scraped home by one wicket in an equally engrossing final Test at The Oval, Jessop's famous 104 rescuing the home side, chasing 263, from the depths of 48 for 5.

1905

Rain, which had ruined the 1902 Lord's Test, returned three years later to wash out what promised to be an interesting final day's play, with England looking to build on an already substantial lead of 252. In a way, the teams and spectators were fortunate to get in as much cricket as they did, as 10 days of rain preceded the match and thunderstorms punctuated each night during the game.

England went into the match one-up, having recorded a convincing victory at Trent Bridge, where MacLaren made 140 and Bosanquet, the 'inventor' of the googly, spun out the tourists with 8 for 107 in the final innings. Australia seemed more fallible than in 1902: bowlers Trumble, Jones and Saunders were missing, and captain Darling had played little cricket in the interim. The tourists' swiftest bowler, Cotter, was injured, which led to both sides taking the field without a recognised fast bowler.

The Hon. F.S. Jackson won the toss, as he was to do in all five Tests of the summer against Darling. Coincidentally, both captains shared the same date of birth. England started well enough, considering that the light was generally dismal and the ground soggy, and MacLaren scored 56 in 2½ hours. Armstrong, bowling defensively down the leg side, had a three-hour spell, emerging with 2 for 41 from 30 overs. Equally gritty innings from Tyldesley and Fry took England to the strong position of 208 for 3, but from there they declined to 258 for 9 before a late flourish on the second morning took the score to 282. The stylish Fry, whose 73 was his highest score in a Lord's Test, recalled that he was not happy when given out by 'that obstinate umpire Jim Phillips (who had no-balled Fry for throwing a few years previously) when I hit the toe of my front boot at least a foot away from the ball'. Fry adds that he queried the caught-behind decision '. . . of course, after the match . . .'

Overnight rain had gingered up the pitch on the second day, and Trumper (barely recovered from a back strain that he had suffered during the first Test) and Duff decided that attack was the best policy, hitting up 57 in 33 minutes before being separated – one nonchalant stroke over the ropes leading to a new shot, the 'Trumper flick', being added to cricket's glossary. Armstrong and Darling were the only other batsmen to pass 16 as Australia were bustled out for 181, conceding a lead of 101. All England's bowlers enjoyed success, with Rhodes taking three wickets and Jackson four. It was to be a golden year for Jackson, who topped the batting (492 runs at 70.29) and bowling (13 wickets at 15.46) averages for both sides in this series, as well as winning all five tosses.

Another fine innings from MacLaren was the highlight of England's second innings, which saw them reach 151 for 5 by the close, at which point Fry had survived 90 minutes for 36.

There was no resumption on the third day, more rain leading to the formal abandonment at lunchtime. In some ways, this was justice for Australia, who had suffered the worst of the conditions, but it was unfortunate for England that the sterling efforts of MacLaren and Fry had gone unrewarded.

Trumper faces Yorkshire's Schofield Haigh in the 1905 Lord's Test, another match ruined by bad weather

ENGLAND v AUSTRALIA
June 15, 16, 17 (no play), 1905

ENGLAND

A.C. MacLaren	b Hopkins	56	b Armstrong	79
T.W. Hayward	lbw b Duff	16	c Laver b McLeod	8
J.T. Tyldesley	c Laver b Armstrong	43	b Noble	12
C.B. Fry	c Kelly b Hopkins	73	not out	36
* Hon.F.S. Jackson	c Armstrong b Laver	29	b Armstrong	0
A.O. Jones	b Laver	1	c Trumper b Armstrong	5
B.J.T. Bosanquet	c and b Armstrong	6	not out	4
W. Rhodes	b Hopkins	15		
† A.F.A. Lilley	lbw b McLeod	0		
S. Haigh	b Laver	14		
E.G. Arnold	not out	7		
Extras	(b20, lb2)	22	(b2, lb4, nb1)	7
	(140 overs)	282	(5 wkts) (50 overs)	151

Fall: 59,97,149,208,210,227,257,258,258.   18,63,136,136,146.

Bowling: McLeod 20-7-40-1, Laver 34-8-64-3, Armstrong 30-11-41-2, Noble 34-13-61-0, Duff 7-4-14-1, Hopkins 15-4-40-3.

Second innings: McLeod 15-5-33-1, Laver 10-4-39-0, Noble 13-2-31-1, Armstrong 10-2-30-3, Hopkins 2-0-11-0.

AUSTRALIA

V.T. Trumper	b Jackson	31	Bowling:
R.A. Duff	c Lilley b Rhodes	27	Haigh 12-3-40-2,
C. Hill	c Bosanquet b Jackson	7	Rhodes 16.1-1-70-3,
M.A. Noble	c Fry b Jackson	7	Jackson 15-0-50-4,
W.W. Armstrong	lbw b Jackson	33	Arnold 7-3-13-1.
* J. Darling	c Haigh b Arnold	41	
S.E. Gregory	c Jones b Rhodes	5	
A.J.Y. Hopkins	b Haigh	16	
C.E. McLeod	b Haigh	0	
F. Laver	not out	4	
† J.J. Kelly	lbw b Rhodes	2	
Extras	(b3, lb5)	8	
	(50.1 overs)	181	

Fall: 57,73,73,95,131,138,171,175,175.

Toss: England   Umpires: J. Phillips and W. Richards

Close of play: (1) E. 258 for 8 (Lilley 0)
                (2) E. 151 for 5 (Fry 36, Bosanquet 4)

MATCH DRAWN

The third Test at Headingley was drawn, Jackson and Tyldesley scoring centuries, as was the fifth, at The Oval, where Tyldesley (again), Fry and Australia's Duff reached three figures. England clinched the series with another win at Old Trafford, Jackson scoring another century and local man Walter Brearley taking eight wickets on his debut. England thus retained the Ashes, won by P.F. Warner's team in 1903-04: Warner, although a selector, did not play in this 1905 series.

1907

South Africa's first Test match was in 1888-89 (although the participants didn't realise it at the time, the match being accepted as a Test at a later date) and they had made three tours of England and played 16 Tests in their own country before they were judged fit to appear in a Test match in England. Fittingly, South Africa's first overseas Test was to be played at Lord's.

South Africa's strength lay in their renowned quartet of legspin/googly bowlers, who had refined Bosanquet's plaything into a fine art. Schwarz (137 wickets at 11.79), Vogler (119 at 15.62), Faulkner (64 at 15.82) and White (56 at 14.73) took 376 wickets on the tour: Faulkner also scored 1163 runs. Their success was largely responsible for the tourists winning eight of the 11 matches that led up to the first Test, so their confidence was high (so, too, were the crowds, who flocked in to see these spin wizards: about 50,000 attended the two days of this Lord's Test, 30,000 on the second day).

England were captained, for this season only, by R.E. 'Tip' Foster, whose entry into Test cricket is still unmatched: at Sydney in 1903-04 he hit 287, sharing a fifth-wicket stand of 192 with Len Braund, who also scored a century, as he was to do at Lord's in 1907.

After a solid opening stand and 52 from the consistent Tyldesley, the loss of Foster and Hirst in rapid succession saw England decline to 158 for 5, all five wickets having fallen to the versatile spinner Vogler, an interesting character who had been on the groundstaff at Lord's for a while in a vain attempt to qualify for Middlesex. England's captain Foster described Vogler as 'the greatest bowler playing cricket in either hemisphere at the present time'.

Fortunately for England, though, the incoming batsman, Gilbert Jessop, was no respecter of reputations. Braund, who went on to complete a vital century in the only innings of his two Lord's Tests, played the minor role in a partnership of 145 as Jessop went on the rampage, hitting 93 in 76 minutes, to the delight of the large first-day crowd. 'The Croucher' faced only 63 balls, and hit 14 fours, being especially severe on fast bowler Kotze, a Boer farmer, whose pace had impressed on previous tours.

Vogler ended the fun eventually, his final figures 7 for 128 as England rounded off the day with a total of 428. In reply, South Africa made a dreadful start on the second morning, losing openers Shalders and Sherwell, and first-drop man Hathorn, with 18 on the board. A partnership of 98 between Nourse (dropped by Hirst in the slips when 29) and Faulkner (missed by Blythe at mid-on when 31) rectified matters, but from 134 for 4 the tourists' last six wickets clattered for just six runs in the space of 24 balls. Arnold finished up with the flattering figures of 5 for 37, which included the wickets of White and Sinclair in successive deliveries, both being bowled by balls that came back a long way.

Following on, South Africa soon lost Shalders for a duck, and seemed set to succumb in two days. However, their skipper, Percy Sherwell, had other ideas. An accomplished allround sportsman who had played cricket for Cornwall (he was at school there) and went on to play tennis for South Africa, Sherwell had batted at No. 9, 10 or 11 throughout the 1905-06 series between the countries, but promoted himself to open in this match because of the poor form of other

One of the earliest examples of the scorer's 'run-chart' illustrates Jessop's rapid 93 during South Africa's first overseas Test, at Lord's in 1907

batsmen. His gamble paid off handsomely, as he sped to his maiden first-class century in just 90 minutes; he was the first wicketkeeper to reach three figures in a Test in England. Sherwell, whose late-cut was particularly productive, shared a stand of 139 with Hathorn, who made 30, and although Blythe eventually halted Sherwell's romp after the captain had hit 18 fours in his 105-minute stay, by the close South Africa had reached 185 for 3, still 103 behind but much better off than seemed likely at one stage.

The scene was set for an interesting third day, but rain set in and, infuriatingly, the final day of the Lord's Test was washed out for the third time running.

ENGLAND v SOUTH AFRICA
July 1, 2, 3 (no play), 1907

ENGLAND

C.B. Fry	b Vogler	33	Bowling:
T.W. Hayward	st Sherwell b Vogler	21	Kotze 12-2-43-0,
J.T. Tyldesley	b Vogler	52	Schwarz 34-7-90-0,
* R.E. Foster	st Sherwell b Vogler	8	Vogler 47.2-12-128-7,
L.C. Braund	c Kotze b Faulkner	104	White 15-2-52-0,
G.H. Hirst	b Vogler	7	Nourse 1-0-2-0,
G.L. Jessop	c Faulkner b Vogler	93	Faulkner 12-1-59-1,
J.N. Crawford	c Sherwell b Schwarz	22	Sinclair 6-1-22-0.
E.G. Arnold	b Schwarz	4	
† A.F.A. Lilley	c Nourse b Vogler	48	
C. Blythe	not out	4	
Extras	(b24, lb6, w2)	32	
	(127.2 overs)	428	

Fall: 54,55,79,140,158,303,335,347,401.

SOUTH AFRICA

W.A. Shalders	c Lilley b Arnold	2	b Hirst	0
*† P.W. Sherwell	run out	6	b Blythe	115
C.M.H. Hathorn	c Foster b Hirst	6	c Fry b Blythe	30
A.W. Nourse	b Blythe	62	not out	11
G.A. Faulkner	c Jessop b Braund	44	not out	12
S.J. Snooke	lbw b Blythe	5		
G.C. White	b Arnold	0		
J.H. Sinclair	b Arnold	0		
R.O. Schwarz	not out	0		
A.E.E. Vogler	c Lilley b Arnold	3		
J.J. Kotze	b Arnold	0		
Extras	(b9, lb2, w1)	12	(b15, lb2)	17
	(65 overs)	140	(3 wkts) (58 overs)	185

Fall: 8,8,18,116,134,135,135,137,140.   1,140,153.

Bowling: Hirst 18-7-35-1, Arnold 22-7-37-5, Jessop 2-0-8-0, Crawford 8-1-20-0, Blythe 8-3-18-2, Braund 7-4-10-1.

Second innings: Hirst 16-8-26-1, Arnold 13-2-41-0, Blythe 21-5-56-2, Braund 4-0-26-0, Crawford 4-0-19-0.

Toss: England   Umpires: A. Millward and A.A. White

Close of play: (1) E. 428 all out

(2) S.A. 185 for 3 (Nourse 11, Faulkner 12)

MATCH DRAWN

England won the second Test, a low-scoring affair at Headingley, with left-arm spinner Colin Blythe taking 15 wickets for just 99 runs. The final Test, at The Oval, was drawn, despite Fry's 129, his last Test century. Blythe took seven more wickets to finish with 26 in the three-match series.

1909

Australia were once again the visitors in 1909, with their captain Monty Noble making his fourth and last tour of England. It was the last tour, too, for Trumper, Hill, Cotter and Ransford, although they were not aware of it at the time: a dispute with the fledgling Australian Board of Control (formed in May 1905) would keep them out of the 1912 tour.

England, once again under the captaincy of Archie MacLaren, won the first Test by 10 wickets, the visitors being bowled out for 74 and 151. Blythe, who took 11 wickets at Edgbaston, and Fry (giving evidence in defence of his brother-in-law, who was facing fraud charges at the Old Bailey; he was acquitted) were not available for the Lord's Test, and the selectors rather surprisingly made three further changes, sending England into the match without a fast bowler.

Noble, correctly forecasting that the pitch would pose problems, put England in after winning the toss, the first time that a captain had opted to field first in a Test in this country. Noble won the toss in each of the five Tests, making up for F.S. Jackson's similar success for England in 1905.

The Surrey pair of Hobbs, in his first Lord's Test, and Hayward, in his last, put on 23, but then three quick wickets reduced England to 44 for 3. Cotter, who took 4 for 80, posed problems to the middle-order batsmen. Tyldesley made 46, and at the end Lilley, in his sixth and last Lord's Test, contributed a plucky 47, but the top-scorer in the disappointing total of 269 was J.H. King, the 38-year-old allrounder from Leicestershire who was making his one and only Test appearance. A left-hander with bat and ball, he contributed a useful 60 with the willow and later, rather surprisingly opening the bowling, had the mortifying experience of seeing Trumper and Ransford dropped in the same over.

Hirst had earlier removed Laver, but Relf chipped away at Australia's batting to good effect, finishing with 5 for 85 as a memento of his only Lord's Test appearance. The great Trumper's last Test innings at Lord's brought him 28 runs: he missed the 1912 tour and, much-mourned, died of Bright's disease in 1915.

Although the pitch was easier on the second day, Bardsley's 46 was topped only by fellow left-hander Ransford, who was lucky to survive three chances, two off the luckless King, MacLaren at slip dropping one and wicketkeeper Lilley grassing another. Ransford gave another chance in the slips off Relf's bowling when he had reached 61, but made the most of his luck by going on to 143 not out, batting in all for 245 minutes and hitting 21 fours. Ransford, whose only Test century this was, later in life succeeded the former Test bowler Hugh Trumble as secretary of Melbourne Cricket Club, defeating Don Bradman – then at the height of his fame – in a ballot in 1938.

Facing a deficit of 81, England made 16, for the loss of Hobbs, on the second evening. For the first time since 1899 rain did not wash out the third day of a Lord's Test, but England no doubt wished that it had. The home side slumped to 41 for 6, in the face of fine bowling from Armstrong, who achieved plentiful turn and, thanks to his huge frame, a lot of bounce. Only Jones, MacLaren and, at the death, Lilley reached double figures as England subsided embarrassingly to 121, and Armstrong, the 'Big Ship', had taken 6 for 35, the best Test figures of his distinguished career.

Vernon Ransford, who rode his luck to make the only Test century of his career at
Lord's in 1909

Australia needed only 41 to square the series, and achieved this for the loss of
Bardsley's wicket.

ENGLAND v AUSTRALIA
June 14, 15, 16, 1909

ENGLAND

T.W. Hayward	st Carter b Laver	16	run out		6
J.B. Hobbs	c Carter b Laver	19	c and b Armstrong		9
J.T. Tyldesley	lbw b Laver	46	st Carter b Armstrong		3
G. Gunn	lbw b Cotter	1	b Armstrong		0
J.H. King	c Macartney b Cotter	60	b Armstrong		4
* A.C. MacLaren	c Armstrong b Noble	7	(8) b Noble		24
G.H. Hirst	b Cotter	31	b Armstrong		1
A.O. Jones	b Cotter	8	(6) lbw b Laver		26
A.E. Relf	c Armstrong b Noble	17	(10) b Armstrong		3
† A.F.A. Lilley	c Bardsley b Noble	47	(9) not out		25
S. Haigh	not out	1	run out		5
Extras	(b8, lb3, w3, nb2)	16	(b2, lb3, nb10)		15
	(107.2 overs)	269	(60.5 overs)		121

Fall: 23,41,44,123,149,175,199,205,258. 16,22,22,23,34,41,82,90,101.

Bowling: Laver 32-9-75-3, Macartney 8-3-10-0, Cotter 23-1-80-4, Noble 24.2-9-42-3, Armstrong 20-6-46-0.

Second innings: Laver 13-4-24-1, Cotter 18-3-35-0, Noble 5-1-12-1, Armstrong 24.5-11-35-6.

AUSTRALIA

P.A. McAlister	lbw b King	22	not out		19
F. Laver	b Hirst	14			
W. Bardsley	b Relf	46	(2) c Lilley b Relf		0
W.W. Armstrong	c Lilley b Relf	12			
V.S. Ransford	not out	143			
V.T. Trumper	c MacLaren b Relf	28			
* M.A. Noble	c Lilley b Relf	32			
S.E. Gregory	c Lilley b Relf	14	(3) not out		18
A. Cotter	run out	0			
C.G. Macartney	b Hirst	5			
† H. Carter	b Hirst	7			
Extras	(b16, lb8, w1, nb2)	27	(b4)		4
	(119.5 overs)	350	(1 wkt) (15.4 overs)		41

Fall: 18,84,90,119,198,269,317,317,342. 4.

Bowling: Hirst 26.5-2-83-3, King 27-5-99-1, Relf 45-14-85-5, Haigh 19-5-41-0, Jones 2-0-15-0.

Second innings: Hirst 8-1-28-0, Relf 7.4-4-9-1.

Toss: Australia Umpires: C.E. Dench and J. Moss
Close of play: (1) A. 17 for 0 (McAlister 4, Laver 13)
(2) E. 16 for 1 (Hayward 5)

AUSTRALIA WON BY 9 WICKETS

Australia, whose early tour form had been patchy, went from strength to strength after their Lord's Test success. They lost only once more, some three months later in a festival match at Scarborough. The tourists won the third Test at Headingley, with Macartney, who was to become much better known as a batsman, taking 11 wickets. The remaining two Tests were drawn, Bardsley becoming, at The Oval, the first to score centuries in each innings of a Test. Noble thus retained the Ashes, which he had won in 1907-08.

1912i

The 1912 season was a busy one, with Lord's – for the one and only time – staging three Test matches. In all, nine Tests were crammed into the summer's programme as the first (and last) Triangular Tournament was played. The brainchild of South African businessman Sir Abe Bailey, a triangular competition between the three Test-playing countries of the day nearly came off in 1909, but in the event it became a reality three years later.

Several factors doomed the event to failure. First, the weather interfered with several matches – notably the first two England-Australia encounters – and secondly the South Africans were not the force they had been during their impressive first Test tour of England in 1907. On the largely damp pitches of 1912, their famed googly bowlers were not as effective as five years previously (although Faulkner again achieved the 'double'), and the most potent of the 1907 quartet, Vogler, was missing, apparently after a disagreement with Sir Abe. Finally, the Australian team was decidedly second-rate, after a dispute over the choice of tour manager between the top players and the Australian Board led to the so-called 'Big Six' – Armstrong, Carter, Cotter, Hill, Ransford and Trumper – withdrawing from the tour. In their absence Australia, captained by the 42-year-old Syd Gregory, stood little chance of success. Gregory, who first appeared at the ground in 1890, played his eighth and ninth Lord's Tests during the tournament, to establish a record by an overseas player which is unlikely ever to be beaten.

The tournament started with Australia's easy victory over South Africa at Old Trafford, where legspinner Jimmy Matthews, whose international career otherwise was unremarkable, took a hat-trick in both innings, a feat unique at Test level.

Reeling from their innings defeat, South Africa came to Lord's to face the England side, captained by C.B. Fry. A great theorist, the mercurial Fry had had but one meeting with his fellow selectors – Harry Foster and John Shuter – during May, at which they chose the England sides, together with agreed reserves, for each of the six Tests. England's team for the first match saw master bowler S.F. Barnes and Kent genius Frank Woolley making their first Test appearances at HQ, while Pelham Warner, in his last international season, fittingly made his first Test appearance at his beloved Lord's.

Rain, the bugbear of the season and of recent Lord's Tests, delayed the start of play until soon after three o'clock, but England made up for lost time by demolishing South Africa on the damp pitch for a paltry 58. Extras (17) top-scored, and only Nourse managed to reach double figures. England's opening bowlers, Barnes and Frank Foster, were irresistible, as they had been in Australia the previous winter, where they shared 66 wickets in England's 4-1 series win. In South Africa's innings, which lasted under an hour and a half, Foster hit the stumps five times and also took two catches off Barnes: no other player was involved in any of the 10 dismissals.

England had an early setback when Hobbs (4) played on to Nourse, but Rhodes and Spooner (dropped at 50) took the score to 122 for 1 by the close. Rhodes left early on the second morning, but the elegant Spooner, whose cricket

The three captains for Test cricket's one and only Triangular Tournament: South
Africa's Yorkshire-born leader Frank Mitchell (left); the great allround athlete
C.B. Fry, having his only taste of Test captaincy for England (centre); and the
veteran Australian skipper Syd Gregory, who had made his first tour of England in
1890 and, in 1912, appeared in his eighth and ninth Lord's Tests – a record by an
overseas player that is unlikely to be beaten

opportunities were limited by the demands of his business career, went on to
reach his only Test century, hitting 13 fours and a six in all during his three-hour
stay. Woolley hit out well, striking seven fours and a six in his 73, and put on 113
in 75 minutes with Warner. At 320 for 4 a huge score seemed to be on the cards,
but the last six wickets went down for only 17 runs, all to Pegler; bowling now
from the Pavilion end, he finished with the splendid figures of 7 for 65. Yet
another high-class legspinner, Pegler took 189 wickets on the tour.

South Africa still faced a sizable deficit of 279, and a two-day defeat seemed
likely when three wickets went down for 36. Llewellyn and Faulkner, however,
had other ideas, and although the latter was out soon before bad light brought an
early close, Llewellyn was still there with 60. 'Buck' Llewellyn was an interesting
character who played for Hampshire for a dozen seasons from 1899 and, despite
the fact that he was born and bred in South Africa, he was included in England's
squad of 14 for the first Test in 1902, only to be omitted from the final XI.

Foster removed Llewellyn early on the final morning, and from then on South
Africa slid quietly to defeat before the lunch interval, although their total of 217
represented a vast improvement on their first-innings effort. Barnes picked up six
more wickets and Foster three, with Nourse being run out. Unusually, of the 29
wickets to fall to bowlers in the match, 20 were bowled.

ENGLAND v SOUTH AFRICA
June 10, 11, 12, 1912

SOUTH AFRICA

G.P.D. Hartigan	c Foster b Barnes	0	b Foster		1
H.W. Taylor	lbw b Barnes	1	b Barnes		5
A.W. Nourse	b Foster	13	run out		17
C.B. Llewellyn	b Foster	9	c Smith b Foster		75
G.A. Faulkner	b Foster	7	b Barnes		15
S.J. Snooke	b Barnes	2	b Foster		16
* F. Mitchell	c and b Barnes	1	b Barnes		1
R.O. Schwarz	c Foster b Barnes	4	b Barnes		28
S.J. Pegler	b Foster	4	b Barnes		10
C.P. Carter	b Foster	0	not out		27
† T. Campbell	not out	0	c Jessop b Barnes		3
Extras	(b12, lb3, nb2)	17	(b17, lb1, nb1)		19
	(26.1 overs)	58	(82 overs)		217

Fall: 2,3,28,35,36,42,45,54,55. 5,17,36,104,132,135,147,176,197.

Bowling: Foster 13.1-7-16-5, Barnes 13-3-25-5.
Second innings: Foster 27-10-54-3, Barnes 34-9-85-6, Brearley 6-2-4-0, Woolley 4-0-19-0, Hobbs 11-2-36-0.

ENGLAND

J.B. Hobbs	b Nourse	4	**Bowling:**
W. Rhodes	b Nourse	36	Nourse 16-5-46-3,
R.H. Spooner	c Llewellyn b Nourse	119	Pegler 31-8-65-7,
* C.B. Fry	b Pegler	29	Faulkner 29-6-72-0,
P.F. Warner	st Campbell b Pegler	39	Carter 4-0-15-0,
F.E. Woolley	b Pegler	73	Llewellyn 9-0-60-0,
G.L. Jessop	b Pegler	3	Schwarz 20-3-44-0,
F.R. Foster	lbw b Pegler	11	Hartigan 10-2-14-0.
† E.J. Smith	b Pegler	2	
S.F. Barnes	not out	0	
W. Brearley	b Pegler	0	
Extras	(b11, lb9, w1)	21	
	(119 overs)	337	

Fall: 4,128,183,207,320,323,324,330,337.

Toss: South Africa   Umpires: W. Richards and W.A.J. West
Close of play: (1) E. 122 for 1 (Rhodes 36, Spooner 67)
(2) S.A. 114 for 4 (Llewellyn 60, Snooke 5)

ENGLAND WON BY AN INNINGS AND 62 RUNS

1912ii

With South Africa showing such poor form, the matches pitting England against Australia held the key to the tournament. The Lord's encounter between the old rivals therefore was keenly awaited, and more than 35,000 paid to come into the ground over the three days – but rain again did its worst and condemned the match to end in a draw.

England made two changes from the previous match, Dean and Hearne coming in for Brearley and Jessop. For Australia, Victorian batsman David Smith made his debut.

Fry won the toss and chose to bat, but rain drove the players from the field after only 11 balls had been bowled. Returning after lunch to an ever more unpredictable pitch, Hobbs and Rhodes applied themselves diligently, the Yorkshireman for once outscoring his more illustrious partner with 52 of the first 77 runs of their partnership, which eventually reached 112. One of the delights of their association was their perfectly-judged running between the wickets, honed during their monumental stand of 323 at Melbourne earlier in the year, which remained an Ashes record until surpassed by Marsh and Taylor of Australia in 1989.

After another delay for rain, Hobbs continued to defy the treacherous pitch, reaching one of his greatest centuries before he was bowled by a perfect legbreak from Emery, having batted for 167 minutes and hit 15 fours. England reached a satisfactory 211 for 4 by the end of the truncated day.

One discordant note was sounded by critics of the bowling action of Australian medium-pacer Gervys Hazlitt, *Wisden* recording that 'two famous cricketers, who were in the pavilion, condemned it in no measured terms'. Hazlitt tried to correct his action, with some success, during the later stages of the tour, and was never no-balled for throwing during his career, which was cut short by his untimely death through heart trouble in 1915. Hazlitt, just 27, joined Trumper and Duff as Australian Test players who were cut off in their prime.

The unlucky spectators had plenty of time to ponder the rights and wrongs of Hazlitt's bowling action on the second day. After a delayed start, rain drove the players off again after little more than 20 minutes, in which time England had added 30 runs without further loss. The drizzle hung around all day, turning to heavier rain later on: play was finally abandoned at 5.45.

In the presence of the Prince of Wales (later King Edward VIII) on the final day, England went for quick runs, scoring 69 in 50 minutes before the declaration came at 310 for 7. Fry, the eternal optimist, encouraged his fielders to change round quickly at first, in the hope of bowling Australia out twice in less than six hours, but this was never realistic: after Jennings departed for 21, Kelleway and Bardsley, in their contrasting styles, combined in a stand of 146. Macartney opened up after reaching 50 in 90 minutes: he struck one of Australia's 1911-12 tormentors, Barnes, for a satisfying six, and had hit 13 fours in 140 minutes when he got a faint edge to one of several legside deliveries from Foster and was caught behind, becoming the first man to be dismissed for 99 in a Lord's Test.

In the meantime Kelleway, exhibiting what *Wisden* termed 'rigid defence and inexhaustible patience', took 4½ hours over his 61, which ended when Rhodes bowled him.

Australia had reached 282 for 7 by the time stumps were drawn. Rhodes ended up with 3 for 59, in what turned out to be his last Lord's Test (although he was to make his last Test appearance in West Indies in 1930, when he was 52 years old). As far as Lord's was concerned, it was the end of an era for England: only Hearne, Hobbs and Woolley were to reappear in a Lord's Test after the Great War.

ENGLAND v AUSTRALIA
June 24, 25, 26, 1912

ENGLAND

J.B. Hobbs	b Emery	107	Bowling:
W. Rhodes	c Carkeek b Kelleway	59	Whitty 12-2-69-1,
R.H. Spooner	c Bardsley b Kelleway	1	Hazlitt 25-6-68-1,
* C.B. Fry	run out	42	Matthews 13-4-26-0,
P.F. Warner	b Emery	4	Kelleway 21-5-66-2,
F.E. Woolley	c Kelleway b Hazlitt	20	Emery 12-1-46-2,
F.R. Foster	c Macartney b Whitty	20	Macartney 7-1-13-0.
J.W. Hearne	not out	21	
† E.J. Smith	not out	14	
S.F. Barnes	} did not bat		
H. Dean			
Extras	(b16, lb4, nb2)	22	
	(7 wkts dec) (90 overs)	310	

Fall: 112,123,197,211,246,255,285.

AUSTRALIA

C.B. Jennings	c Smith b Foster	21	Bowling:
C. Kelleway	b Rhodes	61	Foster 36-18-42-2,
C.G. Macartney	c Smith b Foster	99	Barnes 31-10-74-0,
W. Bardsley	lbw b Rhodes	21	Dean 29-10-49-2,
* S.E. Gregory	c Foster b Dean	10	Hearne 12-1-31-0,
D.B.M. Smith	not out	24	Rhodes 19.2-5-59-3.
T.J. Matthews	b Dean	0	
G.R. Hazlitt	b Rhodes	19	
S.H. Emery	} did not bat		
W.J. Whitty			
† W. Carkeek			
Extras	(b17, lb5, w1, nb4)	27	
	(7 wkts) (127.2 overs)	282	

Fall: 27,173,226,233,243,243,282.

Toss: England   Umpires: J. Moss and A.E. Street
Close of play: (1) E. 211 for 4 (Fry 24)
                 (2) E. 241 for 4 (Fry 41, Woolley 8)

MATCH DRAWN

In the fourth match of the competition, at Headingley, England beat the downcast South Africans by 174 runs, Barnes taking another 10 wickets.

1912iii

One inevitable by-product of the Triangular Tournament was that Australia and South Africa faced each other in three matches, to date the only Tests which have taken place in a neutral country. Not surprisingly, these matches were the least attractive as far as the British public were concerned. The second encounter between the two teams took place at Lord's, the only one of the 84 Tests held there which has not involved England.

South Africa were virtually out of contention in the tournament, and they made a hesitant start again, only Tancred, who scored 31 in 105 minutes, passing 11 as the score dipped to 74 for 5. At this point, however, Taylor and Stricker counterattacked to such good effect that 97 runs were added in little more than an hour. They were aided by dreadful Australian fielding, with some nine catches going down in the day. Taylor, reprieved at 27 and 83, confirmed his status as South Africa's first great batsman with a 170-minute innings of 93. He hit 12 fours and a five (a single plus four overthrows). His partner Stricker hit nine fours in his highest Test score of 48.

A useful knock of 25 from Pegler swelled the total to 263, but Australia's left-arm fast bowler Whitty, who had earlier dismissed the dangerous Faulkner, rounded up the tailenders to finish with 4 for 68.

Australia's reply began badly, Nourse bowling Jennings in his first over and rattling Macartney's stumps soon afterwards. From 14 for 2, Kelleway and Bardsley set about repairing the damage, and had taken the score to 86 by the close, the obdurate Kelleway earning sarcastic applause from the restive crowd for his defensive approach.

The second-day crowd, which included King George V, had no cause for complaint. Shaking off their shackles, Kelleway and Bardsley took their third-wicket stand to 242, with 170 coming in less than two hours. Bardsley moved from 32 to 150 in the morning session, becoming the first player to score a century before lunch in a Lord's Test. The compact left-hander was out soon after lunch for 164, having hit 16 fours and a five. An easy chance to White at third man when he had made 131 and a difficult catch dropped earlier by wicketkeeper Ward were the only blemishes on Bardsley's fine innings.

Kelleway also reached his century, hitting seven fours in a display inevitably overshadowed by Bardsley's brilliance. When Mayne, playing in his first Test, and Minnett took the score past 350 a big score seemed likely, but the persistent Pegler snapped up four quick wickets to restrict the Australians to 390.

Facing a deficit of 127, South Africa were soon in trouble again at 62 for 3. Then Llewellyn, whose 75 had prolonged the first Lord's Test of 1912, hit nine fours in an entertaining innings which staved off another innings defeat, but after he had gone for 59 South Africa slid to 146 for 8 by the close, a slender lead of 19.

A meagre crowd watched the last rites on the final morning – more might have turned up had they realised that Lord's would be starved of Test cricket for nine long years – and saw South Africa reach 173. Matthews, the tormentor of South Africa at Old Trafford, took four wickets and the versatile Macartney three. Australia needed 47 to win, and Jennings and Mayne hit off the runs without being parted, a fitting end to captain Syd Gregory's ninth and last Lord's Test. Of the Australians, only Bardsley and Macartney were to grace a Lord's Test again.

AUSTRALIA v SOUTH AFRICA
July 15, 16, 17, 1912

SOUTH AFRICA

G.A. Faulkner	b Whitty	5	(6) c and b Matthews	6
L.J. Tancred	lbw b Matthews	31	c Bardsley b Hazlitt	19
G.C. White	c Carkeek b Minnett	0	b Matthews	18
C.B. Llewellyn	c Jennings b Minnett	8	b Macartney	59
A.W. Nourse	b Hazlitt	11	lbw b Kelleway	10
H.W. Taylor	c Kelleway b Hazlitt	93	(7) not out	10
L.A. Stricker	lbw b Kelleway	48	(1) b Hazlitt	13
* F. Mitchell	b Whitty	12	b Matthews	3
R.O. Schwarz	b Whitty	0	c Macartney b Matthews	1
S.J. Pegler	c Bardsley b Whitty	25	c Kelleway b Macartney	14
† T.A. Ward	not out	1	b Macartney	7
Extras	(b12, lb14, w1, nb2)	29	(b9, lb4)	13
	(89 overs)	263	(57.1 overs)	173

Fall: 24,25,35,56,74,171,203,213,250. 28,54,62,102,134,136,142,146,163.

Bowling: Minnett 15-6-49-2, Whitty 31-9-68-4, Hazlitt 19-9-47-2, Matthews 13-5-32-1, Kelleway 11-3-38-1.
Second innings: Whitty 9-0-41-0, Hazlitt 13-1-39-2, Matthews 13-2-29-4, Kelleway 8-1-22-1, Macartney 14.1-5-29-3.

AUSTRALIA

C.B. Jennings	b Nourse	0	not out	22
C. Kelleway	lbw b Faulkner	102		
C.G. Macartney	b Nourse	9		
W. Bardsley	lbw b Llewellyn	164		
* S.E. Gregory	b Llewellyn	5		
R.E. Mayne	st Ward b Pegler	23	(2) not out	25
R.B. Minnett	b Pegler	39		
T.J. Matthews	c Faulkner b Pegler	9		
G.R. Hazlitt	b Nourse	0		
† W. Carkeek	not out	6		
W.J. Whitty	lbw b Pegler	3		
Extras	(b24, lb3, w2, nb1)	30	(b1)	1
	(128.5 overs)	390	(0 wkt) (12.1 overs)	48

Fall: 0,14,256,277,316,353,375,379,381.

Bowling: Nourse 36-12-60-3, Pegler 29.5-7-79-4, Schwarz 11-1-44-0, Faulkner 28-3-86-1, Llewellyn 19-2-71-2, Taylor 2-0-12-0, Stricker 3-1-8-0.
Second innings: Nourse 6.1-2-22-0, Pegler 4-1-15-0, Faulkner 2-0-10-0.

Toss: South Africa   Umpires: J. Moss and A.E. Street
Close of play: (1) A. 86 for 2 (Kelleway 33, Bardsley 32)
               (2) S.A. 146 for 8 (Taylor 5)

AUSTRALIA WON BY 10 WICKETS

Rain ruined the next two matches of the tournament, after which England defeated South Africa yet again – the match at The Oval was over before lunch on the second day, Barnes taking 13 wickets. The final match, again at The Oval, saw England face Australia in a game which was to be played out to a finish to decide the winners of the competition. England, for whom Woolley took 10 wickets, needed only four days to win by 244 runs. It was announced at the end of the season that it was not planned to stage another Triangular Tournament in the foreseeable future – and to date there has not been another.

1921

When international cricket resumed after the First World War it seemed that Australia were in far better shape than their traditional rivals England. The first post-war rubber, in 1920-21, saw England thrashed 5-0, and it cannot have been much fun for the defeated England party to have to travel home from the Antipodes on the good ship 'Osterley' alongside their opponents, who were undertaking a five-Test tour of England. The 1921 Australians, captained by Warwick Armstrong, the 21-stone veteran of the 1902, 1905 and 1909 tours, are widely regarded as one of the best combinations ever to visit England (although Armstrong reckoned that the 1902 side could have beaten 22 of his 1921 team). They had batting strength in depth, plus the fearsome fast bowling of Gregory and McDonald, who had proved too much for England's batsmen in Australia.

England's prospects, already gloomy, were further upset when Hobbs, their best batsman, missed the first two Tests with a leg strain. During the third Test he underwent an operation for appendicitis and missed the rest of the series.

Australia arrived for the second Test at Lord's already one-up, Gregory and McDonald having taken eight wickets apiece as England were demolished for 112 and 147 at Trent Bridge. England's selectors exhibited the first signs of a panic that was to see a record 30 players employed during the series, and made six changes for the Lord's Test, including four players new to Test cricket, three of whom – Dipper, Durston and Evans – never appeared again. It would have been seven changes had the selectors persuaded the 49-year-old Fry to play, but he declined the invitation as he was unhappy with his form.

J.W.H.T. Douglas, captaining England in his only Lord's Test, chose to bat, but it was the same old story as his side declined to 25 for 3. Knight fell to Armstrong, whose 18 overs during the day cost him only nine runs, but the main destroyer was McDonald, who bowled Dipper for 11 and then castled Hendren with an exceptionally quick delivery before the popular Middlesex man had opened his account. Woolley and Douglas stood firm, putting on 83 before McDonald struck again, taking the wickets of the captain and the nervous debutant Evans in quick succession. A brave soldier who had been decorated for gallantry for his exploits during the war, Evans sadly was not up to the demands of Test cricket.

Woolley, who hit 10 fours, held the innings together with a masterly display in which his back-foot strokes enthralled the crowd. Although he was dropped twice in the slips when he had reached 87, he was unlucky to miss his century, being the last man out for 95, having refused some long singles to keep No. 11 Durston from the strike.

In spite of Woolley's heroics the England total was a mediocre 187, and Australia soon put that into perspective by dashing to 116 for 2 in a mere 65 minutes, the fielding looking pedestrian in contrast with the athleticism displayed by the visitors. Australia took the lead just before the close, Bardsley leading the way with 88.

Bardsley was out immediately on the second morning, and England cherished hopes of restricting Australia's lead to manageable proportions when Armstrong fell for a duck, one of four wickets for Middlesex fast bowler Durston. Allrounder

England were outclassed in the first Lord's Test after the war, despite the efforts of Kent's Frank Woolley, who had an unfortunate double with scores of 95 and 93

Gregory, though, gave two difficult chances on his way to 52, and the veteran wicketkeeper Carter made 46 as the total stretched to 342, a lead of 155. Carter, incidentally, was the only Yorkshire-born player on either side in the match.

England made their almost customary poor start, Gregory disposing of Knight for 1, but then Dipper and Woolley shared a stand of 94. Dipper went for a plucky 40, and then Woolley had the mortification of being dismissed in the nineties for the second time in the match. This time, on 93, he smashed a Mailey long-hop towards short leg, where Hendry – who had earlier dropped him – juggled but hung on to a good catch. A defiant innings from Tennyson kept English hopes alive into the third day.

England's last two wickets added a further 40 runs on the final morning, Tennyson hitting out cheerfully to make 30 of them. The grandson of the Poet Laureate Alfred Lord Tennyson, he owed his place in the side to the perceptive Fry, who urged the selectors to include the aggressive Hampshire captain in the team when the injured Mead withdrew. Tennyson ended up with 74 not out, and took over the captaincy for the rest of the series: after injuring his hand, he was to play two famous innings of 63 and 36 during the next match, at Headingley, batting virtually one-handed.

Australia needed 129 to win, a target they achieved with the minimum of fuss. Bardsley, especially strong on the cut and off his legs, remained unbeaten on 63. He put on 103 for the first wicket with Andrews, and a 10-wicket victory seemed likely until Parkin and Durston took a wicket apiece.

ENGLAND v AUSTRALIA
June 11, 13, 14, 1921

ENGLAND

D.J. Knight	c Gregory b Armstrong	7	c Carter b Gregory	1
A.E. Dipper	b McDonald	11	b McDonald	40
F.E. Woolley	st Carter b Mailey	95	c Hendry b Mailey	93
E.H. Hendren	b McDonald	0	c Gregory b Mailey	10
* J.W.H.T. Douglas	b McDonald	34	b Gregory	14
A.J. Evans	b McDonald	4	lbw b McDonald	14
Hon.L.H. Tennyson	st Carter b Mailey	5	not out	74
N.E. Haig	c Carter b Gregory	3	b McDonald	0
C.H. Parkin	b Mailey	0	c Pellew b McDonald	11
† H. Strudwick	c McDonald b Mailey	8	b Gregory	12
F.J. Durston	not out	6	b Gregory	2
Extras	(b1, lb11, w1, nb1)	14	(b4, lb3, nb5)	12
	(68.2 overs)	187	(90.2 overs)	283

Fall: 20,24,25,108,120,145,156,157,170. 3,97,124,165,165,198,202,235,263.

Bowling: Gregory 16-1-51-1, McDonald 20-2-58-4, Armstrong 18-12-9-1, Mailley 14.2-1-55-4.

Second innings: Gregory 26.2-4-76-4, McDonald 23-3-89-4, Armstrong 12-6-19-0, Mailey 25-4-72-2, Hendry 4-0-15-0.

AUSTRALIA

W. Bardsley	c Woolley b Douglas	88	not out	63
T.J.E. Andrews	c Strudwick b Durston	9	lbw b Parkin	49
C.G. Macartney	c Strudwick b Durston	31	b Durston	8
C.E. Pellew	b Haig	43	not out	5
J.M. Taylor	lbw b Douglas	36		
* W.W. Armstrong	b Durston	0		
J.M. Gregory	c and b Parkin	52		
H.S.T.L. Hendry	b Haig	5		
† H. Carter	b Durston	46		
A.A. Mailey	c and b Parkin	5		
E.A. McDonald	not out	17		
Extras	(b2, lb5, nb3)	10	(b3, lb2, nb1)	6
	(84.1 overs)	342	(2 wkts) (30.3 overs)	131

Fall: 19,73,145,191,192,230,263,277,289. 103,114.

Bowling: Durston 24.1-2-102-4, Douglas 9-1-53-2, Parkin 20-5-72-2, Haig 20-4-61-2, Woolley 11-2-44-0.

Second innings: Durston 9.3-0-34-1, Douglas 6-0-23-0, Parkin 9-0-31-1, Haig 3-0-27-0, Woolley 3-0-10-0.

Toss: England   Umpires: J. Moss and W. Phillips
Close of play: (1) A. 191 for 3 (Bardsley 88, Taylor 15)
                   (2) E. 243 for 8 (Tennyson 44, Strudwick 6)

AUSTRALIA WON BY 8 WICKETS

Despite Tennyson's heroics, Australia went 3-0 up at Headingley, so retaining the Ashes. England fared better in the remaining two Tests, which were both drawn. Rain ruined the Old Trafford match, and Australia scored 389 at The Oval in reply to England's 403 for 8, of which Mead scored 182 not out.

1924

South Africa, making their first tour of England for 12 years, were the visitors in 1924. Now captained by Herby Taylor, the South Africans included Nourse for his last tour at the age of 46. 'Old Dave' enjoyed his most successful tour with the bat, scoring 1928 runs: he also took 27 wickets. A left-handed allrounder, he played on in domestic cricket until he was nearly 56, and the Nourse name was not long absent from South Africa's representative side: his son, Dudley, first appeared in 1935, and captained the 1951 tourists in England.

The South Africans were not as strong as the 1907 tourists had been. The bowlers, used to receiving help from the matting pitches of their own country, struggled to such an extent that Pegler and the veteran Faulkner were called up, as was George Parker, a fastish bowler from Cape Town who was spending the season as a professional in the Bradford League. Parker played in three matches on the tour, including the first two Tests, and that was the extent of his first-class career, as he never appeared in domestic cricket in South Africa.

The England captaincy had passed to Arthur Gilligan, the genial allrounder from Sussex who formed, with his county colleague Maurice Tate, a decidedly useful opening attack. After England's strong batting side made 438 in the first Test at Edgbaston, Gilligan (6 for 7) and Tate (4 for 12, including a wicket with his first ball in Tests) bundled out the visitors for 30. South Africa fared much better in the follow-on, Catterall hitting 120 out of 390, but nonetheless England recorded a comfortable victory by an innings and 18 runs.

The margin of victory was to be exactly repeated in the Lord's Test, as was Catterall's score. Taylor won the toss, batted, and South Africa were soon in trouble again at 17 for 3, Taylor himself going in the first over. Susskind, whose style was awkward but productive, then scored 64 in a century partnership with the in-form Catterall, who made the most of two let-offs, the first of them (to wicketkeeper Wood) when he had made only 5. An exciting, free-hitting batsman from Rhodesia, Catterall reached his second century in successive Test innings and went on to match exactly the 120 he had scored at Edgbaston.

Helped by useful contributions from Deane and the 42-year-old Faulkner, Catterall's 200-minute innings, which included 16 fours, took South Africa to 273, and England scored 28 without loss in the remaining 15 minutes.

The second day was one of the most remarkable that Lord's has ever seen. Hobbs and Sutcliffe, whose successful association had started at Birmingham with a stand of 136 in Sutcliffe's debut match, had no difficulty with the friendly South African bowling, and piled on 200 runs before lunch, Hobbs moving from 12 overnight to 114 at the interval. The Surrey maestro might have been stumped off Faulkner when he had made 109, but otherwise his innings was without blemish.

The runs continued to flow in the afternoon session, Sutcliffe reaching his first Test century soon after the interval. He had made 122, and the opening stand was worth 268, when he played on to the persevering Parker. Hobbs, though, was in superb form, and with Woolley also scoring freely the second-wicket stand of 142 came up in 80 minutes, before Hobbs's highest Test innings came to an end at 211, made in 280 minutes with 15 fours – and 85 singles. Still the punchdrunk bowlers had no respite. Woolley raced to the third century of the innings, and his

Probably England's greatest-ever opening pair, Jack Hobbs (left) and Herbert Sutcliffe, who in 1924 recorded the highest first-wicket partnership in a Lord's Test. Hobbs made 211, Sutcliffe 122 – and England ran up 531 for 2

unbroken stand of 121 with Hendren was posted in less than an hour.

Gilligan called a halt to the slaughter just before the close, England having scored 503 in the day, still the Test record by one side. South Africa scored 19 without loss before stumps, the overall aggregate of 522 in the day being a record at the time and only once exceeded since (by England and India at Old Trafford in 1936).

The visitors' only hope was to bat out the final day, but although Commaille (37) and Susskind (53) played useful innings, once Catterall departed for 45 it was only a matter of time. South Africa were all out soon after tea for 240, leaving England the winners, as in the first Test, by an innings and 18 runs.

ENGLAND v SOUTH AFRICA
June 28, 30, July 1, 1924

SOUTH AFRICA

* H.W. Taylor	c Wood b Gilligan	4	(5) b Gilligan	8
J.M.M. Commaille	b Gilligan	0	lbw b Tyldesley	37
M.J. Susskind	c Tate b Hearne	64	lbw b Tyldesley	53
A.W. Nourse	c Woolley b Tate	4	lbw b Gilligan	11
R.H. Catterall	b Gilligan	120	(6) c Gilligan b Tyldesley	45
J.M. Blanckenberg	b Tate	12	(7) c Hobbs b Fender	15
H.G. Deane	b Tyldesley	33	(1) c Sutcliffe b Hearne	24
G.A. Faulkner	b Fender	25	run out	12
† T.A. Ward	b Tyldesley	1	(10) not out	3
S.J. Pegler	c Fender b Tyldesley	0	(9) b Tate	8
G.M. Parker	not out	1	b Tate	0
Extras	(b3, lb2, nb4)	9	(b13, lb8, nb3)	24
	(116 overs)	273	(123.4 overs)	240

Fall: 4,5,17,129,182,212,265,271,272.   50,78,103,117,171,204,224,231,240.

Bowling: Gilligan 31-7-70-3, Tate 34-12-62-2, Tyldesley 24-10-52-3,
Hearne 18-3-35-1, Fender 9-1-45-1.

Second innings: Gilligan 24-6-54-2, Tate 26.4-8-43-2, Tyldesley 36-18-50-3,
Fender 14-5-25-1, Hearne 19-4-35-1, Woolley 4-1-9-0.

ENGLAND

J.B. Hobbs	c Taylor b Parker	211	Bowling:	
H. Sutcliffe	b Parker	122	Parker 24-0-121-2,	
F.E. Woolley	not out	134	Blanckenberg 28-3-113-0,	
E.H. Hendren	not out	50	Pegler 31-4-120-0,	
J.W. Hearne	⎫		Nourse 15-1-57-0,	
A.P.F. Chapman	⎪		Faulkner 17-0-87-0,	
P.G.H. Fender	⎪		Catterall 3-0-19-0.	
* A.E.R. Gilligan	⎬ did not bat			
† G.E.C. Wood	⎪			
M.W. Tate	⎪			
R.K. Tyldesley	⎭			
Extras	(b11, lb1, nb2)	14		
	(2 wkts dec) (118 overs)	531		

Fall: 268,410.

Toss: South Africa   Umpires: F. Chester and H.I. Young
Close of play: (1) E. 28 for 0 (Hobbs 12, Sutcliffe 12)
                 (2) S.A. 19 for 0 (Deane 13, Commaille 5)

ENGLAND WON BY AN INNINGS AND 18 RUNS

England clinched the series with another convincing win in the third Test, at Headingley. Rain ruined the final two matches, permitting only 50 minutes' play on the third day of the final Test at The Oval, and just 165 minutes in total in the previous encounter at Old Trafford.

1926

Australia were back in 1926, still in possession of the Ashes (retained 4-1 in 1924-25), but generally a less imposing side than the great 1921 line-up. Armstrong and McDonald were gone, Gregory was struggling with a knee injury (he took only 36 wickets on the tour) and the other survivors were, of course, five years older. The side did include new names destined for stardom in Woodfull, Ponsford and Grimmett, but their great days were as yet largely in the future.

The uncompromising Nottinghamshire skipper Arthur Carr was now in charge of an England side which retained the formidable batting line-up of 1924, while Tate was still the spearhead of the bowling attack; for the Lord's Test he was joined by a young Nottinghamshire paceman making his Test debut, 21-year-old Harold Larwood.

Neither side learnt anything from the first Test, which was limited to 50 minutes' play on the first day before rain, which was to plague much of the summer, set in.

Moving to Lord's, 'Lucky' Collins guessed right with the toss but, a few minutes later, wrong with a cutter from Root. The Australian captain let the ball go, but it nipped back and bowled him. When Bardsley had made 6, wicketkeeper Strudwick made an expensive mistake, putting down a very difficult low chance off Tate, an error he was to repeat when the opener had moved on to 112.

Bardsley and Macartney needed to be watchful against testing England bowling, and they had added 73 when Larwood had Macartney caught behind. Bardsley continued, scoring most of his runs with deft cuts and legside deflections, and reached his hundred at 3.30, but wickets fell regularly at the other end, Taylor receiving a particularly nasty ball from Tate which 'popped'. Bardsley shared an important stand with Richardson, and was still there at the close, with 173 to his name: just before the end Strudwick rounded off a miserable day by dropping him again, off Woolley, when the left-hander had made 172.

A mysterious wet patch appeared on the ground during an otherwise dry night. Foul play was hinted at, but eventually it was discovered that a careless groundstaff member had left a hose running all night. The pitch was affected, but only in the middle, so play was able to proceed only 10 minutes late after a liberal application of sawdust: Sydney Smith, the Australian manager, recalled that 'the area outside the wicket looked like a leopard's skin'.

Australia added a further 45 runs, Mailey just being unable to see Bardsley to his double-century, but the New South Welshman did have the satisfaction of becoming the second man, after his compatriot J.E. Barrett in 1890, to carry his bat at Lord's. In all he survived for 398 minutes, hitting 14 fours, and he remains the oldest player to score a century for Australia, at 43 years 201 days (a year older than was generally supposed at the time: he was born five months after his parents were married, which might explain!).

The home side's batsmen took up where they left off against South Africa two years previously. Hobbs and Sutcliffe shared another large stand – 182 this time – starting off briskly with 77 in 70 minutes before lunch. Only Arthur Richardson, bowling offbreaks to four short legs, restricted the batsmen, and he eventually removed Sutcliffe for 82. Hobbs remained, however, reaching 88 in 130 minutes

The durable Australian Warren Bardsley, rising 44, carried his bat for 193 in 1926.
Bardsley scored more runs in Lord's Tests (575) than any other overseas player

but taking a further 70 minutes to reach three figures, his third century in successive Lord's Test innings spanning 14 years. During his chanceless 119, which contained 10 fours, he became the first player to reach an aggregate of 4000 runs in Tests.

After Hobbs's dismissal, Woolley and Hendren shared a stand, worth 78 by the close, which they extended to 140 on the third morning. After Woolley fell for 87, Hendren shared a brisk partnership of 116 with Chapman which ended when Carr declared at lunchtime. Hendren had batted for 208 minutes, hitting 18 fours, and rather surprisingly is still the only Middlesex player to score a century in a Lord's Test against Australia. Equally surprisingly, the 37-year-old Patsy was the youngest of the match's four centurions.

With two sessions remaining, Australia needed only to avoid a startling collapse to be safe from defeat, and this they did, despite the loss of makeshift opener Gregory for a duck. Collins and Macartney made the match safe with a partnership of 123, the captain hanging on doggedly for 145 minutes, scoring 24 (he was becalmed on 14 for 52 minutes). Macartney, who had celebrated his 43rd birthday on the rest day, played a delightful innings, hitting 13 fours in his unbeaten 133. A few late wickets as the batting order was juggled mattered little, and honours were even.

ENGLAND v AUSTRALIA
June 26, 28, 29, 1926

AUSTRALIA

* H.L. Collins	b Root	1	c Sutcliffe b Larwood	24
W. Bardsley	not out	193		
C.G. Macartney	c Sutcliffe b Larwood	39	not out	133
W.M. Woodfull	c Strudwick b Root	13	(6) c Root b Woolley	0
T.J.E. Andrews	c and b Kilner	10	(4) b Root	9
J.M. Gregory	b Larwood	7	(2) c Sutcliffe b Root	0
J.M. Taylor	c Carr b Tate	9		
A.J. Richardson	b Kilner	35		
J. Ryder	c Strudwick b Tate	28	(7) not out	0
† W.A.S. Oldfield	c Sutcliffe b Kilner	19	(5) c Sutcliffe b Tate	11
A.A. Mailey	lbw b Kilner	1		
Extras	(b12, lb16)	28	(b5, lb12)	17
	(154.5 overs)	383	(5 wkts) (88 overs)	194

Fall: 11,84,127,158,187,208,282,338,379. 2,125,163,187,194.

Bowling: Tate 50-12-111-2, Root 36-11-70-2, Kilner 34.5-11-70-4, Larwood 32-2-99-2, Woolley 2-0-5-0.

Second innings: Tate 25-11-38-1, Root 19-9-40-2, Kilner 22-2-49-0, Larwood 15-3-37-1, Woolley 7-1-13-1.

ENGLAND

J.B. Hobbs	c Richardson b Macartney	119	Bowling:
H. Sutcliffe	b Richardson	82	Gregory 30-3-125-0,
F.E. Woolley	lbw b Ryder	87	Macartney 33-8-90-1,
E.H. Hendren	not out	127	Mailey 30-6-96-0,
A.P.F. Chapman	not out	50	Richardson 48-18-73-1,
* A.W. Carr			Ryder 25-3-70-1,
R. Kilner			Collins 2-0-11-0.
M.W. Tate	did not bat		
H. Larwood			
C.F. Root			
† H. Strudwick			
Extras	(b4, lb4, w1, nb1)	10	
	(3 wkts) (168 overs)	475	

Fall: 182,219,359.

Toss: Australia   Umpires: L.C. Braund and A.E. Street
Close of play: (1) A. 338 for 8 (Bardsley 173)
                          (2) E. 297 for 2 (Woolley 50, Hendren 42)

MATCH DRAWN

Woodfull, Macartney and Richardson all scored centuries in a high-scoring drawn third Test at Headingley, and the first two reached three figures again in another draw at Old Trafford. The series depended on the final Test at The Oval, where England replaced captain Carr with Chapman and recalled the 48-year-old Rhodes, who took four important wickets on the last day as England cruised home by 289 runs to take the Ashes. Earlier, Hobbs and Sutcliffe had shared perhaps their greatest partnership, 172 on a rain-affected pitch.

1928

The period between 1928 and 1932 saw the number of Test-playing sides double, with the rise to international cricket of West Indies (1928), New Zealand (1929-30) and India (1932). Tours by one country or another became an annual event, with the result that Lord's has staged at least one Test each summer since 1928, apart from the war years and 1970, when an unofficial match against the Rest of the World replaced the planned Test against South Africa.

The first 'new recruits' were West Indies. Their 1928 team had some formidable fast bowlers, one of whom, Learie Constantine, was also an explosive batsman and arguably the greatest fieldsman of all time. The batting, although appearing strong on paper, did not come to terms with English conditions, and the selectors must have regretted leaving out the man destined to become West Indies' first great Test batsman, George Headley, on the grounds that he was too young at 19. At this time – and for some years afterwards – West Indies cricket also suffered from inter-island rivalries, selections often being determined as much by nationality as by ability, which meant that team spirit was difficult to encourage. Walter Hammond recalled that 'they were still ragged and unreliable as a team'.

Wicketkeeper-batsman Karl Nunes was West Indies' first Test captain. He was a white Jamaican, who had been educated at Dulwich College: at this time it was unthinkable that a black man might skipper the side.

West Indies approached their first-ever Test match with guarded confidence, Constantine having raised morale with a stunning performance against Middlesex at Lord's, where he scored 86 and 103 in quick time, as well as taking 7 for 57. Unfortunately for the tourists, Constantine was unable to reproduce this sort of form in any of the three Tests.

England were without the unfit Hobbs, Sutcliffe's opening partner being the Lancastrian Charles Hallows, who had recently become the third (and last to date) batsman to score 1000 runs *in* May.

Chapman won the toss, and England made an uncertain start against the pace of Francis, Constantine and Griffith. Sutcliffe was quite often hit, but Hallows was the first to go after the openers had added 51 in 80 minutes. Sutcliffe went on to 45, and useful contributions came from Hammond, Jardine (on his Test debut) and Chapman, although the skipper's 50 came in less flamboyant manner than usual. The innings of the day, though, came from Lancashire's Ernest Tyldesley who, playing his only innings in a Lord's Test at the age of 39, scored 122, reaching his century in 160 minutes. His brother, J.T., appeared in five Tests at Lord's around the turn of the century.

England, 382 for 8 overnight, added only 19 next morning, Constantine taking both wickets to finish with 4 for 82. West Indies flattered to deceive in reply, Challenor and Martin taking the score to 70 for 0 at lunch. After the interval, though, wickets tumbled. Five went down before three figures were posted, Fernandes and Roach making ducks, and although Nunes, with a determined 37, stayed for a while, the eventual total of 177 was disappointing. Jupp, with four wickets, outshone three bowlers of greater celebrity in Larwood, Tate and Freeman.

Lancashire stalwart Ernest Tyldesley hit 122 against West Indies in 1928 – it was his only innings in a Lord's Test

Challenor was out without scoring in the follow-on, and another clatter of wickets saw West Indies precariously placed at 55 for 6 at the close, 16 wickets having gone down during the day.

On the third morning, with Larwood absent with a strain, the tourists reached exactly 100 before another wicket fell, whereupon Small (who recorded West Indies' first Test half-century) and Browne laid about them and added another 47. Jupp ended the fun with two quick wickets, and Freeman polished off the innings before lunch, leaving England the victors by an innings and 58 runs.

ENGLAND v WEST INDIES
June 23, 25, 26, 1928

ENGLAND

H. Sutcliffe	c Constantine b Francis	48	Bowling:
C. Hallows	c Griffith b Constantine	26	Francis 25-4-72-2,
G.E. Tyldesley	c Constantine b Francis	122	Constantine 26.4-9-82-4,
W.R. Hammond	b Constantine	45	Griffith 29-9-78-2,
D.R. Jardine	lbw b Griffith	22	Browne 22-5-53-0,
* A.P.F. Chapman	c Constantine b Small	50	Small 15-1-67-2,
V.W.C. Jupp	b Small	14	Martin 8-2-22-0.
M.W. Tate	c Browne b Griffith	22	
† H. Smith	b Constantine	7	
H. Larwood	not out	17	
A.P. Freeman	b Constantine	1	
Extras	(b6, lb19, nb2)	27	
	(125.4 overs)	401	

Fall: 51,97,174,231,327,339,360,380,389.

WEST INDIES

G. Challenor	c Smith b Larwood	29	b Tate	0
F.R. Martin	lbw b Tate	44	b Hammond	12
M.P. Fernandes	b Tate.	0	c Hammond b Freeman	8
*† R.K. Nunes	b Jupp	37	lbw b Jupp	10
W.H. St Hill	c Jardine b Jupp	4	lbw b Freeman	9
C.A. Roach	run out	0	c Chapman b Tate	16
L.N. Constantine	c Larwood b Freeman	13	b Freeman	0
J.A. Small	lbw b Jupp	0	c Hammond b Jupp	52
C.R. Browne	b Jupp	10	b Freeman	44
G.N. Francis	not out	19	c Jardine b Jupp	0
H.C. Griffith	c Sutcliffe b Freeman	2	not out	0
Extras	(b13, lb6)	19	(b10, lb5)	15
	(83.3 overs)	177	(73.1 overs)	166

Fall: 86,86,88,95,96,112,123,151,156. 0,22,35,43,44,44,100,147,147.

Bowling: Larwood 15-4-27-1, Tate 27-8-54-2, Freeman 18.3-5-40-2, Jupp 23-9-37-4.

Second innings: Tate 22-10-28-2, Hammond 15-6-20-1, Jupp 15-4-66-3, Freeman 21.1-10-37-4.

Toss: England   Umpires: L.C. Braund and F. Chester
Close of play: (1) E. 382 for 8 (Smith 7, Larwood 2)
(2) W.I. 55 for 6 (Roach 3, Small 8)

ENGLAND WON BY AN INNINGS AND 58 RUNS

England recorded comfortable innings victories in the remaining two Tests, giving rise to suggestions that West Indies were not up to the rigours of Test cricket. Freeman took 10 wickets at Old Trafford, where Jardine top-scored with 83, while Hobbs's 159 set up England's winning total of 438 at The Oval.

1929

The tourists in 1929 were H.G. 'Nummy' Deane's South Africans, a popular band who were hard hit by injuries which kept leading batsmen Siedle and the veteran Taylor out of the Lord's Test. Taylor's absence – he first toured with the 1912 side – meant that there were only two survivors from South Africa's 1924 Lord's Test side: skipper Deane and Catterall, who scored a memorable 120 in that match.

For England, Somerset farmer J.C. White was having a brief taste of Test captaincy, and his side for the Lord's Test, the second of the series, included two players new to international cricket in Essex batsman Jack O'Connor and Middlesex legspinner Walter Robins. The first Test, at Edgbaston, had ended in a draw, Sutcliffe and Hammond scoring hundreds for England while Catterall and Mitchell shared two century opening stands for the visitors.

At Lord's, England made a poor start after winning the toss. Killick, given the onerous task of filling in for Hobbs, who was missing his second successive Lord's Test, was out for 3. With the score at 18, Hammond went for 8 and O'Connor was bowled without scoring, all three wickets having gone to medium-paced allrounder Morkel. Sutcliffe had scored only 14 when he was dropped by Mitchell in the slips, Morkel again being the bowler. It was to be an expensive miss for South Africa, as Sutcliffe went on to score exactly 100, his first century in a Lord's Test and his second in successive innings in this series. In partnership with Hendren, the Yorkshireman put on 93 in 75 minutes, while his stand of 88 with his county colleague Leyland took little more than an hour. A late flourish from Larwood took England to 302, with 'Sandy' Bell, in his first Test, swerving the ball about at a brisk fast-medium, taking the last six wickets to become the first bowler to take five or more wickets in a Test innings at Lord's since Barnes in 1912.

South Africa lost Catterall before a run was scored, but Mitchell dropped anchor and, with the more free-scoring Christy, survived until the close, taking the score to 57.

Applying themselves well, South Africa took a slender first-innings lead of 20 on the second day. Hammond, during a brief spell, removed Mitchell, but Christy went on to 70 and the impressive Morkel – who should have been stumped when 12 – made 88. The 20-year-old 'Tuppy' Owen-Smith, who a few years later played rugby for England, chipped in with an unbeaten half-century.

England's second innings began indifferently, two wickets going down before the close. Morkel had a hand in both, catching Killick and having Sutcliffe caught by Catterall.

That man Morkel further embarrassed England on the final morning, hitting the stumps twice to dismiss Hammond and Hendren. Hammond (5) was batting with a runner (12th man Aidan Crawley) after picking up a strain in the field. When Ochse (pronounced 'Oosh') removed O'Connor, England were struggling at 117 for 5, only 97 ahead, but a barnstorming partnership of 129 in 70 minutes between Leyland and Tate redressed the balance. Leyland, in his first Lord's Test, was caught behind for 102, but Tate continued on his merry way, reaching his only Test century in less than two hours. When the Sussex man reached three figures White declared, leaving South Africa an unlikely target of 293. Ochse took

The 1929 Lord's Test saw Maurice Leyland record a notable double with the bat –
73 and 102. South Africa's wicketkeeper 'Jock' Cameron, however, had a less
memorable match: in indifferent light he was laid out by a Larwood bouncer and
was stretchered off the field. Maurice Tate, for one, thought he was dead

two late wickets to finish with 4 for 99.

South Africa's attempt to avoid defeat took a knock when Catterall again went
cheaply, but Mitchell and Christy combined in a stand that looked likely to save
the match. However, Robins and Larwood took three quick wickets before, in
murky light, the Nottinghamshire paceman laid out Cameron with a sickening
blow to the head. Tate, who helped carry him off the field, thought Cameron was
dead. Happily he survived, although he missed three weeks' cricket while he
recovered. Shortly after this incident, the umpires decided that the light was too
bad for play to continue, and the match was left drawn.

ENGLAND v SOUTH AFRICA
June 29, July 1, 2, 1929

ENGLAND

H. Sutcliffe	c Mitchell b Bell	100	c Catterall b Morkel		10
E.T. Killick	b Morkel	3	c Morkel b Christy		24
W.R. Hammond	c Christy b Morkel	8	(5),b Morkel		5
J. O'Connor	b Morkel	0	(6) c Cameron b Ochse		11
E.H. Hendren	b Morkel	43	(4) b Morkel		11
M. Leyland	b Bell	73	(3) c Cameron b Ochse		102
M.W.Tate	c Cameron b Bell	15	not out		100
R.W.V. Robins	c Mitchell b Bell	4	c Mitchell b Ochse		0
H. Larwood	b Bell	35	b Ochse		9
* J.C. White	b Bell	8	not out		18
† G. Duckworth	not out	8			
Extras	(lb4, w1)	5	(b11, lb6, w2, nb3)		22
	(99.4 overs)	302	(8 wkts dec) (82.2 overs)		312

Fall: 8,18,18,111,199,243,249,252,287.   28,46,83,93,117,246,250,260.

Bowling: Ochse 24-5-51-0, Morkel 31-6-93-4, Bell 30.4-7-99-6, Christy 6-2-20-0, McMillan 7-0-31-0, Owen-Smith 1-0-3-0.

Second innings: Ochse 20-0-99-4, Morkel 24-6-63-3, Bell 18.2-2-60-0, Christy 3-0-15-1, McMillan 13-0-34-0, Mitchell 4-0-19-0.

SOUTH AFRICA

R.H. Catterall	b Larwood	0	b Tate		3
B. Mitchell	st Duckworth b Hammond	29	c Hendren b Robins		22
J.A.J. Christy	run out	70	c Hendren b Robins		41
D.P.B. Morkel	lbw b Tate	88	not out		17
* H.G. Deane	b Tate	1	(6) st Duckworth b Robins		2
† H.B. Cameron	c Leyland b Robins	32	(7) retired hurt		0
H.G. Owen-Smith	not out	52	(8) not out		1
E.L. Dalton	b Tate	6	(5) c Killick b Larwood		1
Q. McMillan	c Killick b White	17			
A.L. Ochse	c Duckworth b White	1			
A.J. Bell	b Robins	13			
Extras	(b9, lb4)	13	(b2, lb1)		3
	(131 overs)	322	(5 wkts) (51 overs)		90

Fall: 0,82,125,126,189,237,253,272,279.   9,60,77,82,85.

Bowling: Larwood 20-4-65-1, Tate 39-9-108-3, Hammond 8-3-19-1, White 35-12-61-2, Robins 24-5-47-2, Leyland 5-2-9-0.

Second innings: Larwood 12-3-17-1, Tate 11-3-27-1, Robins 19-4-32-3, White 9-3-11-0.

Toss: England   Umpires: W. Bestwick and F. Chester

Close of play: (1) S.A. 57 for 1 (Mitchell 15, Christy 42)
(2) E. 49 for 2 (Leyland 12, Hendren 0)
Cameron retired hurt at 86 for 5

MATCH DRAWN

England won the third Test, at Headingley, Woolley hitting 83 and 95 not out to answer Owen-Smith's whirlwind hundred for South Africa, and the home side clinched the series with an innings win at Old Trafford, where Wyatt and Woolley both made centuries and Freeman took 12 wickets. The final Test, at The Oval, was drawn, Sutcliffe hitting his third and fourth centuries of the rubber. Hammond also reached three figures, as did the 40-year-old Taylor for the visitors.

1930

The Lord's Test of 1930 saw probably the greatest innings ever played on the historic old ground. Don Bradman, aged 21 and on his first tour of England, scored 254, in his own judgment 'technically the best innings of my life. Practically without exception every ball went where it was intended to go, even the one from which I was dismissed, but the latter went slightly in the air.' Percy Fender, who before the tour had suggested that Bradman would not do well in England, had to alter his opinion: 'His 254 was as perfect an example of real batting in its best sense as anyone could wish to see.'

Bradman had already stamped his mark on the series with 131 in the first Test, although England had emerged victorious by 93 runs in the end. Australia fielded an unchanged side at Lord's, but injuries forced Sutcliffe and Larwood to withdraw from the England side, their replacements being Duleepsinhji and the Australian-born 'Gubby' Allen, whose first Test it was.

Chapman, back in charge, won the toss, but England suffered an early setback when Hobbs, in his sixth and last Lord's Test at the age of 47, was caught behind for a single. Woolley, a comparative youngster at 43, hit out from his unaccustomed position as opener, but he mixed brilliant strokes with less memorable swipes and it was no great surprise when he went for 41. Hammond was deceived by Grimmett at 105, after which Duleepsinhji and Hendren combined in a stand of 104 in only 91 minutes; later 'Duleep' and Tate put on 98. The Indian was missed twice, at 65 and 98, but soon after the second miss he emulated his uncle Ranjitsinhji in scoring a century in his first Test against Australia. It was also his first Test at Lord's.

Duleep's cutting and his on-side shots were a delight to watch, and it was a shock when, shortly before the close, he played a wild shot at Grimmett to be caught by Bradman for 173. He had batted for 292 minutes, hitting 21 fours.

Wall broke an annoying last-wicket stand of 38 early on the second day, England finishing with 425, which seemed likely to insure them against defeat, even allowing for the fact that the Tests in this series had been extended from three to four days.

With Ponsford as his partner, Australia's captain Woodfull set about reducing the deficit. The Victorians had carried the score to 162 when play was interrupted while the teams were presented to King George V: in the first over afterwards Ponsford gave a catch to Hammond after scoring 81, in what turned out to be the only Lord's Test of his illustrious career: injury and illness kept him out of the 1926 and 1934 matches.

Woodfull was now joined by Bradman. Runs came at a great rate: Bradman's fifty came up in 46 minutes, and he needed only another hour to reach his hundred, by which time the stand was worth 152. By now Woodfull was well past his own century, batting in a style that caused Pelham Warner to remark that 'Bowling to Woodfull was like throwing stones at the Rock of Gibraltar.' The stand was worth 231, made in 154 minutes, when Woodfull (155) finally was stumped off Robins, having given a similar chance at 52. The captain had batted for 328 minutes, and hit only nine fours. By the close, a few minutes later, Australia had moved to 404 for 2, Bradman's share being 155, with 101 coming

Despite a respectable first-innings total of 425, England were overwhelmed in a recordbreaking match at Lord's in 1930. Australia's captain Bill Woodfull (right) scored 155, but the main contributor to the visitors' record total of 729 for 6 was the great Don Bradman (left), whose flawless 254 remains the highest individual Test score at Lord's

since the tea interval. He had not lifted the ball off the ground, and the only suggestion of a false stroke came when, on 111, he almost played on.

The slaughter continued on the third day, Bradman and Kippax sharing a stand of 192. Bradman, a little more circumspect, took 73 minutes to reach his double-century, and at 191 he aimed to turn Hammond on the leg side but succeeded only in edging the ball down through the slips (still the ball went along the ground!). Eventually it came to an end, the first lofted shot being brilliantly caught right-handed by a relieved Chapman at extra cover. Bradman's 254, the highest score in any Lord's Test, took him 339 minutes and contained 25 fours.

McCabe (44), Richardson (30) and Oldfield (43 not out) piled on the agony for England, and Woodfull was able to declare at tea with 729 for 6 on the board, still the highest total recorded in any match at Lord's. After the interval England were batting again, remarkably enough (after their first innings of 425) facing a deficit of 304.

Two wickets went down before the close, both to the wily Grimmett: Hobbs was bowled behind his legs, while the unlucky Woolley trod on his wicket in hitting a boundary.

Hammond and Duleepsinhji raised the hundred on Day 4, but two more wickets from Grimmett plus Oldfield's brilliant catch off Hornibrook to get rid of Duleep reduced England to 147 for 5. Chapman had a slice of luck before he scored, skying a simple chance between Richardson and Ponsford, who left the catch to each other. After this, though, Chapman knuckled down and, shielding the nervous Allen from Grimmett's legspin, dominated a partnership of 125. He took the long handle to Grimmett, three times swinging him into the Mound Stand for six, and he collected a bonus when a wild throw swelled a hit for two into another six. Chapman went on to his only Test century, and when he was out for 121 – gulping in discomfort after swallowing a bluebottle – he had hit 12 fours in addition to those four sixes. Grimmett eventually snared Allen for 57, finishing with 6 for 167 from 53 overs as England were all out for 375 just before 3.30.

Australia needed only 72 to win, but they had their problems, Robins taking two wickets and Tate making up for his first-innings pasting (1 for 148) by having Bradman caught, again by Chapman, for a single. Woodfull and McCabe stopped the rot, however, and Australia reached their target without further loss.

ENGLAND v AUSTRALIA
June 27, 28, 30, July 1, 1930

ENGLAND

J.B. Hobbs	c Oldfield b Fairfax	1	b Grimmett		19
F.E. Woolley	c Wall b Fairfax	41	hit wkt b Grimmett		28
W.R. Hammond	b Grimmett	38	c Fairfax b Grimmett		32
K.S. Duleepsinhji	c Bradman b Grimmett	173	c Oldfield b Hornibrook		48
E.H. Hendren	c McCabe b Fairfax	48	c Richardson b Grimmett		9
* A.P.F. Chapman	c Oldfield b Wall	11	c Oldfield b Fairfax		121
G.O.B. Allen	b Fairfax	3	lbw b Grimmett		57
M.W. Tate	c McCabe b Wall	54	c Ponsford b Grimmett		10
R.W.V. Robins	c Oldfield b Hornibrook	5	not out		11
J.C. White	not out	23	run out		10
† G. Duckworth	c Oldfield b Wall	18	lbw b Fairfax		0
Extras	(b2, lb7, nb1)	10	(b16, lb13, w1)		30
	(128.4 overs)	425	(116.4 overs)		375

Fall: 13,53,105,209,236,239,337,363,387.   45,58,129,141,147,272,329,354,372.

Bowling: Wall 29.4-2-118-3, Fairfax 31-6-101-4, Grimmett 33-4-105-2, Hornibrook 26-6-62-1, McCabe 9-1-29-0.

Second innings: Wall 25-2-80-0, Fairfax 12.4-2-37-2, Grimmett 53-13-167-6, Hornibrook 22-6-49-1, Bradman 1-0-1-0, McCabe 3-1-11-0.

AUSTRALIA

* W.M. Woodfull	st Duckworth b Robins	155	not out		26
W.H. Ponsford	c Hammond b White	81	b Robins		14
D.G. Bradman	c Chapman b White	254	c Chapman b Tate		1
A.F. Kippax	b White	83	c Duckworth b Robins		3
S.J. McCabe	c Woolley b Hammond	44	not out		25
V.Y. Richardson	c Hobbs b Tate	30			
† W.A.S. Oldfield	not out	43			
A.G. Fairfax	not out	20			
C.V. Grimmett	⎫				
P.M. Hornibrook	⎬ did not bat				
T.W. Wall	⎭				
Extras	(b6, lb8, w5)	19	(b1, lb2)		3
	(6 wkts dec) (232 overs)	729	(3 wkts) (28.2 overs)		72

Fall: 162,393,585,588,643,672.   16,17,22.

Bowling: Allen 34-7-115-0, Tate 64-16-148-1, White 51-7-158-3, Robins 42-1-172-1, Hammond 35-8-82-1, Woolley 6-0-35-0.

Second innings: Tate 13-6-21-1, Hammond 4.2-1-6-0, Robins 9-1-34-2, White 2-0-8-0.

Toss: England   Umpires: F. Chester and T.W. Oates

Close of play: (1) E. 405 for 9 (White 14, Duckworth 7)
(2) A. 404 for 2 (Bradman 155, Kippax 7)
(3) E. 98 for 2 (Hammond 20, Duleepsinhji 27)

AUSTRALIA WON BY 7 WICKETS

Bradman continued his astonishing run of success with 334 in the drawn match at Headingley, where Hammond made 113 for England. The fourth Test, at Old Trafford, was ruined by rain, but in the final match, on their captain Woodfull's 33rd birthday, they clinched the series and regained the Ashes with an innings victory, Bradman scoring 232 and Ponsford 110 in a total of 695. The incredible Bradman took his series aggregate to 974 runs, still a Test record.

1931

New Zealand made their first Test tour of England in 1931, their original itinerary allowing for one Test match, which of course was to be played at Lord's. The tourists' impressive showings in the early county matches inspired suggestions that another Test or two might be played, and eventually the remaining fixtures were juggled to allow a three-Test series.

At Lord's, England were captained for the first time by Douglas Jardine, but he was without Sutcliffe and Larwood, both of whom were injured. With Hobbs having retired from international cricket, England had a brand-new opening pair – Fred Bakewell of Northants and Hampshire's Johnny Arnold, the latter playing in his only Test: he later joined the select band of 'double internationals' by playing football for England.

New Zealand's captain was Tom Lowry, a Cambridge Blue who had played a number of matches for Somerset in the early 1920s. His side had a number of fine batsmen, Stewart Dempster being arguably the best. The scorer of the Kiwis' first Test century, Dempster, who later played for Leicestershire with great success, started the tour with 212 against Essex at Leyton.

Lowry won the toss and watched with pride as his openers laid a good foundation. The 50 came up in 40 minutes, 100 in 88: although Dempster fell just before lunch for 53, the interval saw the visitors well placed at 132 for 2. After the break, however, a collapse set in, the last eight wickets going down for 92. Peebles started the slide in the first over after lunch, trapping Weir lbw, and Robins had Kerr well stumped in the next over. The stumping was a relief for wicketkeeper Ames, who had had an indifferent time in the morning session.

The Middlesex legspinners continued to dominate the batsmen, who seemed reluctant to use their feet. Peebles finished with 5 for 77 and Robins 3 for 38 as New Zealand subsided to 224.

England could hardly have made a worse start, slumping to 31 for 3, with the energetic fast bowler Cromb dismissing Arnold, Bakewell and Hammond for single-figure scores. The Indian-born pair of Duleepsinhji and Jardine took the score to 62 before Duleep fell to Merritt's legspin. Despite some uncertainty early on when facing the legspinner, Woolley then played a scintillating innings of 80 in even time: but he, Jardine and nightwatchman Peebles (stumped!) all fell to Merritt before the close, which saw England at 190 for 7, 17 wickets having fallen during the day.

England's rather dicey position was rescued by a marvellous stand on the second morning. Taking full advantage of some wayward New Zealand bowling, Ames and Allen added 210 in the morning's play, lifting the score to 400 for 7 by lunch. Ames, who offered two chances, had reached 106, while Allen had progressed to 98. He reached his only Test century shortly after the break. Weir, belatedly brought back into the attack, ended the stand after 165 minutes, during which time Ames and Allen had put on 246, still a Test record for the eighth wicket. Weir quickly took the last two wickets as well, finishing with 3 for 38 from only eight overs in England's total of 454.

Faced with a deficit of 230, New Zealand needed a good start, but lost Mills to the second ball of the innings, a full-toss from Allen flattening his off stump.

Kent wicketkeeper-batsman Les Ames was a consistent runscorer for England at Lord's, and in 1931 he (137) and Gubby Allen (122) shared a record eighth-wicket stand of 246 against first-time visitors New Zealand

Dempster and Weir put things to rights with a stand of 99, and by the close New Zealand had reached 161 for 2, Dempster being still there with 86. The stylish opener, with 'Curly' Page as his partner, reached his century early on the final morning, and the pair took their stand to 118 in 95 minutes before Hammond bowled Dempster for 120. Page now assumed the senior role, and had advanced to 99 by lunch, having successfully negotiated a series of short-pitched deliveries from Voce, who was bowling fast left-arm to a close-set legside field.

Page reached his century immediately after lunch, but was then out, bringing a stand of 142 with Blunt to an end. Blunt hit 96 in nearly three hours, and although England's legspinners once again worked their way through the order, they were much more expensive than in the first innings.

Lowry made a determined 34, despite having injured his hand in catching Robins to end England's first innings, and when the captain was out he declared at 469 for 9, leaving England a token target of 240 in 140 minutes. Bakewell and Arnold added 62 before both fell at the same score, and despite Cromb's gallant two-hour spell there was never much likelihood of a surprise win. Hammond reached 46 – his highest score in four Lord's Tests to this point – but was run out soon before the close, which found England at 146 for 5.

ENGLAND v NEW ZEALAND
June 27, 29, 30, 1931

NEW ZEALAND

J.E. Mills	b Peebles	34	(2) b Allen		0
C.S. Dempster	lbw b Peebles	53	(1) b Hammond		120
G.L. Weir	lbw b Peebles	37	b Allen		40
J.L. Kerr	st Ames b Robins	2	(6) lbw b Peebles		0
R.C. Blunt	c Hammond b Robins	7	b Robins		96
M.L. Page	b Allen	23	(4) c and b Peebles		104
* T.C. Lowry	c Hammond b Robins	1	(9) b Peebles		34
I.B. Cromb	c Ames b Peebles	20	(7) c Voce b Robins		14
C.F.W. Allcott	c Hammond b Peebles	13	(10) not out		20
W.E. Merritt	c Jardine b Hammond	17	(8) b Peebles		5
† K.C. James	not out	1			
Extras	(b2, lb12, w1, nb1)	16	(b23, lb10, w1, nb2)		36
	(74.3 overs)	224	(9 wkts dec) (157.4 overs)		469

Fall: 58,130,136,140,153,161,190,191,209.   1,100,218,360,360,389,404,406,469.

Bowling: Voce 10-1-40-0, Allen 15-2-45-1, Hammond 10.3-5-8-1, Peebles 26-3-77-5, Robins 13-3-38-3.
Second innings: Allen 25-8-47-2, Voce 32-11-60-0, Peebles 42.4-6-150-4, Robins 37-5-126-2, Hammond 21-2-50-1.

ENGLAND

A.H. Bakewell	lbw b Cromb	9	c Blunt b Cromb		27
J. Arnold	c Page b Cromb	0	c and b Blunt		34
W.R. Hammond	b Cromb	7	run out		46
K.S. Duleepsinhji	c Kerr b Merritt	25	c James b Allcott		11
* D.R. Jardine	c Blunt b Merritt	38	(7) not out		0
F.E. Woolley	lbw b Merritt	80	(5) b Cromb		9
† L.E.G. Ames	c James b Weir	137	(6) not out		17
I.A.R. Peebles	st James b Merritt	0			
G.O.B. Allen	c Lowry b Weir	122			
R.W.V. Robins	c Lowry b Weir	12			
W. Voce	not out	1			
Extras	(b15, lb8)	23	(lb2)		2
	(134 overs)	454	(5 wkts) (55 overs)		146

Fall: 5,14,31,62,129,188,190,436,447.   62,62,94,105,144.

Bowling: Cromb 37-7-113-3, Weir 8-1-38-3, Blunt 46-9-124-0, Allcott 17-3-34-0, Merritt 23-2-104-4, Page 3-0-18-0.
Second innings: Cromb 25-5-44-2, Weir 5-1-18-0, Blunt 14-5-54-1, Allcott 10-2-26-1, Merritt 1-0-2-0.

Toss: New Zealand   Umpires: F. Chester and J. Hardstaff snr
Close of play: (1) E. 190 for 7 (Ames 15)
                  (2) N.Z. 161 for 2 (Dempster 86, Page 31)

MATCH DRAWN

A fit-again Sutcliffe made 117 in the second Test at The Oval, Duleepsinhji and Hammond also reaching three figures in England's imposing 416 for 4 dec. England took the match and the series by shooting the visitors out for 193 (Allen 5 for 14) and 197. Only 195 minutes' play (all on the third day) was possible in the third Test, at Old Trafford, Sutcliffe scoring 109 not out in that time.

1932

England geared up for what became known as the 'Bodyline' tour of Australia with a solitary match in 1932 against India, newly elevated to Test-match status. It was necessary, for political reasons as well as India's self-esteem, that her side should be captained by someone of princely blood: when the Maharajah of Patiala found himself unable to make the tour, the Maharajah of Porbandar was chosen, even though his cricket ability was strictly limited.

Rather sensibly, the Maharajah (who, it was said, acquired more Rolls-Royces than runs during the tour) stood down for the Test, and with his vice-captain (and brother-in-law) K.S. Ganshyamsinhji of Limbdi having an injury, the captaincy for India's inaugural Test devolved, somewhat unexpectedly, on a commoner, C.K. Nayudu. 'C.K.' was one of the legendary names of Indian cricket: uniquely, he played first-class cricket in six different decades, playing on until he was 68.

England fielded a near full-strength side, with 45-year-old Percy Holmes returning to partner Sutcliffe only 10 days after the pair's then-world record 555 for the first wicket for Yorkshire against Essex at Leyton. Sadly, Holmes failed in what turned out to be his final Test, and indeed England were soon in trouble after Jardine won the toss, losing their first three wickets for 19. Bowling to an attacking field of three slips and three short legs, Nissar, a well-built fast bowler from the Punjab, removed both openers, and Woolley was run out. Hammond and Jardine rectified matters with a stand of 82 in 100 minutes, the captain going on to 79 in the face of some rapid bowling from Nissar and Amar Singh.

The crowd, disappointing at first, swelled to around 20,000 after lunch as the news spread of India's good start, but England's recovery continued, with the consistent Ames hitting nine fours in his 65, and adding 63 in only half an hour with Robins. Ames unintentionally struck another blow, cracking a ball to gully where Nayudu injured his hand in trying to stop it. The innings closed at 259, the impressive Nissar finishing with 5 for 93. India's openers scored 30 without loss by stumps.

India's injury-hit side struggled against Bowes (making his Test debut) and Voce on the second day. Nayudu made 40, despite his injured hand, and Naoomal and Wazir Ali both passed 30 as India reached 153 for 4 by lunch, but after the interval, with Nazir Ali and Palia troubled by leg injuries, the innings declined to 189 all out, the tall Yorkshireman Bowes taking 4 for 49 in 30 overs.

Once again England made a poor start, losing four wickets for 67 – three to Jahangir Khan – before Jardine, once again, steadied the ship. He led his side to 141 for 4 by the close, and on the final morning took his partnership with Paynter to 89 before the Lancastrian fell to Jahangir for 54. Useful innings from Robins and Brown allowed Jardine to declare at 275 for 8, a lead of 345. The skipper had batted superbly for 85 not out, cementing his place as captain for the winter tour of Australia.

Indian wickets tumbled after an opening stand of 41. Nayudu was still troubled by his hand injury, and although Wazir Ali again batted well for 39, India soon declined to 108 for 7. Lall Singh, the first Malayan-born Test cricketer, and Amar Singh hit out, the latter racing to his half-century (India's first in Tests) as 74 were added in 40 minutes. It couldn't last, however, Hammond taking a late turn at the

C.K. Nayudu, who had the honour of leading India in their first-ever Test match, at Lord's in 1932, after the tourists' princely captain and vice-captain diplomatically withdrew from the team

bowling crease and removing the last three wickets. Ordered to bat by his captain, Palia hobbled in at No. 11 with a pulled muscle at the back of his left thigh, but his gesture was in vain, England winning by 158 runs.

ENGLAND v INDIA
June 25, 27, 28, 1932

ENGLAND

P. Holmes	b Nissar	6	b Jahangir		11
H. Sutcliffe	b Nissar	3	c Nayudu b Amar Singh		19
F.E. Woolley	run out	9	c Colah b Jahangir		21
W.R. Hammond	b Amar Singh	35	b Jahangir		12
* D.R. Jardine	c Navle b Nayudu	79	not out		85
E. Paynter	lbw b Nayudu	14	b Jahangir		54
† L.E.G. Ames	b Nissar	65	b Amar Singh		6
R.W.V. Robins	c Lall Singh b Nissar	21	c Jahangir b Nissar		30
F.R. Brown	c Amar Singh b Nissar	1	c Colah b Naoomal		29
W. Voce	not out	4	not out		0
W.E. Bowes	c Nissar b Amar Singh	7			
Extras	(b3, lb9, nb3)	15	(b2, lb6)		8
	(105.1 overs)	259	(8 wkts dec) (110 overs)		275

Fall: 8,11,19,101,149,166,229,231,252.   30,34,54,67,156,169,222,271.

Bowling: Nissar 26-3-93-5, Amar Singh 31.1-10-75-2, Jahangir 17-7-26-0,
                  Nayudu 24-8-40-2, Palia 4-3-2-0, Naoomal 3-0-8-0.

Second innings: Nissar 18-5-42-1, Amar Singh 41-13-84-2, Jahangir 30-12-60-4,
                        Nayudu 9-0-21-0, Naoomal 8-0-40-1, Palia 3-0-11-0, Wazir Ali 1-0-9-0.

INDIA

† J.G. Navle	b Bowes	12	lbw b Robins		13
Naoomal Jeoomal	lbw b Robins	33	b Brown		25
S. Wazir Ali	lbw b Brown	31	c Hammond b Voce		39
* C.K. Nayudu	c Robins b Voce	40	b Bowes		10
S.H.M. Colah	c Robins b Bowes	22	b Brown		4
S. Nazir Ali	b Bowes	13	c Jardine b Bowes		6
P.E. Palia	b Voce	1	(11) not out		1
Lall Singh	c Jardine b Bowes	15	(7) b Hammond		29
M. Jahangir Khan	b Robins	1	(8) b Voce		0
L. Amar Singh	c Robins b Voce	5	(9) c and b Hammond		51
Mahomed Nissar	not out	1	(10) b Hammond		0
Extras	(b5, lb7, w1, nb2)	15	(b5, lb2, nb2)		9
	(93 overs)	189	(59.3 overs)		187

Fall: 39,63,110,139,160,165,181,182,188.   41,41,52,65,83,108,108,182,182.

Bowling: Bowes 30-13-49-4, Voce 17-6-23-3, Brown 25-7-48-1, Robins 17-4-39-2,
                  Hammond 4-0-15-0.

Second innings: Bowes 14-5-30-2, Voce 12-3-28-2, Brown 14-1-54-2, Robins 14-5-57-1,
                        Hammond 5.3-3-9-3.

Toss: England   Umpires: F. Chester and J. Hardstaff snr
Close of play: (1) I. 30 for 0 (Navle 11, Naoomal 11)
                  (2) E. 141 for 4 (Jardine 25, Paynter 50)

ENGLAND WON BY 158 RUNS

1933

When West Indies arrived for their second Test tour of England in 1933, the cricket world was still reeling from the ructions caused by the acrimonious Bodyline series in Australia. The tourists' batting had been strengthened by the inclusion of the brilliant George Headley, the 'Black Bradman' (some West Indians preferred to tag Bradman the 'White Headley'), but the exciting allrounder from the 1928 tour, Learie Constantine, had taken up an appointment as professional to Lancashire League club Nelson, and was able to play in only a few matches. Indeed, despite frantic negotiations, Nelson refused to release him to play in the Lord's Test.

Jackie Grant, West Indies' popular captain, had partial compensation for Constantine's absence when Bolton League club Radcliffe agreed to release their fast bowler, George Francis, but in reality Constantine was irreplaceable, even though he often failed to produce his best in Test matches. The Lord's Test saw another genuinely fast bowler, 'Mannie' Martindale, make his international debut for the visitors.

England's line-up was based largely on the successful 1932-33 touring team, although the chief Bodyline bowlers Larwood and Voce were both absent. One newcomer was the elegant Worcestershire opener Cyril Walters, who had a brief but productive Test career, which started with 51 in this match.

King George V was present on the first day, but the weather was decidedly unkind to the royal visitor, allowing only two brief periods of play, amounting to 45 minutes in all. Walters and Sutcliffe survived, adding 43 runs.

The second day was much brighter, and England, batting on a pitch which took turn later on, reached 100 for the loss of Sutcliffe, before three wickets went down for as many runs, Griffith obtaining the prize scalps of Hammond and Leyland. Skipper Jardine, aided by Turnbull, took the score past 150, but then both fell to Ellis 'Puss' Achong, a left-arm spinner of Chinese descent who is often credited with inventing the Chinaman – left-armer's googly – although this attribution seems to have little or no basis in fact.

Ames, as so often at Lord's, was England's saviour: he scored an unbeaten 83 and, with the help of the tailenders, shepherded the score to 296. Newcomer Martindale ended up with 4 for 85, and Griffith had 3 for 48.

The tourists made a poor start when Roach, who in 1929-30 had become the first man to score a Test century for West Indies, was bowled by Allen for a duck. Verity, soon called into the attack, disposed of Barrow, but surprisingly this was to be the left-armer's only wicket of the innings. Allen trapped the dangerous Headley lbw, then two quick wickets from Robins left West Indies in a sorry state at the end of the day at 55 for 6 – by a remarkable coincidence, the same score that they reached at the end of the second day of their only previous Lord's Test, in 1928.

Captain Grant led a fightback on the third morning, but after he hit his own wicket for 26 West Indies subsided to 97 all out. Legspinner Robins took all four wickets to fall, finishing with 6 for 32. The tourists were soon batting again, and made the worst possible start: Roach completed his 'pair' when Macaulay (a last-minute inclusion for the injured E.W. 'Nobby' Clark, who thus missed what

Walter Robins won only 19 Test caps, but seven of them came at Lord's. In 1933, his legspin claimed 6 for 32 as West Indies were routed for 97

would have been his only Lord's Test) had him caught from the first ball of the follow-on. Headley, who had warmed up for the match with 200 against Derbyshire the previous week, made light of an ankle injury to share a partnership of 56 with the obdurate Barrow, but after Headley reached 50 he fell to Allen, for the second time in the match. Hoad, who defended well for 36, raised another half-century partnership with Grant, but after they fell it became something of a procession, Verity working his way through the later batsmen to finish with four wickets, as did Macaulay. A brief flourish by the last pair lifted West Indies to 172, but they were all out with two hours remaining for play, England winning by an innings, as they had in 1928.

ENGLAND v WEST INDIES
June 24, 26, 27, 1933

ENGLAND

C.F. Walters	c Barrow b Martindale	51	Bowling:
H. Sutcliffe	c Grant b Martindale	21	Martindale 24-3-85-4,
W.R. Hammond	c Headley b Griffith	29	Francis 18-3-52-0,
M. Leyland	c Barrow b Griffith	1	Griffith 20-7-48-3,
* D.R. Jardine	c Da Costa b Achong	21	Achong 35-9-88-2,
M.J.L. Turnbull	c Barrow b Achong	28	Da Costa 4-0-15-0.
† L.E.G. Ames	not out	83	
G.O.B. Allen	run out	16	
R.W.V. Robins	b Martindale	8	
H. Verity	c Achong b Griffith	21	
G.G. Macaulay	lbw b Martindale	9	
Extras	(b3, lb5)	8	
	(101 overs)	296	

Fall: 49,103,105,106,154,155,194,217,265.

WEST INDIES

C.A. Roach	b Allen	0	c Sutcliffe b Macaulay	0	
† I. Barrow	c and b Verity	7	lbw b Robins	12	
G.A. Headley	lbw b Allen	13	b Allen	50	
E.L.G. Hoad	lbw b Robins	6	c and b Verity	36	
* G.C. Grant	hit wkt b Robins	26	lbw b Macaulay	28	
O.C. Da Costa	b Robins	6	lbw b Verity	1	
C.A. Merry	lbw b Macaulay	9	b Macaulay	1	
E.E. Achong	b Robins	15	c Hammond b Verity	10	
G.N. Francis	b Robins	4	(10) not out	11	
E.A. Martindale	b Robins	4	(9) b Macaulay	4	
H.C. Griffith	not out	1	b Verity	18	
Extras	(b3, lb1, nb2)	6	(b1)	1	
	(58.5 overs)	97	(61.1 overs)	172	

Fall: 1,17,27,31,40,51,87,92,96.   0,56,64,116,119,120,133,138,146.

Bowling: Macaulay 18-7-25-1, Allen 13-6-13-2, Verity 16-8-21-1, Robins 11.5-1-32-6.
Second innings: Macaulay 20-6-57-4, Allen 11-2-33-1, Verity 18.1-4-45-4, Robins 12-2-36-1.

Toss: England   Umpires: F. Chester and A. Dolphin
Close of play: (1) E. 43 for 0 (Walters 21, Sutcliffe 19)
(2) W.I. 55 for 6 (Grant 11, Achong 2)

ENGLAND WON BY AN INNINGS AND 27 RUNS

Constantine was released for the drawn second Test, at Old Trafford, where he scored a brisk 64 after earlier, with Martindale, indulging in an exhibition of Bodyline bowling which brought home to English eyes the full meaning of those tactics. Despite their efforts, Jardine scored 127. Earlier Headley (169 not out) and Barrow had made centuries for West Indies. England won the third Test, at The Oval, again by an innings: for the home side, Bakewell made his only Test century and C.S. 'Father' Marriott, in his only Test, took 11 wickets.

1934

The Lord's Test of 1934 saw one of those rare matches which have taken the name of their star performer. For two days of 'Verity's Match' it looked like business as usual, as England ran up a more than useful score and Australia reached 192 for 2 in reply: but it rained on the rest day, and on a pitch that was sometimes spiteful but hardly unplayable, the 29-year-old Yorkshire slow left-armer Hedley Verity took 14 wickets for 80 runs on the third day.

Australia went into the match without the prolific Ponsford (influenza), but both their 1930 centurymakers, Woodfull and the peerless Bradman, were back, while the bowling attack had been bolstered since the previous tour by the arrival of the fiery O'Reilly, probably the greatest legspinner of them all. For England, Jardine and Larwood had both disappeared from the scene, Wyatt being the new captain, although a broken thumb had kept him out of the first Test, which Australia won comfortably, O'Reilly and Grimmett taking 19 of the wickets to fall.

Wyatt, his thumb encased in a guard, won the toss and saw Walters (who had captained England at Trent Bridge) and Sutcliffe take the score to 70, before the Yorkshireman was lbw to Chipperfield, who captured the important wicket of Hammond soon afterwards. Hendren, playing his last Lord's Test at the age of 45, also went cheaply, Walters made 82, and when Wyatt fell to Chipperfield for a brave 33, England were an unimpressive 182 for 5. However, they were rescued by Leyland, playing the spinners well, and the consistent Ames, who took the score to 293, Leyland being just five runs short of his century by the close.

The Yorkshire left-hander reached three figures after 10 minutes on the second morning, but added only nine more before he was yorked by Wall. Leyland's chanceless innings had lasted 211 minutes, and included 14 fours and a six off Chipperfield. His partnership with Ames was worth 129, and now the wicketkeeper took command: he dominated a stand of 48 with Geary (9), and had reached 96 when his fellow wicketkeeper Oldfield put down a chance off Wall. Ames put this escape behind him and soon reached three figures with a square cut off the same bowler. It was Ames's second century in a Lord's Test, and he became the first wicketkeeper to score a hundred in England-Australia matches. Just before lunch, Ames was out for 120, having hit 14 fours during his·262 minutes at the crease.

Oldfield made up for missing Ames by stumping Verity off Grimmett to end the innings soon after lunch, in the process becoming the first wicketkeeper to make 100 Test dismissals.

Replying to England's 440, Woodfull and Brown put on 68 before Bowes, the only survivor among the fast bowlers from the Bodyline tour, castled the 'unbowlable' Woodfull. The new batsman was Bradman, whose 1930 innings was still fresh in the memory. The Don's 1934 form had been patchy, however, and although he and Brown rattled up 73 in 46 minutes, *Wisden* described him as 'making many of his strokes without restraint'. Bradman hit three consecutive fours off Verity, and seven in all, without ever resembling the clinical, perfect batsman of 1930, whose only half-mistake had come at 254. The 1934 Bradman gave a return catch to Verity when he had scored 36.

Yorkshire's Hedley Verity took 14 wickets on the third day of the 1934 Lord's Test as Australia collapsed twice on a helpful pitch. England's victory was their last to date against Australia at Lord's

Brown continued to impress, notwithstanding two hard chances to short leg off Bowes at 21 and 68. Now in concert with McCabe, the 21-year-old Queenslander reached his century just before the close on Saturday night, which saw Australia comfortably placed at 192 for 2. Three of England's side were less comfortable, however, with Farnes (leg), Geary (knee) and Hammond (back) all carrying injuries.

The situation changed with heavy rain on the rest day, which transformed the bland pitch into one receptive to Verity's turn. The spinner, though, tempted fate on his journey to the ground on that third morning: his car ran over a black cat, and a distraught Verity was nearly late after trying to locate the owner.

Play started only 17 minutes late, and almost immediately Brown fell to Bowes for 105, his 199-minute innings having contained 14 fours. Verity now took over, dismissing McCabe for 34 and Darling for a duck as Australia declined from 203 for 2 to 205 for 5. Soon Bromley, too, was gone, and although the resourceful Chipperfield put on 40 with Oldfield (who survived a nasty knock from Hammond), by lunch the visitors were 273 for 8, Bowes having removed Grimmett after Verity ended Oldfield's resistance. While Chipperfield was there Australia harboured hopes of avoiding the follow-on, but two rapid strikes from the inevitable Verity, whose final figures were 7 for 61 (22-9-37-6 on the third day) saw them all out seven runs short.

First-innings centurion Brown went cheaply second time around, hooking Bowes to long leg, and then Verity, whose line and length on the difficult pitch were immaculate, imposed his stranglehold once again. Woodfull and McCabe took the score to 43 before the latter was caught by Hendren, bringing Bradman to the crease. Verity placed his field shrewdly for The Don, leaving the outfield empty in an attempt to encourage the big hit, and when he had made 13 the trap was sprung. As *The Times* put it, Bradman 'suddenly perpetrated the worst shot he has ever made in his life', lashing out at Verity. The ball went straight up in the air. Any one of the close fielders might have caught it, but they sensibly left it to Ames, who grasped the important chance with relief.

Next to go was Woodfull, whose two hours of defiance for 43 ended when Hammond clung on to a sharp catch. That made it 94 for 4, and within a few minutes it was 95 for 8, Hammond bowling Darling, and the tigerish Verity removing Bromley, Oldfield and Grimmett, the last two with successive balls. There was no escape as England sought to square the series, and Australia finally reached 118, losing by an innings and 38 runs. Verity's second-innings figures were 8 for 43, and he had taken 15 for 104 in the match (14 for 80 on the third and last day), a record for a Lord's Test until Bob Massie surpassed it in 1972.

England thus celebrated their first win over Australia at Lord's since 1896 – and to date they have not managed another victory.

70

ENGLAND v AUSTRALIA
June 22, 23, 25, 1934

ENGLAND

C.F. Walters	c Bromley b O'Reilly	82	Bowling:
H. Sutcliffe	lbw b Chipperfield	20	Wall 49-7-108-4,
W.R. Hammond	c and b Chipperfield	2	McCabe 18-3-38-1,
E.H. Hendren	c McCabe b Wall	13	Grimmett 53.3-13-102-1,
* R.E.S. Wyatt	c Oldfield b Chipperfield	33	O'Reilly 38-15-70-1,
M. Leyland	b Wall	109	Chipperfield 34-10-91-3,
† L.E.G. Ames	c Oldfield b McCabe	120	Darling 6-2-19-0.
G. Geary	c Chipperfield b Wall	9	
H. Verity	st Oldfield b Grimmett	29	
K. Farnes	b Wall	1	
W.E. Bowes	not out	10	
Extras	(lb12)	12	
	(198.3 overs)	440	

Fall: 70,78,99,130,182,311,359,409,410.

AUSTRALIA

* W.M. Woodfull	b Bowes	22	c Hammond b Verity	43
W.A. Brown	c Ames b Bowes	105	c Walters b Bowes	2
D.G. Bradman	c and b Verity	36	(4) c Ames b Verity	13
S.J. McCabe	c Hammond b Verity	34	(3) c Hendren b Verity	19
L.S. Darling	c Sutcliffe b Verity	0	b Hammond	10
A.G. Chipperfield	not out	37	c Geary b Verity	14
E.H. Bromley	c Geary b Verity	4	c and b Verity	1
† W.A.S. Oldfield	c Sutcliffe b Verity	23	lbw b Verity	0
C.V. Grimmett	b Bowes	9	c Hammond b Verity	0
W.J. O'Reilly	b Verity	4	not out	8
T.W. Wall	lbw b Verity	0	c Hendren b Verity	1
Extras	(b1, lb9)	10	(b6, nb1)	7
	(109 overs)	284	(53.3 overs)	118

Fall: 68,141,203,204,205,218,258,273,284.   10,43,57,94,94,95,95,95,112.

Bowling: Farnes 12-3-43-0, Bowes 31-5-98-3, Geary 22-4-56-0, Verity 36-15-61-7, Hammond 4-1-6-0, Leyland 4-1-10-1.

Second innings: Farnes 4-2-6-0, Bowes 14-4-24-1, Verity 22.3-8-43-8, Hammond 13-0-38-1.

Toss: England   Umpires: F. Chester and J. Hardstaff snr

Close of play: (1) E. 293 for 5 (Leyland 95, Ames 44)
                 (2) A. 192 for 2 (Brown 103, McCabe 24)

ENGLAND WON BY AN INNINGS AND 38 RUNS

The third Test was drawn, Hendren and Leyland scoring centuries in England's 627 for 9. McCabe made 137 in Australia's 491. Bradman, who was to undergo an emergency appendix operation after the tour, returned to form with 304 at Leeds (his second triple-century there) as Australia scored 584. England emerged with a draw, but there was no escape at The Oval, where Ponsford (266) and Bradman (244) shared a Test-record 451 partnership in Australia's 701. England's 321 and 145 looked pale in comparison, and Australia regained the Ashes – as in 1930, on their captain Woodfull's birthday.

1935

Those used to the immaculate greensward at Lord's would have been dismayed by the look of the hallowed turf in 1935, for that year a plague of leatherjackets – the larvae of the cranefly, or daddy-longlegs – attacked the grass, leaving the ground looking like a sandy beach. The South Africans, making their fifth full tour, recorded their first Test win in England on this strange surface.

The tourists had drawn the rain-affected first Test at Trent Bridge, where opposing captain Wyatt had scored 149 in England's 384 for 7. More than half the South African side, including captain Herby Wade, made their Test debuts in that match. Two of the newcomers, Dudley Nourse and Eric Rowan, were destined to be ranked among their country's greatest batsmen.

Sir Pelham Warner recalled that the selection meeting to finalise the England side for the Lord's Test was the longest he could remember. It lasted about eight hours, with most of the time being taken up by Wyatt's insistence on including Tommy Mitchell, rather than Robins, as the legspinner. Wyatt had his way, but ironically Mitchell bowled below his best and fell out with his captain during the match. The home side also included, for the last time, the great Herbert Sutcliffe, whose eighth Lord's Test it was. One of the original selections, Somerset's N.S. 'Mandy' Mitchell-Innes, had to withdraw from what would have been his only Lord's Test, suffering from severe hay fever.

Some 30,000 spectators were present on the first day, and saw South Africa reach 228 after winning the toss. After the early loss of the obdurate Siedle, Bruce Mitchell and Rowan took the score to 59, but two quick wickets from Verity, who dismissed Rowan and the nervous Nourse, put England on top. The visitors were rescued by a scintillating innings from wicketkeeper 'Jock' Cameron, who used the drive and cut to great effect in reaching 90 out of 126, hitting three sixes and batting for only 105 minutes. Six years previously, this same Cameron had been carried off the field at the end of the Lord's Test, after being struck a fearsome blow in murky light by Larwood. Tragically, on the voyage home after this tour, Cameron contracted enteric fever and died, at the age of 30, less than three months after the final Test.

Cameron's innings lifted the total to 228, and although England soon lost Sutcliffe (under the new law which could see a batsman lbw to a ball pitching outside off stump, provided that it hit the striker between wicket and wicket and would have hit the stumps), Wyatt and Leyland took the score to 46 before the latter was bowled by Xenophon Balaskas, an intriguing legspinner of Greek extraction. England reached 75 without further loss that night.

On the rest day, the South Africans took afternoon tea at Buckingham Palace, and their trip seemed to inspire them, for on the second day England were shot out for 198, only Wyatt (53) making more than the 27 managed by both Hammond and Langridge. Balaskas, with 5 for 49, was South Africa's main destroyer.

Once more, Siedle was an early casualty when South Africa batted again, but Bruce Mitchell was determined to build on his side's hard-fought first-innings lead of 30. He combined in a stand of 134 with Rowan, but after the latter fell for 44, four quick wickets left South Africa at 177 for 6, with England back on top.

The imperturbable Bruce Mitchell made 164 not out in 1935 – the highest score for South Africa in a Lord's Test

Verity had three scalps and Mitchell one, the dangerous Cameron being caught by Ames, who was playing as a batsman in this match, the wicketkeeping gloves having passed temporarily to Farrimond of Lancashire. By now, Mitchell had reached a splendid century, and he had moved to 129 by the close, which saw South Africa at 208 for 6, 238 ahead.

Mitchell and Langton took their partnership past three figures on the third morning. 'Chud' Langton was eventually caught-and-bowled by Hammond for an invaluable 44, at which point Wade declared, leaving Mitchell undefeated with a masterly 5½-hour 164, the highest score by a South African at Lord's. Mitchell ended his career many years later as his country's leading runscorer with 3471 runs in 42 Tests.

The declaration set England 309 to win in 4¾ hours. Balaskas removed Wyatt for 16, and although Sutcliffe, batting with a runner (Middlesex's George Hart) because of a strained thigh, made a solid 38, once again no-one else could exceed 27, a score which Hammond made in both innings. Langton, fresh from his important innings, took four wickets, as did Balaskas as England subsided to 151 all out, leaving South Africa the proud victors by 157 runs.

ENGLAND v SOUTH AFRICA
June 29, July 1, 2, 1935

SOUTH AFRICA

B. Mitchell	lbw b Nichols	30	not out	164
I.J. Siedle	b Mitchell	6	c Farrimond b Mitchell	13
E.A.B. Rowan	c Farrimond b Verity	40	lbw b Nichols	44
A.D. Nourse	b Verity	3	b Verity	2
* H.F. Wade	c Hammond b Langridge	23	(7) b Verity	0
† H.B. Cameron	b Nichols	90	(5) c Ames b Mitchell	3
E.L. Dalton	c and b Langridge	19	(6) c Wyatt b Verity	0
X.C. Balaskas	b Verity	4		
A.B.C. Langton	c Holmes b Hammond	4	(8) c and b Hammond	44
R.J. Crisp	not out	4		
A.J. Bell	b Hammond	0		
Extras	(b1, lb1, w1, nb2)	5	(b3, lb5)	8
	(91.3 overs)	228	(7 wkts dec) (121.4 overs)	278

Fall: 27,59,62,98,158,187,196,224,228.   32,136,158,169,169,177,278.

Bowling: Nichols 21-5-47-2, Wyatt 4-2-9-0, Hammond 5.3-3-8-2, Mitchell 20-3-71-1, Verity 28-10-61-3, Langridge 13-3-27-2.

Second innings: Nichols 18-4-64-1, Hammond 14.4-4-26-1, Mitchell 33-5-93-2, Verity 38-16-56-3, Langridge 10-4-19-0, Holmes 4-2-10-0, Wyatt 4-2-2-0.

ENGLAND

* R.E.S. Wyatt	c Nourse b Dalton	53	b Balaskas	16
H. Sutcliffe	lbw b Bell	3	lbw b Langton	38
M. Leyland	b Balaskas	18	b Crisp	4
W.R. Hammond	b Dalton	27	c Cameron b Langton	27
L.E.G. Ames	b Balaskas	5	lbw b Langton	8
E.R.T. Holmes	c Bell b Balaskas	10	b Langton	8
J. Langridge	c Mitchell b Balaskas	27	lbw b Balaskas	17
† W. Farrimond	b Balaskas	13	b Crisp	13
M.S. Nichols	c Cameron b Langton	10	not out	7
H. Verity	lbw b Langton	17	c Langton b Balaskas	8
T.B. Mitchell	not out	5	st Cameron b Balaskas	1
Extras	(b4, lb5, w1)	10	(lb4)	4
	(80.3 overs)	198	(67 overs)	151

Fall: 5,46,100,109,116,121,158,161,177.   24,45,89,90,102,111,129,141,149.

Bowling: Crisp 8-1-32-0, Bell 6-0-16-1, Langton 21.3-3-58-2, Balaskas 32-8-49-5, Dalton 13-1-33-2.

Second innings: Crisp 15-4-30-2, Bell 12-3-21-0, Balaskas 27-8-54-4, Mitchell 2-0-11-0, Langton 11-3-31-4.

Toss: South Africa   Umpires: E.J. Smith and F.I. Walden
Close of play: (1) E. 75 for 2 (Wyatt 37, Hammond 12)
                        (2) S.A. 208 for 6 (Mitchell 129, Langton 11)

SOUTH AFRICA WON BY 157 RUNS

South Africa clinched their first series victory in England when the three remaining Tests were all drawn. Robins made his only Test century for England at Old Trafford, while Leyland (161) and Ames (148 not out) shared a stand of 179 at The Oval. Viljoen, Mitchell and Dalton also reached three figures for the visitors.

1936

Not for the first (or last) time, the composition of India's touring team in 1936 was shrouded in mystery. First, MCC agreed that the Nawab of Pataudi (who had represented England in a Test as recently as 1934) might play for and lead India, but he eventually pulled out of the tour with health problems. Eventually the captaincy devolved on the Maharajah of Vizianagram, who proved to be something of a liability on the field. In the Tests he batted at No. 9 and did not bowl, and seemed reluctant to seek advice from his senior players, one of whom, the legendary C.K. Nayudu, had an indifferent tour anyway.

Almost from the start there were rumours of splits and factions within the unnecessarily large touring party – some 22 players turned out for the Indians on tour – and even before the Tests Lala Amarnath, probably the team's best allrounder, was sent home for alleged indiscipline. It was therefore a ragged Indian team which assembled for the first Test of the tour, at Lord's.

Under a new captain in 'Gubby' Allen, who was to lead MCC in Australia the following winter, England had an experimental side: in the absence of Hammond, recovering from a tonsillectomy, Gimblett made his Test debut, while Allen took the new ball with his predecessor as captain, occasional medium-pacer Bob Wyatt.

Typically, in one of the wettest summers on record, rain had soaked the pitch before the match, but on the first morning the sun was beating down as the captains tossed. Allen won, and put India in, only the second time that a captain had fielded first in a Lord's Test. After a few desultory overs from Wyatt the spinners were on, but they failed to make the expected breakthrough as Merchant, who emerged on this tour as a batsman of the highest class, and Hindlekar took the score to 62. At this point, Allen put himself on at the Nursery end, meaning to bowl only one over to allow the spinners to change ends. However, he immediately bowled Merchant with a full-toss, and had Mushtaq Ali caught in the same over. Two runs later, the captain trapped Nayudu leg-before, and when Robins bowled the stubborn Hindlekar India had declined to 66 for 4. The next five in the order reached double figures but did not pass 20, Vizianagram finishing with 19 not out as India fell to 147 all out. Allen's final figures were 5 for 35.

In reply, England had to contend with the bowling of Amar Singh, who extracted pace and bounce from the helpful pitch. He took four quick wickets for 13 as England declined to 41 for 5, and the Indian's impressive display caused Walter Hammond to suggest: 'With the new ball he was perhaps better than anyone I have ever seen.'

England were saved from embarrassment by Leyland, who made 60, but both he and Langridge were out before the close, which found England 132 for 7 at the end of a day that had seen 17 wickets go down.

Heavy overnight rain meant that no play was possible before lunch on the second day. For the first time, artificial means were used to dry the playing area. When play did begin, India claimed a surprise first-innings lead of 13 when England were all out almost immediately. Allen and Duckworth both fell without addition to the overnight score, the captain mistiming an attempted legside shot

The lively Amar Singh took 6 for 35 as India claimed a narrow first -innings lead in 1936. Although England emerged victorious, Walter Hammond was moved to write of Amar Singh that 'With the new ball he was perhaps better than anyone I have ever seen'

and sending a catch to slip off the back of the bat, giving the impressive Amar Singh his sixth wicket.

India's second innings had a disastrous start, Duckworth – playing his first Lord's Test since 1930 – clinging on to a splendid legside catch off Allen to send back Merchant for a duck. Although Hindlekar, handicapped by a chipped finger, survived for an hour and a half for 17, wickets fell regularly at the other end, where only Palia and Jahangir reached double figures. When bad light and drizzle forced an early close, India had limped to 80 for 7.

More heavy rain prevented a resumption until three o'clock on the final afternoon, but India were soon despatched for 93, Allen taking five more wickets to finish with match figures of 10 for 78.

England needed only 107 to win, but looked set for a struggle when a ball from Nissar climbed on the scoreless Arthur Mitchell, who fended it off with his glove to Merchant at backward point. The debutant Gimblett, however, hit out: he hooked four successive short-pitched balls from Nissar to the boundary, and ended up with 11 fours in his unbeaten 67. He and Turnbull put on 108 for the second wicket: both, however, gave difficult chances off Amar Singh. Gimblett hit the winning run off the unlucky Amar Singh, taking England to victory with some 50 minutes remaining.

India's bowling hero, Amar Singh, seemed set for a long and fruitful career, but this proved to be his last Test series. After this tour, India played no more Test cricket until 1946, by which time Amar Singh had died of pneumonia, aged only 29.

ENGLAND v INDIA
June 27, 29, 30, 1936

INDIA

V.M. Merchant	b Allen	35	c Duckworth b Allen		0
† D.D. Hindlekar	b Robins	26	lbw b Robins		17
S. Mushtaq Ali	c Langridge b Allen	0	lbw b Allen		8
C.K. Nayudu	lbw b Allen	1	c Robins b Allen		3
S. Wazir Ali	b Allen	11	c Verity b Allen		4
L. Amar Singh	c Langridge b Robins	12	lbw b Verity		7
P.E. Palia	c Mitchell b Verity	11	c Leyland b Verity		16
M. Jahangir Khan	b Allen	13	c Duckworth b Verity		13
* Maharajah of Vizianagram	not out	19	c Mitchell b Verity		6
C.S. Nayudu	c Wyatt b Robins	6	c Hardstaff b Allen		9
Mahomed Nissar	st Duckworth b Verity	9	not out		2
Extras	(b4)	4	(b4, lb3, nb1)		8
	(55.1 overs)	147	(46 overs)		93

Fall:	62,62,64,66,85,97,107,119,137.	0,18,22,28,39,45,64,80,90.

Bowling: Allen 17-7-35-5, Wyatt 3-2-7-0, Verity 18.1-5-42-2,
Langridge 4-1-9-0, Robins 13-4-50-3.
Second innings: Allen 18-1-43-5, Wyatt 7-4-8-0, Verity 16-8-17-4, Robins 5-1-17-1.

ENGLAND

A. Mitchell	b Amar Singh	14	c Merchant b Nissar		0
H. Gimblett	c Mushtaq Ali b Amar Singh	11	not out		67
M.J.L. Turnbull	b Amar Singh	0	not out		37
M. Leyland	lbw b Amar Singh	60			
R.E.S. Wyatt	c Jahangir b Amar Singh	0			
J. Hardstaff jnr	b Nissar	2			
J. Langridge	c Jahangir b C.K. Nayudu	19			
* G.O.B. Allen	c Jahangir b Amar Singh	13			
† G. Duckworth	c Vizianagram b Nissar	2			
R.W.V. Robins	c C.K. Nayudu b Nissar	0			
H. Verity	not out	2			
Extras	(b4, lb4, nb3)	11	(b4)		4
	(61.1 overs)	134	(1 wkt) (39.3 overs)		108

Fall:	16,16,30,34,41,96,129,132,132.	0.

Bowling: Nissar 17-5-36-3, Amar Singh 25.1-11-35-6, Jahangir 9-0-27-0,
C.K. Nayudu 7-2-17-1, C.S. Nayudu 3-0-8-0.
Second innings: Nissar 6-3-26-1, Amar Singh 16.3-6-36-0, Jahangir 10-3-20-0,
C.K. Nayudu 7-2-22-0.

Toss: England   Umpires: A. Dolphin and F.I. Walden
Close of play: (1) E. 132 for 7 (Allen 13, Duckworth 2)
                 (2) I. 80 for 7 (Palia 15, Vizianagram 6)

ENGLAND WON BY 9 WICKETS

Merchant (114) and Mushtaq Ali (112) shared an opening stand of 203 in the second Test, which ended in a draw. Hammond, who had scored 167 in England's 571 for 8 at Old Trafford, made 217 in the final Test, at The Oval, where England won by nine wickets. Worthington also made a century for England, while Allen took 7 for 80 in the second innings.

1937

New Zealand, who had impressed on their Lord's Test 'debut' in 1931, returned six years later with an inexperienced side. One of their 1931 centurymakers, 'Curly' Page, was now captain, but Stewie Dempster, who had made a memorable 120 in the previous match, was now captaining Leicestershire in the County Championship and therefore was unavailable. Kerr was New Zealand's only other survivor from Lord's in 1931.

England, too, were a changed side: Allen played little cricket in 1937 after the rigours of his Ashes tour (which saw Australia come back from 2-0 down to take the series 3-2, the only time this has been done in Tests), and his Middlesex team-mate Robins, in his seventh and last Lord's Test, assumed the captaincy.

Robins came in for some criticism when, after winning the toss, he sent in Parks and the 21-year-old Hutton to open. Both were making their Test debuts, and Robins's side included Barnett, who had opened in all five Tests in Australia the previous winter. The gamble did not pay off, the crowd – which swelled to 20,000 later on – being disappointed to see Cowie bring a ball back a long way to bowl Hutton for a duck after 25 minutes. Parks made 22 before he too was bowled by Cowie, but then Hardstaff and Hammond combined in a partnership of 245 in 219 minutes. Both scored centuries, Hardstaff's being his first in Tests. Hammond, however, put his poor form in his previous eight Lord's Tests behind him (his best score before this innings was 46), and hit 14 fours and a six in his 140. When he had made 23, he passed Jack Hobbs's then-record Test aggregate of 5410 runs.

New Zealand, whose keen fielding was a feature of the first day's play, kept in the game with three quick wickets, and by the close England had reached 370 for 7. Paynter took his score to 74 on the second morning, as England were all out for 424: New Zealand's persevering opening bowlers, Cowie and Roberts, both took four wickets.

In reply, the visitors soon lost Vivian, lbw to Gover for 5, and then saw Kerr retire after being hit on the chin by Hammond. A sparkling innings of 52 from Wallace enlivened proceedings: he hit six fours and two sixes, one of which was well caught by a spectator. The young Martin Donnelly, destined for greater things in 1949, emulated Hutton by collecting a duck on his Test debut: both he and Wallace were lbw to Parks, who was playing the only Test of his career in the middle of a season which saw him achieve the unique double of 3000 runs and 100 wickets.

At 176 for 7, New Zealand were facing the follow-on, but a sensible stand between Moloney and Roberts averted this possibility. They hit out judiciously amid periods of watchful defence, and had posted the century partnership when play was interrupted as the sides were presented to King George VI. As so often happens, the break in play affected the players' concentration, and Moloney was out immediately afterwards. Dunning, too, was out before the close, which saw the Kiwis still 142 adrift. Voce ended the innings early on the final morning, trapping Cowie lbw to leave Roberts undefeated with 66.

England, searching for quick runs, again lost both openers cheaply, but Hardstaff and Barnett (batting at No. 4 in the absence of Hammond with water

79

In eight Test appearances at Lord's prior to 1937 the great Walter Hammond had, remarkably, failed to record a single half-century. He put this poor run behind him with 140 against the touring New Zealanders then, against Bradman's Australians the following year, played a memorable innings of 240, the highest score for England at Lord's

on the knee) piled on 104 in 52 minutes. Barnett's 83 not out, which contained 14 fours, took 100 minutes. Ames and Robins also made useful contributions, and the lunchtime declaration saw England at 226 for 4, those runs coming from only 42 overs.

New Zealand needed to survive the final two sessions, their theoretical victory target being 355. They were in trouble almost from the start, three wickets falling with the score at 15. Wallace again hit out, making light of two painful blows on the hand to such effect that he hit four fours in one Verity over. Staunch defence from the injured Kerr, who lasted 105 minutes for his 38, hitting eight fours, and Roberts took the visitors almost to safety, and although Donnelly, after 47 minutes of defiance, succumbed to the last ball of the match, New Zealand had preserved their unbeaten record at Lord's.

ENGLAND v NEW ZEALAND
June 26, 28, 29, 1937

ENGLAND

J.H. Parks	b Cowie	22	b Cowie		7
L. Hutton	b Cowie	0	c Vivian b Cowie		1
J. Hardstaff jnr	c Moloney b Roberts	114	c Tindill b Roberts		64
W.R. Hammond	c Roberts b Vivian	140			
E. Paynter	c Dunning b Roberts	74			
C.J. Barnett	b Cowie	5	(4) not out		83
† L.E.G. Ames	b Vivian	5	(5) c sub (J.R. Lamason) b Roberts		20
* R.W.V. Robins	c Tindill b Roberts	18	(6) not out		38
W. Voce	c Tindill b Cowie	27			
H. Verity	c Cowie b Roberts	3			
A.R. Gover	not out	2			
Extras	(b4, lb9, w1)	14	(b5, lb8)		13
	(155.3 overs)	424	(4 wkts dec) (42 overs)		226

Fall: 13,31,276,284,302,307,339,402,415.   8,19,123,163.

Bowling: Cowie 41-10-118-4, Roberts 43.3-11-101-4, Dunning 20-3-64-0, Vivian 46-10-106-2, Moloney 2-1-9-0, Page 3-0-12-0.
Second innings: Cowie 15-2-49-2, Roberts 14-3-73-2, Dunning 9-0-60-0, Vivian 4-0-31-0.

NEW ZEALAND

J.L. Kerr	c Ames b Robins	31	(7) not out		38
H.G. Vivian	lbw b Gover	5	c Verity b Voce		11
W.A. Hadlee	c Verity b Voce	34	b Voce		3
* M.L. Page	c Paynter b Robins	9	(5) c and b Robins		13
W.M. Wallace	lbw b Parks	52	(4) lbw b Parks		56
M.P. Donnelly	lbw b Parks	0	(9) c Ames b Voce		21
D.A.R. Moloney	c and b Verity	64	(1) run out		0
† E.W.T. Tindill	c Hammond b Robins	8	lbw b Verity		3
A.W. Roberts	not out	66	(6) c sub (G.E. Hart) b Gover		17
J.A. Dunning	b Gover	0			
J. Cowie	lbw b Voce	2			
Extras	(b4, lb18, nb2)	24	(b4, lb8, w1)		13
	(111.2 overs)	295	(8 wkts) (76.5 overs)		175

Fall: 9,36,66,131,131,147,176,280,281.   15,15,15,85,87,143,146,175.

Bowling: Gover 22-8-49-2, Voce 24.2-2-74-2, Hammond 6-2-12-0, Robins 21-5-58-3, Verity 25-13-48-1, Parks 11-3-26-2, Hutton 2-1-4-0.
Second innings: Gover 18-7-27-1, Voce 18.5-8-41-3, Parks 10-6-10-1, Robins 16-3-51-1, Verity 14-7-33-1.

Toss: England   Umpires: F. Chester and F.I. Walden
Close of play: (1) E. 370 for 7 (Paynter 42, Voce 12)
           (2) N.Z. 282 for 9 (Roberts 58, Cowie 1)
           Kerr retired hurt at 20 for 1, resumed at 66 for 3

MATCH DRAWN

England took the series with a 130-run win in the next match, at Old Trafford, Hutton making 100 in his second Test. Gloucestershire offspinner Tom Goddard, making one of his rare Test appearances, took 6 for 29 in the second innings. The third Test, at The Oval, was drawn, Hardstaff scoring 103 and Denis Compton, on his Test debut, 65.

1938

Bradman's majestic 254 at Lord's in 1930 was probably the finest innings ever seen at the great ground, but Walter Hammond's 240 eight years later ran it close. Hammond had not had the best of luck in Test matches at Lord's until 1937, when he converted his maiden Test half-century at HQ into 140. Having broken his duck and having become an amateur in order to take on the England captaincy, Hammond was ready for Bradman's invaders in 1938.

Bradman had assumed the Australian captaincy in 1936-37, suffering a bad shock when Gubby Allen's tourists went two-up. Uniquely, the Australians fought back to win the series, Bradman himself scoring two double-centuries and another hundred. The great man's 1938 side was largely familiar, although the selectors (of which Bradman was one) caused a stir by leaving the wily legspinner Grimmett at home (he was 46).

The drawn first Test foreshadowed a high-scoring series. England ran up 658 for 8, Paynter scoring 216 not out and three others – Barnett, Hutton and the 20-year-old Compton – making centuries. Australia replied with 411, McCabe's 232 being another of Test cricket's legendary innings, and Brown and Bradman passed three figures in the follow-on.

England batted first again at Lord's, but on a green pitch and facing McCormick's genuinely fast bowling, Barnett and Hutton were never likely to repeat their opening stand of 219 at Nottingham. Obtaining sharp lift from the pavilion end, McCormick had both openers caught at short leg, while Edrich played on before he had scored. Paynter came out to join Hammond at 31 for 3, and the experienced pair rescued the situation. Hammond was in good form from the start: his half-century came up in 68 minutes, and he reached his eighth hundred against Australia in 145 minutes. At 87, he gave a hard chance to O'Reilly in the covers, but otherwise his innings was flawless. The power of his shots is best illustrated by the fact that when bowler Chipperfield tried to intercept a ferocious drive, he damaged his hand so much that he had to leave the field immediately.

Paynter, meanwhile, was making his own way to a century, but he was cruelly denied one run short by O'Reilly, who bowled better as the day wore on. The legspinner soon accounted for Compton, too, but Hammond sailed regally on, now in concert with Ames. The pair raised another century partnership, Hammond reaching his double-century not long before the close. Hammond's great day – neatly, he scored 70 in each session – was marred just before the end when he pulled a leg muscle running a quick single.

Even though this was the first Lord's Test to be televised, so many spectators crowded in on the Saturday that the authorities made more room by shortening the boundaries, but even this did not enable England to make much of a fist of extending their overnight 409 for 5, their task being hampered by Hammond's indisposition. The captain reached 240 before McCormick uprooted his leg stump, and apart from Ames, who hit 10 fours in his 83, no-one else reached double figures as the innings declined to 494 all out. In all, Hammond lasted 367 minutes and hit 32 fours, and his 240 remains the highest for England in a Lord's Test. Neville Cardus wrote: 'Hammond batted with an ease and style beyond anything

Queenslander Bill Brown made a Lord's century in 1934, but surpassed that four years later by carrying his bat for 206

he has ever done before: more handsome cricket could not be imagined.'

Australia's openers took the score to 69 with little fuss until Fingleton fell to Wright. Brown and Bradman raised the century, but then Verity made a vital breakthrough when Bradman misjudged his arm ball and played on. McCabe threatened briefly, until he was well caught by Verity at gully, and it was left to Brown and Hassett, who put on 124, to retrieve the situation. Hassett fell to Wellard soon before stumps, but Brown was still there at the close with 140, his second century in his second Lord's Test.

Brown was still there, too, when the Australian innings came to an end next day. He batted for 369 minutes and hit 22 fours and a five in his 206 not out, becoming the third player after his compatriots Barrett and Bardsley to carry his bat at Lord's. When 184, he was missed by Paynter at mid-on off Wellard (Paynter later put down O'Reilly as well). Australia's 422 is the highest Test innings through which an opener has carried his bat. For all Brown's heroics, the visitors would probably have followed on without an aggressive 42 from O'Reilly, who lofted two sixes off Verity: the pair added 85 in 46 minutes. Farnes, who was to die in the war, should have ended the Australian innings with a hat-trick, but Compton at slip dropped Fleetwood-Smith after the Essex fast bowler had disposed of O'Reilly and McCormick.

After a three-hour interruption for rain, England made a poor start as they attempted to build on their lead of 72, two wickets going down before the close. Wickets continued to tumble on the final morning, Hammond appearing briefly with a runner, and the home side were in some danger at 76 for 5 and 142 for 7. A stand of 74 between Compton, whose 76 not out included 14 fours, and the big-hitting Wellard (he belted McCabe into the Grand Stand) made things safe and, 314 ahead, Hammond was able to make a teasing declaration, giving Australia nearly three hours to survive on a testing pitch. England's prospects were hampered by an injury to Ames, who had fractured a finger while batting. Paynter took his place behind the stumps, and caught Barnett, despite having 'not kept wicket since he was a boy in knickerbockers,' as Sir Pelham Warner put it.

Although Fingleton was soon out, a nonchalant century from Bradman – his 14th in Tests – prevented any thoughts of an England win. The Don's chanceless innings, the 200th century in England-Australia Tests, included 15 fours. Australia finished up at 204 for 6, Badcock having the misfortune to complete a 'pair'.

ENGLAND v AUSTRALIA
June 24, 25, 27, 28, 1938

ENGLAND

C.J. Barnett	c Brown b McCormick	18	c McCabe b McCormick	12
L. Hutton	c Brown b McCormick	4	c McCormick b O'Reilly	5
W.J. Edrich	b McCormick	0	(4) c McCabe b McCormick	10
* W.R. Hammond	b McCormick	240	(6) c sub (M.G. Waite) b McCabe	2
E. Paynter	lbw b O'Reilly	99	run out	43
D.C.S. Compton	lbw b O'Reilly	6	(7) not out	76
† L.E.G. Ames	c McCormick b Fleetwood-Smith	83	(8) c McCabe b O'Reilly	6
H. Verity	b O'Reilly	5	(3) b McCormick	11
A.W. Wellard	c McCormick b O'Reilly	4	b McCabe	38
D.V.P. Wright	b Fleetwood-Smith	6	not out	10
K. Farnes	not out	5		
Extras	(b1, lb12, w1, nb10)	24	(b12, lb12, w1, nb4)	29
	(137.3 overs)	494	(8 wkts dec) (72 overs)	242

Fall: 12,20,31,253,271,457,472,476,483.   25,28,43,64,76,128,142,216.

Bowling: McCormick 27-1-101-4, McCabe 31-4-86-0, Fleetwood-Smith 33.5-2-139-2, O'Reilly 37-6-93-4, Chipperfield 8.4-0-51-0.

Second innings: McCormick 24-5-72-3, O'Reilly 29-10-53-2, McCabe 12-1-58-2, Fleetwood-Smith 7-1-30-0.

AUSTRALIA

J.H.W. Fingleton	c Hammond b Wright	31	c Hammond b Wellard	4
W.A. Brown	not out	206	b Verity	10
* D.G. Bradman	b Verity	18	not out	102
S.J. McCabe	c Verity b Farnes	38	c Hutton b Verity	21
A.L. Hassett	lbw b Wellard	56	b Wright	42
C.L. Badcock	b Wellard	0	c Wright b Edrich	0
† B.A. Barnett	c Compton b Verity	8	c Paynter b Edrich	14
A.G. Chipperfield	lbw b Verity	1		
W.J. O'Reilly	b Farnes	42		
E.L. McCormick	c Barnett b Farnes	0		
L.O'B. Fleetwood-Smith	c Barnett b Verity	7		
Extras	(b1, lb8, nb6)	15	(b5, lb3, w2, nb1)	11
	(121.4 overs)	422	(6 wkts) (48.2 overs)	204

Fall: 69,101,152,276,276,307,308,393,393.   8,71,111,175,180,204.

Bowling: Farnes 43-6-135-3, Wellard 23-2-96-2, Wright 16-2-68-1, Verity 35.4-9-103-4, Edrich 4-2-5-0.

Second innings: Farnes 13-3-51-0, Wellard 9-1-30-1, Verity 13-5-29-2, Wright 8-0-56-1, Edrich 5.2-0-27-2.

Toss: England   Umpires: E.J. Smith and F.I. Walden
Close of play: (1) E. 409 for 5 (Hammond 210, Ames 50)
                 (2) A. 299 for 5 (Brown 140, Barnett 6)
                 (3) E. 39 for 2 (Verity 5, Edrich 6)

MATCH DRAWN

Rain completely washed out the Old Trafford Test, and Australia took a 1-0 lead at Headingley, yet another century from Bradman and O'Reilly's 10 wickets being the decisive factors. Australia thus retained the Ashes, but England had some revenge at The Oval, where Hutton made his Test-record 364 in England's huge total of 903 for 7. Australia, without Bradman and Fingleton (both injured), could muster only 201 and 123 in reply.

1939

The crowds for the Lord's Test were becoming accustomed to witnessing great batting feats, and they had another display to savour in 1939 when George Headley, the West Indian maestro, became the only player so far to score two centuries in the same Test at Lord's.

Headley's heroics lightened the gloomy atmosphere prevalent at the time. War with Germany seemed unavoidable: Hammond broadcast army recruitment messages over the loudspeakers during the match.

West Indies, in their third Lord's Test, were hopeful of avoiding their third straight innings defeat. They had the great Headley, and they also had Constantine, who had been largely unavailable in 1933. Jeff Stollmeyer, just 18 but destined to become a great name in West Indian cricket, made his Test debut at Lord's, as did Cameron, Clarke and Kenneth 'Bam Bam' Weekes (no relation to Everton). Cameron was an interesting player who, as a schoolboy at Taunton School, had taken all 10 wickets in an innings during a schools' game at Lord's in 1931. For England, still captained by Hammond, Derbyshire fast bowler Bill Copson was playing in his first Test. As a matter of interest, the England professionals' match fee for this Test was £27/10/0 (£27.50).

For the only time in England, eight-ball overs were used in this season, as part of an intended two-year experiment which was abandoned with the outbreak of war.

Rolph Grant, the brother of West Indies' 1933 skipper Jack, won the toss and braved a bitterly cold wind on a dull day by going in first himself with Stollmeyer. Grant left for 22, well caught left-handed by Compton, close in at forward short leg, but Stollmeyer and Headley managed to survive on a bland pitch, deadened after recent rains. Bowes, who had difficulty controlling the new ball, eventually bowled Stollmeyer for a three-hour 59, but Headley, although he was not at his best, showed flashes of his back-foot brilliance and went on to 106, made in around four hours.

From 226 for 3, West Indies declined to 277 all out. Weekes fell to a marvellous catch by Gimblett, running backwards at cover, and Copson had both Constantine and Barrow lbw: he finished with 5 for 85.

England made 11 without loss that evening, and on the second day, despite two brief interruptions for bad light, they moved to 404 for 5. The openers added 49 before Gimblett was bowled by Cameron's second ball in Tests, then Hutton and Paynter put on 70 more. Hammond became the third victim in a good spell from Cameron, but then Hutton and Compton (dropped twice in two balls) stopped the rot, combining to add 248 for the fourth wicket in 140 minutes. Hutton, who had not passed 5 in his previous four Test innings at Lord's, made amends now as he went on to 196. After their epic partnership, Hutton and Compton departed within seven runs of each other, the Yorkshireman falling to Hylton (who later found unwanted notoriety when he became the first Test cricketer to be hanged for murder), while Compton, hitting out, sent a difficult catch to Stollmeyer at deep square leg. West Indies bowled well, although Constantine (13-0-67-0) received heavy punishment, Compton once thrashing him for three fours in an over.

Jamaica's master batsman George Headley, who hit 106 and 107 in 1939, remains the only man to hit centuries in each innings of a Lord's Test

Hammond declared at the overnight score with a lead of 127, and Copson continued his fine debut by having Stollmeyer caught off a lifter for a duck. Grant and Headley added 42 before Bowes flattened the captain's off stump, and of the rest only Sealy, with 29, kept Headley company for long in the face of some excellent England fielding. Although he had his problems against the spin of Wright and Compton, overall Headley batted with more certainty than in the first innings. He went on to his second century of the match – a unique feat in a Lord's Test – becoming the first player to achieve this feat twice in Tests, having also taken twin centuries off England at Georgetown in 1929-30.

Wickets tumbled quickly at the death, Hardstaff taking a fine low catch to dismiss Hylton and Bowes sticking out his hand to collect a hard-hit stroke from Martindale. West Indies were all out for 225, Copson finishing with four more wickets for match figures of 9 for 152.

England had 110 minutes to score the 99 needed for victory, and reached their target in 17.7 overs, Hammond making the winning hit with 35 minutes to spare. Gimblett took a four and a six off successive balls from Martindale before that player bowled him, and England also lost Hutton before achieving a win in the last Lord's Test for seven long, dark years.

ENGLAND v WEST INDIES
June 24, 26, 27, 1939

WEST INDIES

* R.S. Grant	c Compton b Copson	22	b Bowes	23
J.B. Stollmeyer	b Bowes	59	c Verity b Copson	0
G.A. Headley	c Wood b Copson	106	c Hutton b Wright	107
J.E.D. Sealy	c Wood b Wright	13	c Wood b Copson	29
K.H. Weekes	c Gimblett b Copson	20	c Wood b Verity	16
L.N. Constantine	lbw b Copson	14	c Hammond b Verity	17
J.H. Cameron	c Hutton b Bowes	1	c and b Wright	0
† I. Barrow	lbw b Copson	2	not out	6
E.A. Martindale	lbw b Wright	22	c Bowes b Wright	3
L.G. Hylton	not out	2	c Hardstaff b Copson	13
C.B. Clarke	b Bowes	1	c and b Copson	0
Extras	(b3, lb9, nb3)	15	(b6, lb4, w1)	11
	(81.4 overs)	277	(69.4 overs)	225

Fall: 29,147,180,226,245,250,250,261,276.   0,42,105,154,190,199,200,204,225.

Bowling: Bowes 28.4-5-86-3, Copson 24-2-85-5, Wright 13-1-57-2, Verity 16-3-34-0.
Second innings: Bowes 19-7-44-1, Copson 16.4-2-67-4, Wright 17-0-75-3, Verity 14-4-20-2, Compton 3-0-8-0.

ENGLAND

L. Hutton	c Grant b Hylton	196	b Hylton	16
H. Gimblett	b Cameron	22	b Martindale	20
E. Paynter	c Barrow b Cameron	34	not out	32
* W.R. Hammond	c Grant b Cameron	14	not out	30
D.C.S. Compton	c Stollmeyer b Clarke	120		
J. Hardstaff jnr	not out	3		
† A. Wood	not out	0		
D.V.P. Wright				
H. Verity	did not bat			
W.H. Copson				
W.E. Bowes				
Extras	(b8, lb6, w1)	15	(lb2)	2
	(5 wkts dec) (95 overs)	404	(2 wkts) (17.7 overs)	100

Fall: 49,119,147,395,402.   35,39.

Bowling: Martindale 20-2-86-0, Hylton 24-4-98-1, Constantine 13-0-67-0, Cameron 26-6-66-3, Clarke 6-0-28-1, Sealy 3-0-21-0, Grant 3-0-23-0.
Second innings: Martindale 7.7-0-51-1, Hylton 7-1-36-1, Constantine 3-0-11-0.

Toss: West Indies   Umpires: E.J. Smith and F.I. Walden
Close of play: (1) E. 11 for 0 (Hutton 4, Gimblett 5)
  (2) E. 404 for 5 (Hardstaff 3, Wood 0)

ENGLAND WON BY 8 WICKETS

The remaining Tests were both drawn. At Old Trafford, in a rain-affected match, Bowes took 6 for 33 as West Indies slumped to 133 all out. At The Oval, the visitors made 498, Weekes scoring 137, but a stand of 264 between Hutton (165 not out) and Hammond (138) cemented England's 1-0 series win.

1946

The Nawab of Pataudi, who might have led India in 1936, finally was persuaded to lead his country 10 years later, when they were the opponents for England's first summer of international cricket after the Second World War. Pataudi, now 36, had played three Tests for England in the 1930s, starting with a Test-debut century against Australia on the 'Bodyline' tour.

England's postwar side was still led by Hammond, and the batting was largely unchanged from before the war, Ikin being the only newcomer. The bowling department, however, had been badly depleted by the wartime deaths of Farnes and Verity, but Alec Bedser, one of the Surrey twins, had given distinct signs of promise – and he was to confirm them in this match.

The Indians gave notice of their capabilities early in the tour, during a remarkable match with Surrey. The last two batsmen, Sarwate and Banerjee, both hit centuries, and put on 249 for the last wicket, a record in England.

The cricket-starved public flocked to Lord's for England's first postwar Test, and the gates were closed on the first two days. Pataudi won the toss, and chose to bat even though the ground was heavy and the outfield slow after recent rain. All day, Hammond kept four close fielders, sometimes more: the pressure told on the Indians, who declined to 87 for 6 in the face of accurate bowling from Bedser. Modi, a lithe batsman with a great reputation, belatedly found his timing and shared a stand of 57 with Kardar, who later captained Pakistan at Lord's. When Kardar departed for an aggressive 43, Modi found another staunch ally in last man Shinde, and they raised 200 before the No. 11 became Bedser's seventh wicket of the innings. Modi remained unbeaten on 57.

England, too, made an indifferent start, Hutton going for 7 and Compton falling first ball, both to Amarnath, the 'bad boy' of the 1936 tour (he was sent home for 'indiscipline' before the Tests started). Amarnath had a short run to the wicket, but his speed was deceptive, and he added two more wickets as England lurched to 70 for 4 after little more than an hour. Hardstaff and Gibb avoided further problems, and took the score to 135 for 4 by stumps.

The fifth-wicket pair took their stand to 182 on the second morning, Gibb making 60 before he was caught at slip off the tireless Mankad. Hardstaff, who otherwise had a moderate season, went on to his century – the first in any Test after the war – and then to his only double-century in Tests. In all, he batted for 315 minutes, and remained 205 not out when the innings closed for 428. Amarnath ended up with 5 for 118 from 57 overs.

Mankad had also done a lot of work, sending down 48 overs, but nonetheless he opened the innings with Merchant, and they shared a partnership of 67 before Ikin claimed his first Test wicket. Merchant, the man out, was the batting star of the Indian side: he comfortably exceeded 2000 runs in all matches on the trip, and indeed had been narrowly defeated (10-8) for the captaincy in a vote among Indian Board members before the tour.

Mankad and Modi put on another 50, but England had winkled out two more wickets by the close, which found India 162 for 4, still 66 adrift. On the final morning Wright produced a perfect legbreak to bowl Pataudi, and when Hazare fell to Bedser only a pugnacious 50 from Amarnath staved off the threat of an

Alec Bedser, who took 11 wickets in his first Test, at Lord's in 1946

innings defeat. As it was, India were all out for 275, Bedser wrapping up the innings to finish with debut match figures of 11 for 145.

England needed only 46 to win, which they achieved without losing a wicket. The proud Indians, however, did not give up, and made England fight for their victory: the final seven runs all came in singles, the last one coming on the stroke of lunch.

ENGLAND v INDIA
June 22, 24, 25, 1946

INDIA

V.M. Merchant	c Gibb b Bedser	12	lbw b Ikin		27
M.H. Mankad	b Wright	14	c Hammond b Smailes		63
L. Amarnath	lbw b Bedser	0	(8) b Smailes		50
V.S. Hazare	b Bedser	31	c Hammond b Bedser		34
R.S. Modi	not out	57	(3) lbw b Smailes		21
* Nawab of Pataudi snr	c Ikin b Bedser	9	b Wright		22
Gul Mahomed	b Wright	1	lbw b Wright		9
A.H. Kardar	b Bowes	43	(5) b Bedser		0
† D.D. Hindlekar	lbw b Bedser	3	c Ikin b Bedser		17
C.S. Nayudu	st Gibb b Bedser	4	b Bedser		13
S.G. Shinde	b Bedser	10	not out		4
Extras	(b10, lb6)	16	(b10, lb2, nb3)		15
	(76.1 overs)	200	(81.1 overs)		275

Fall: 15,15,44,74,86,87,144,147,157.   67,117,126,129,174,185,190,249,263.

Bowling: Bowes 25-7-64-1, Bedser 29.1-11-49-7, Smailes 5-1-18-0, Wright 17-4-53-2.
Second innings: Bowes 4-1-9-0, Bedser 32.1-3-96-4, Wright 20-3-68-2, Ikin 10-1-43-1, Smailes 15-2-44-3.

ENGLAND

L. Hutton	c Nayudu b Amarnath	7	not out		22
C. Washbrook	c Mankad b Amarnath	27	not out		24
D.C.S. Compton	b Amarnath	0			
* W.R. Hammond	b Amarnath	33			
J. Hardstaff jnr	not out	205			
† P.A. Gibb	c Hazare b Mankad	60			
J.T. Ikin	c Hindlekar b Shinde	16			
T.F. Smailes	c Mankad b Amarnath	25			
A.V. Bedser	b Hazare	30			
D.V.P. Wright	b Mankad	3			
W.E. Bowes	lbw b Hazare	2			
Extras	(b11, lb8, nb1)	20	(lb1, w1)		2
	(169.4 overs)	428	(0 wkt) (16.5 overs)		48

Fall: 16,16,61,70,252,284,344,416,421.

Bowling: Hazare 34.4-4-100-2, Amarnath 57-18-118-5, Gul Mahomed 2-0-2-0, Mankad 48-11-107-2, Shinde 23-2-66-1, Nayudu 5-1-15-0.
Second innings: Amarnath 4-0-15-0, Hazare 4-2-7-0, Mankad 4.5-1-11-0, Nayudu 4-0-13-0.

Toss: India   Umpires: H.G. Baldwin and J.A. Smart
Close of play: (1) E. 135 for 4 (Hardstaff 42, Gibb 23)
               (2) I. 162 for 4 (Hazare 26, Pataudi 16)

ENGLAND WON BY 10 WICKETS

The remaining Tests were both drawn, India's last pair hanging on for 13 minutes to draw at Old Trafford, where Bedser took another 11 wickets. Rain ruined the Oval Test, England reaching 95 for 3 in reply to India's 331, of which Merchant made 128.

1947

The 'golden summer' of 1947 forever will be remembered as the year of Compton and Edrich. The 'Middlesex Twins' could do no wrong, especially when confronted by the touring South Africans. In all matches that season, the duo made more than 7000 runs, Compton's 3816 and 18 centuries both being records which are unlikely ever to be beaten.

Once again, crowds flooded in to cricket matches in numbers rarely seen since. The popular South Africans ran up a big score – 533 – in the first Test at Trent Bridge, skipper Alan Melville scoring 189 and Dudley Nourse 149. England, all out for 208, followed on: this time Compton, with 163, led the way to a total of 551. In the 138 minutes remaining, South Africa made 166 of the 227 they had needed to win, Melville making another century.

At Lord's, the gates were closed on a 30,000 crowd half an hour before the start. Norman Yardley was England's captain, Hammond's Test career having ended after a disappointing series in Australia, where the home side retained the Ashes convincingly. Yardley, who had made 99 at Nottingham, won the toss, and saw his openers make a solid start. They survived until lunch, although Hutton in particular was bogged down (Washbrook hit the only boundary of the first session). After the interval Hutton, who had survived 121 balls for his 18, was bowled by a fine offspinner from Rowan, and not long afterwards Washbrook went for 65, Tuckett juggling but hanging on to a slip chance.

This brought together the famous 'twins', and they did not disappoint their public. After a careful start, which featured Compton almost visibly restricting the power of his strokes as he played himself in, the pair opened out, and the South Africans, for all the tenacity of their fielding, could do little to stem the flow. Edrich, specialising in the pull-drive, and Compton, unveiling all his strokes, including his patent sweep, continued almost run-for-run for the rest of the day. Both reached three figures shortly before the close, and had it not been for rain interrupting play for half an hour, they might have put on more than 216 in 190 minutes. Skipper Melville, who had enough to contend with in the shape of two master batsmen, received a nasty blow in the face when he was hit by a fielder's return. He developed a lurid black eye over the weekend.

The second day saw Edrich and Compton anxious for further glory. Left-arm spinner Mann once turned a ball past Compton's groping bat, but such events were rare indeed as the stand wore on. Edrich fell to the tidy Mann soon after the lunch interval, his 355-minute 189 containing a six off Rowan and 26 fours, four of them off consecutive balls from legspinner Smith. Compton carried on, reaching his first Test double-century before falling to Tuckett for 208, made in 350 minutes and containing 20 fours.

Barnett knocked up a brisk 33 as quick runs were sought, and Tuckett's figures benefited greatly as he took 5 for 20 in the space of seven overs (5 for 115 overall). England piled on 111 in 65 minutes after the interval before Yardley declared at 554 for 8.

South Africa made a sound start in reply, Mitchell and Melville (who survived a return chance to Wright when 40) putting on 95, at which point that man Compton had the former stumped. Viljoen immediately played on to Wright, but

The 'Middlesex Twins', Bill Edrich (left) and Denis Compton: they shared a stand of 370 – the highest in any Lord's Test – against the long-suffering 1947 South Africans

Melville and Nourse survived to the close with few alarms, although the captain should have been caught behind when 93.

Melville, 96 overnight, reached his fourth century in successive Test innings (a feat achieved previously only by Australia's Jack Fingleton) with a four in the first over of the third morning, and he and Nourse took their stand to 118, before both departed within eight runs of each other. Dawson and Harris subdued their natural attacking instincts to add 60 in 85 minutes, but when Compton broke the stand South Africa swiftly declined to 327 all out, Wright taking three quick wickets to finish with 5 for 95.

Following on, South Africa had reached 15 when the innings was interrupted while the teams were presented to the King and Queen and their two daughters (the current Queen and Princess Margaret). According to Dudley Nourse, the King said to Melville: 'I do hope I do not turn out to hold the reputation of my father. He was regarded as England's best change bowler, you know.'

Almost inevitably – and unhappily for the tourists – the King turned out to be just as good a change bowler as his father. With one run added, Melville's middle stump was flattened by Edrich, who then proceeded to uproot Viljoen's middle peg as well (Edrich later recalled that the flying stump nearly knocked out wicketkeeper Evans). Nourse made Edrich pay, with three fours in an over, and South Africa lost no more wickets before the close, which found them still 107 behind.

The match was virtually decided by the first ball of the final day, when Edrich bowled Nourse. Mitchell's 255-minute graft ended at 80, when Edrich pulled off an acrobatic slip catch, and the same fielder's effort to dispose of Dawson off Compton was nearly as good. Yardley also made two good catches – one of them a rebound off the chest of Pope, who was playing in his only Test – as South Africa descended to 252 all out, Wright taking another five wickets. Only a brave unbeaten 38 from Rowan staved off the innings defeat, but England knocked off the 26 runs needed for victory in little more than half an hour.

ENGLAND v SOUTH AFRICA
June 21, 23, 24, 25, 1947

ENGLAND

L. Hutton	b Rowan	18	not out	13
C. Washbrook	c Tuckett b Dawson	65	not out	13
W.J. Edrich	b Mann	189		
D.C.S. Compton	c Rowan b Tuckett	208		
C.J. Barnett	b Tuckett	33		
* N.W.D. Yardley	c Rowan b Tuckett	5		
† T.G. Evans	b Tuckett	16		
G.H. Pope	not out	8		
A.V. Bedser	b Tuckett	0		
D.V.P. Wright	did not bat			
W.E. Hollies				
Extras	(b2, lb10)	12		0
	(8 wkts dec) (215 overs)	554	(0 wkt) (12.1 overs)	26

Fall: 75,96,466,515,526,541,554,554.

Bowling: Tuckett 47-8-115-5, Dawson 33-11-81-1, Mann 53-16-99-1, Rowan 65-11-174-1, Smith 17-2-73-0.
Second innings: Tuckett 3-0-4-0, Dawson 6-2-6-0, Mann 3.1-1-16-0.

SOUTH AFRICA

B. Mitchell	st Evans b Compton	46	c Edrich b Wright	80
* A. Melville	c Bedser b Hollies	117	b Edrich	8
K.G. Viljoen	b Wright	1	b Edrich	6
A.D. Nourse	lbw b Wright	61	b Edrich	58
O.C. Dawson	c Barnett b Hollies	36	c Edrich b Compton	33
T.A. Harris	st Evans b Compton	30	c Yardley b Compton	3
A.M.B. Rowan	b Wright	8	not out	38
L. Tuckett	b Wright	5	lbw b Wright	9
N.B.F. Mann	b Wright	4	b Wright	5
† J.D. Lindsay	not out	7	c Yardley b Wright	5
V.I. Smith	c Edrich b Pope	11	c Edrich b Wright	0
Extras	(lb1)	1	(b3, lb4)	7
	(142.2 overs)	327	(128.2 overs)	252

Fall: 95,104,222,230,290,300,302,308,309.   16,28,120,192,192,201,224,236,252.

Bowling: Edrich 9-1-22-0, Bedser 26-1-76-0, Pope 19.2-5-49-1, Wright 39-10-95-5, Hollies 28-10-52-2, Compton 21-11-32-2.
Second innings: Pope 17-7-36-0, Bedser 14-6-20-0, Wright 32.2-6-80-5, Edrich 13-5-31-3, Compton 32-10-46-2, Hollies 20-7-32-0.

Toss: England   Umpires: H.G. Baldwin and D. Davies
Close of play: (1) E. 312 for 2 (Edrich 109, Compton 110)
                (2) S.A. 167 for 2 (Melville 96, Nourse 24)
                (3) S.A. 120 for 2 (Mitchell 47, Nourse 58)

ENGLAND WON BY 10 WICKETS

The 'twins' did it again at Old Trafford: Edrich 191, Compton 115, and England won by seven wickets despite Nourse's 115. England took a 3-0 lead at Headingley, where Hutton made 100, while the final Test was drawn, Mitchell saving the day for South Africa with 120 and 189 not out after Compton's fourth century of the series.

1948

When the question of the 'strongest-ever' Test side is raised, before long the merits of the 1948 Australians receive prolonged discussion. This side had the great fast bowlers Lindwall and Miller, backed up by the consistent Johnston and Toshack (the fast men's task was aided by a short-sighted, short-lived ruling that permitted a new ball every 55 overs), and they had batsmen of the calibre of Barnes, Morris, Harvey, Hassett and Brown, not all of whom could be accommodated in the same side. Above all, though, they had the incomparable Bradman, making his farewell tour, and although at nearly 40 he was not the bowler-killer of previous years, his skill and experience enabled him to score more than 2000 runs at an average of 89.

The powerful tourists swept all before them in the run-up to the Tests, winning the first eight matches, seven of them by an innings. Against Essex, they ran up 721 runs in the day, a first-class record. In the first Test Compton, continuing his great form of the previous year, rescued England with an innings of 184, after centuries from Bradman and Hassett had taken Australia to a big first-innings lead of 344.

All square, the teams moved to Lord's, where the gates were closed before the start on the first day, some people having queued all night. Bradman won the toss, and found himself batting as early as the fourth over when Coxon, playing in his only Test, had Barnes caught by Hutton at short fine leg, a position in which he had twice caught Bradman off Bedser at Trent Bridge. Showing unusual fallibility, at 17 The Don came close to giving Hutton another catch there, and when he had made 38 the trap worked, to England's great delight.

Meanwhile Morris, after a careful start, was doing the bulk of the scoring, and after nearly 3½ hours he reached his century, out of 166. Six minutes later his chanceless innings came to an end when Hutton took his third catch. Morris, who at times disturbed the purists by moving right across his stumps to Bedser, batted for 209 minutes and hit 14 fours and a six off a Wright no-ball. Miller played no stroke at Bedser to be lbw, and Australia rather lost their way as Yardley picked up the wickets of Hassett, who had stayed nearly three hours for his 47, and Brown. By the end of a satisfactory day for England, Tallon and Lindwall had taken the score to 258 for 7.

On the second day the pitch had lost the tinge of green which had bothered the batsmen on Day 1, and the tailenders made the most of some undistinguished English fielding to conjure up 92 runs in 70 minutes. Tallon made 53, and Johnston and Toshack made 49 between them, their batting being described by John Arlott as 'gaily incorrect'.

Although a back injury prevented Miller from bowling, partner-in-crime Lindwall was in top form. Soon working up to his top pace, he had Washbrook caught behind in his fourth over, and then, after offspinner Johnson had deceived Hutton, Lindwall shattered the stumps of Edrich and Dollery in the space of three balls.

From 46 for 4, it fell to Compton and Yardley to put things to rights. They carried the score to 126 by tea, but both were out soon afterwards, Compton falling to an excellent catch by Miller. Laker, dropped twice, and Coxon added 41

Among the batting stars of Don Bradman's powerful 1948 Australian touring team was left-hander Arthur Morris, who scored 105 and 62 in the Lord's Test. He added innings of 30 and 89 in 1953

for the eighth wicket, but when Lindwall, who finished with 5 for 70, bowled Bedser early on the third morning England's final total was a disappointing 215.

Australia built impressively on their lead of 135, the openers adding 122 before Morris, who had looked set for his second century of the match, played on to Wright. Barnes, though, would not be denied: in his only Lord's Test, he made the most of a possible stumping chance at 18 to reach a dogged hundred in just over four hours. After he reached three figures he hit out, at one point hitting successive balls from Laker for 2, 2, 4, 6 and 6 in an over that cost 21 in all. Eventually Yardley, something of a partnership-breaker, removed Barnes and Hassett with successive balls (Miller just avoided the hat-trick). In all, Barnes batted for 277 minutes, hitting 14 fours and two sixes: he put on 174 with Bradman, who was now homing in on his own century.

The Australian captain had already passed 50, this being the 14th consecutive Test in which he batted against England that he had managed at least one half-century, and he seemed intent on making a hundred jn his last Test at Lord's, the scene of his greatest innings in 1930. When he had progressed to 89, however, he gave Edrich a catch off Bedser: it was the closest Bradman ever approached a Test century without getting one, and it was also Bedser's fifth consecutive dismissal of the great man.

Miller, who made 74, hit out boldly on the fourth morning as Australia piled on the runs. The eventual declaration set England's victory target at a distant 596, but the final innings was delayed by rain, the Australians twice being driven from the field before a ball was bowled.

When play did begin, the pitch was playing a few tricks, and Hutton was lucky to escape when Miller at slip dropped a catch off Johnston before the Yorkshireman had scored. Soon Hutton was gone, though, Lindwall again making the breakthrough, and Edrich and Washbrook soon followed. Compton and Dollery made 41 in the last half-hour, England's deficit at stumps being a daunting 489 runs.

Any faint hopes England may have harboured of saving the match disappeared with the second ball of the final morning. Left-armer Johnston found the edge of Compton's bat and Miller at slip took another good, low catch at the second attempt. It was all over a few minutes before lunch: Lindwall removed the stubborn Dollery, and added the wicket of Laker in the same over, while Toshack, who also had two wickets in one over, finished with 5 for 40. Australia's margin of victory is the greatest in any Lord's Test, using runs as the yardstick (England defeated India by an innings and 285 runs in 1974).

ENGLAND v AUSTRALIA
June 24, 25, 26, 28, 29, 1948

AUSTRALIA

S.G. Barnes	c Hutton b Coxon	0	c Washbrook b Yardley	141
A.R. Morris	c Hutton b Coxon	105	b Wright	62
* D.G. Bradman	c Hutton b Bedser	38	c Edrich b Bedser	89
A.L. Hassett	b Yardley	47	b Yardley	0
K.R. Miller	lbw b Bedser	4	c Bedser b Laker	74
W.A. Brown	lbw b Yardley	24	c Evans b Coxon	32
I.W. Johnson	c Evans b Edrich	4	(8) not out	9
† D. Tallon	c Yardley b Bedser	53		
R.R. Lindwall	b Bedser	15	(7) st Evans b Laker	25
W.A. Johnston	st Evans b Wright	29		
E.R.H. Toshack	not out	20		
Extras	(b3, lb7, nb1)	11	(b22, lb5, nb1)	28
	(129.3 overs)	350	(7 wkts dec) (130.2 overs)	460

Fall: 3,87,166,173,216,225,246,275,320.   122,296,296,329,416,445,460.

Bowling: Bedser 43-14-100-4, Coxon 35-10-90-2, Edrich 8-0-43-1, Wright 21.3-8-54-1, Laker 7-3-17-0, Yardley 15-4-35-2.

Second innings: Bedser 34-6-112-1, Coxon 28-3-82-1, Yardley 13-4-36-2, Edrich 2-0-11-0, Wright 19-4-69-1, Laker 31.2-6-111-2, Compton 3-0-11-0.

ENGLAND

L. Hutton	b Johnson	20	c Johnson b Lindwall	13
C. Washbrook	c Tallon b Lindwall	8	c Tallon b Toshack	37
W.J. Edrich	b Lindwall	5	c Johnson b Toshack	2
D.C.S. Compton	c Miller b Johnston	53	c Miller b Johnston	29
H.E. Dollery	b Lindwall	0	b Lindwall	37
* N.W.D. Yardley	b Lindwall	44	b Toshack	11
A. Coxon	c and b Johnson	19	lbw b Toshack	0
† T.G. Evans	c Miller b Johnston	9	not out	24
J.C. Laker	c Tallon b Johnson	28	b Lindwall	0
A.V. Bedser	b Lindwall	9	c Hassett b Johnston	9
D.V.P. Wright	not out	13	c Lindwall b Toshack	4
Extras	(lb3, nb4)	7	(b16, lb4)	20
	(102.4 overs)	215	(78.1 overs)	186

Fall: 17,32,46,46,133,134,145,186,197.   42,52,65,106,133,133,141,141,158.

Bowling: Lindwall 27.4-7-70-5, Johnston 22-4-43-2, Johnson 35-13-72-3, Toshack 18-11-23-0.

Second innings: Lindwall 23-9-61-3, Johnston 33-15-62-2, Toshack 20.1-6-40-5, Johnson 2-1-3-0.

Toss: Australia   Umpires: D. Davies and C.N. Woolley
Close of play: (1) A. 258 for 7 (Tallon 25, Lindwall 3)
　　　　　　　 (2) E. 207 for 9 (Bedser 6, Wright 8)
　　　　　　　 (3) A. 343 for 4 (Miller 22, Brown 7)
　　　　　　　 (4) E. 106 for 3 (Compton 29, Dollery 21)

AUSTRALIA WON BY 409 RUNS

Honours were even at Old Trafford, where Compton completed a famous century after being hit on the head by Lindwall. Australia won the last two Tests decisively, scoring 404 for 3 on the last day to win at Headingley (Morris 182, Bradman 173 not out). At The Oval Lindwall (6 for 20) was instrumental in bowling England out for 52. Morris scored 196 for Australia, but their 389 was more notable, in some ways, for Bradman's duck in his final Test innings. Bradman was comforted, no doubt, by his side's 3-0 series win and their unbeaten record in all matches on the tour.

1949

The tourists in 1949 were New Zealand, who were rather put out at being allocated four Tests of only three days' duration. Their captain Walter Hadlee, the father of New Zealand's greatest allrounder Richard, is reputed to have told his team they would just have to draw all four Tests – and that is what happened. The tourists were a little weak in bowling, but their batsmen included two of the best left-handers to grace the Test arena, Bert Sutcliffe and Martin Donnelly.

Hutton, Compton and Washbrook scored centuries for England in the first Test, at Headingley, but Washbrook suffered a leg injury during his innings which kept him out at Lord's, Middlesex opener Robertson taking his place. New Zealand drew at Leeds without undue difficulty, despite Bailey, on his Test debut, taking 6 for 118.

At Lord's Mann, the Middlesex captain who had led England in South Africa the previous winter, won the toss and saw his openers make a sound start, putting on 48 before Hutton was bowled by left-arm spinner Burtt's first delivery. Something of a collapse followed Hutton's dismissal, three more wickets going down before lunch. Cowie, a survivor of New Zealand's 1937 tour, was bowling well, finding occasional lift from a good length at a high pace. He had Robertson caught behind, and had Edrich caught in the gully off a lifter.

Mann fell soon after lunch, making England 112 for 5, but now the impressive Cowie was feeling his 37 years in the blazing sun that was beating down. Compton and Bailey embarked on a rescue act which was to take England to 301 before another wicket fell. Compton, who went on to 116 (11 fours) in 225 minutes, played the minor role, cutting out all risks as the Essex allrounder hit out in a manner which will surprise those who know only of 'Barnacle' Bailey the stonewaller. Starting with two legside fours off Cowie, Bailey hit 16 boundaries in all in his brisk 93, which inspired the watching Arthur Mailey to pronounce that his near-namesake was 'rapidly becoming England's most entertaining batsman'. The hundred partnership came up in just 68 minutes, and in all the pair added 189.

Three more wickets tumbled before Mann declared at 313 for 9, leaving New Zealand an awkward 15 minutes' batting, which they negotiated without loss. Mann's declaration – the first on the first day of any Test – was later found to be illegal, as the regulation which permitted such an act on the first day in county cricket did not apply to this Test series. Mann apologised, and the New Zealanders took the matter no further.

Sutcliffe, who unleashed some grand strokes in his 57, and Scott took their opening stand to 89 on the second morning before Gladwin struck. Compton soon trapped Scott for a patient 42, but Hadlee, making light of a painful bruise he had acquired in a previous match, made a gritty 43 before he fell to the last ball before lunch, bowled by Hollies, who had also captured the wicket of Wallace.

The elegant Donnelly took control after the interval, to such effect that only one wicket (Smith) went down between lunch and tea. Donnelly, who shared a stand of 76 with Rabone, reached his century in 3½ hours, and was still there at the close, unbeaten on 126, having taken New Zealand into their first-ever first-innings lead against England (skipper Hadlee ordered drinks all round in the

The highest score by a New Zealander in a Lord's Test is 206, by the elegant left-hander Martin Donnelly in 1949. His innings completed a rare hat-trick of centuries at Lord's in a Test, a Varsity Match and for Gentlemen v Players – Percy Chapman (another left-hander) is the only other batsman to achieve the feat

Press-box – 36 glasses of beer – to celebrate).

Donnelly's century rounded off a notable treble for the batsman who had impressed as a 19-year-old with the 1937 side. After the war he went to Oxford, for whom he scored 142 in the 1946 Varsity match; in 1947, playing for Gentlemen against Players, he made 162 not out. Only Percy Chapman, another left-hander, has equalled Donnelly's three-century feat at Lord's, and even he had to give best as a sporting allrounder to the New Zealander, a noted rugby player who won one cap for *England* against Ireland in 1947.

On the final day Donnelly continued to 206, his 355-minute innings containing 26 fours, many from powerful pulls or neat late cuts. After an eighth-wicket stand of 85 with Burtt, Donnelly was 197 when last man Cowie came to the crease. Showing confidence in his partner, Donnelly reached 200 with three singles, the last a quick one to mid-off, where Hollies might have been feeling the effects of his 58 overs (he took 5 for 133).

England were 171 behind, but were in little danger of defeat. Hutton, surviving an early close shout for lbw against Cowie, made 66, adding 143 for the first wicket with Robertson, whose 225-minute innings of 121 was not enough to keep him in the side for the next Test, when a fit-again Washbrook replaced him. Wallace took the new ball for the last over of the match, the close finding England at 306 for 5, with Watkins just short of his half-century.

ENGLAND v NEW ZEALAND
June 25, 27, 28, 1949

ENGLAND

L. Hutton	b Burtt	23	c Cave b Rabone	66
J.D.B. Robertson	c Mooney b Cowie	26	c Cave b Rabone	121
W.J. Edrich	c Donnelly b Cowie	9	c Hadlee b Burtt	31
D.C.S. Compton	c Sutcliffe b Burtt	116	b Burtt	6
A.J. Watkins	c Wallace b Burtt	6	not out	49
* F.G. Mann	b Cave	18	c Donnelly b Rabone	17
T.E. Bailey	c Sutcliffe b Rabone	93	not out	6
† T.G. Evans	b Burtt	5		
C. Gladwin	run out	5		
J.A. Young	not out	1		
W.E. Hollies	did not bat			
Extras	(b9, lb2)	11	(b9, lb1)	10
	(9 wkts dec) (103.1 overs)	313	(5 wkts) (103 overs)	306

Fall: 48,59,72,83,112,301,307,307,313.   143,216,226,226,252.

Bowling: Cowie 26.1-5-64-2, Cave 27-2-79-1, Rabone 14-5-56-1, Burtt 35-7-102-4, Sutcliffe 1-0-1-0.

Second innings: Cowie 14-3-39-0, Cave 7-1-23-0, Rabone 28-6-116-3, Burtt 37-12-58-2, Sutcliffe 16-1-55-0, Wallace 1-0-5-0.

NEW ZEALAND

B. Sutcliffe	c Compton b Gladwin	57	Bowling:
V.J. Scott	c Edrich b Compton	42	Bailey 33-3-136-0,
* W.A. Hadlee	c Robertson b Hollies	43	Gladwin 28-5-67-1,
W.M. Wallace	c Evans b Hollies	2	Edrich 4-0-16-0,
M.P. Donnelly	c Hutton b Young	206	Hollies 58-18-133-5,
F.B. Smith	b Hollies	23	Compton 7-0-33-1,
G.O. Rabone	b Hollies	25	Young 26.4-4-65-3,
† F.L.H. Mooney	c Watkins b Young	33	Watkins 3-1-11-0.
T.B. Burtt	c Edrich b Hollies	23	
H.B. Cave	c and b Young	6	
J. Cowie	not out	1	
Extras	(b16, lb3, w3, nb1)	23	
	(159.4 overs)	484	

Fall: 89,124,137,160,197,273,351,436,464.

Toss: England   Umpires: W.H. Ashdown and F. Chester
Close of play: (1) N.Z. 20 for 0 (Sutcliffe 12, Scott 8)
                       (2) N.Z. 372 for 7 (Donnelly 126, Burtt 5)

MATCH DRAWN

Hadlee fulfilled his 'four-draws' prediction with some ease and style, most of his batsmen scoring well in the final two Tests. Bowlers on both sides had a hard time of it, Bailey taking 6 for 84 and Burtt 6 for 162 at Old Trafford, and New Zealander Fen Cresswell 6 for 168 on his Test debut at The Oval.

1950

Before the Second World War England had not been inclined to take West Indies cricket entirely seriously. Below-strength England sides toured the Caribbean, where some interesting series were fought out, but each of West Indies' three pre-war Test tours saw England, at full strength, take the series. The first postwar rubber, however (in 1947-48), saw the emergence of a famous trio of batsmen, the 'Three Ws' from Barbados, Walcott, Weekes and Worrell: they soon found their feet at Test level as West Indies recorded a comfortable victory over 45-year-old 'Gubby' Allen's touring side, which again lacked several of England's more celebrated players.

The Three Ws, together with the dependable opening pair of Rae and Stollmeyer, formed a powerful batting line-up for West Indies' 1950 tour. The team had a capable fast-bowling attack, and two useful allrounders in captain Goddard and Gomez, but the slow bowling was in the hands of two virtually unknown spinners, who had played just two matches apiece prior to the tour: left-armer Alf Valentine and the mysterious Sonny Ramadhin, whose mixture of right-arm off- and legbreaks were sent down with virtually the same action, to the discomfort of opposing batsmen.

West Indies displayed their powerful batting in the early matches of their tour, but an underprepared pitch led to their downfall in the first Test, at Old Trafford, where a brisk century from Evans set up England's 202-run victory. Valentine, however, showed his promise by taking the first eight wickets to fall.

England had injury problems before the Lord's Test: already without Compton (knee injury), the home side were forced to replace Bailey, Hollies and Simpson from the successful first-Test side. The injuries allowed Parkhouse to win his first Test cap, while Doggart (later MCC's president and treasurer) appeared in his only Lord's Test.

Interest in the match was high, the gates being closed before the start. Goddard won the toss from Yardley, who had returned as England's captain, and after the teams were presented to the King the visitors set off. Stollmeyer, the only survivor of West Indies' 1939 Lord's Test side, produced one sublime shot off his pads for four, but he was the first to go, falling lbw to Wardle's first ball in Test cricket in England. The left-hander Rae was solid, but Worrell played a charming innings, his late-cuts delighting an appreciative crowd and inspiring the watching Sir Neville Cardus to write that 'An innings by Worrell knows no dawn. It begins at high noon!' Worrell's innings was ended at 52 by a superb ball from Bedser. Anchorman Rae and Weekes saw the 200 up, both escaping when Doggart, normally a reliable fielder, put down chances at slip off Bedser. Weekes was soon into his stride, cracking 10 fours in his 90-minute 63 before Bedser had his revenge.

Rae moved to his century, eventually falling after 280 minutes for 106: he hit 15 fours, three of them in one over from Jenkins before eventually falling to the legspinner, who improved England's position with two more quick wickets. By stumps West Indies had moved to 320 for 7, but within a few minutes on the second morning the innings was over, Bedser's third ball of the day accounting for the dangerous Christiani and the persevering Jenkins taking two more wickets to finish with 5 for 116.

England's reply began well, the openers adding 62 before Hutton had a rush of blood against Valentine and was stumped by Walcott not long before lunch: the spinners then imposed such a stranglehold on proceedings that no further runs were added in 7.4 overs before the interval. After lunch England slumped to 86 for 5, Washbrook being stumped off Ramadhin, who then removed Edrich (1½ hours for 8) and the bemused Doggart for a duck. Parkhouse also went without scoring, Valentine this time being the executioner.

Yardley made 16 and his fellow Yorkshireman Wardle a bright undefeated 33, his last-wicket stand of 29 with Berry being the best of the innings after the openers' 62. Paceman Jones took the last wicket, but spinners Ramadhin and Valentine – 'Ram' and 'Val' – took the other nine, bowling a remarkable 55 maidens between them in their combined tally of 88 overs.

Leading by 175, West Indies added another 45 without loss in 75 minutes before the close, Rae giving two unaccepted chances. Jenkins removed both openers early on Day 3, and he also disposed of Worrell for 45. Weekes, though, was once again in prime form, and had equalled his first-innings 63 when he answered Walcott's call for a quick single and was run out by Yardley.

Walcott had been dropped at slip when 9 by the unfortunate Doggart, who earlier put down Weekes off the same bowler, Edrich. A stumping chance off Jenkins was the only other chance offered by the well-built Walcott, who powered his way to a memorable century during the course of a long stand with Gomez. Walcott had shaved off a short-lived moustache before the match, in a superstitious bid to regain his elusive form.

West Indies, 386 for 5 overnight, batted on for 40 minutes on the fourth day to reach 425, Walcott ending up with an undefeated 168, the highest score for West Indies at Lord's until Desmond Haynes surpassed it in 1980. Walcott, whose stand with Gomez realised 211, hit 24 fours, the majority coming from ferocious drives and sweeps.

England, for whom Jenkins had match figures of 9 for 290, needed an improbable 601 to win, and they soon lost Hutton, who played no shot at Valentine's arm ball and was bowled. Edrich, too, was soon gone, but Washbrook, despite never looking at home against the mysterious Ramadhin, applied himself well, sharing a stand of 83 with Doggart, who concentrated grimly for his 25. Washbrook and Parkhouse then added a further 78, the Glamorgan player – according to wicketkeeper Walcott, the only Englishman who seemed to be able to 'read' Ramadhin – making an attractive 48 before hammering a rare full-toss from Valentine to short mid-off, where Goddard took a good one-handed catch. This setback came just before the close, by which time England were 218 for 4, with Washbrook undefeated with 114, having hit 14 fours and a six in his defiant innings.

Washbrook kept out six maidens from Ramadhin on the final morning before falling without having added to his score. His downfall signalled the end of England's serious resistance, the remaining batsmen raising the score to 274 before Worrell was recalled to dispose of the troublesome Wardle, who had hit Valentine for three fours in an over.

The crowd, many of them West Indians, celebrated West Indies' 326-run victory in a manner previously unknown at Lord's: they danced on the playing area, singing Caribbean calypsos, the most famous of which immortalised 'Those two little pals of mine', Ramadhin and Valentine, who had taken 11 and seven wickets respectively in their side's famous victory.

The powerful Clyde Walcott, seen here keeping wicket, scored 168 not out as West Indies overwhelmed England in 1950. The batsman is Glamorgan's Gilbert Parkhouse, considered by Walcott to have been one of the few to 'read' the mystery spin of Sonny Ramadhin

ENGLAND v WEST INDIES
June 24, 26, 27, 28, 29, 1950

WEST INDIES

A.F. Rae	c and b Jenkins	106	b Jenkins		24
J.B. Stollmeyer	lbw b Wardle	20	b Jenkins		30
F.M.M. Worrell	b Bedser	52	c Doggart b Jenkins		45
E.D. Weekes	b Bedser	63	run out		63
† C.L. Walcott	st Evans b Jenkins	14	(6) not out		168
G.E. Gomez	st Evans b Jenkins	1	(7) c Edrich b Bedser		70
R.J. Christiani	b Bedser	33	(8) not out		5
* J.D.C. Goddard	b Wardle	14	(5) c Evans b Jenkins		11
P.E. Jones	c Evans b Jenkins	0			
S. Ramadhin	not out	1			
A.L. Valentine	c Hutton b Jenkins	5			
Extras	(b10, lb5, w1, nb1)	17	(lb8, nb1)		9
	(131.2 overs)	326	(6 wkts dec) (178 overs)		425

Fall: 37,128,233,262,273,274,320,320,320.   48,75,108,146,199,410.

Bowling: Bedser 40-14-60-3, Edrich 16-4-30-0, Jenkins 35.2-6-116-5,
Wardle 17-6-46-2, Berry 19-7-45-0, Yardley 4-1-12-0.

Second innings: Bedser 44-16-80-1, Edrich 13-2-37-0, Jenkins 59-13-174-4,
Wardle 30-10-58-0, Berry 32-15-67-0.

ENGLAND

L. Hutton	st Walcott b Valentine	35	b Valentine		10
C. Washbrook	st Walcott b Ramadhin	36	b Ramadhin		114
W.J. Edrich	c Walcott b Ramadhin	8	c Jones b Ramadhin		8
G.H.G. Doggart	lbw b Ramadhin	0	b Ramadhin		25
W.G.A. Parkhouse	b Valentine	0	c Goddard b Valentine		48
* N.W.D. Yardley	b Valentine	16	c Weekes b Valentine		19
† T.G. Evans	b Ramadhin	8	c Rae b Ramadhin		2
R.O. Jenkins	c Walcott b Valentine	4	b Ramadhin		4
J.H. Wardle	not out	33	lbw b Worrell		21
A.V. Bedser	b Ramadhin	5	b Ramadhin		0
R. Berry	c Goddard b Jones	2	not out		0
Extras	(b2, lb1, w1)	4	(b16, lb7)		23
	(106.4 overs)	151	(191.3 overs)		274

Fall: 62,74,74,75,86,102,110,113,122.   28,57,140,218,228,238,245,248,258.

Bowling: Jones 8.4-2-13-1, Worrell 10-4-20-0, Valentine 45-28-48-4,
Ramadhin 43-27-66-5.

Second innings: Jones 7-1-22-0, Worrell 22.3-9-39-1, Valentine 71-47-79-3,
Ramadhin 72-43-86-6, Gomez 13-1-25-0, Goddard 6-6-0-0.

Toss: West Indies   Umpires: D. Davies and F.S. Lee
Close of play: (1) W.I. 320 for 7 (Christiani 33, Jones 0)
                      (2) W.I. 45 for 0 (Rae 16, Stollmeyer 29)
                      (3) W.I. 386 for 5 (Walcott 148, Gomez 57)
                      (4) E. 218 for 4 (Washbrook 114, Yardley 0)

WEST INDIES WON BY 326 RUNS

*West Indies won both remaining Tests by wide margins to take the series 3-1.
Worrell (261) and Weekes (129) shared a partnership of 283 at Trent Bridge, where
an opening stand of 212 between Hutton and Washbrook could not save England.
Rae and Worrell made centuries at The Oval, where Hutton's 202 not out could not
even avert the follow-on. Valentine finished the series with 33 wickets, his 'little pal'
Ramadhin with 26.*

1951

English cricket, put in its place by West Indies in 1950, suffered another blow to its self-esteem in Australia in 1950-51, Freddie Brown's side going down 4-1, although an overdue victory in the final Test gave some hope for the future.

Brown retained the captaincy for the 1951 home series against South Africa, in the process playing his second Lord's Test 19 years after his first. The tourists, captained by third-time tourist Dudley Nourse, were largely a young, promising side, although opener Eric Rowan – a member of the 1935 side and a surprise omission in 1947 – returned for his second tour.

England collapsed to 114 all out in the first Test at Trent Bridge, presenting South Africa with their first Test victory since the 1935 Lord's Test. Nourse made light of a recently-broken thumb to score an epic 208.

At Lord's, Brown won the toss, but England soon suffered a serious blow when Hutton, facing the pacey McCarthy, played back, missed, and was lbw. Ikin and Simpson then shared a stand of 69, the Lancashire left-hander hitting splendidly to leg and collecting six fours in his 51. Simpson, meanwhile, drove offspinner Athol Rowan's first delivery, a no-ball, straight into the pavilion for six.

Ikin eventually fell to the accurate Mann, whose first-day figures were economy itself: 24-11-28-1. In a sad echo of the death of 'Jock' Cameron after the 1935 tour, the popular Mann missed the end of the tour, suffering from the first stages of cancer: the left-arm spinner died in July 1952, aged 30.

Simpson, undone by the first ball of a new spell from McCarthy, soon followed Ikin back to the pavilion, whereupon Compton and Watson embarked on a stand which grew to be worth 122. Compton, the scourge of the 1947 South Africans, threatened to repeat his domination this time (he had already scored 112 in the first Test), but when he had made 79, with seven fours, he too fell to McCarthy, whose loose-limbed, open-chested action was causing some concern. Watson, who the previous summer had been playing World Cup football for England, hit nine fours before holing out to McCarthy at long leg. The innings folded for 311 in the face of accurate bowling from McCarthy (4 for 76) and 40-year-old Geoff Chubb, who took 5 for 77 and generally performed admirably during his one and only Test series.

South Africa had 10 minutes to survive before stumps, which they did without alarms, but an overnight thunderstorm changed the face of the match. Tattersall, who earlier in the tour had taken 8 for 51 for MCC against the South Africans on a similarly wet pitch, this time snapped up 7 for 52, his best Test figures, as the tourists crumbled to 115. Eric Rowan top-scored with 24 before his innings was ended by a brilliant catch by Ikin, one of several fine efforts from the fielders in Tattersall's leg-trap. The Lancashire offspinner bowled beautifully, operating at a brisk pace over the wicket with deadly accuracy: scarcely any of the 138 balls he sent down could be left alone. Nourse hit out, but was well caught by Watson on the square-leg boundary after scattering the close fielders, and the last six wickets went down for 37 in an hour.

Following on, the visitors were soon in trouble again at 58 for 4, raising the prospect of a two-day defeat, but Cheetham and Fullerton hung on through the 75

Lancashire offspinner Roy
Tattersall, whose Test
career was largely
overshadowed by the great
Jim Laker, took 12 wickets
on a helpful pitch to
demolish South Africa
in 1951

minutes to the close, the latter somehow surviving one marvellous over from Bedser, who four times beat him and shaved the stumps.

England's failure to wrap things up inside two days was good news for the members of the Cricket-Writers' Club, whose annual dinner was planned to take place on the evening of the third day. Part of the celebrations included the presentation of the inaugural 'Young Cricketer of the Year' award – ironically to Tattersall, whose nine wickets on the second day had done much to endanger the event.

Play continued on the third day despite poor light and drizzle. Cheetham, handicapped by a stiff neck, survived for half an hour before Statham removed his middle stump. Cheetham had battled it out for 135 minutes, and hit seven fours. Fullerton soon followed, and Tattersall mopped up the innings to finish with 5 for 49 (12 for 101 in the match). The innings ended five minutes before lunch, and by 2.20 England had won by 10 wickets to square the series.

To entertain the sell-out crowd, the two sides played a knockabout exhibition match, the first such event to take place at Lord's. South Africa salvaged a modicum of pride by winning this game.

ENGLAND v SOUTH AFRICA
June 21, 22, 23, 1951

ENGLAND

L. Hutton	lbw b McCarthy	12	not out		12
J.T. Ikin	b Mann	51	not out		4
R.T. Simpson	lbw b McCarthy	26			
D.C.S. Compton	lbw b McCarthy	79			
W. Watson	c McCarthy b Chubb	79			
* F.R. Brown	b Chubb	1			
† T.G. Evans	c Fullerton b McCarthy	0			
J.H. Wardle	lbw b Chubb	18			
A.V. Bedser	not out	26			
J.B. Statham	b Chubb	1			
R. Tattersall	b Chubb	1			
Extras	(b8, lb9)	17			0
	(107.4 overs)	311	(0 wkt) (3.5 overs)		16

Fall: 20,89,103,225,226,231,265,299,301.

Bowling: McCarthy 23-2-76-4, Chubb 34.4-9-77-5, A.M.B. Rowan 13-1-63-0, Mann 32-12-51-1, Van Ryneveld 5-0-27-0.
Second innings: Nourse 2-0-9-0, E.A.B. Rowan 1.5-0-7-0.

SOUTH AFRICA

E.A.B. Rowan	c Ikin b Tattersall	24	c Ikin b Statham	10
† J.H.B. Waite	c Hutton b Wardle	15	c Compton b Tattersall	17
D.J. McGlew	c Evans b Tattersall	3	b Tattersall	2
* A.D. Nourse	c Watson b Tattersall	20	lbw b Wardle	3
J.E. Cheetham	c Hutton b Tattersall	15	b Statham	54
G.M. Fullerton	b Tattersall	12	lbw b Bedser	60
C.B. van Ryneveld	lbw b Wardle	0	c Ikin b Tattersall	18
A.M.B. Rowan	c Ikin b Tattersall	3	c Brown b Bedser	10
N.B.F. Mann	c Brown b Tattersall	14	c Brown b Tattersall	13
G.W.A. Chubb	c Tattersall b Wardle	5	b Tattersall	3
C.N. McCarthy	not out	1	not out	2
Extras	(lb3)	3	(b11, lb8)	19
	(64.5 overs)	115	(2 wkts) (96.2 overs)	211

Fall: 25,38,47,72,88,91,91,103,112. 21,29,32,58,152,160,178,196,200.

Bowling: Bedser 8-5-7-0, Statham 6-3-7-0, Tattersall 28-10-52-7, Wardle 22.5-10-46-3.
Second innings: Bedser 24-8-53-2, Statham 18-6-33-2, Tattersall 32.2-14-49-5, Wardle 20-5-44-1, Compton 2-0-13-0.

Toss: England Umpires: H. Elliott and F.S. Lee
Close of play: (1) S.A. 4 for 0 (E.A.B. Rowan 0, Waite 4)
(2) S.A. 137 for 4 (Cheetham 46, Fullerton 50)

AUSTRALIA WON BY 10 WICKETS

England took a 2-1 lead with a nine-wicket win at Old Trafford, Bedser taking 12 wickets as South Africa totalled only 158 and 191. After a high-scoring draw at Headingley, where centuries from Hutton and May answered Eric Rowan's 236, England clinched the series with a close-run victory at The Oval, where the home side's successful quest for 163 in the second innings was marked by Hutton's dismissal for obstructing the field.

107

1952

A fairly weak MCC side had drawn 1-1 with India in the winter of 1951-52, but the Indian touring side of 1952 found the full-strength England team an altogether different proposition. Vijay Hazare's side was outclassed, and had great problems against the pace of the young Trueman and the accurate Bedser, who reduced them to 0 for 4 wickets at one stage on the first Test at Headingley, which England won by seven wickets.

History was made at Lord's on June 19 when a professional, Len Hutton, led England out. England's premier batsman, Hutton took over from Brown, who had announced his retirement from Test cricket. The Yorkshireman's side included, for his first Lord's Test, his eventual successor as captain, Peter May.

India had chosen a young side, without Merchant (retired), Mushtaq Ali or Amarnath, and were further handicapped by the non-availability of Vinoo Mankad, who was playing for Lancashire League club Haslingden. India's wretched showing at Leeds prompted the manager to negotiate Mankad's release for the remaining Tests, and the allrounder was to turn in a memorable performance at Lord's.

India won the toss, and the openers batted through the first session, defying all that England's five bowlers could produce. Roy was watchful, but Mankad attacked, lofting legspinner Jenkins's fourth ball over the sightscreen for six. The stand swelled to 106 after lunch, but then Mankad was well caught by Watkins at leg slip. A disappointing collapse set in, irresolute batting leading to seven wickets going down between lunch and tea. Hazare stood firm, hitting nine fours in his 170-minute undefeated innings of 69, but received little support until the last two batsmen stuck at their task in a manner which shamed the recognised batsmen. Shinde and Ghulam Ahmed made only 5 and 0 respectively, but they survived for 75 minutes and helped the captain put on another 55. Shinde's resistance was ended by a brilliant stumping from Evans, who became the first England wicketkeeper to make 100 Test dismissals.

England, 8 for 0 overnight, made a leisurely start the next morning, the openers scoring 60 in two hours before lunch. After the interval Hutton and Simpson raised three figures before the first wicket went down at 106, as India's had done. Hutton was in fine form, however, and had no intention of allowing a collapse: he and May added 158 for the second wicket in 2½ hours before Hutton was caught behind for 150. The skipper had hit 20 fours in his 315-minute innings, his first century against India.

Three quick wickets, including May's, went down after Hutton's departure, Watkins falling to the last ball of the day, bowled by Mankad, who had already sent down 42 overs of left-arm spin. He was to deliver a further 31 next day, when India wilted in the face of a spectacular assault from Evans, who raced to 98 before lunch. He reached three figures soon afterwards, and was out for 104, having hit 16 fours. He shared a stand of 159 with Graveney, who made a cultured 73.

India faced a deficit of 302, and the indefatigable Mankad, whose 73 overs yielded figures of 5 for 196, strode out to open the innings, but soon lost his partner Roy, bowled by Bedser for a duck. Mankad renewed his assault on

Queen Elizabeth II made her first visit to Lord's as Sovereign in 1952: here she shakes the hand of 'Vinoo' Mankad, who put in an exceptional allround performance in that year's Lord's Test – he scored 72 and 184, as well as sending down 97 overs of left-arm spin

Jenkins, this time hitting his first ball for six, and at the end of a day which had seen 382 runs scored, Mankad had made 86 of India's 137 for 2.

Mankad and Hazare took their partnership to 211 on the fourth morning. Showers on Sunday had freshened up the pitch, but Mankad was indomitable, taking his score to a magnificent 184 before he misjudged a ball from Laker and was bowled. He hit 19 fours and a six in his marvellous 270-minute innings. Hazare was out soon afterwards, for a stoic 49 in 225 minutes, but Ramchand, with a few lusty blows, ensured that Mankad's heroics were not in vain and that England would have to bat again.

England needed 77 to win in 80 minutes on the fourth evening but, apparently uninspired by Queen Elizabeth's first visit as sovereign, they batted cautiously, against accurate bowling, notably from the apparently tireless Mankad. *Wisden* rather uncharitably described England's batting as 'a pathetic display', and there were other discontented murmurs as the home side took 45 minutes on the final morning to reach their target.

ENGLAND v INDIA
June 19, 20, 21, 23, 24, 1952

INDIA

M.H. Mankad	c Watkins b Trueman	72	b Laker	184
P. Roy	c and b Bedser	35	b Bedser	0
P.R. Umrigar	b Trueman	5	(7) b Trueman	14
* V.S. Hazare	not out	69	c Laker b Bedser	49
V.L. Manjrekar	lbw b Bedser	5	b Laker	1
D.G. Phadkar	b Watkins	8	b Laker	16
H.R. Adhikari	lbw b Watkins	0	(3) b Trueman	16
G.S. Ramchand	b Trueman	18	(9) b Trueman	42
† M.K. Mantri	b Trueman	1	(8) c Compton b Laker	5
S.G. Shinde	st Evans b Watkins	5	c Hutton b Trueman	14
Ghulam Ahmed	b Jenkins	0	not out	1
Extras	(b7, nb10)	17	(b29, lb3, nb4)	36
	(94.3 overs)	235	(122 overs)	378

Fall: 106,116,118,126,135,139,167,180,221.

7,59,270,272,289,312,314,323,377.

Bowling: Bedser 33-8-62-2, Trueman 25-3-72-4, Jenkins 7.3-1-26-1,
Laker 12-5-21-0, Watkins 17-7-37-3.

Second innings: Bedser 36-13-60-2, Trueman 27-4-110-4, Jenkins 10-1-40-0,
Laker 39-15-102-4, Watkins 8-0-20-0, Compton 2-0-10-0.

ENGLAND

* L. Hutton	c Mantri b Hazare	150	not out	39
R.T. Simpson	b Mankad	53	run out	2
P.B.H. May	c Mantri b Mankad	74	c Roy b Ghulam Ahmed	26
D.C.S. Compton	lbw b Hazare	6	not out	4
T.W. Graveney	c Mantri b Ghulam Ahmed	73		
A.J. Watkins	b Mankad	0		
† T.G. Evans	c and b Ghulam Ahmed	104		
R.O. Jenkins	st Mantri b Mankad	21		
J.C. Laker	not out	23		
A.V. Bedser	c Ramchand b Mankad	3		
F.S. Trueman	b Ghulam Ahmed	17		
Extras	(b8, lb5)	13	(b4, lb4)	8
	(206.4 overs)	537	(2 wkts) (49.2 overs)	79

Fall: 106,264,272,292,292,451,468,506,514.

8,71.

Bowling: Phadkar 27-8-44-0, Ramchand 29-8-67-0, Hazare 24-4-53-2,
Mankad 73-24-196-5, Ghulam Ahmed 43.4-12-106-3, Shinde 6-0-43-0,
Umrigar 4-0-15-0.

Second innings: Ramchand 1-0-5-0, Mankad 24-12-35-0, Ghulam Ahmed 23.2-9-31-1,
Hazare 1-1-0-0.

Toss: India

Umpires: F. Chester and F.S. Lee

Close of play: (1) E. 8 for 0 (Hutton 6, Simpson 2)
(2) E. 292 for 5 (Graveney 8)
(3) I. 137 for 2 (Mankad 86, Hazare 24)
(4) E. 40 for 1 (Hutton 27, May 8)

ENGLAND WON BY 8 WICKETS

England took a 3-0 lead in the series at Old Trafford, India managing only 58 and 82 in the face of express bowling from Trueman, who took 8 for 31 in the first innings. England were set for a clean sweep when rain set in at The Oval after India had again failed to reach three figures, Bedser and Trueman sharing all 10 wickets.

1953

Quite often, a Test will be remembered for a matchwinning performance by a player, but only rarely does a match*saving* effort impress itself so clearly on the mind. One instance was the magnificent defensive effort by Willie Watson and Trevor Bailey on the last day of the 1953 Lord's Test, which saved England from certain defeat.

Watson and Bailey came together at 12.42 on the final day, with England, 73 for 4, still 270 short of their unlikely victory target. Left-hander Watson, who hit 16 fours, ground out a characterful century in his first Test against Australia: no-one present, at least among Englishmen, minded that his 109 took five hours 46 minutes, or that his second fifty, which took 201 minutes, was the slowest in Tests at the time. Similarly Bailey, whose defensive displays occasionally riled spectators, won nothing but praise for his 4¼-hour marathon. Bailey, whose previous-highest score against Australia was 15, scored 71 in 257 minutes and made light of three painful blows on the knuckles from the new ball: *Wisden* recalls that he played a 'deadbat pendulum stroke to every ball on his wicket'. The epic stand was not broken until ten-to-six, leaving England an anxious 40 minutes to survive before the close, but some bold hitting from Brown saw England safely to a draw.

The first Test of the series had also ended in a draw, rain spoiling an evenly-balanced match in which Bedser took 14 wickets. Hassett, who had taken over from Bradman as Australia's captain and retained the Ashes in 1950-51, had scored a studious 115 at Trent Bridge, and he was soon in action again at Lord's after winning the toss. The diminutive skipper, who had moved up the list after the failure of his regular openers, shared a solid opening stand with Morris, who fell to Bedser 20 minutes before lunch when Evans pulled off a lightning stumping. Hassett, although bothered by a strained arm, made the most of his luck: he might have been caught off Bedser early on, but Compton at leg slip moved the wrong way, and at 55 Hutton at second slip dropped him off Brown's medium-pace.

Hassett and Harvey took the score to 190, the left-hander finally falling to the persevering Bedser after nearly three hours. Hassett continued to his second century in successive Tests, reaching three figures with an exquisite square cut for his 11th four. Immediately afterwards, though, he retired hurt, having suffered an attack of cramp in the leg. England took advantage of his temporary departure, Wardle snapping up three wickets in 10 balls, the only scoring shot being Miller's six off the ball before his downfall.

Hassett resumed on the fall of Ring's wicket on the second morning, but added only three runs, his innings lasting 296 minutes in all. England were thwarted by an aggressive innings from Davidson, who struck 13 fours and a six and reached 50 in 16 scoring shots. He was missed twice, however, and England put down eight catchable chances during the innings, of which Hutton dropped three, the last of which injured his thumb and forced him to leave the field for a while. Chairman of selectors Brown, recalled for this match, took over in his captain's absence.

Bedser ended the resistance, removing Davidson and Langley and taking his

200th Test wicket in the process, but England's reply began badly when Lindwall, from the pavilion end, dismissed Kenyon for 3. There now followed some of the best batting of the season, Hutton and Graveney matching each other shot-for-shot in a partnership which swelled to 168 by stumps, one minor criticism being that the pair scored slowly in the final hour, just 32 runs being gathered from some tired bowlers.

Sadly for England, Graveney was out without addition on the third morning, Lindwall's fourth ball crashing into the stumps. Compton, whose place had been in jeopardy after some indifferent form, played the minor role in a stand of 102 with Hutton, who soon reached a marvellous century, his fifth, last and arguably best against Australia. He continued his innings with scarcely a false stroke to 145, at which point he completed 2000 runs against Australia, but then, tiring, he 'holed' out (literally) off Johnston after batting for 325 minutes and hitting 16 fours.

From the prosperous position of 279 for 2, England declined to 372 all out. Compton went for 57, and Watson was unluckily stumped when the ball hit Langley's pads and bounced back onto the wicket after the batsman overbalanced, but the rest were unequal to the pace of Lindwall, who took the wickets of Brown and Evans with successive balls and finished with 5 for 66. Australia cleared the deficit of 26 for the loss of Hassett, Morris and Miller – who once lofted Wardle for six – taking the score to 96 by the close.

An uncharacteristic but vital innings of 109 from Miller was the backbone of Australia's fourth-day score of 368. Whereas the great allrounder had done the bulk of scoring on Saturday evening, on the fourth morning Morris took over, reaching 89 before Compton had him brilliantly caught by a running Statham, who fell as he made the catch and banged his head hard. Miller had added only 35 by lunch, but the crowd's ribbing seemed to aid his concentration, and he eventually went on to a chanceless 109, his 292-minute innings being probably the longest of his life. He hit 14 fours and a six.

England clawed their way back into the match, Brown taking three quick wickets, but a broadside from Lindwall's bat changed things again: the allrounder added 54 with Langley in a mere 25 minutes, and his 50 included five fours and two sixes.

England's distant target was 343 for victory, but in the final hour of the fourth day that became academic as Lindwall removed Kenyon and Hutton. Graveney was brilliantly caught by a diving Langley, and England were floundering at 12 for 3. The new batsman, Watson, might have been caught twice in the final over, Lindwall at short leg dropping one difficult chance and moving the wrong way for the other . . . so Watson survived to fight another day.

Bailey joined Watson when Compton was out for a defiant 33 after 92 minutes on the final morning, and the Watson-Bailey stand rolled on throughout the day. Few spectators were there at the start, but the crowd grew as news of the rearguard action spread, and the overall crowd figure of 137,915 for the five days remains an alltime Lord's Test record.

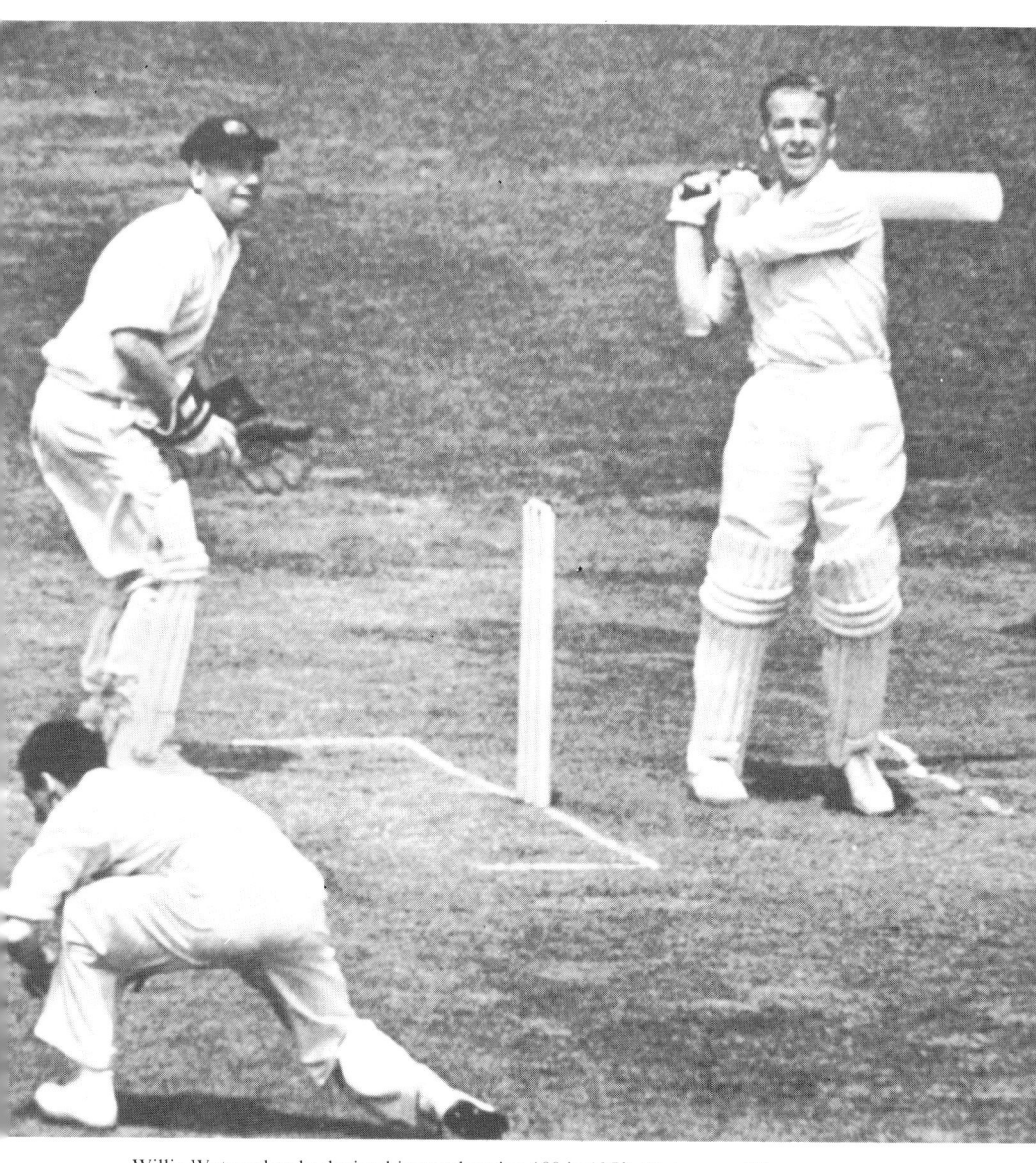

Willie Watson hooks during his matchsaving 109 in 1953. Watson and Trevor
Bailey defied the Australian bowlers for 257 minutes in their epic stand. Behind
the stumps is Gil Langley, who three years later established the Lord's Test record
of nine dismissals in a match

ENGLAND v AUSTRALIA
June 25, 26, 27, 29, 30, 1953

AUSTRALIA

* A.L. Hassett	c Bailey b Bedser	104	c Evans b Statham		3
A.R. Morris	st Evans b Bedser	30	c Statham b Compton		89
R.N. Harvey	lbw b Bedser	59	(4) b Bedser		21
K.R. Miller	b Wardle	25	(3) b Wardle		109
G.B. Hole	c Compton b Wardle	13	lbw b Brown		47
R. Benaud	lbw b Wardle	0	c Graveney b Bedser		5
A.K. Davidson	c Statham b Bedser	76	c and b Brown		15
D.T. Ring	lbw b Wardle	18	lbw b Brown		7
R.R. Lindwall	b Statham	9	b Bedser		50
† G.R.A. Langley	c Watson b Bedser	1	b Brown		9
W.A. Johnston	not out	3	not out		0
Extras	(b4, lb4)	8	(b8, lb5)		13
	(140.4 overs)	346	(132.5 overs)		368

Fall: 65,190,225,229,240,280,291,330,331.   3,168,227,235,248,296,305,308,362.

Bowling: Bedser 42.4-8-105-5, Statham 28-7-48-1, Brown 25-7-53-0, Bailey 16-2-55-0, Wardle 29-8-77-4.

Second innings: Bedser 31.5-8-77-3, Statham 15-3-40-1, Wardle 46-18-111-1, Brown 27-4-82-4, Bailey 10-4-24-0, Compton 3-0-21-1.

ENGLAND

* L. Hutton	c Hole b Johnston	145	c Hole b Lindwall		5
D. Kenyon	c Davidson b Lindwall	3	c Hassett b Lindwall		2
T.W. Graveney	b Lindwall	78	c Langley b Johnston		2
D.C.S. Compton	c Hole b Benaud	57	lbw b Johnston		33
W. Watson	st Langley b Johnston	4	c Hole b Ring		109
T.E. Bailey	c and b Miller	2	c Benaud b Ring		71
F.R. Brown	c Langley b Lindwall	22	c Hole b Benaud		28
† T.G. Evans	b Lindwall	0	not out		11
J.H. Wardle	b Davidson	23	not out		0
A.V. Bedser	b Lindwall	1			
J.B. Statham	not out	17			
Extras	(b11, lb1, w1, nb7)	20	(b7, lb6, w2, nb6)		21
	(126.5 overs)	372	(7 wkts) (126 overs)		282

Fall: 9,177,279,291,301,328,328,332,341.   6,10,12,73,236,246,282.

Bowling: Lindwall 23-4-66-5, Miller 25-6-57-1, Johnston 35-11-91-2, Ring 14-2-43-0, Benaud 19-4-70-1, Davidson 10.5-2-25-1.

Second innings: Lindwall 19-3-26-2, Johnston 29-10-70-2, Ring 29-5-84-2, Miller 17-8-17-0, Benaud 17-6-51-1, Davidson 14-5-13-0, Hole 1-1-0-0.

Toss: Australia   Umpires: H.G. Baldwin and F.S. Lee

Close of play: (1) A. 263 for 5 (Davidson 17, Ring 10)
(2) E. 177 for 1 (Hutton 83, Graveney 78)
(3) A. 96 for 1 (Morris 35, Miller 58)
(4) E. 20 for 3 (Compton 5, Watson 3)
Hassett retired hurt at 201 for 2, resumed at 280 for 6

MATCH DRAWN

The third and fourth Tests were both drawn, rain severely curtailing proceedings at Old Trafford, where Wardle (4 for 7) enlivened the last half-hour by reducing Australia to 35 for 8. Bailey, with defensive bowling this time, denied Australia victory at Headingley, and England took the series – and regained the Ashes after 19 years – with an emotional win at The Oval.

114

1954

Pakistan, who had made their bow in Test cricket against neighbours India in 1952-53, made their first Test tour of England in 1954. Like South Africa, West Indies, New Zealand and India before them (and, later, Sri Lanka) they played their first Test match on English soil at Lord's. Their captain, Abdul Hafeez Kardar, completed a unique double when he went out to toss: he had played for India in 1946, and became the only player to appear for two countries in Tests at Lord's.

Kardar's young side contained Pakistan's first great players, the fast-medium bowler Fazal Mahmood and the compact opener Hanif Mohammad, then only 19.

The tourists had no real chance to display their talents in their first Test in England. Rain completely washed out the first three days, and when play eventually got under way at 3.45 on Day 4, Pakistan were put in on a treacherous pitch. The tourists scored 50 in the 155 minutes' play possible before bad light brought an early close. Hanif dropped anchor, and had moved to 11 by stumps, but Pakistan had lost three prime wickets, all to Wardle, whose 21-over spell had cost just 21 runs.

Pakistan were all out in 80 minutes on the final morning, Statham mopping up the tail to finish with 4 for 18, including a spell of 3 for 0 in 13 balls. Hanif top-scored with 20, but the visitors' struggle is best illustrated by the fact that only 81 runs came off the bat in 83.5 overs.

Hutton, in his last Lord's Test, fell to Khan Mohammad's first ball, and England continued to lose wickets in the search for quick runs. Simpson scored the first 23 runs, and after 100 minutes Hutton declared at 117 for 9, Fazal and Khan having bowled throughout the innings.

When Alimuddin lost his off stump to the eighth ball of the second innings, England sensed a surprise victory, but Hanif defended stoutly again, before falling to the last ball of the match. He shared half-century stands with Waqar Hassan, who made 53, and Maqsood Ahmed (29 not out).

Len Hutton ended his Lord's Test career in 1954 as he had begun it in 1937 – with a duck. In between, however, he joined the select band of those who have made three Test centuries at Lord's. Jack Hobbs was the first member of that club, and he, Denis Compton and Hutton were later joined by Geoff Boycott, John Edrich, Graham Gooch, Allan Lamb and India's Dilip Vengsarkar

ENGLAND v PAKISTAN
June 10 (no play), 11 (no play), 12 (no play), 14, 15, 1954

PAKISTAN

Hanif Mohammad	b Tattersall	20	lbw b Laker	39
Alimuddin	c Edrich b Wardle	19	b Bailey	0
Waqar Hassan	c Compton b Wardle	9	c Statham b Compton	53
Maqsood Ahmed	st Evans b Wardle	0	not out	29
† Imtiaz Ahmed	b Laker	12		
* A.H. Kardar	b Statham	2		
Fazal Mahmood	b Wardle	5		
Khalid Wazir	b Statham	3		
Khan Mohammad	b Statham	0		
Zulfiqar Ahmed	b Statham	11		
Shujauddin	not out	0		
Extras	(b4, lb1, nb1)	6		0
	(83.5 overs)	87	(3 wkts) (52.2 overs)	121

Fall: 24,42,43,57,67,67,71,71,87.　　0,71,121.

Bowling: Statham 13-6-18-4, Bailey 3-2-1-0, Wardle 30.5-22-33-4,
Tattersall 15-8-12-1, Laker 22-12-17-1.

Second innings: Statham 5-2-17-0, Bailey 6-2-13-1, Wardle 8-6-6-0, Laker 10.2-5-22-1,
Tattersall 10-1-27-0, Compton 13-2-36-1.

ENGLAND

* L. Hutton	b Khan	0	Bowling:	
R.T. Simpson	lbw b Fazal	40	Fazal 16-2-54-4,	
P.B.H. May	b Khan	27	Khan 15-3-61-5.	
D.C.S. Compton	b Fazal	0		
W.J. Edrich	b Khan	4		
J.H. Wardle	c Maqsood b Fazal	3		
† T.G. Evans	b Khan	25		
T.E. Bailey	b Khan	3		
J.C. Laker	not out	13		
J.B. Statham	b Fazal	0		
R. Tattersall	did not bat			
Extras	(b2)	2		
	(9 wkts dec) (31 overs)	117		

Fall: 9,55,59,72,75,79,85,110,117.

Toss: England　　　　　　　　　　　　Umpires: T.J. Bartley and D. Davies
Close of play: (4) P. 50 for 3 (Hanif 11, Imtiaz 6)

MATCH DRAWN

*England went one-up with a comfortable innings victory at Trent Bridge, Compton
scoring 278 and Simpson, on his home ground, 101. Three days of the third Test
were lost to rain, but Pakistan squared the series with a shock win in the final match
at The Oval, where a rather makeshift England side was bundled out for 130 and
143 by Fazal, who took 12 wickets.*

1955

England had retained the Ashes with a resounding 4-1 series win in 1954-55, but suffered a cruel blow early the following season when Len Hutton, their captain, had to withdraw from the Test series against South Africa suffering from lumbago. Hutton never played Test cricket again, and retired altogether at the end of the season.

The tourists, captained now by Jack Cheetham, arrived with a high reputation after contesting a pulsating series in Australia in 1952-53, but a collapse against Frank Tyson (6 for 28), the hero of the previous winter's Ashes triumph, sent the tourists to Lord's one-down after defeat in a low-key first Test at Trent Bridge.

England's new captain, Peter May, won the toss at Lord's and, on viewing the well-grassed pitch, must have been tempted to field first. Instead he batted, and the first ball of the match, from South Africa's tall debutant fast bowler Peter Heine, climbed at opener Kenyon and passed him head-high. Kenyon soon fell to the other opening bowler, Adcock, and South Africa were cock-a-hoop when May, before he had scored, provided the aggressive Heine with his first Test wicket by edging to third slip where Tayfield took a fine catch. Compton made 20, becoming the fifth player to reach 5000 runs in Tests, before he too fell to Heine, and it was left to Barrington, in only his second Test, to hold the innings together. He top-scored with 34 in an hour and a half, but was fortunate that more than one uppish hook fell out of reach of the eager Springbok fielders. Bailey lingered an hour for 13, Evans and Wardle made 20 apiece, the Yorkshireman clouting successive sixes off Goddard, and in 190 minutes England were all out for 133. Heine (5 for 60) and Goddard (4 for 59) were applauded from the field by their delighted team-mates.

Now it was South Africa's turn to struggle, McGlew being caught behind off Statham's first ball of the innings, to register his first Test duck in 27 innings. Goddard also failed to score, whereupon Cheetham and Endean embarked on an important partnership during which both were dropped. The stubborn Cheetham received a nasty blow on the hand from Statham, and afterwards played some deliveries one-handed as he grafted his way to 13 in 70 minutes before he was lbw to Bailey. McLean and Endean added another 50, but England struck twice more before the close, which saw the tourists nine runs in front.

McLean made the most of his luck to complete a memorable century next morning. In all he was dropped no fewer than six times – at 48, 62, 64, 78, 80 and 91 – but he went on to 142, his innings featuring many fierce drives. In all, McLean lasted for 213 minutes, hitting 21 fours and a six, before he fell to Statham's last ball before lunch. Keith, who went on to 57, helped McLean add 109 for the sixth wicket.

South Africa's final total gave them a healthy lead of 171, and the tourists' prospects looked even rosier when Kenyon, whose scores in his two Lord's Tests were 3, 2, 1 and 2, was lbw offering no shot to Goddard after the highest opening partnership of the match – 9. Graveney and May, however, altered the picture with the best batting display of the match: both took toll of some wayward bowling, May taking four fours in two overs as Heine persisted in pitching short.

Graveney fell early on the third morning, to an acrobatic airborne catch by

118

South Africa's Roy McLean, dropped six times, rode his luck to score 142 in 1955. Here he cuts Johnny Wardle, watched by Godfrey Evans (who ended his career with more Lord's Test dismissals – 37 – than any other wicketkeeper) and Tom Graveney

Heine at fine leg, but May went on, reaching a chanceless century just before lunch. When 102, he gave a return chance to Mansell, who dropped it, but it was an inexpensive miss, as after the interval May trod on his stumps while playing back to Heine after batting 4½ hours and hitting 15 fours.

Barrington was brilliantly caught by McLean, and three more wickets went down before tea. Controversy flared when Bailey edged Goddard low to slip, where Mansell claimed the catch. Bailey waited for the decision of umpire Gray, whose first Test it was, and after consultation with his colleague Chester he ruled in favour of Bailey. Compton seemed affected by this, and soon departed to the same combination for 69, having hit 11 fours. Bailey stayed to score 22, but Tayfield worked his way through the tail, finishing with 5 for 80 and becoming South Africa's leading Test wicket-taker in the process.

Only 38 minutes remained on the third day as South Africa began their quest for the 183 runs needed to square the series, but once more they made a dreadful start, McGlew again falling to Statham for a duck, second ball this time. Goddard, perhaps feeling the effects of his marathon bowling spell, departed for 10, and the Springboks suffered a cruel blow when Cheetham turned his back on Trueman's last ball of the day: the ball hit his elbow and broke it.

The unfortunate Cheetham was unable to continue on the fourth morning, and indeed missed the next two Tests. Nightwatchman Tayfield and Endean took the score to 40, but neither looked happy against Statham, who had embarked on a spell which was to see him bowl throughout the 3¾-hour innings. Only Tayfield succumbed during the first session, although Endean survived a confident appeal for a gully catch by Titmus off the irrepressible Statham. A shower drove the players from the field at 12.30, and they returned two hours later. A refreshed Statham swept the middle order aside, taking the first seven wickets to fall in all and ending with 7 for 39, which remained his best figures in Tests.

From 78 for 7, Mansell and Heine posted the hundred, but both fell in rapid succession to Wardle, and by five o'clock England had completed a victory which had looked unlikely for most of the match.

ENGLAND v SOUTH AFRICA
June 23, 24, 25, 27, 1955

ENGLAND

D. Kenyon	b Adcock	1	lbw b Goddard	2
T.W. Graveney	c Waite b Heine	15	c Heine b Goddard	60
* P.B.H. May	c Tayfield b Heine	0	hit wkt b Heine	112
D.C.S. Compton	c Keith b Heine	20	c Mansell b Goddard	69
K.F. Barrington	b Heine	34	c McLean b Tayfield	18
T.E. Bailey	lbw b Goddard	13	c Adcock b Tayfield	22
† T.G. Evans	c Waite b Heine	20	c and b Tayfield	14
F.J. Titmus	lbw b Goddard	4	(9) c Waite b Adcock	16
J.H. Wardle	c Tayfield b Goddard	20	(8) c Heine b Tayfield	4
J.B. Statham	c McLean b Goddard	0	b Tayfield	11
F.S. Trueman	not out	2	not out	6
Extras	(b2, lb2)	4	(b15, lb2, nb2)	19
	(54.2 overs)	133	(149.5 overs)	353

Fall: 7,8,30,45,82,98,111,111,111.

9,141,237,277,285,302,306,336,336.

Bowling: Heine 25-7-60-5, Adcock 8-3-10-1, Goddard 21.2-8-59-4.
Second innings: Heine 29-5-87-1, Adcock 25-5-64-1, Goddard 55-23-96-3, Tayfield 38.5-12-80-5, Mansell 2-0-7-0.

SOUTH AFRICA

D.J. McGlew	c Evans b Statham	0	lbw b Statham	0
T.L. Goddard	c Evans b Trueman	0	c Evans b Statham	10
* J.E. Cheetham	lbw b Bailey	13	retired hurt	3
W.R. Endean	lbw b Wardle	48	(5) c Evans b Statham	28
R.A. McLean	b Statham	142	(6) b Statham	8
† J.H.B. Waite	c Evans b Trueman	8	(8) lbw b Statham	9
H.J. Keith	c Titmus b Wardle	57	c Graveney b Statham	5
P.N.F. Mansell	c Graveney b Wardle	2	(9) c Kenyon b Wardle	16
H.J. Tayfield	b Titmus	21	(4) c Evans b Statham	3
P.S. Heine	st Evans b Wardle	2	c Kenyon b Wardle	14
N.A.T. Adcock	not out	0	not out	0
Extras	(b6, lb1, nb4)	11	(b11, lb3, nb1)	15
	(102 overs)	304	(57.4 overs)	111

Fall: 0,7,51,101,138,247,259,302,304.

0,17,40,54,63,75,78,111,111.

Bowling: Statham 27-9-49-2, Trueman 16-2-73-2, Bailey 16-2-56-1, Wardle 29-10-65-4, Titmus 14-3-50-1.
Second innings: Statham 29-12-39-7, Trueman 19-2-39-0, Wardle 9.4-4-18-2.

Toss: England
Close of play: (1) S.A. 142 for 5 (McLean 62, Keith 0)
(2) E. 108 for 1 (Graveney 53, May 50)
(3) S.A. 17 for 2 (Cheetham 3, Tayfield 0)
Cheetham retired hurt at 17 for 2

Umpires: F. Chester and L.H. Gray

ENGLAND WON BY 71 RUNS

Remarkably, South Africa won the next two Tests to square the series, stand-in captain McGlew scoring centuries in both matches. However, England took an absorbing series 3-2 in a low-scoring match at The Oval, where Lock and Laker, on home territory, took 15 wickets between them. This was the first time that a five-Test series in England had produced five definite results.

1956

The 1956 summer is now remembered mainly for the exploits of Jim Laker, who took a staggering 19 wickets in the fourth Test at Old Trafford, and overall took 46 wickets in the series, which England won 2-1 to retain the Ashes. At Lord's, however, as so often, Australia turned the tables and defeated the home side.

Australia's side in 1956 was an interesting blend of youth and experience. Captained by offspinner Ian Johnson, a survivor from Bradman's great 1948 side, the fast bowlers included the incomparable Miller and Lindwall, although the latter was unfit to play at Lord's after picking up an injury in the drawn first Test at Trent Bridge. Davidson, too, was unfit, and Australia gave a first cap to NSW fast bowler Pat Crawford, who was destined to break down himself during his fifth over of the match. Australia's batting was led by Harvey, and for added solidity at Lord's the tourists included 30-year-old allrounder Ken Mackay, who like Crawford was making his Test debut.

For England, Laker, now at his peak, had taken six wickets at Nottingham, but his Surrey partner-in-spin Lock was omitted at Lord's in favour of Wardle. Generally the England side bore a solid, comforting look.

Johnson won the toss, and on a firm, easy-paced pitch his openers batted solidly to post a stand of 137, the only blemish coming when McDonald, at 43, was dropped by May in the gully off Statham. Just before tea, Bailey broke the stand when McDonald fell to an excellent catch by Trueman at second slip, and three balls later Harvey was caught behind for a duck. Burke's 250-minute resistance ended at 65, and after a bad-light stoppage of nearly an hour Australia moved to 180 for 3 by the close, May dropping another slip catch near the end when Burge had made 16.

Australia added another 105 runs on the second day, Mackay battling it out for 160 minutes for 38. England's reply began poorly, when Richardson was caught behind – as he was in all eight of his innings in the series. Graveney soon followed, and a promising third-wicket stand was ended when Benaud in the gully clung on to a phenomenal catch from a hard-hit cut from Cowdrey, who had made 23. England had limped to 74 for 3 at the end of a day that had seen only 179 runs scored.

May and Bailey were the only batsmen to resist for long on an exciting, see-saw third day. May's 63 took 2½ hours, and Bailey defended in typical style, but Miller, trying to make up for the loss of regular partner Lindwall and stand-in Crawford, bowled beautifully to take 5 for 72.

Leading by 114, Australia saw half their side out for 79, with Trueman bowling at top speed to take three quick wickets, including the important one of Harvey who, having taken 10 runs from his first three balls, was brilliantly caught by Bailey at leg slip from the fourth. Just before the close, which saw Australia 115 for 6, Trueman had Miller caught behind for 30.

The match took a decisive turn back Australia's way on the fourth morning. Mackay, whose 31 occupied 265 minutes, was virtually a spectator as Benaud flayed the bowling around the historic ground. Benaud, whose previous-highest score in nine Tests against England was 34, sailed past this figure, piling on 90 before lunch. He became Trueman's fifth victim of the innings soon after the

Gully fieldsman Richie Benaud brings off a stunning catch to dismiss Colin
Cowdrey in 1956. The Australians went on to their almost customary Lord's Test
victory

break, skying a ball to the wicketkeeper after hitting 14 fours and a six in his 97,
which took 143 minutes: he scored all but 20 of his partnership of .117 with
Mackay. Two late wickets from Bailey ended the innings at 257, leaving England
372 to win. Laker, who had removed three batsmen in the first innings, was
wicketless this time.

The teams were presented to the Queen at tea, and she proved to be just as
good a 'change bowler' as her father had been, Richardson flicking Archer to the
wicketkeeper. Graveney followed, the same way, at 59, but Cowdrey and Watson
held out to stumps.

England needed a round 300 on the final day, but Watson was unable to repeat
his 1953 heroics from a very similar situation, and Cowdrey eventually left after
three hours' resistance for 27. Some felt that Cowdrey was unfairly inhibited by
the presence of the bulky Burge, who often fielded within touching distance of the
striker, but Ian Johnson denied that his tactics were unfair, pointing out that
Cowdrey could have driven the fielder away by hitting the ball at him.

May compiled his second half-century of the match, but when he left it was
only a matter of time, and Archer mopped up the tail, finishing with 4 for 71 as
the match ended at 2.53 pm. Miller, though, with five more wickets making 10 in
his last Lord's Test, was Australia's real bowling hero. Wicketkeeper Langley,
with eight catches and a stumping in the match, established a new Test record:
although his aggregate record has been beaten elsewhere, it remains a record for
any Lord's Test.

ENGLAND v AUSTRALIA
June 21, 22, 23, 25, 26, 1956

AUSTRALIA

C.C. McDonald	c Trueman b Bailey	78	c Cowdrey b Bailey	26
J.W. Burke	st Evans b Laker	65	c Graveney b Trueman	16
R.N. Harvey	c Evans b Bailey	0	c Bailey b Trueman	10
P.J.P. Burge	b Statham	21	b Trueman	14
K.R. Miller	b Trueman	28	(7) c Evans b Trueman	30
K.D. Mackay	c Bailey b Laker	38	(5) c Evans b Statham	31
R.G. Archer	b Wardle	28	(6) c Evans b Bailey	1
R. Benaud	b Statham	5	c Evans b Trueman	97
* I.W. Johnson	c Evans b Trueman	6	lbw b Bailey	17
† G.R.A. Langley	c Bailey b Laker	14	not out	7
W.P.A. Crawford	not out	0	lbw b Bailey	0
Extras	(lb2)	2	(b2, lb2, nb4)	8
	(146.1 overs)	285	(92.5 overs)	257

Fall: 137,137,151,185,196,249,255,265,285.   36,47,69,70,79,112,229,243,257.

Bowling: Statham 35-9-70-2, Trueman 28-6-54-2, Bailey 34-12-72-2, Laker 29.1-10-47-3, Wardle 20-7-40-1.

Second innings: Statham 26-5-59-1, Trueman 28-2-90-5, Bailey 24.5-8-64-4, Laker 7-3-17-0, Wardle 7-2-19-0.

ENGLAND

P.E. Richardson	c Langley b Miller	9	c Langley b Archer	21
M.C. Cowdrey	c Benaud b Mackay	23	lbw b Benaud	27
T.W. Graveney	b Miller	5	c Langley b Miller	18
* P.B.H. May	b Benaud	63	(5) c Langley b Miller	53
W. Watson	c Benaud b Miller	6	(4) b Miller	18
T.E. Bailey	b Miller	32	c Harvey b Archer	18
† T.G. Evans	st Langley b Benaud	0	c Langley b Miller	20
J.C. Laker	b Archer	12	c Langley b Archer	4
J.H. Wardle	c Langley b Archer	0	b Miller	0
F.S. Trueman	c Langley b Miller	7	b Archer	2
J.B. Statham	not out	0	not out	0
Extras	(lb14)	14	(lb5)	5
	(82 overs)	171	(99.2 overs)	186

Fall: 22,32,60,87,128,128,161,161,170.   35,59,89,91,142,175,180,184,184.

Bowling: Miller 34.1-9-72-5, Crawford 4.5-2-4-0, Archer 23-9-47-2, Mackay 11-3-15-1, Benaud 9-2-19-2.

Second innings: Miller 36-12-80-5, Archer 31.2-8-71-4, Benaud 28-14-27-1, Johnson 4-2-3-0.

Toss: Australia   Umpires: D.E. Davies and F.S. Lee

Close of play: (1) A. 180 for 3 (Burge 18, Miller 19)
(2) E. 74 for 3 (May 23, Watson 4)
(3) A. 115 for 6 (Mackay 9, Benaud 3)
(4) E. 72 for 2 (Cowdrey 21, Watson 9)

AUSTRALIA WON BY 185 RUNS

England squared the series with an innings victory at Headingley, where May made 101 and the recalled Washbrook 98: Laker took 11 wickets and Lock seven. Laker's heroics at Old Trafford took England into the lead and retained the Ashes, while the final match, at The Oval, was drawn, Laker taking seven more wickets. Compton, with 94, completed a hat-trick of successful comebacks (Sheppard had made a century at Manchester).

1957

After their exploits seven years previously, the 1957 West Indians were expected to pose a serious threat to Peter May's England side, but in the end the tourists were very disappointing. Of the great 'Three Ws', only Worrell enhanced his reputation on the tour, while the two great spinners of 1950, Ramadhin and Valentine, were much less of a threat, especially after May and Cowdrey broke Ramadhin's spirit with frequent pad-play during a marathon partnership of 411 to save the first Test at Edgbaston. Ramadhin, who had taken 7 for 49 in the first innings, toiled through 98 overs in the second, ending up with 2 for 179. He was never the same bowler again.

At Lord's, West Indies made a poor start after winning the toss, Asgarali, in his first Test, being trapped lbw by Trueman's yorker before he had scored. The batsmen could not come to terms with the pitch's variable bounce, and Bailey, in his 50th Test, exploited the conditions superbly, moving the ball both ways off the seam. Kanhai, who shaped well for an hour and a half, top-scored with 34, but although all the middle-order batsmen reached double figures only the adventurous Collie Smith passed 20, and he had the benefit of two escapes: Close at slip dropped him on 8, and his namesake Don Smith at short leg put him down again when he had reached 12, Statham being the unlucky bowler each time.

Bailey, well supported by the fielders, ended up with 7 for 44 as the visitors were bowled out for 127 in less than four hours.

In reply, England too made an uncertain start. Smith, in his first Test, went lbw for 8, then the tearaway Gilchrist bagged a double prize by disposing of Graveney and May in the same over, both for ducks. Richardson and Cowdrey changed the tone, putting on 95 in 85 minutes before the opener also succumbed to Gilchrist, having hit 11 fours in his 130-minute innings of 76.

Cowdrey, now partnered by Bailey, reached the close without further ado, but England's bowling hero was out without addition on the second morning. Cowdrey, however, seemed in good touch, his innings being marked by several exquisite cover-drives and square-cuts, and he and Close put on 58 for the sixth wicket. When Close was caught behind by Kanhai, Cowdrey was joined by his county colleague Evans, and the pair put West Indies to the sword with a riproaring partnership of 174 in just 115 minutes. West Indian heads began to droop as Cowdrey continued towards his second successive score in excess of 150, and Evans was dropped no fewer than five times in his quickfire 82, which included 11 fours. In all, West Indies reportedly dropped 12 chances. Cowdrey, who hit 14 fours, eventually departed for 152, but England were not finished: Trueman weighed in with a brisk undefeated 36, slamming the miserable Ramadhin for three sixes towards the pavilion in one over.

Facing a deficit of 297, West Indies made another poor start, a Statham lifter taking the shoulder of Kanhai's bat before the opener had scored. Smith, opening in the absence of Asgarali who had pulled muscles in both legs, was lbw to Statham, and Walcott also left before the close, which found West Indies deep in trouble at 45 for 3.

Asgarali, batting with 12th man Atkinson as his runner, stayed for an hour to make 26 next morning, but it was a stand of exactly 100 between Sobers and

Trevor Bailey, a hero with the bat in 1953, leads his side off after a sterling performance with the ball in 1957: he took 7 for 44 as West Indies were shot out for 127, and added four more wickets as England completed their last Test win to date against West Indies at Lord's

Weekes that gave West Indies faint hope. Sobers, showing signs of his great promise, took nearly three hours over his 66, while Weekes played his best innings of the series. Making light of a cracked finger (he also injured a thumb during his innings), he batted for 169 minutes, hitting 16 spanking fours in his 90. Few would have begrudged him the extra runs needed for his century.

After Bailey, who ended the match with 11 wickets, removed both Sobers and Weekes, the tourists crumbled to 261 all out, giving England victory by an innings with more than two days to spare. One disturbing feature of the match was the apparent existence of what *Wisden* termed a 'peculiar ridge' at the Nursery end of the pitch, which seemed to cause the uneven bounce that had seen several of the West Indies batsmen hit during their innings. The 'ridge' was to rear its head on several occasions in the future.

The England team, however, were unconcerned about the problems of the pitch as they celebrated what remains their last win to date against West Indies at Lord's.

ENGLAND v WEST INDIES
June 20, 21, 22, 1957

WEST INDIES

N.S. Asgarali	lbw b Trueman	0	(4) c Trueman b Wardle	26
† R.B. Kanhai	c Cowdrey b Bailey	34	(1) c Bailey b Statham	0
C.L. Walcott	lbw b Bailey	14	c Trueman b Bailey	21
G.S. Sobers	c May b Statham	17	(5) c May b Bailey	66
E.D. Weekes	c Evans b Bailey	13	(6) c Evans b Bailey	90
F.M.M. Worrell	c Close b Bailey	12	(7) c Evans b Trueman	10
O.G. Smith	c Graveney b Bailey	25	(2) lbw b Statham	5
* J.D.C. Goddard	c Cowdrey b Bailey	1	c Evans b Trueman	21
S. Ramadhin	b Trueman	0	c Statham b Bailey	0
R. Gilchrist	c and b Bailey	4	not out	11
A.L. Valentine	not out	0	b Statham	1
Extras	(b2, lb1, w4)	7	(b4, lb6)	10
	(51.3 overs)	127	(96.1 overs)	261

Fall: 7,34,55,79,85,118,120,123,127.   0,17,32,80,180,203,233,241,256.

Bowling: Statham 18-3-46-1, Trueman 12.3-2-30-2, Bailey 21-8-44-7.
Second innings: Statham 29.1-9-71-3, Trueman 23-5-73-2, Bailey 22-6-54-4, Wardle 22-5-53-1.

ENGLAND

P.E. Richardson	b Gilchrist	76	Bowling:
D.V. Smith	lbw b Worrell	8	Worrell 42-7-114-2,
T.W. Graveney	lbw b Gilchrist	0	Gilchrist 36.3-7-115-4,
* P.B.H. May	c Kanhai b Gilchrist	0	Ramadhin 22-5-83-1,
M.C. Cowdrey	c Walcott b Sobers	152	Valentine 3-0-20-0,
T.E. Bailey	b Worrell	1	Goddard 13-1-45-1,
D.B. Close	c Kanhai b Goddard	32	Sobers 7-0-28-2.
† T.G. Evans	b Sobers	82	
J.H. Wardle	c Sobers b Ramadhin	11	
F.S. Trueman	not out	36	
J.B. Statham	b Gilchrist	7	
Extras	(b7, lb11, w1)	19	
	(123.3 overs)	424	

Fall: 25,34,34,129,134,192,366,379,387.

Toss: West Indies   Umpires: D.E. Davies and C.S. Elliott
Close of play: (1) E. 134 for 4 (Cowdrey 39, Bailey 1)
                 (2) W.I. 45 for 3 (Asgarali 12, Sobers 7)

ENGLAND WON BY AN INNINGS AND 36 RUNS

England ran up 619 for 6 at Trent Bridge, Graveney (258), Richardson and May making centuries. Worrell carried his bat through West Indies' first innings for 191, and Smith (who was to die in a car crash two years later) saved the tourists with a brilliant 168 in the second innings. England, however, took the series 3-0 with innings victories at Headingley (where Loader of Surrey took a hat-trick) and The Oval (Richardson and Graveney made hundreds, and Lock took 11 wickets as West Indies were bundled out for 89 and 86).

1958

Nine years after Walter Hadlee's successful tourists had drawn all four Tests, New Zealand returned to do battle with England in, for the first and last time, a full five-Test series. John Reid, the 'baby' of the 1949 side, returned as captain, but his side was largely an inexperienced one, and proved to be easy meat for England's bowlers, in particular the wily spinners Lock and Laker. Many, Reid included, felt that the selectors had not chosen the best available side for the tour. One survivor of the 1949 tour was the brilliant left-hander Sutcliffe, but he had missed the first Test with a broken wrist. He was fit for Lord's, where he batted with his right forearm encased in a felt cover to protect the joint.

England won the first Test, at Edgbaston, with over a day to spare, the Kiwis being bowled out for 94 and 137.

The first day of the Lord's Test was a sombre occasion, flags flying at half-mast in memory of the former England captain Douglas Jardine, who had died of cancer in a Swiss clinic. There also was sadness in the New Zealand dressing-room, where 22-year-old John D'Arcy was mourning his father, who had died a few days before the match.

England won the toss and batted on a placid pitch, but the openers made a cautious start, Mike Smith taking 25 minutes to get off the mark. Richardson was caught behind just before lunch, and at the break Smith had progressed to 17, having hit his first boundary after 90 minutes. The batsmen continued to show little imagination in the face of tight New Zealand bowling and fielding, and Smith's vigilant 230-minute innings came to an end shortly before tea, when he jabbed at a short ball from Hayes and was caught behind for 47. May went to the first ball after tea, but a stand of 60 between Cowdrey and Bailey, who was playing in his last Lord's Test, took England past 200. Cowdrey, again specialising in his textbook cover-drive, hit nine fours, but was bowled in the day's last over as Hayes summoned up some extra pace.

With England 237 for 7, honours were even at the end of the first day, with New Zealand perhaps having done better than many expected. During the night, though, it began to rain . . . and enough fell to prevent a restart before 3.20 on the second day, the New Zealand batsmen having plenty of time to muse over their likely fate on a spiteful, rain-affected pitch.

When play did start, England lost the last three wickets in 40 minutes and, after tea, New Zealand began their thankless task. The pitch was taking a degree of turn, though it was not a true 'sticky dog', but the tourists were not technically equipped to survive. D'Arcy struggled for 50 minutes, scoring 14, but only Sutcliffe of the others reached double figures. Miller left in the first over, while D'Arcy's defiance ended as soon as he faced Laker. Reid's only scoring shot was a six off Lock, but he skyed the same bowler to mid-on in trying to repeat the shot. Wicketkeeper Petrie hung around for 40 scoreless minutes, but Lock ended the tourists' misery after 110 minutes, finishing with 5 for 17 in the puny total of 47, at the time the lowest score in a Lord's Test. Laker took 4 for 13.

Following on, 222 behind, New Zealand survived the 10 minutes before the close without further loss.

More rain delayed the third-day resumption by half an hour, but the Kiwis

The left-arm spin of the aggressive Tony Lock proved too hot for the 1958 New Zealanders to handle. At Lord's Lock took 9 for 29 as the tourists were bundled out for 47 and 74

were soon back on the rack. Miller failed to score, and only D'Arcy, who played a defiant two-hour innings of 33 containing four fours, held up England for long. Of the other batsmen, no-one exceeded MacGibbon's 7 until last man Hayes swept Laker for two sixes. Lock soon ended the fun, however, the last-wicket stand of 18 being New Zealand's best in either innings. In the second innings Lock took 4 for 12, his match figures being 24-15-29-9. It was all over at 3.30 on the Saturday, the match itself being concluded in 11½ hours of actual playing time.

ENGLAND v NEW ZEALAND
June 19, 20, 21, 1958

ENGLAND

P.E. Richardson	c Petrie b Hayes	36	Bowling:
M.J.K. Smith	c Petrie b Hayes	47	Hayes 22-5-36-4,
T.W. Graveney	c Petrie b Alabaster	37	MacGibbon 36.4-11-86-4,
* P.B.H. May	c Alabaster b MacGibbon	19	Blair 25-6-57-0,
M.C. Cowdrey	b Hayes	65	Reid 24-12-41-1,
T.E. Bailey	c Petrie b Reid	17	Alabaster 16-6-48-1.
† T.G. Evans	c Hayes b MacGibbon	11	
G.A.R. Lock	not out	23	
F.S. Trueman	b Hayes	8	
J.C. Laker	c Blair b MacGibbon	1	
P.J. Loader	c Playle b MacGibbon	4	
Extras	(lb1)	1	
	(123.4 overs)	269	

Fall: 54,113,139,141,201,222,237,259,260.

NEW ZEALAND

L.S.M. Miller	lbw b Trueman	4	c Trueman b Loader	0
J.W. D'Arcy	c Trueman b Laker	14	c Bailey b Trueman	33
W.R. Playle	c Graveney b Laker	1	b Loader	3
N.S. Harford	c and b Laker	0	c May b Lock	3
* J.R. Reid	c Loader b Lock	6	c Cowdrey b Trueman	5
B. Sutcliffe	b Lock	18	b Bailey	0
A.R. MacGibbon	c May b Lock	2	c May b Lock	7
J.C. Alabaster	c and b Lock	0	b Laker	5
† E.C. Petrie	c Trueman b Laker	0	not out	4
R.W. Blair	not out	0	b Lock	0
J.A. Hayes	c Cowdrey b Lock	1	c and b Lock	14
Extras	(lb1)	1		0
	(32.3 overs)	47	(50.3 overs)	74

Fall: 4,12,12,19,25,31,34,46,46.   11,21,34,41,44,44,56,56,56.

Bowling: Trueman 4-1-6-1, Loader 4-2-6-0, Laker 12-6-13-4, Lock 11.3-7-17-5, Bailey 1-0-4-0.

Second innings: Trueman 11-6-24-2, Loader 9-6-7-2, Laker 13-8-24-1, Lock 12.3-8-12-4, Bailey 5-1-7-1.

Toss: England   Umpires: D. Davies and C.S. Elliott
Close of play: (1) E. 237 for 7 (Lock 4)
                 (2) N.Z. 0 for 0 (Miller 0, D'Arcy 0)

ENGLAND WON BY AN INNINGS AND 148 RUNS

Despite more rain England had little difficulty in winning the next two Tests by an innings, Lock taking 11 wickets at Headingley and eight at Old Trafford. England lost only two wickets in winning the third Test. Rain did prevent an England clean sweep, however, only 12 hours' play being possible in the final Test at The Oval.' Lock ended the series with 34 wickets at the startling average of 7.47.

1959

Having been denied by the weather of the opportunity of winning all five Tests the previous year, England managed to achieve the feat in 1959, against an admittedly weak Indian side. For England, it was a tonic after a comprehensive Ashes defeat the previous winter at the hands of Richie Benaud's Australians.

England scored 422 in the first Test, May scoring 106, then bowled India out twice to win by an innings, Statham taking seven wickets and India's old tormentor Trueman six.

For the Lord's Test, the already downcast Indians were without their captain, Dattajirao Gaekwad, who had bronchitis, and allrounders Borde (broken finger) and Nadkarni (injured back). So it was the bespectacled opener Pankaj Roy, having his only taste of Test captaincy, who tossed up with Peter May. Roy won the toss, but on a lively pitch his was the first wicket to fall. Statham was working up a good pace, and fizzed one past the back of Roy's neck: later on he broke one of Contractor's ribs. The opening stand was worth 32 when Roy provided Statham with his 150th Test wicket, touching a ball to Evans. Umrigar soon followed, for a single, and Trueman removed Manjrekar with the last ball before lunch.

Despite his injury, Contractor continued gamely, adding 83 with Ghorpade. After tea, though, Contractor – by now batting with a runner – succumbed after 255 minutes (nine fours and a six) to Greenhough, who promptly removed Surendranath with his next ball. Gupte prevented his rival legspinner from taking a hat-trick, but Greenhough's 5 for 12 spell ruined India's hopes of a large score: the last seven wickets tumbled for 24 runs. Horton tidied up the innings at 168 with his first two Test wickets. England's main worry concerned wicketkeeper Evans, who had missed four possible stumpings during the innings. As it turned out, the Kent man was playing in his last Test match – his 91st in all and his 13th at Lord's, both figures being records at the time.

India's opening bowler 'Tiny' Desai, whose whippy action produced more pace than seemed likely, removed both openers as England made an indifferent start. Taylor mishooked a bouncer, and Milton was caught by Surendranath, who made another important breakthrough himself when he knocked back May's off stump.

The struggle continued on the second morning, England dipping to 80 for 6 when Evans, hit on the ear first ball by Desai, was out for a duck to Surendranath. However, the opening bowlers were tired now, and although Gupte trapped Trueman for 7, Barrington and Statham laid about them, taking England into the lead with a stand of 84 in 80 minutes. Barrington, who batted for 225 minutes and hit 10 fours, and Moss added a further 42 in 29 before both fell at the same score, the total of 226 giving England a lead of 58. The diminutive Desai took 5 for 89.

India could hardly have made a worse start, Trueman removing Roy (caught at third slip) and Umrigar (caught in the gully) for ducks with the third and fourth balls of the innings. Jaisimha, moved up to open in his first Test in place of the injured Contractor, soon went for 8, and when Ghorpade was caught behind India were deep in trouble at 42 for 4. Manjrekar, who once took 14 off a Statham over, and Kripal Singh put India in the black and extended their stand to 66 at a run a minute by the close.

Brian Statham excelled with the ball during his Lord's Test career, but also shone with the bat in 1959, scoring a breezy 38 (his best Test score) as England recorded their second victory on the way to a 5-0 'whitewash'

Manjrekar reached his half-century with an on-driven four off Trueman's first ball of the third day, but when the stand had grown to 89, Manjrekar was lbw for the fourth time in four innings in the series. Another collapse followed, only Contractor, from No. 8, managing to reach double figures. Two late wickets from Greenhough rounded off the innings for 165, leaving England a victory target of 108.

When both openers went cheaply again, India sensed a possible sensation, but Cowdrey, in particularly good form, and May knocked off the last 96 runs required in 70 minutes. However, both gave difficult chances early on, Cowdrey edging high and wide past wicketkeeper Joshi and May driving a catch back at bowler Surendranath.

England completed their third successive three-day win in Lord's Tests in the third over after tea on Saturday afternoon.

ENGLAND v INDIA
June 18, 19, 20, 1959

INDIA

* P. Roy	c Evans b Statham	15	c May b Trueman		0
N.J. Contractor	b Greenhough	81	(8) not out		11
P.R. Umrigar	b Statham	1	c Horton b Trueman		0
V.L. Manjrekar	lbw b Trueman	12	(5) lbw b Statham		61
J.M. Ghorpade	lbw b Greenhough	41	(4) c Evans b Statham		22
A.G. Kripal Singh	b Greenhough	0	b Statham		41
M.L. Jaisimha	lbw b Greenhough	1	(2) lbw b Moss		8
† P.G. Joshi	b Horton	4	(7) b Moss		6
R. Surendranath	b Greenhough	0	run out		0
S.P. Gupte	c May b Horton	0	st Evans b Greenhough		7
R.B. Desai	not out	2	b Greenhough		5
Extras	(lb11)	11	(lb4)		4
	(77.4 overs)	168	(79.1 overs)		165

Fall: 32,40,61,144,152,158,163,163,164.   0,0,22,42,131,140,147,147,159.

Bowling: Trueman 16-4-40-1, Statham 16-6-27-2, Moss 14-5-31-0, Greenhough 16-4-35-5, Horton 15.4-7-24-2.

Second innings: Trueman 21-3-55-2, Statham 17-7-45-3, Moss 23-10-30-2, Greenhough 18.1-8-31-2.

ENGLAND

C.A. Milton	c Surendranath b Desai	14	c Joshi b Desai	3
K. Taylor	c Gupte b Desai	6	lbw b Surendranath	3
M.C. Cowdrey	c Joshi b Desai	34	not out	63
* P.B.H. May	b Surendranath	9	not out	33
K.F. Barrington	c sub (V.M. Muddiah) b Desai	80		
M.J. Horton	b Desai	2		
† T.G. Evans	b Surendranath	0		
F.S. Trueman	lbw b Gupte	7		
J.B. Statham	c Surendranath b Gupte	38		
A.E. Moss	b Surendranath	26		
T. Greenhough	not out	0		
Extras	(b5, lb4, w1)	10	(b5, lb1)	6
	(84.4 overs)	226	(2 wkts) (27.2 overs)	108

Fall: 9,26,35,69,79,80,100,184,226.   8,12.

Bowling: Desai 31.4-8-89-5, Surendranath 30-17-46-3, Umrigar 1-1-0-0, Gupte 19-2-62-2, Kripal Singh 3-0-19-0.

Second innings: Desai 7-1-29-1, Surendranath 11-2-32-1, Jaisimha 1-0-8-0, Gupte 6-2-21-0, Kripal Singh 1-1-0-0, Umrigar 1-0-8-0, Roy 0.2-0-4-0.

Toss: India   Umpires: D.E. Davies and C.S. Elliott
Close of play: (1) E. 50 for 3 (Cowdrey 19, Barrington 1)
              (2) I. 108 for 4 (Manjrekar 46, Kripal Singh 28)

ENGLAND WON BY 8 WICKETS

Another three-day win at Headingley, where Cowdrey made 160, clinched the series for England. India batted better at Old Trafford, Baig and Umrigar registering hundreds, but England, for whom Pullar and Smith also reached three figures, came out on top. The clean sweep was completed with another innings win at The Oval.

1960

Two unique events make the 1960 Lord's Test stand out, the major achievement coming from the blond South African fast bowler Geoff Griffin, who had turned 21 during the first Test, which England had won by 100 runs. At Lord's, Griffin became the only bowler to take a Test hat-trick there, dismissing Smith (for 99), Walker and Trueman. His joy should have been unconfined, but, as Ian Peebles put it, 'There was a very sizable fly in this most pleasant ointment': Griffin had also chalked up an unwanted 'first', becoming the only player to be no-balled for throwing in a Lord's Test.

There had been much comment about Griffin's bowling action in the early matches of the tour, and he had already been 'called' 17 times in county matches before the Lord's Test. It was a time when the game's rulers were starting to take a hard line with the so-called 'chuckers', and there are those – notably South Africans – who believe that Griffin was made a scapegoat. Film of his action, though, does seem to support the view that he threw the ball.

All this lay in the future as the teams took the field on the first day, the start of which was delayed by 45 minutes after rain. In an attempt to negate the effects of the 'ridge', the pitch had been moved a yard nearer the pavilion than was usual. England's captain was Cowdrey, who had taken over from May (ill) during the winter series in West Indies, which England had won 1-0. South African cricket was at an interim stage between the useful 1950s side and the powerful mid- to late-1960s line-up. None of this team, captained by third-time tourist Jackie McGlew, was to appear in another Lord's Test.

Cowdrey won the toss and, on a day shortened by rain by 3¼ hours in all, saw his side progress to 114 for 2. Cowdrey himself was out early on, caught at slip off Griffin after taking several blows on the body from Adcock, but Subba Row and Dexter, both in their maiden Lord's Tests, put on 96 before Dexter, unsettled by the various stoppages, edged Adcock to second slip.

Griffin, bowling from the pavilion end, had made his piece of unwanted history as early as his third over, which contained two no-ball shouts from square-leg umpire Frank Lee. In all, he was called five times on the first day: curiously, he was bowling to Dexter on each occasion.

Subba Row continued his patient innings on the second day, surviving for two minutes short of five hours and hitting just five fours before Adcock trapped him lbw for 90. Barrington and Parks did not last long, the latter being beaten seven times in the space of two overs from Griffin before Adcock dismissed him. However, a spirited partnership of 120 between Smith and Walker took the score to a respectable 347, at which point Smith was out. With the close looming, Smith, on 97, had seen certain fours cut off by brilliant fielding from Fellows-Smith and Wesley, and although he moved to 99 the unfortunate Warwickshire man was caught behind from the last ball of a Griffin over. Two sixes from Walker in Goddard's next over took the Glamorgan allrounder to his only Test half-century, but he was beaten and bowled by the first ball of Griffin's next over. Unaware that the bowler was on a hat-trick, Trueman swished at his first ball and was bowled as well, the signal for great rejoicing in the South African ranks.

England scored two more runs that evening, and Cowdrey declared at the

South African fast bowler Geoff Griffin had a mixed time of it in 1960. He took the only hat-trick ever recorded in a Lord's Test – but he chalked up another unwanted first after being no-balled for throwing on 11 occasions. Here umpire Syd Buller scrutinises Griffin's unusual bowling action

overnight score. During the day, umpire Lee had called Griffin for throwing six more times.

None of South Africa's batsmen settled on the second day as the tourists were shot out for 152 in a little over three hours. Eight players reached double figures but only Fellows-Smith passed 20. Statham, who always seemed to bowl well at Lord's, performed superbly, ending up with 6 for 63 while Moss, on his home ground, claimed the other four wickets. The visitors' captain, McGlew, seemed unlucky to have been given out lbw after the ball apparently hit his bat, but there was little room for argument in the other dismissals, two fine slip catches by Cowdrey (one a one-handed diving effort to remove Carlstein) being the highlights.

South Africa were batting again before tea, and they lost McGlew, bowled off the inside edge, before a thunderstorm ended the day's entertainment. McGlew, a prolific scorer elsewhere, ended his Lord's Test career with 37 runs in six innings.

Another disappointing display on the third day saw South Africa slide to defeat, the coup de grace being administered by Statham, appropriately enough, 15 minutes after lunch. First to go was Goddard, who 'walked' for a catch behind, then with no addition Trueman took his first wicket of the match by removing the stubborn former Charlton Athletic footballer O'Linn. Although McLean, the hero of the 1955 Lord's Test, survived an hour for 13, South Africa seemed to be sliding to an embarrassingly low score before left-hander Wesley and Fellows-Smith, a mighty hitter on his day, enjoyed a stand of 54.

After lunch, Statham rounded off a triumphant match by hitting the stumps twice to dismiss Griffin (breaking a stump in the process) and Adcock. The Lancastrian had taken 11 for 97 in the match, his best Test figures.

Although the match was over, the drama was not. The teams agreed to play an exhibition match to entertain the crowd, and during this piece of supposed levity the unfortunate Griffin's first-class career was effectively ended. Operating for the first time with Syd Buller, that most fearless of umpires, at square leg, Griffin found that four successive deliveries in his only over were ruled as throws. Distraught, he tried to complete the over underarm, but now umpire Lee stepped in with a no-ball shout as the bowler had not informed the batsman of his change of action. A more miserable state of affairs in a light-hearted match is difficult to imagine. Griffin did not bowl again on the tour, and faded out of first-class cricket after three more seasons in South Africa.

ENGLAND v SOUTH AFRICA
June 23, 24, 25, 27, 1960

ENGLAND

* M.C. Cowdrey	c McLean b Griffin	4	Bowling:	
R. Subba Row	lbw b Adcock	90	Adcock 36-11-70-3,	
E.R. Dexter	c McLean b Adcock	56	Griffin 30-7-87-4,	
K.F. Barrington	lbw b Goddard	24	Goddard 31-6-96-1,	
M.J.K. Smith	c Waite b Griffin	99	Tayfield 27-9-64-0,	
† J.M. Parks	c Fellows-Smith b Adcock	3	Fellows-Smith 5-0-13-0.	
P.M. Walker	b Griffin	52		
R. Illingworth	not out	0		
F.S. Trueman	b Griffin	0		
J.B. Statham	not out	2		
A.E. Moss	did not bat			
Extras	(b6, lb14, w1, nb11)	32		
	(8 wkts dec) (129 overs)	362		

Fall: 7,103,165,220,227,347,360,360.

SOUTH AFRICA

* D.J. McGlew	lbw b Statham	15	b Statham	17
T.L. Goddard	b Statham	19	c Parks b Statham	24
S. O'Linn	c Walker b Moss	18	lbw b Trueman	8
R.A. McLean	c Cowdrey b Statham	15	c Parks b Trueman	13
† J.H.B. Waite	c Parks b Statham	3	lbw b Statham	0
P.R. Carlstein	c Cowdrey b Moss	12	c Parks b Moss	6
C. Wesley	c Parks b Statham	11	b Dexter	35
J.P. Fellows-Smith	c Parks b Moss	29	not out	27
H.J. Tayfield	c Smith b Moss	12	b Dexter	4
G.M. Griffin	b Statham	5	b Statham	0
N.A.T. Adcock	not out	8	b Statham	2
Extras	(lb4, nb1)	5	(nb1)	1
	(43.3 overs)	152	(57 overs)	137

Fall: 33,48,56,69,78,88,112,132,138. 26,49,49,50,63,72,126,132,133.

Bowling: Statham 20-5-63-6, Trueman 13-2-49-0, Moss 10.3-0-35-4.
Second innings: Statham 21-6-34-5, Trueman 17-5-44-2, Moss 14-1-41-1,
Illingworth 1-1-0-0, Dexter 4-0-17-2.

Toss: England Umpires: J.S. Buller and F.S. Lee
Close of play: (1) E. 114 for 2 (Subba Row 36, Barrington 5)
(2) E. 362 for 8 (Illingworth 0, Statham 2)
(3) S.A. 34 for 1 (Goddard 11, O'Linn 6)

ENGLAND WON BY AN INNINGS AND 73 RUNS

England clinched the series with an eight-wicket win at Trent Bridge, the third year running they had won the first three Tests of a series. The remaining two matches were drawn, rain ruining the Old Trafford match. In the final Test, at The Oval, South Africa built a first-innings lead of 264, only to see Pullar (175) and Cowdrey (155) wipe off the deficit with an opening stand of 290.

1961

For the second time in three years the touring captain had the ill-luck to miss the Lord's Test on fitness grounds. In 1959, Dattajirao Gaekwad had been forced to withdraw from the match suffering from bronchitis: in 1961, Richie Benaud's troublesome shoulder kept him on the sidelines. Australia were captained by the experienced Neil Harvey, making his fourth tour of England: like Gaekwad's deputy Pankaj Roy, Harvey's only taste of Test captaincy came at Lord's.

The sides came to Lord's all square, England having fought back to draw the first Test, at Edgbaston, after conceding a first-innings lead of 321.

England were strengthened at Lord's by the return of May, who had not played Test cricket for 16 months. Cowdrey, however, retained the captaincy for this match (but May took over afterwards for the rest of the series).

After Cowdrey won the toss England made an uncertain start, with the Australian fast bowlers Davidson, McKenzie (on his debut) and Misson exploiting the lively pitch, where from time to time the ball flew on the mysterious 'ridge' (after this Test, MCC called in surveyors to determine the extent of the problem). Pullar had made 5 when the simplest of gully chances was floored by Burge off Davidson, but the Lancastrian did not profit unduly, adding only half-a-dozen before Davidson had his revenge.

Subba Row and Dexter, both given lives off Misson, took the score to 87 before both fell minutes before lunch. The teams were presented to the Queen during the interval, after which – as had become almost traditional – the Monarch presided over something of an England collapse, five wickets going down for 80. Bogged down, Cowdrey had shown a hint of desperation in hitting out at McKenzie, managing three fours off successive balls but giving a catch to the fourth, becoming the young paceman's first Test wicket. May produced some pedigree shots before falling to an awkward lifter from Davidson, and Barrington went to a juggling catch by Mackay at second slip.

A jolly stand of 39 between Trueman and Statham took the score to 206, Davidson finally removing the Yorkshireman to finish with 5 for 42. Faced with an hour's batting, Australia lost two wickets before the close, Simpson going for a duck after McDonald had become Statham's 200th Test victim. The lithe Lancastrian, the second Englishman to reach this figure (Alec Bedser was the first), ended his career with 252 Test wickets, but this was to be his last Lord's Test.

A superb innings from Lawry dominated an absorbing second day's play. The slim left-hander defied the varied England bowling attack and the vagaries of the pitch, surviving in all for 369 minutes and hitting 18 fours in his maiden Test century. It was a chanceless innings, although occasionally Statham beat him outside the off stump.

Earlier, Harvey had fallen to Trueman for 27, straight after taking two successive blows on the body, and O'Neill was bowled by Dexter for a single. Burge made a gritty 46, putting on 95 with Lawry in 140 minutes.

When Dexter removed Grout for a duck (238 for 8) it seemed that Australia's lead would be kept within reasonable bounds, but a typical innings from Mackay, in conjunction with sensible innings from McKenzie and Misson, eventually

136

Bill Lawry hooks during his defiant 130 in 1961

swelled the advantage to 134. At one point Mackay, struck on the pad by Statham, lost feeling in his leg and called for Simpson as a runner. However, the stodgy 'Slasher' was soon fit again, and when both batsman and runner set off for a single, 'Simpson withdrew his services,' as John Arlott put it.

In front of a capacity crowd (the gates were closed for the first time at Lord's since 1957), Mackay and McKenzie added only five runs on the third morning before McKenzie, whose 20th birthday it was, fell to Trueman. Misson helped put on another 49 before Mackay finally succumbed to Illingworth.

Pullar made a lively start, tucking fours off his legs and making 24 of the first 31 runs in the 25 minutes remaining before lunch. The first setback, however, came in the first over after the interval, when Subba Row was caught behind. Dexter was bowled off his body, having been hit in the chest by the previous ball, and Pullar soon gave Grout another catch. Cowdrey, in introspective mood, gave a simple catch to cover, and the arrears had still not been cleared when May was caught behind off the enthusiastic McKenzie. Illingworth survived for 20 minutes without scoring, then Barrington and Murray dug in, taking England to 178 for 6 – a slender lead of 44.

Barrington continued his resistance on the fourth morning, taking his score to 66 in 200 minutes (11 fours) before he padded up to Davidson and was lbw. McKenzie wrapped up the innings with three wickets in 12 balls, ending with impressive debut figures of 5 for 37.

Australia's target was a mere 60, but Statham and Trueman made the most of the variable pitch, taking two wickets apiece as Australia slumped to 19 for 4. Burge, misjudging a hook, gave a difficult chance to square leg off the last ball before lunch: had the fielder, the usually reliable Lock, been able to hang on to the ball the score would have been 33 for 5. Instead, Australia notched up another two runs, and although Simpson fell just before the end, some meaty blows from Burge settled the issue, two consecutive fours off Statham ending the match at 2.50 on the fourth afternoon.

Australia's victory brought to an end England's five-year unbeaten home run, their last defeat having come, again at Australia's hands, in the 1956 Lord's Test.

ENGLAND v AUSTRALIA
June 22, 23, 24, 26, 1961

ENGLAND

G. Pullar	b Davidson	11	c Grout b Misson		42
R. Subba Row	lbw b Mackay	48	c Grout b Davidson		8
E.R. Dexter	c McKenzie b Misson	27	b McKenzie		17
* M.C. Cowdrey	c Grout b McKenzie	16	c Mackay b Misson		7
P.B.H. May	c Grout b Davidson	17	c Grout b McKenzie		22
K.F. Barrington	c Mackay b Davidson	4	lbw b Davidson		66
R. Illingworth	b Misson	13	c Harvey b Simpson		0
† J.T. Murray	lbw b Mackay	18	c Grout b McKenzie		25
G.A.R. Lock	c Grout b Davidson	5	b McKenzie		1
F.S. Trueman	b Davidson	25	c Grout b McKenzie		0
J.B. Statham	not out	11	not out		2
Extras	(lb9, w2)	11	(b1, lb10, w1)		12
	(78.3 overs)	206	(97 overs)		202

Fall: 26,87,87,111,115,127,156,164,167. 33,63,67,80,127,144,191,199,199.

Bowling: Davidson 24.3-6-42-5, McKenzie 26-7-81-1, Misson 16-4-48-2, Mackay 12-3-24-2.

Second innings: Davidson 24-8-50-2, McKenzie 29-13-37-5, Misson 17-2-66-2, Mackay 8-6-5-0, Simpson 19-10-32-1.

AUSTRALIA

W.M. Lawry	c Murray b Dexter	130	c Murray b Statham	1
C.C. McDonald	b Statham	4	c Illingworth b Trueman	14
R.B. Simpson	c Illingworth b Trueman	0	(6) c Illingworth b Statham	15
* R.N. Harvey	c Barrington b Trueman	27	(3) c Murray b Trueman	4
N.C. O'Neill	b Dexter	1	(4) b Statham	0
P.J.P. Burge	c Murray b Statham	46	(5) not out	37
A.K. Davidson	lbw b Trueman	6	not out	0
K.D. Mackay	c Barrington b Illingworth	54		
† A.T.W. Grout	lbw b Dexter	0		
G.D. McKenzie	b Trueman	34		
F.M. Misson	not out	25		
Extras	(b1, lb12)	13		0
	(139.3 overs)	340	(5 wkts) (20.5 overs)	71

Fall: 5,6,81,88,183,194,238,238,291. 15,15,19,19,58.

Bowling: Statham 44-10-89-2, Trueman 34-3-118-4, Dexter 24-7-56-3, Lock 26-13-48-0, Illingworth 11.3-5-16-1.

Second innings: Statham 10.5-3-31-3, Trueman 10-0-40-2.

Toss: England   Umpires: C.S. Elliott and W.E. Phillipson
Close of play: (1) A. 42 for 2 (Lawry 32, Harvey 6)
(2) A. 286 for 8 (Mackay 32, McKenzie 29)
(3) E. 178 for 6 (Barrington 59, Murray 14)

AUSTRALIA WON BY 5 WICKETS

England squared the series with a three-day victory at Headingley, where Trueman took 11 wickets. Australia, though, retained the Ashes (won in 1958-59) with a stunning win at Old Trafford, where the fit-again Benaud, as a last resort, bowled round the wicket into the rough and took 6 for 70 after England seemed to be cruising to victory. The final Test, at The Oval, was drawn.

1962

Pakistan, making only their second Test tour of England, were the visitors in 1962, but their trip was a disappointing one, only rain at Trent Bridge preventing a probable England clean sweep.

Pakistan's captain, the former Oxford Blue Javed Burki, was perhaps too young, at 24, to take charge of a Test side, and he was beset by problems. His best batsman, Hanif Mohammad, was troubled by a knee injury throughout the tour, and Fazal Mahmood, a late reinforcement to a touring party of already epic proportions (21 players appeared in first-class matches on the tour), was a shadow of his former self. The batting star was Mushtaq Mohammad, reputedly only 18, who topped the tour averages.

England, captained now by Ted Dexter, won the first Test by an innings, running up 544 for 5 at Edgbaston, where deposed captain Cowdrey and Parfitt both made centuries.

On an overcast day at Lord's, Burki rather unwisely elected to bat on a green pitch, and saw his side skittled for 100, Trueman taking 6 for 31, including his 200th wicket in Tests when he disposed of the opposing captain. Coldwell, making his debut, bowled Imtiaz with his fifth ball, and Pakistan were in disarray at 76 for 6 at lunch, having exhibited some distaste for the swinging, lifting ball. The innings ended 45 minutes after lunch, a last-wicket stand of 22 at least ensuring that three figures were reached. Cowdrey took three good catches at second slip.

More accustomed to such conditions, England soon took the lead. Cowdrey scored 41 of the first 59 before he fell to the lively Farooq, whereupon the debutant Stewart and Dexter (destined to become England's management team in 1989) put on a further 78. Dexter hit 10 fours in his fine 65, but he and Barrington fell to successive balls from Farooq shortly before the close, which found England 176 for 4.

Graveney, with a vintage innings of 153, dominated the second day's play as England worked themselves into an impregnable position. Batting for a shade over four hours before being the last to go, Graveney hit 22 fours in an innings marked by several superb cover-drives. Wickets fell regularly at the other end, and the biggest stand of the day was 76 for the ninth wicket between Graveney and Trueman.

Faced with a deficit of 270, Pakistan made a useful start but then lost both openers at 36. Saeed and Mushtaq also departed before stumps, at which point Pakistan, at 103 for 4, were still 167 adrift.

Nightwatchman Nasim-ul-Ghani, who had come in 30 minutes before the close the previous day, displayed a hidden talent on the third morning, taking the lead role in a partnership which eventually reached 197 and ensured that England would have to bat again. The left-hander, who had never previously reached three figures in first-class cricket, hit 15 fours and a six in his brave 101, and the partnership was not broken until after lunch, when Coldwell had Nasim caught by Graveney.

Burki also reached a plucky century, his third in five Tests against England, before he too fell to Coldwell, having hit 15 fours in his 3¾-hour innings.

The resistance eventually ended at 355, Coldwell finishing with 6 for 85,

Tom Graveney is bowled by Pakistan's Antao D'Souza in 1962 – but not before the graceful Worcestershire batsman had reached 153

making nine in his first Test. Left-arm spinner Lock had come in for some heavy punishment, conceding 78 runs in 14 overs, giving rise to some rather cynical speculation that Dexter had kept Lock on to avoid the possibility of becoming involved in one of the knockabout exhibition matches which the crowd enjoyed but the players disliked.

Needing 86 to win, England started circumspectly, but when Cowdrey was out for 20 Stewart and Dexter knocked off the remaining 50 runs in less than half an hour, Dexter helping himself to four boundaries in one D'Souza over. The home side went 2-0 up in the series, the victory having been achieved with more than two days to spare.

ENGLAND v PAKISTAN
June 21, 22, 23, 1962

PAKISTAN

Hanif Mohammad	c Cowdrey b Trueman	13	lbw b Coldwell		24
† Imtiaz Ahmed	b Coldwell	1	(7) c Trueman b Coldwell		33
Saeed Ahmed	b Dexter	10	b Coldwell		20
* Javed Burki	c Dexter b Trueman	5	(5) lbw b Coldwell		101
Mushtaq Mohammad	c Cowdrey b Trueman	7	(4) c Millman b Trueman		18
Alimuddin	b Coldwell	9	(2) c Graveney b Allen		10
Wallis Mathias	b Trueman	15	(8) c Graveney b Trueman		1
Nasim-ul-Ghani	c Millman b Trueman	17	(6) c Graveney b Coldwell		101
Mahmood Hussain	c Cowdrey b Coldwell	1	b Coldwell		20
Antao D'Souza	not out	6	not out		12
Mohammad Farooq	c Stewart b Trueman	13	b Trueman		1
Extras	(b1, lb2)	3	(b6, lb4, w4)		14
	(43.4 overs)	100	(119.3 overs)		355

Fall: 2,23,25,31,36,51,77,78,78. 36,36,57,77,274,299,300,333,354.

Bowling: Trueman 17.4-6-31-6, Coldwell 14-2-25-3, Dexter 12-3-41-1.
Second innings: Trueman 33.3-6-85-3, Coldwell 41-13-85-6, Dexter 15-4-44-0, Allen 15-6-41-1, Lock 14-1-78-0, Barrington 1-0-8-0.

ENGLAND

M.J. Stewart	c Imtiaz b D'Souza	39	not out		34
M.C. Cowdrey	c D'Souza b Farooq	41	c Imtiaz b D'Souza		20
* E.R. Dexter	c Imtiaz b Farooq	65	not out		32
T.W. Graveney	b D'Souza	153			
K.F. Barrington	c Imtiaz b Farooq	0			
D.A. Allen	lbw b Farooq	2			
P.H. Parfitt	b Mahmood	16			
† G. Millman	c Hanif b Mahmood	7			
G.A.R. Lock	c Mathias b Saeed	7			
F.S. Trueman	lbw b Saeed	29			
L.J. Coldwell	not out	0			
Extras	(b1, lb5, nb5)	11			0
	(101.4 overs)	370	(1 wkt) (17 overs)		86

Fall: 59,137,168,168,184,221,247,290,366. 36.

Bowling: Mahmood 40-9-106-2, Farooq 19-4-70-4, D'Souza 35.4-3-147-2, Nasim 2-0-15-0, Saeed 5-1-21-2.
Second innings: Farooq 7-1-37-0, D'Souza 7-0-29-1, Saeed 2-0-12-0, Mushtaq 1-0-8-0.

Toss: Pakistan Umpires: J.S. Buller and N. Oldfield
Close of play: (1) E. 176 for 4 (Graveney 23, Allen 0)
  (2) P. 103 for 4 (Burki 15, Nasim 13)

ENGLAND WON BY 9 WICKETS

England enjoyed another three-day win at Headingley, Parfitt scoring 119, and another century from Parfitt and 114 from Graveney nearly brought another victory at Trent Bridge, where Mushtaq became the youngest Test centurymaker as Pakistan hung on for a draw in a rain-affected match. Tall scoring from Cowdrey (182) and Dexter (172) set up another convincing win at The Oval, where David Larter, making his Test debut, took nine wickets.

1963

Probably the best-remembered and most famous of all the 84 Lord's Tests was the epic 1963 match between England and West Indies. Indeed, it is one of the few Tests to have inspired a book of its own (*West Indies at Lord's*, by Alan Ross). West Indies, under their first regular black captain, Frank Worrell, went into the match one-up, after a 10-wicket victory at Old Trafford, where Hunte's 182 was the backbone of a winning total of 501 for 6.

At Lord's, though, the final act was without doubt the most dramatic in the long history of Tests there. England began the final day needing 118 more to win with seven wickets in hand – the overall target was 234 – but the equation was complicated by rain, which delayed the start until 2.20, and also by the fact that one of England's premier batsmen, Cowdrey, had had his left arm broken by Hall in murky light the previous day.

Hall, who had also been a key figure at the death in the famous Australia-West Indies tied Test in 1960-61, bowled throughout the shortened final day, and his fearsome new-ball partner Griffith did likewise, apart from five overs from offspinner Gibbs. With no minimum overs requirement in the last hour, this further reduced England's victory chances.

England made slow progress when play began, Barrington remaining on his overnight 55 for 40 minutes, and eventually falling for 60 after just 14 had been added in the first 13 overs. Close and Parks inched the score to 158 before Parks fell to Griffith, then Titmus joined the Yorkshire captain in adding a further 45. At 203, though, disaster struck: Hall removed Titmus and Trueman with successive deliveries.

This double calamity persuaded Close to abandon his previous tactics, which had involved taking the ball on the body to avoid giving a close catch. Suddenly he walked down the pitch to Hall, who pulled up in surprise at this audacity, hurting his back in the process. Close frequently repeated these advances, coupling them with violent swishes at the ball. He collected a boundary or two, but his 230-minute innings ended at 219 when he tickled a catch to Murray. Close's brave 70 – like Dexter's similar score earlier in the match – is one of the best-remembered of all Lord's Test innings.

Close's departure brought in Shackleton, playing his only Lord's Test (and his first anywhere for nearly 12 years), to join Allen. With 19 minutes remaining, 15 were needed, and the pair nudged a few runs here and there until Hall began the final over with eight required. Singles came off the second and third balls, then non-striker Allen tried to steal a bye. Worrell collected Murray's shy at the stumps and engaged Shackleton – who had hesitated fatally before setting off – in a stately race to the bowler's stumps (both men were 38). Unencumbered by pads and bat, Worrell won, forcing Cowdrey to come out for two balls. Fortunately for England, the batsmen had crossed, leaving Allen to face Hall: although only six runs were needed, Allen blocked the last two balls to earn the draw. Cowdrey, who would have faced up one-handed from a left-hander's stance with his injured arm out of sight behind his back, was not required to put his new technique to the test.

So ended the most dramatic of all Lord's Tests. If rain had not intervened, and

Ted Dexter on the attack – as he was for most of his best-remembered innings, a savage 70 against West Indies in 1963

if West Indies had needed to bowl 20 overs in the final hour, England probably would have won with some ease . . . but then the match would not be so fondly remembered today, and, in any case, 'if' is a word beloved of cricket and cricketers.

From the very beginning this match was unusual. After a brief rain delay, Hunte gave the game a sensational start by taking fours from Trueman's first three balls. The first over yielded 13 runs, the next 31 overs only 34 as Trueman, who was to finish with 6 for 100, and the recalled Shackleton applied the brakes. 'Shack' had execrable luck, having McMorris put down by Stewart and Hunte dropped twice by the normally-reliable pair of Stewart and Cowdrey. Close also dropped Hunte off Trueman before gratefully hanging on to a chance when the opener had made 44. Sobers made a useful 42, and Kanhai played well before Trueman removed him for 73: the new ball also accounted for Worrell, who failed to score, and Butcher.

West Indies advanced to 297 for 7 on the second morning, Solomon completing a patient half-century before Shackleton's luck finally turned: he took three wickets in four balls to bring the innings to an abrupt halt at 301.

England's reply began badly, Edrich failing to score and Stewart falling for 2, but Dexter came in to play probably the finest (and certainly best-remembered) innings of his career. Dexter later wrote, 'I was not going to be the Aunt Sally for Hall and Griffith,' and accordingly he took the pair on in a vintage display of power hitting: in all he galloped to 70 from only 73 balls, hitting 10 fours, with two particularly powerful boundaries in one over screaming back past the bemused Griffith. He saw off the pacemen, only to fall in Sobers's second over.

Barrington rarely looked comfortable, but nonetheless survived for 190 minutes for 60: he added 55 in an hour with Parks. Although Titmus completed a watchful half-century on the third morning, England's eventual total of 297 – four

Colin Cowdrey, broken arm and all, surveys the scene from the pavilion as the 1963 Lord's Test reaches its exciting climax. Cowdrey, who had practised batting one-handed with his injured arm behind his back, eventually had to go out to the crease, but was not called upon to face a ball

behind – was a disappointment after Dexter's onslaught. Griffith finished with 5 for 91.

Hunte gave West Indies' second innings another adventurous start, hoisting a six in Trueman's second over and breaking his bat in the process; he then gave a slip catch to Cowdrey, who earlier had dropped him. Cowdrey also caught McMorris and, a little later, Kanhai, but England were held at bay by a splendid innings from Butcher, who rode his luck to score 133, hitting two sixes off Allen and 17 fours in nearly 4½ hours at the crease. Apart from Kanhai, only Worrell, who played the minor role in a stand of 110 with Butcher, reached double figures. The innings folded when five wickets fell for 15 in 25 minutes on the fourth morning, Trueman finishing with 11 wickets in the match.

Although England's victory target of 234 seemed modest enough, it would nevertheless have been the biggest fourth-innings score to win a Lord's Test at the time, and it seemed very distant when Hall, perhaps finding the 'ridge', shot out both openers. Dexter, who had injured a knee during his memorable 70 (he had not fielded during the tourists' second innings), could not repeat the medicine, this time falling to a looping offbreak from Gibbs for 2. England were reeling at 31 for 3, but Cowdrey and Barrington steadied the ship before, at 72, an ominous crack told those watching that Cowdrey's arm had been broken. Soon afterwards, bad light drove the players from the pitch (there was no sightscreen at the pavilion end at the time – it was installed the following year after the events of this match). After two brief resumptions England ended the day at 116 for 3, 118 short of victory. The stage was set for the thrilling climax.

ENGLAND v WEST INDIES
June 20, 21, 22, 24, 25, 1963

WEST INDIES

C.C. Hunte	c Close b Trueman	44	c Cowdrey b Shackleton	7
E.D.A.S. McMorris	lbw b Trueman	16	c Cowdrey b Trueman	8
G.S. Sobers	c Cowdrey b Allen	42	(5) c Parks b Trueman	8
R.B. Kanhai	c Edrich b Trueman	73	(3) c Cowdrey b Shackleton	21
B.F. Butcher	c Barrington b Trueman	14	(4) lbw b Shackleton	133
J.S. Solomon	lbw b Shackleton	56	c Stewart b Allen	5
* F.M.M. Worrell	b Trueman	0	c Stewart b Trueman	33
† D.L. Murray	c Cowdrey b Trueman	20	c Parks b Trueman	2
W.W. Hall	not out	25	c Parks b Trueman	2
C.C. Griffith	c Cowdrey b Shackleton	0	b Shackleton	1
L.R. Gibbs	c Stewart b Shackleton	0	not out	1
Extras	(b10, lb1)	11	(b5, lb2, nb1)	8
	(133.2 overs)	301	(98 overs)	229

Fall: 51,64,127,145,219,219,263,297,297.   15,15,64,84,104,214,224,226,228.

Bowling: Trueman 44-16-100-6, Shackleton 50.2-22-93-3, Dexter 20-6-41-0, Close 9-3-21-0, Allen 10-3-35-1.

Second innings: Trueman 26-9-52-5, Shackleton 34-14-72-4, Titmus 17-3-47-0, Allen 21-7-50-1.

ENGLAND

M.J. Stewart	c Kanhai b Griffith	2	c Solomon b Hall	17
J.H. Edrich	c Murray b Griffith	0	c Murray b Hall	8
* E.R. Dexter	lbw b Sobers	70	b Gibbs	2
K.F. Barrington	c Sobers b Worrell	80	c Murray b Griffith	60
M.C. Cowdrey	b Gibbs	4	not out	19
D.B. Close	c Murray b Griffith	9	c Murray b Griffith	70
† J.M. Parks	b Worrell	35	lbw b Griffith	17
F.J. Titmus	not out	52	c McMorris b Hall	11
F.S. Trueman	b Hall	10	c Murray b Hall	0
D.A. Allen	lbw b Griffith	2	not out	4
D. Shackleton	b Griffith	8	run out	4
Extras	(b8, lb8, nb9)	25	(b5, lb8, nb3)	16
	(102 overs)	297	(9 wkts) (91 overs)	228

Fall: 2,20,102,115,151,206,235,271,274.   15,27,31,130,158,203,203,219,228.

Bowling: Hall 18-2-65-1, Griffith 26-6-91-5, Sobers 18-4-45-1, Gibbs 27-9-59-1, Worrell 13-6-12-2.

Second innings: Hall 40-9-93-4, Griffith 30-7-59-3, Gibbs 17-7-56-1, Sobers 4-1-4-0.

Toss: West Indies   Umpires: J.S. Buller and W.E. Phillipson
Close of play: (1) W.I. 245 for 6 (Solomon 34, Murray 12)
                  (2) E. 244 for 7 (Titmus 23, Trueman 5)
                  (3) W.I. 214 for 5 (Butcher 129, Worrell 33)
                  (4) E. 116 for 3 (Barrington 55, Close 7)
                  Cowdrey retired hurt at 72 for 3, resumed at 228 for 9

MATCH DRAWN

England squared the series with a 217-run victory at Edgbaston, where Trueman took 12 for 119. West Indies, though, took the series (and the new Wisden Trophy) 3-1, with wins in the final two Tests. Sobers, with 102, starred with the bat at Headingley, while Hunte (80 and 108 not out) saw his side home at The Oval. Griffith took nine wickets in both matches, ending the series with 32 wickets: Trueman bettered that with 34.

1964

The weather was unkind to the Lord's Test yet again in 1964, over half the scheduled playing time being lost to rain, with the first two days of the match being washed out. A result was therefore never likely, even though the visitors had been written off before the tour as the 'worst team ever to leave Australia'. This uncharitable assessment was based largely on the fact that three of Australia's greatest players – Benaud, Davidson and Harvey – had retired since the 1962-63 series in Australia, when the home side had retained the Ashes. The captaincy had passed to Bob Simpson, a talented allrounder whose 26 Tests before this tour had, surprisingly, not produced a century.

Rain had already spoiled the drawn first Test, at Trent Bridge, and on arrival at Lord's for the second Test the teams were greeted by another torrential downpour which soon put paid to any hope of play on the first day. The rain held off on the Friday, but the Lord's drains proved unequal to the task of disposing of the previous day's precipitation. After a frustrating day for all concerned, the umpires announced after tea that no play would be possible.

There was better news on the third day, when play started on time, Dexter winning the toss and putting Australia in. England shuffled their side, including an extra batsman in Sharpe, who had originally been named as 12th man, in place of fast bowler Jack Flavell, who thus rather unluckily missed what would have been his only Lord's Test appearance.

Trueman started with a wild legside delivery that went for four wides, but after two unimpressive overs he settled down and immediately bowled Lawry, the Lord's centurymaker of 1961. The bowlers all obtained some help from the pitch, and batting was difficult all day. Redpath and O'Neill added 38 before Dexter removed O'Neill and Burge, after which Australia moved carefully to 79 for 3 at lunch.

After the interval three quick wickets went down, Parfitt taking two excellent diving catches to remove the stubborn Redpath for 30 and Simpson for a duck. Allrounder Veivers now led a recovery of sorts, hitting eight fours in his 54, and sharing an important stand of 44 with McKenzie, whose defensive innings of 10 included one remarkable stroke, when he swung Coldwell for six into St John's Wood Road, where the ball broke the spectacles of newspaper-seller Richard Horton.

Trueman, who went on to take 5 for 48, eventually bowled McKenzie, but Grout helped Veivers add a further 31 before offering Dexter a catch which the England captain eventually clung to despite first almost slipping over, then nearly colliding with Edrich. This gave the debutant Gifford his first Test wicket, and he picked up another shortly afterwards to end Veivers' 2½-hour resistance.

A shower briefly delayed England's reply to Australia's 176, and when play did restart the second ball of the innings accounted for Dexter, who had, unwisely in the opinion of some, elected to open in the absence of the injured Boycott. Edrich and Cowdrey ensured that there were no further alarms that night, but Cowdrey fell to Hawke early on the fourth morning.

A fine innings from Edrich, playing his first Test against Australia, was the feature of Day 4. Losing partners regularly at the other end (Sharpe's 35 was the

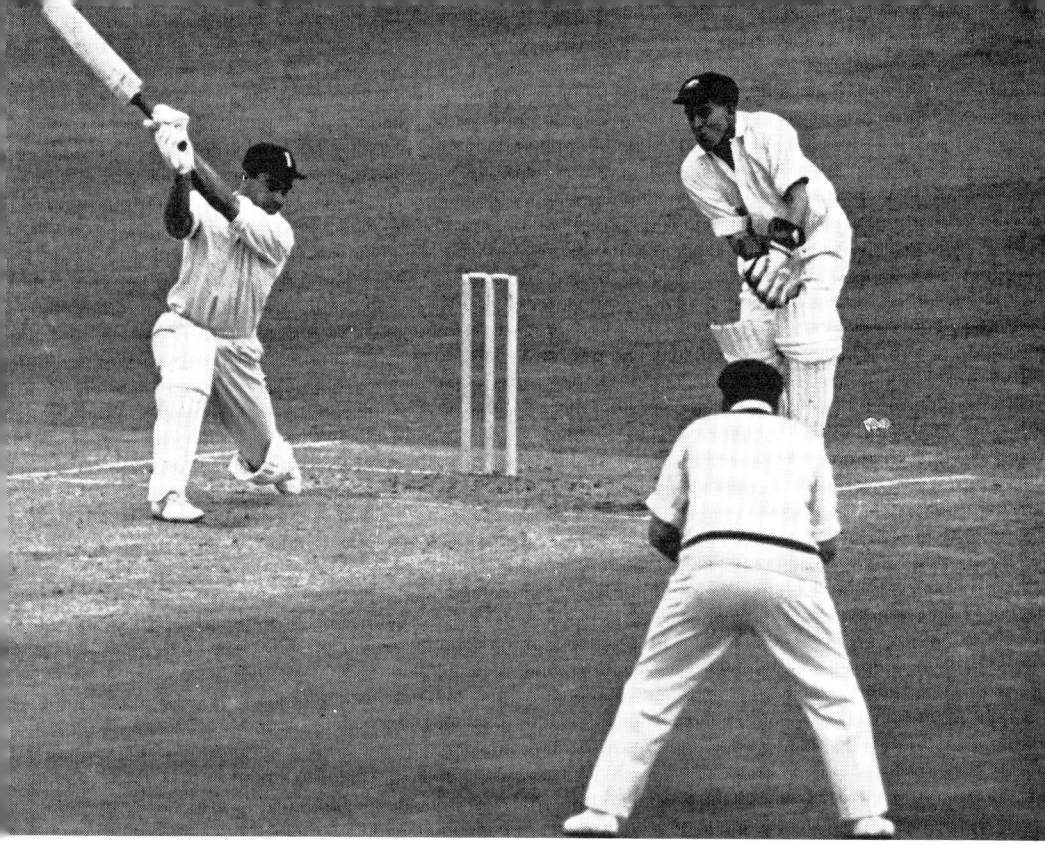

John Edrich flashes at a wide one in 1964, but does not get a touch as the ball goes through to Wally Grout. An unconcerned Edrich went on to 120, the first of his three Test centuries at HQ

next-best effort), the Surrey left-hander grafted his way to 120, reaching three figures soon after the Queen arrived to watch some of the afternoon's play. Although lucky to escape early on when he spooned a ball just out of reach of backward point, Edrich gave no other chance until Redpath at slip dropped him off Corling at 117; three runs later, the same fielder made amends, but only after juggling the chance. Edrich batted for 379 minutes in all, hitting two sixes off Simpson as well as nine fours.

A good running catch from Simpson disposed of Parks, then Corling took the last three wickets to contain England's lead to 70. Australia had 66 minutes to bat before the close, which they negotiated for the loss of Lawry, who gave a bat-pad catch off the only ball to misbehave.

Early on the final morning O'Neill mishooked Trueman straight to backward short leg, and this breakthrough and an unaccepted chance shortly afterwards when Burge snicked the Yorkshireman between wicketkeeper and first slip persuaded Dexter to rely on his faster bowlers for nearly two hours. When the spinners belatedly appeared the scoring rate dropped markedly, but Burge, with a hard-hitting half-century including a big six over long-on off Coldwell, had already taken Australia into the black. The spinners ended Redpath's long vigil: he batted for 3¼ hours for his 36, and was scoreless for the last 53 minutes of his innings. Burge, too, departed before rain interrupted at 2.30 with Australia 98 runs on with six wickets standing . . . no further play was possible, bringing a watery end to what had promised to be an exciting match.

ENGLAND v AUSTRALIA
June 18 (no play), 19 (no play), 20, 22, 23, 1964

AUSTRALIA

W.M. Lawry	b Trueman	4	c Dexter b Gifford		20
I.R. Redpath	c Parfitt b Coldwell	30	lbw b Titmus		36
N.C. O'Neill	c Titmus b Dexter	26	c Parfitt b Trueman		22
P.J.P. Burge	lbw b Dexter	1	c Parfitt b Titmus		59
B.C. Booth	lbw b Trueman	14	not out		2
* R.B. Simpson	c Parfitt b Trueman	0	not out		15
T.R. Veivers	b Gifford	54			
G.D. McKenzie	b Trueman	10			
† A.T.W. Grout	c Dexter b Gifford	14			
N.J.N. Hawke	not out	5			
G.E. Corling	b Trueman	0			
Extras	(b8, lb5, nb5)	18	(b8, lb4, nb2)		14
	(84 overs)	176	(4 wkts) (74 overs)		168

Fall: 8,46,58,84,84,88,132,163,167. 35,76,143,148.

Bowling: Trueman 25-8-48-5, Coldwell 23-7-51-1, Gifford 12-6-14-2, Dexter 7-1-16-2, Titmus 17-6-29-0.

Second innings: Trueman 18-6-52-1, Coldwell 19-4-59-0, Dexter 3-0-5-0, Gifford 17-9-17-1, Titmus 17-7-21-2.

ENGLAND

* E.R. Dexter	b McKenzie	2	Bowling:
J.H. Edrich	c Redpath b McKenzie	120	McKenzie 26-8-69-3,
M.C. Cowdrey	c Burge b Hawke	10	Corling 27.3-9-60-4,
K.F. Barrington	lbw b McKenzie	5	Hawke 16-4-41-3,
P.H. Parfitt	lbw b Corling	20	Veivers 9-4-17-0,
P.J. Sharpe	lbw b Hawke	35	Simpson 21-8-51-0.
† J.M. Parks	c Simpson b Hawke	12	
F.J. Titmus	b Corling	15	
F.S. Trueman	b Corling	8	
N. Gifford	c Hawke b Corling	5	
L.J. Coldwell	not out	6	
Extras	(lb7, nb1)	8	
	(99.3 overs)	246	

Fall: 2,33,42,83,138,170,227,229,235.

Toss: England Umpires: J.S. Buller and J.F. Crapp
Close of play: (3) E. 26 for 1 (Edrich 15, Cowdrey 9)
(4) A. 49 for 1 (Redpath 15, O'Neill 9)

MATCH DRAWN

Australia threw off their 'worst-ever' tag with a convincing win in the third Test at Headingley, Burge's 160 setting up the seven-wicket victory. At Old Trafford, Simpson stretched his maiden Test century to 311 out of his side's 656 for 8: England replied in kind with 611, Barrington making 256 and Dexter 174. This match was drawn, as was the rain-affected final Test at The Oval, which was notable for Trueman's becoming the first bowler to reach 300 wickets in Tests. Australia therefore retained the Ashes.

1965i

After the enterprising, exciting cricket played by Frank Worrell's 1963 tourists, many people bemoaned the fact that West Indies were not due to make another visit to England until 1971. A letter to the *Daily Telegraph*, from a Mr T.J.R. Dashwood, suggested that one solution might be to invite two teams over per summer for three Tests apiece. The authorities acted on his idea with unusual speed, to such effect that 1965 saw the first 'twin-tour' summer, featuring New Zealand and South Africa.

Much persuasion was needed to convince some countries that they were not being downgraded by having a three-Test tour, but the lure of more frequent visits won the day (New Zealand, for example, had made only two postwar Test tours of England, in 1949 and 1958: after 1965, they were to return in 1969, 1973, 1978, 1983 and 1986).

For the financial success of the twin tours it was important that both touring teams should play a Test match at Lord's, so from 1965 the ground has frequently staged two Tests in a summer, a state of affairs previously unknown except during the 1912 Triangular Tournament (when, in fact, *three* Tests were played at Lord's).

One of the system's problems proved to be that the first of the summer's tourists often had to contend with miserable May weather, giving them little chance to prepare properly for a brief Test series, and the 1965 New Zealanders were the first sufferers from the weather. They were largely an inexperienced team, and their seasoned captain John Reid was struggling with a cartilage injury which restricted his bowling. Captained for the first time at home by Mike Smith, England won the first Test, at Edgbaston, where Bert Sutcliffe – like Reid a veteran of the '49 and '58 tours – was hit on the head by Trueman and played little part in the rest of the tour. Another 'casualty' at Birmingham was Barrington, who scored his 137 too slowly (437 minutes) for the selectors' liking and was dropped for the Lord's Test as a disciplinary measure.

At Lord's England gave a first cap to the promising Sussex fast bowler John Snow, but it was Rumsey who reduced New Zealand, who won the toss, to 28 for 4 after little more than an hour's batting. The Somerset left-armer trapped Congdon lbw with the second ball of the match to start a spell which brought him 4 for 7 in 46 balls. Reid hit about him for 21 before becoming Snow's first Test wicket, but when Dick was bowled in the last over before lunch New Zealand were floundering at 62 for 6.

The tourists were revived by a sensible seventh-wicket stand of 92 between Pollard and Taylor, both of whom passed 50. Titmus eventually removed Pollard, then Trueman, in what proved to be his last Test, snapped up the last two wickets to end the innings at 175.

Motz had both openers caught behind in his initial spell, but Dexter, whose unbeaten 30 included six fours, led England to 72 for 2 by the close. Dexter continued to bat attractively on the second morning, hitting 12 fours in his 62 and sharing a partnership of 93 with Cowdrey, who made light of a back strain to compile 119 in a little under five hours at the crease. He hit 13 fours in his innings, which was marked by several silky drives and cuts. Cowdrey and Smith

Freddie Trueman played his last Test at Lord's in 1965. At Lord's alone he took 63 of his 307 Test wickets: among others only Ian Botham (68 to date) has reached the 50-wicket mark at Lord's

shared a stand of 105 in even time before both fell to catches by the substitute Terry Jarvis, who was fielding for the temporarily indisposed Motz, but from 271 for 4 England declined to 307 all out, the last six wickets going down for 36 in the face of a fiery display from left-armer Collinge, who took 4 for 17 with the new ball.

Starting afresh on the third morning, New Zealand found the pitch – by now easy-paced and getting slower – to their liking as they wiped off the deficit of 132 for the loss of Congdon. Dowling and Sinclair shared a stand of 90 before the latter miscued a sweep against legspinner Barber and gave an easy catch to wicketkeeper Parks. Dowling fell to Parfitt's occasional offspin for 66, and although Reid and Morgan took the score past 200, three late wickets left the visitors uncomfortably placed at 261 for 7 at stumps, a lead of 129.

After rain had prevented any play until 2.15 on the fourth day, selective hitting from Collinge and another diligent half-century from the Lancashire-born Pollard took New Zealand past 300. Last pair Pollard and Cameron prolonged matters with a stand of 44 in 75 minutes, before Pollard was run out for 55. Cameron's 9 not out left him with a tour aggregate of 80 for once out – he raised this to 90, and was threatening Bill Johnston's freak 1953 average of 103, before an inopportune duck in his last innings of the tour halved his average to a less Bradmanesque 45.

England reduced their target of 216 by 64 before the close, Barber falling to Motz just before stumps. Rain delayed a start on the final day until 2.45, by which time England needed a further 152 in just under three hours. Although nightwatchman Titmus was out almost immediately, Boycott and Dexter – who hit 10 fours in his last Lord's Test innings – put on 126 in 2¼ hours. Although Boycott became the third victim of the persistent Motz with 20 still needed, Dexter and Cowdrey saw England home with just 15 minutes to spare.

ENGLAND v NEW ZEALAND
June 17, 18, 19, 21, 22, 1965

NEW ZEALAND

B.E. Congdon	lbw b Rumsey	0	lbw b Titmus	26
G.T. Dowling	lbw b Rumsey	12	b Parfitt	66
B.W. Sinclair	b Rumsey	1	c Parks b Barber	72
* J.R. Reid	c Parks b Snow	21	b Titmus	22
R.W. Morgan	c Parfitt b Rumsey	0	lbw b Rumsey	35
V. Pollard	c and b Titmus	55	run out	55
† A.E. Dick	b Snow	7	c Parks b Snow	3
B.R. Taylor	b Trueman	51	c Smith b Snow	0
R.C. Motz	c Parks b Titmus	11	(10) c Snow b Barber	8
R.O. Collinge	b Trueman	7	(9) c Parks b Barber	21
F.J. Cameron	not out	3	not out	9
Extras	(b3, lb2, nb2)	7	(b8, lb12, nb10)	30
	(74.5 overs)	175	(149 overs)	347

Fall: 0,4,24,28,49,62,154,160,171.   59,149,196,206,253,258,259,293,303.

Bowling: Rumsey 13-4-25-4, Trueman 19.5-8-40-2, Dexter 8-2-27-0, Snow 11-2-27-2, Titmus 15-7-25-2, Barber 8-2-24-0.

Second innings: Rumsey 26-10-42-1, Trueman 26-4-69-0, Snow 24-4-53-2, Titmus 39-12-71-2, Parfitt 6-2-25-1, Barber 28-10-57-3.

ENGLAND

G. Boycott	c Dick b Motz	14	lbw b Motz	76
R.W. Barber	c Dick b Motz	13	b Motz	34
E.R. Dexter	c Dick b Taylor	62	(4) not out	80
M.C. Cowdrey	c sub (T.W. Jarvis) b Collinge	119	(5) not out	4
P.H. Parfitt	c Dick b Cameron	11		
* M.J.K. Smith	c sub (T.W. Jarvis) b Taylor	44		
† J.M. Parks	b Collinge	2		
F.J. Titmus	run out	13	(3) c Dick b Motz	1
F.S. Trueman	b Collinge	3		
F.E. Rumsey	b Collinge	3		
J.A. Snow	not out	2		
Extras	(b1, lb7, w1, nb12)	21	(b9, lb5, nb9)	23
	(100.2 overs)	307	(3 wkts) (60.5 overs)	218

Fall: 18,38,131,166,271,285,292,300,302.   64,70,196.

Bowling: Collinge 28.2-4-85-4, Motz 20-1-62-2, Taylor 25-4-66-2, Cameron 19-6-40-1, Morgan 8-1-33-0.

Second innings: Collinge 15-1-43-0, Motz 19-5-45-3, Taylor 10-0-53-0, Cameron 13-0-39-0, Morgan 3-0-11-0, Reid 0.5-0-4-0.

Toss: New Zealand   Umpires: J.S. Buller and W.E. Phillipson
Close of play: (1) E. 72 for 2 (Dexter 30, Cowdrey 10)
                 (2) E. 307 all out
                 (3) N.Z. 261 for 7 (Pollard 14, Collinge 0)
                 (4) E. 64 for 1 (Boycott 28, Titmus 0)

ENGLAND WON BY 7 WICKETS

England completed a 3-0 clean sweep with an innings victory at Headingley, where Edrich (310 not out) and the restored Barrington (163) shared a stand of 369 in England's imposing total of 546 for 4. New Zealand could muster only 193 and 166 in reply.

1965ii

The second visitors in the first twin-tour were South Africa, making what turned out to be their last official visit to this country. England had pulled off a narrow victory in the previous winter's series between the two sides, but the South Africans, unimpressed by being allocated only three Tests, were a strong combination which, within a few years, had developed into arguably the strongest side in the world. Sadly, politics meant that they were unable to confirm this ranking.

The tourists' line-up was much-changed from the disappointing 1960 side, the only survivor being Atholl McKinnon, who did not appear in the Lord's Test on either visit: the South African team for the 1965 Lord's Test – the first of the three-match series – therefore showed 11 changes from the 1960 side, the first time this had occurred (the 1967 Indians were later to field an entirely different line-up from 1959). Among the 11 players making their first (and last) appearance in a Lord's Test were Barlow, Bacher, Lindsay, skipper van der Merwe and the Pollock brothers.

England had Barrington back in the fold but were without Dexter, who had contrived to run himself over with his own car and had injured his leg. The fast-bowling attack had a strange look about it, lacking either Trueman or Statham for the first time since 1950: Brown of Warwickshire made his Test debut.

Mike Smith lost the first battle of two bespectacled captains when van der Merwe won the toss, but the South African soon saw his side reduced by good fielding from England. Barlow was the first to go, to a fine catch by Barber at forward short leg, then Lance and Lindsay, after a useful partnership of 59, fell in quick succession, Brown's ankle-high caught-and-bowled to send back Lance giving the bowler his first Test wicket. Lindsay then fell victim to a fine diving effort in the gully by Titmus, leaving the visitors 75 for 3. Graeme Pollock and Bland, two gifted strokemakers, put on 80 for the fourth wicket, but a late flurry of wickets saw South Africa end the day at 227 for 8.

Rain spoiled the second day, allowing only 2½ hours' play and none before lunch, but when the innings did restart the tailenders lifted the score to 280. Botten made 33, while Peter Pollock (34) and Bromfield (9 not out) shared a last-gasp stand of 39. England had time to reach 26 without loss before stumps were drawn.

An expectant crowd of around 26,000 watched England progress without alarms to 82 on the third morning, at which point three quick wickets went down. Barber was bowled by offspinner Bromfield for 56, Boycott gave a catch off Botten for 36, and Edrich fell lbw to the pacey Pollock before he had scored. Barrington and Cowdrey steadied the ship with a stand of 56, then Smith combined with the Surrey stalwart in a partnership worth 96 before both fell at the same total, Barrington's three-hour innings, which contained 11 fours and a six, ending when he rashly took on Bland, undoubtedly the best fielder in the world at the time: the resultant direct hit found Barrington some way out of his ground. Sensible batting from Parks and Titmus took England into the lead just before the close.

Bland struck again early on the fourth morning, when Parks ignored the

152

South Africa's Colin Bland was the best fieldsman in the world during the 1960s – a fact that Ken Barrington and Jim Parks found out the hard way in 1965

warning of Barrington's dismissal and chanced a quick run. Although the running Parks was obscuring his view of the wicket, the remarkable Rhodesian took deliberate aim under the batsman's body and shattered the stumps again. Titmus, who scored 59, shepherded the score to 338, a useful lead of 58.

Barlow began the second innings in aggressive style, dominating an opening stand of 55 with Lance, who made only 9. Brown eventually dismissed both, and added a third scalp when he bowled the dangerous Graeme Pollock for 5. England scented victory, but Bland shone again, batting well for 70 and sharing useful stands with Lindsay and Bacher. By stumps, South Africa had moved to 186 for 5.

England were happy to wrap up the South African innings for 248 on the final day, Rumsey taking three of the wickets to fall, including the adhesive van der Merwe for 31. England's victory target was a modest one – 191 in 235 minutes – but the home side never looked likely to force a win in the face of hostile South African bowling and a slow over rate. Barber was caught behind for 12, then Edrich – a triple-centurion in the previous Test – was hit on the side of the head by a decidedly brisk delivery from Peter Pollock and was taken to hospital.

Cowdrey made 37 before he too fell to Pollock, and with Edrich unlikely to be able to return to the crease England were relieved to salvage a draw when stumps were drawn for the last time with the score at 145 for 7. South Africa's final Test at Lord's thus ended with the visitors having won just one of their 10 encounters there against England (in 1935). England won six, with three draws. South Africa also lost their 1912 Lord's Test against Australia.

ENGLAND v SOUTH AFRICA
July 22, 23, 24, 26, 27, 1965

SOUTH AFRICA

E.J. Barlow	c Barber b Rumsey	1	c Parks b Brown	52
H.R. Lance	c and b Brown	28	c Titmus b Brown	9
† D.T. Lindsay	c Titmus b Rumsey	40	c Parks b Larter	22
R.G. Pollock	c Barrington b Titmus	56	b Brown	5
K.C. Bland	b Brown	39	c Edrich b Barber	70
A. Bacher	lbw b Titmus	4	b Titmus	37
* P.L. van der Merwe	c Barrington b Rumsey	17	c Barrington b Rumsey	31
R. Dumbrill	b Barber	3	c Cowdrey b Rumsey	2
J.T. Botten	b Brown	33	b Rumsey	0
P.M. Pollock	st Parks b Barber	34	not out	14
H.D. Bromfield	not out	9	run out	0
Extras	(lb14, nb2)	16	(b4, lb2)	6
	(119.3 overs)	280	(110 overs)	248

Fall: 1,60,75,155,170,170,178,212,241.   55,62,68,120,170,216,230,230,247.

Bowling: Larter 26-10-47-0, Rumsey 30-9-84-3, Brown 24-9-44-3,
Titmus 29-10-59-2, Barber 10.3-3-30-2.

Second innings: Larter 17-2-67-1, Rumsey 21-8-49-3, Brown 21-11-30-3,
Titmus 26-13-36-1, Barber 25-5-60-1.

ENGLAND

G. Boycott	c Barlow b Botten	31	c and b Dumbrill	28
R.W. Barber	b Bromfield	56	c Lindsay b P.M. Pollock	12
J.H. Edrich	lbw b P.M. Pollock	0	retired hurt	7
K.F. Barrington	run out	91	lbw b Dumbrill	18
M.C. Cowdrey	b Dumbrill	29	lbw b P.M. Pollock	37
* M.J.K. Smith	c Lindsay b Botten	26	c Lindsay b Dumbrill	13
† J.M. Parks	run out	32	c van der Merwe b Dumbrill	7
F.J. Titmus	c P.M. Pollock b Bromfield	59	not out	9
D.J. Brown	c Bromfield b Dumbrill	1	c Barlow b R.G. Pollock	5
F.E. Rumsey	b Dumbrill	3	not out	0
J.D.F. Larter	not out	0		
Extras	(b1, lb4, w1, nb4)	10	(lb7, w1, nb1)	9
	(150.2 overs)	338	(7 wkts) (68 overs)	145

Fall: 82,88,88,144,240,240,294,314,338.   23,70,79,113,121,135,140.

Bowling: P.M. Pollock 39-12-91-1, Botten 33-11-65-2, Barlow 19-6-31-0,
Bromfield 25.2-5-71-2, Dumbrill 24-11-31-3, Lance 5-0-18-0,
R.G. Pollock 5-1-21-0.

Second innings: P.M. Pollock 20-6-52-2, Botten 12-6-25-0, Dumbrill 18-8-30-4,
Barlow 9-1-25-0, Bromfield 5-4-4-0, R.G. Pollock 4-4-0-1.

Toss: South Africa   Umpires: J.S. Buller and A.E.G. Rhodes
Close of play: (1) S.A. 227 for 8 (Botten 27, P.M. Pollock 2)
                 (2) E. 26 for 0 (Boycott 11, Barber 15)
                 (3) E. 287 for 6 (Parks 25, Titmus 22)
                 (4) S.A. 186 for 5 (Bacher 27, van der Merwe 1)
                 Edrich retired hurt at 37 for 1

MATCH DRAWN

South Africa won the second Test – and with it the series – at Trent Bridge, Graeme Pollock scoring a memorable 125 on a difficult pitch. Cowdrey replied with 105 for England, but the pace of Peter Pollock (10 for 87) proved too much for England. A potentially exciting climax to the final Test, at The Oval, was nipped in the bud when rain set in with England needing 91 to win in 70 minutes, Bland's 127 being the best innings of the match. For England, the recalled Statham, in his final Test, took seven wickets.

1966

The desired result of the twin-tour experiment came about in 1966, with the exciting West Indies team returning for another full tour only three years after the previous one. Frank Worrell had retired (sadly, he was to die of leukaemia in 1967) and Garfield Sobers had assumed the captaincy of the side whose victory over Australia at home in 1964-65 had earned them the unofficial title of 'world champions'.

West Indies reinforced their position with an innings win in the first Test, at Old Trafford. Hunte and Sobers scored centuries before Gibbs, with five wickets in each innings, spun out England for 167 and 277. Among the England casualties from that match was captain Mike Smith, who was dropped after scores of 5 and 6. He was replaced as captain for the Lord's Test by Cowdrey, while Graveney found himself restored to the Test side on his 39th birthday after three years out of favour. Graveney's Worcestershire team-mate Basil D'Oliveira made his Test debut at Lord's, completing a fairytale rise to fame for the Cape Coloured South African.

Rain, the enemy of countless Lord's Tests, reduced the playing time on the first day to 2¾ hours, in which time West Indies reached 155 for 4 after winning the toss. Moving the ball both ways off a good length, Higgs, who was to be the only England player to appear in all five Tests of the summer, took 3 for 14 in the course of his first nine overs, as West Indies dipped to 53 for 3, but a solid innings from 1963 centurymaker Butcher rescued matters. Butcher had added 66 with Nurse when, on 49, he was caught by the tubby Milburn. The bowler, Knight, then had wretched luck as Sobers edged his first ball to the left of first slip, where Titmus was unable to latch onto the chance.

The overnight pair lasted another hour on the second morning before Nurse allowed a ball from D'Oliveira to come back up the hill and remove his leg stump, presenting the bowler with his first Test wicket. Soon afterwards, Sobers played no stroke at Knight and was lbw. From 247 for 6 at lunch, West Indies declined to 269 all out against the new ball, used cleverly by Higgs, who finished with 6 for 91, and Jones.

England's reply began badly when Milburn, who had already been rapped several times on the pads, was adjudged lbw to Hall, but Boycott and Graveney matched each other run for run in a stand of 115 – both players brought up their half-centuries in the same Griffith over – before the Yorkshireman was out shortly before the close.

Runs were harder to come by on the third morning. The bowling was tighter, and Graveney was troubled by a bruised thumb, received the previous evening. Nonetheless it was a surprise when, having reached 96 (11 fours) in 260 minutes, Graveney tried to run Hall down through the slips and was caught behind by Allan, a bright spot for the wicketkeeper in an otherwise undistinguished display.

With Barrington and Cowdrey (9 in 52 minutes) having departed earlier, D'Oliveira now arrived to play his first Test innings, and after an early chance behind off Sobers, he had looked comfortable, scoring 27 and adding 48 with Parks. Then, however, tragedy struck as Parks drove Hall back down the pitch. The ball hit D'Oliveira's heel and broke the wicket, and in the heat of the moment the batsman thought he was out and did not try to regain his ground. Hall, however, knew otherwise, grabbed the ball and uprooted a stump to run out the unfortunate D'Oliveira.

Parks, though, continued to 91, adding 59 with the obdurate Higgs, before Sobers, in desperation, turned to part-time bowler Carew, who immediately trapped Parks lbw. Gibbs soon removed Higgs to wrap up the innings for 355, giving England a handy lead of 86. Bowling hero Carew, however, was soon back in the pavilion when he batted, Higgs having him caught by Knight for a duck. By stumps, West Indies had reached 18 for 1.

Rain gingered up the pitch before the fourth day, and two quick wickets soon accounted for Hunte and Butcher. Kanhai and Nurse shared a stand of 66, but both departed in the space of four runs to leave the visitors teetering at 95 for 5, a slender overall lead of nine runs.

Joining Sobers at the crease was his cousin Holford, an inexperienced allrounder playing only his second Test. The captain had confidence in the batting ability of the young man, who had just recorded his maiden first-class century in the tour match against Lancashire, and Sobers told his junior partner: 'You just stay there.' Cowdrey allowed Sobers to take singles in order to attack the junior partner, and Holford's confidence grew as he realised that Sobers was happy to allow him the strike. D'Oliveira worried Holford, but gradually he blossomed out until both batsmen were well set.

Not surprisingly, Sobers dominated the partnership at first, reaching 50 out of 73 with a single off Jones. By the time bad light drove the players from the field, West Indies had moved to 182 for 5, and when play resumed after tea – the teams having been presented to the Queen during the interval – Holford reached his half-century, then Sobers, let off at 93 when Cowdrey at second slip dropped a difficult chance off Higgs, flew to three figures with a glorious cover-drive off Jones. It was his 16th Test century, a West Indies record. By the close the partnership had grown to 193, Sobers having reached 121 and Holford 71.

The pair continued in similar vein on the final morning, a shower interrupting briefly when Holford had progressed to 92. When play resumed Holford moved to 96 in singles, then powered a classic back-foot stroke to the Warner Stand railings to reach his century. At the end of that over Sobers declared, the cousins' unbeaten stand having reached 274, still a West Indian sixth-wicket record for all Tests. Sobers's 330-minute innings included 13 fours; Holford hit six fours in 10 fewer minutes at the crease.

England's target was not impossible – 284 in 240 minutes – but two quick wickets apiece from Hall (off successive balls) and Griffith ended any thoughts of a home win. Graveney was forced to bat, despite his bruised thumb, and, aided by a 45-minute rain-break, he and Milburn saw England to a draw, Milburn playing the major role in an unbeaten partnership of 130 and reaching his first century in his second Test. In all he hit 17 fours and smashed sixes off Hall, Gibbs and Griffith: when he reached three figures, some optimistic spectators ran out and attempted to lift Milburn off the ground (the centuries of Sobers and Holford had been celebrated in this way), but the batsman's 17½-stone frame defeated their efforts.

Garry Sobers (left) and David Holford are applauded from the ground during their marvellous partnership at Lord's in 1966. Coming together with their side effectively 9 for 5, Sobers (163 not out) and his cousin (105 not out) put on 274 runs without being parted

ENGLAND v WEST INDIES
June 16, 17, 18, 20, 21, 1966

WEST INDIES

C.C. Hunte	c Parks b Higgs	18	c Milburn b Knight	13
M.C. Carew	c Parks b Higgs	2	c Knight b Higgs	0
R.B. Kanhai	c Titmus b Higgs	25	c Parks b Knight	40
B.F. Butcher	c Milburn b Knight	49	lbw b Higgs	3
S.M. Nurse	b D'Oliveira	64	c Parks b D'Oliveira	35
* G.S. Sobers	lbw b Knight	46	not out	163
D.A.J. Holford	b Jones	26	not out	105
† D.W. Allan	c Titmus b Higgs	13		
C.C. Griffith	lbw b Higgs	5		
W.W. Hall	not out	8		
L.R. Gibbs	c Parks b Higgs	4		
Extras	(b2, lb7)	9	(lb8, nb2)	10
	(94 overs)	269	(5 wkts dec) (133 overs)	369

Fall: 8,42,53,119,205,213,252,252,261. 2,22,25,91,95.

Bowling: Jones 21-3-64-1, Higgs 33-9-91-6, Knight 21-0-63-2, Titmus 5-0-18-0, D'Oliveira 14-5-24-1.

Second innings: Jones 25-2-95-0, Higgs 34-5-82-2, Knight 30-3-106-2, D'Oliveira 25-7-46-1, Titmus 19-3-30-0.

ENGLAND

G. Boycott	c Griffith b Gibbs	60	c Allan b Griffith	25
C. Milburn	lbw b Hall	6	not out	126
T.W. Graveney	c Allan b Hall	96	(6) not out	30
K.F. Barrington	b Sobers	19	(3) b Griffith	5
* M.C. Cowdrey	c Gibbs b Hall	9	(4) c Allan b Hall	5
† J.M. Parks	lbw b Carew	91	(5) b Hall	0
B.L. D'Oliveira	run out	27		
B.R. Knight	b Griffith	6		
F.J. Titmus	c Allan b Hall	6		
K. Higgs	c Holford b Gibbs	13		
I.J. Jones	not out	0		
Extras	(b7, lb10, nb5)	22	(b4, lb2)	6
	(143.3 overs)	355	(4 wkts) (55 overs)	197

Fall: 8,123,164,198,203,251,266,296,355. 37,43,67,67.

Bowling: Sobers 39-12-89-1, Hall 36-2-106-4, Griffith 28-4-79-1, Gibbs 37.3-18-48-2, Carew 3-0-11-1.

Second innings: Hall 14-1-65-2, Griffith 11-2-43-2, Gibbs 13-4-40-0, Sobers 8-4-8-0, Holford 9-1-35-0.

Toss: West Indies   Umpires: J.S. Buller and W.F.F. Price

Close of play: (1) W.I. 155 for 4 (Nurse 40, Sobers 16)
(2) E. 145 for 2 (Graveney 65, Barrington 8)
(3) W.I. 18 for 1 (Hunte 11, Kanhai 7)
(4) W.I. 288 for 5 (Sobers 121, Holford 71)

MATCH DRAWN

West Indies confirmed their superiority and clinched the series with victories at Trent Bridge (139 runs; Butcher 209 not out) and Headingley (innings and 55; Sobers 174, Nurse 137). The home side turned the tables with an innings win at The Oval, where Graveney made 165 and Murray 112 as England, captained for the first time by Brian Close, ran up the imposing total of 528.

1967i

The second twin-tour summer found India, the early visitors, faced with miserable weather which restricted practice and may have contributed to a crop of injuries which never allowed them to field their first-choice fast bowlers in the Tests: in the final match India's bowling was opened by reserve wicketkeeper Kunderan in the first innings and the Nawab of Pataudi – the team's captain but no bowler – in the second.

England exposed the Indians' limitations in the first Test at Headingley, where Boycott's 246 not out was the backbone of a total of 550 for 4. Rolled over for 164, India showed much better form in their second innings, Pataudi scoring 148, but England completed a comfortable six-wicket win. Boycott's slow scoring – he batted for 573 minutes in all – cost him his place at Lord's as a disciplinary measure.

India's side at Lord's was completely different from their last Test at the ground (1959), only the second time this had occurred (South Africa fielded entirely different sides in 1960 and 1965). The tourists' strength was in their spin-bowling triumvirate – offspinner Prasanna, left-armer Bedi and brisk legspinner Chandrasekhar.

It was India's batsmen, however, who were put to the test first after their captain won the toss. England's new skipper Brian Close played despite having acquired an eye infection which bothered him throughout the match and brought home to him the problems faced by Pataudi, who lost an eye as a result of a car accident in 1961.

On a murky day, Engineer gave India a bright start with two fours in Brown's first over, but a rash shot saw him caught behind in the fourth over of the day. The next blow came when Sardesai had to retire hurt after being hit on the left hand by Snow. Wadekar stood firm, hitting nine fours in his stylish 57, but the experienced vice-captain Borde went for a duck and Pataudi followed for 5. Sardesai returned, not knowing that a later X-ray would reveal that the middle finger of his left hand was broken, and battled bravely to 28, but Murray took three more catches to equal the then Test record of six as India slumped to 152 all out in 3½ hours, Snow and Brown taking three wickets apiece.

Edrich fell to Surti for 12 when England batted, but Barrington (opening the innings in the absence of Boycott) and Amiss took the score to 107 before Amiss fell to the last ball of the day.

Only three hours' play was possible on the second day, England moving sedately to 252 for 3 in that time. Treating the spinners with great respect, Barrington moved to within three runs of his first Test century at Lord's before Chandrasekhar hit his off stump. In all, Barrington batted for just over four hours and hit 10 fours. Graveney, who once pulled Bedi for six, also hit 10 fours in reaching 74 by the time rain brought a premature end to the day.

Graveney batted beautifully on the third day, which again was roughly halved by bad weather. Graveney reached 151, his ninth Test century, in five hours, hitting 20 fours and two sixes before Bedi lured him out of his ground with the third ball after lunch. Graveney's stand with D'Oliveira, who managed only six in the first hour of the day, was worth 122.

159

The stoic Ken Barrington came close to his first Lord's Test century against the Indian tourists of 1967; he was dismissed by the wily Chandrasekhar for 97. He made no mistake later in the season, though, knocking up 148 against Pakistan

Graveney's demise brought on a collapse, which saw England's last five wickets go down for 27 in 45 minutes, the tireless Chandrasekhar finishing with 5 for 127 from 53 overs. India faced a deficit of 234, but more rain meant that they did not have to bat until the Monday.

India's batsmen gave another disappointing display on the fourth day. Engineer again went early, and although 52 runs were added before the next wicket fell, a sharp shower during lunch (taken with India 75 for 3) livened up the pitch and the remaining six wickets went down for 35 in less than an hour. Only Kunderan impressed: he opened in place of Sardesai and survived for 2¾ hours, hitting six fours in his fighting 47. Of the others, only Wadekar and Bedi managed double figures as India slumped to 110 all out, to lose by an innings and 124 runs. Illingworth, who came on at 18 for 1, bowled unchanged apart from a change of ends and finished with 6 for 29.

The rapid collapse caught out the royal party, which missed the end of the match by about half an hour. The teams were nonetheless presented to the Queen on the field at the due time.

160

ENGLAND v INDIA
June 22, 23, 24, 26, 1967

INDIA

D.N. Sardesai	c Murray b Illingworth	28	absent hurt		–
† F.M. Engineer	c Murray b Brown	8	(1) c Amiss b Snow		8
A.L. Wadekar	c Illingworth b D'Oliveira	57	b Illingworth		19
C.G. Borde	b Snow	0	c Snow b Close		1
* Nawab of Pataudi jnr	c Murray b Brown	5	c Graveney b Close		5
R.F. Surti	c Murray b D'Oliveira	6	c D'Oliveira b Illingworth		0
V. Subramanya	c Murray b Brown	0	c Edrich b Illingworth		1
B.K. Kunderan	c Murray b Snow	20	(2) lbw b Illingworth		47
E.A.S. Prasanna	run out	17	(8) c D'Oliveira b Illingworth		0
B.S. Bedi	c Amiss b Snow	5	(9) b Illingworth		11
B.S. Chandrasekhar	not out	2	(10) not out		3
Extras	(b2, lb2)	4	(b11, lb4)		15
	(55.4 overs)	152	(56.3 overs)		110

Fall: 12,24,29,45,58,102,112,144,145.

8,60,67,79,80,86,90,101,110.

Bowling: Snow 20.4-5-49-3, Brown 18-3-61-3, D'Oliveira 15-6-38-2,
Illingworth 2-2-0-1.

Second innings: Snow 8-4-12-1, Brown 5-2-10-0, Illingworth 22.3-12-29-6,
Hobbs 6-1-16-0, Close 15-5-28-2.

ENGLAND

J.H. Edrich	c and b Surti	12	Bowling:
K.F. Barrington	b Chandrasekhar	97	Surti 31-10-67-1,
D.L. Amiss	b Chandrasekhar	29	Subramanya 7-1-20-0,
T.W. Graveney	st Engineer b Bedi	151	Chandrasekhar 53-9-127-5,
B.L. D'Oliveira	c and b Chandrasekhar	33	Bedi 31.2-13-68-3,
* D.B. Close	c Borde b Prasanna	7	Prasanna 32-5-78-1.
† J.T. Murray	b Chandrasekhar	7	
R. Illingworth	lbw b Chandrasekhar	4	
R.N.S. Hobbs	b Bedi	7	
D.J. Brown	c Pataudi b Bedi	5	
J.A. Snow	not out	8	
Extras	(b5, lb18, w1, nb2)	26	
	(154.2 overs)	386	

Fall: 46,107,185,307,334,359,365,372,372.

Toss: India Umpires: J.S. Buller and A. Jepson
Close of play: (1) E. 107 for 2 (Barrington 54)
(2) E. 252 for 3 (Graveney 74, D'Oliveira 27)
(3) E. 386 all out
Sardesai retired hurt at 22 for 1, resumed at 102 for 6

ENGLAND WON BY AN INNINGS AND 124 RUNS

*England completed a 3-0 clean sweep by winning at Edgbaston with more than two
days to spare, India being shot out for 92 and 277.*

1967ii

It was felt that the Pakistan tourists of the latter part of the 1967 summer would be more of a handful for England than their Indian predecessors, and so it proved. Captained by the 'Little Master', Hanif Mohammad, Pakistan's side included their captain from 1962, Javed Burki, as well as a number of players who were to form the nucleus of Pakistan's first world-class side in the early- to mid-1970s: Mushtaq Mohammad, Majid Jahangir Khan, Asif Iqbal, Intikhab Alam and Wasim Bari.

As usual, the first Test of the second series of a twin-tour summer was held at Lord's, where Close won the toss and saw his batsmen make merry on the first day. Milburn was out for 3, but Russell of Middlesex, playing his only Lord's Test, helped Barrington to add 77 before the opener fell in legspinner Intikhab's first over. That was the extent of Pakistan's success, however, as Barrington and Graveney combined in a stand which reached exactly 200 as stumps were drawn. Barrington, whose previous-highest Test score at Lord's was his 97 earlier in the year, finally reached three figures at HQ in his 11th Test there. It was the 17th Test hundred of his illustrious career, and he had hit 17 fours in his overnight 147.

Overnight rain delayed the start on the second day by 70 minutes, and when play began Salim and Asif found unexpected life in the pitch. Graveney, who had hit 11 fours the previous day, fell without addition to his score, and Barrington managed only a single before his 310-minute innings was ended by Asif. In all, five wickets went down for nine runs before D'Oliveira, who had been dropped before he had scored, put on 60 with Higgs. D'Oliveira struck out boldly, successive hits for four, four and six off Intikhab taking him to 50: in all he had nine fours and a six in his 59.

Replying to England's 369, Pakistan struggled initially against good bowling from the accurate Higgs, who took two early wickets then returned later to trap the stubborn Burki lbw. Legspinner Hobbs chipped in to remove the dangerous Majid, leaving Pakistan struggling at 78 for 4 at the end of the day.

Bad light and rain claimed nearly two hours of the third day, which was marked by a fine defensive innings from Hanif. Two early strikes from Snow reduced Pakistan to 99 for 6, but Hanif was undaunted, adding 40 with Intikhab then, crucially, 130 with Asif. Milburn, who had been off the field the day before with a blistered hand, dropped the Pakistan captain at long leg when he had made 51, but otherwise the little man was secure, reaching his century just before a premature close at five o'clock.

Hanif and Asif continued their important partnership on the fourth morning, Asif reaching a creditable 76 before Illingworth had him caught. Hanif, though, kept his concentration going admirably (Close described Hanif in this mood as 'sheer murder to bowl to'), and was still there with 187 when the tailenders finally were winkled out with the score at 354. The Pakistan captain had hit 21 fours in his vigil of 542 minutes – quite a brief knock when compared to his record 970-minute marathon to save the Bridgetown Test of 1957-58!

With their first-innings lead restricted to just 15, England made heavy weather of it when they batted again, stumbling to 95 for 4 before D'Oliveira and Close took the score to 131 by stumps: they extended their stand to 104 on the final

Pakistan captain Hanif Mohammad ensured a draw with a nine-hour innings of 187 not out in 1967. Here he pushes a single past his opposite number Brian Close, watched by wicketkeeper John Murray and Basil D'Oliveira

morning, D'Oliveira completing his second half-century of the match and remaining unbeaten on 81 when Close called a halt at 241 for 9.

The declaration set Pakistan to score 257 in 210 minutes, but their attitude was clear when Ibadulla and Burki ground out 23 in the first hour. In all, the tourists managed only 88 runs in 62 overs, 32 of which were maidens, and Close recalls that the match ended with 'boos and catcalls' for the Pakistani batsmen when they left the field at the end of the drawn match.

ENGLAND v PAKISTAN
July 27, 28, 29, 31, August 1, 1967

ENGLAND

C. Milburn	c Wasim b Asif	3	c Asif b Majid	32
W.E. Russell	b Intikhab	43	b Majid	12
K.F. Barrington	c Wasim b Asif	148	b Intikhab	14
T.W. Graveney	b Salim	81	c Ibadulla b Asif	30
B.L. D'Oliveira	c Intikhab b Mushtaq	59	not out	81
* D.B. Close	c sub (Ghulam Abbas) b Salim	4	st Wasim b Nasim	36
† J.T. Murray	b Salim	0	c and b Nasim	0
R. Illingworth	b Asif	4	c and b Nasim	9
K. Higgs	lbw b Mushtaq	14	c Hanif b Intikhab	1
J.A. Snow	b Mushtaq	0	c Hanif b Mushtaq	7
R.N.S. Hobbs	not out	1	not out	1
Extras	(lb5, nb7)	12	(b12, lb5, nb1)	18
	(138.3 overs)	369	(9 wkts dec) (90.3 overs)	241

Fall: 5,82,283,283,287,287,292,352,354.   33,48,76,95,199,201,215,220,239.

Bowling: Salim 33-6-74-3, Asif 28-10-76-3, Ibadulla 3-0-5-0, Majid 11-2-28-0, Nasim 12-1-36-0, Intikhab 29-3-86-1, Mushtaq 11.3-3-23-3, Saeed 11-3-29-0.

Second innings: Salim 0.3-0-4-0, Asif 21-5-50-1, Majid 10-1-32-2, Intikhab 30-7-70-2, Mushtaq 16-4-35-1, Nasim 13-3-32-3.

PAKISTAN

Khalid Ibadulla	b Higgs	8	c Close b Illingworth	32
Javed Burki	lbw b Higgs	31	c and b Barrington	13
Mushtaq Mohammad	c Murray b Higgs	4	(4) not out	30
* Hanif Mohammad	not out	187		
Majid Jahangir Khan	c and b Hobbs	5	(3) c Close b Barrington	5
Nasim-ul-Ghani	c D'Oliveira b Snow	2		
Saeed Ahmed	c Graveney b Snow	6	(5) not out	6
Intikhab Alam	lbw b Illingworth	17		
Asif Iqbal	c Barrington b Illingworth	76		
† Wasim Bari	c Close b Barrington	13		
Salim Altaf	c Milburn b Snow	2		
Extras	(b1, lb2)	3	(b1, lb1)	2
	(182.1 overs)	354	(3 wkts) (62 overs)	88

Fall: 19,25,67,76,91,99,139,269,310.   27,39,77.

Bowling: Snow 45.1-11-120-3, Higgs 39-12-81-3, D'Oliveira 15-7-17-0, Illingworth 31-14-48-2, Hobbs 35-16-46-1, Barrington 11-1-29-1, Close 6-3-10-0.

Second innings: Snow 4-2-6-0, Higgs 6-3-6-0, Hobbs 16-9-28-0, Illingworth 15-11-10-1, Barrington 13-2-23-2, Close 8-5-13-0.

Toss: England   Umpires: C.S. Elliott and A. Jepson

Close of play: (1) E. 282 for 2 (Barrington 147, Graveney 81)
(2) P. 78 for 4 (Hanif 28, Nasim 2)
(3) P. 233 for 7 (Hanif 102, Asif 56)
(4) E. 131 for 4 (D'Oliveira 21, Close 10)

MATCH DRAWN

England took the series 2-0 with comfortable victories in the remaining two Tests, Barrington scoring 109 at Trent Bridge and 142 at The Oval, lifting his series average to 142.00. Close ended his spell as England captain with six wins and a draw from his seven matches in charge.

1968

The 1968 Lord's Test against Australia, the highlight of the cricket calendar, was ruined by the weather, with more than half the scheduled playing time in the 200th match between the two countries being washed out, as had been the case in the 1964 match. It was especially disappointing for England, who had forged a strong position and had looked likely to avenge Australia's surprise victory in the first Test at Old Trafford, which had been a fillip for Lawry who had taken over the captaincy of his country from the retired Simpson.

Some rather eccentric team selection saw England's best performers in that Manchester match, D'Oliveira (87 not out) and Pocock (6 for 79), omitted from the team at Lord's: Pocock never played against Australia again. In some ways this match marked the end of an era for England: none of those longtime pillars of the middle order Cowdrey (restored as captain for the last of his 13 Lord's Tests), Barrington (12) and Graveney (11) was to grace the famous ground again at the highest level. Milburn, too, was making his last appearance: his career was abruptly ended when he lost an eye in a car crash in May 1969.

Using a gold sovereign given to him by Australian Prime Minister Robert Menzies, Cowdrey won the toss and chose to bat, and England lost Edrich to a flyer from McKenzie in reaching 53 for 1 in 88 minutes before a violent hailstorm hit the ground with a solitary ball having been bowled after the lunch interval. Lord's looked as if it had been hit by an unseasonal blizzard, and no more play was possible.

A bright innings from Milburn enlivened the second morning: he announced his intentions by bludgeoning two fours in McKenzie's first over, and lofted offspinner Cowper's first ball high into the Grand Stand for six. In 80 minutes, Milburn added 67 to his overnight score, hitting 12 fours and two sixes in all, before falling to 'mystery spinner' Gleeson for 83. Having shared a stand of 132, Boycott soon followed Milburn back to the pavilion, but Cowdrey and Barrington batted soundly, taking the score to 244 before Cowdrey became McKenzie's third victim. At 271 England suffered a double blow, first losing Graveney then, temporarily, Barrington, who had to retire when 61 after being struck on the hand: two runs earlier, he had completed 2000 runs in Tests against Australia.

Knight dropped anchor, scoring eight in 70 minutes before stumps, leaving the scoring to Knott, who made a bright 30 after an early let-off when he spooned Hawke back over his head and saw the bowler and fielder Walters get in each other's way and spill the catch.

The unrelenting rain allowed only three brief periods of play, amounting to only 53 minutes – 13½ overs – on the third day. In that time England lost Knott for 33 and the restored Barrington, who moved on to 75 (his highest first-class score of his final season) despite receiving two painful blows on his injured hand.

The fourth morning saw an immediate declaration by Cowdrey, whose fast bowlers soon took charge on a helpful pitch. Lawry fell without scoring in the second over, Knott taking a brilliant one-handed catch diving away to his right, and only Walters of the early batsmen resisted for long, reaching 26 before falling to a marvellous full-length diving catch by Knight in the gully. Sheahan became Knight's 1000th first-class wicket after Knight had dropped him in Brown's

Colin Milburn hooks Graham McKenzie during his brisk 83 in 1968

previous over, and by lunch Australia had limped to 63 for 7.

More rain delayed the resumption by 50 minutes, but the innings came to an abrupt end at 78 after Gleeson had become only the second player to reach double figures (Cowdrey's catch to dismiss the spinner was his 111th in Tests, breaking Walter Hammond's old record). Jarman, who had broken his right forefinger in two places while keeping wicket, came in at No. 10, but his bravery was misplaced, as the first ball he received hit him on the hand, adding another fracture, causing him to retire hurt: he missed the next Test. The innings ended at the same score, Australia's lowest in England since 1912 and their lowest in a Lord's Test since 1896.

Following on, Lawry had great difficulty in avoiding a 'pair', but after he had broken his duck he and Redpath played with some assurance, posting a half-century partnership just before the end of another abbreviated day.

No resumption was possible until 3.15 on the final day, and a draw was virtually assured when Australia lost only Lawry's wicket before tea. Three further wickets went down after the interval, the batsmen perhaps losing that fine edge of concentration knowing that a draw was inevitable. Sheahan defied the numerous close fielders to survive for 52 scoreless minutes before the match was left drawn.

166

ENGLAND v AUSTRALIA
June 20, 21, 22, 24, 25, 1968

ENGLAND

J.H. Edrich	c Cowper b McKenzie	7	Bowling:
G. Boycott	c Sheahan b McKenzie	49	McKenzie 45-18-111-3,
C. Milburn	c Walters b Gleeson	83	Hawke 35-7-82-0,
* M.C. Cowdrey	c Cowper b McKenzie	45	Connolly 26.3-8-55-2,
K.F. Barrington	c Jarman b Connolly	75	Walters 3-2-2-0,
T.W. Graveney	c Jarman b Connolly	14	Cowper 8-2-40-0,
B.R. Knight	not out	27	Gleeson 27-11-43-1.
† A.P.E. Knott	run out	33	
J.A. Snow	not out	0	
D.J. Brown D.L. Underwood	did not bat		
Extras	(b7, lb5, w1, nb5)	18	
	(7 wkts dec) (144.3 overs)	351	

Fall: 10,142,147,244,271,330,351.

AUSTRALIA

* W.M. Lawry	c Knott b Brown	0	c Brown b Snow	28
I.R. Redpath	c Cowdrey b Brown	4	b Underwood	53
R.M. Cowper	c Graveney b Snow	8	c Underwood b Barrington	32
K.D. Walters	c Knight b Brown	26	b Underwood	0
A.P. Sheahan	c Knott b Knight	6	not out	0
I.M. Chappell	lbw b Knight	7	not out	12
N.J.N. Hawke	c Cowdrey b Knight	2		
G.D. McKenzie	b Brown	5		
J.W. Gleeson	c Cowdrey b Brown	14		
† B.N. Jarman	retired hurt	0		
A.N. Connolly	not out	0		
Extras	(lb2, nb4)	6	(nb2)	2
	(33.4 overs)	78	(4 wkts) (67 overs)	127

Fall: 1,12,23,46,52,58,63,78,78.   66,93,97,115.

Bowling: Snow 9-5-14-1, Brown 14-5-42-5, Knight 10.4-5-16-3.
Second innings: Snow 12-5-30-1, Brown 19-9-40-0, Knight 16-9-35-0, Underwood 18-15-8-2, Barrington 2-0-12-1.

Toss: England   Umpires: J.S. Buller and A.E. Fagg
Close of play: (1) E. 53 for 1 (Boycott 27, Milburn 16)
               (2) E. 314 for 5 (Knight 8, Knott 30)
               (3) E. 351 for 7 (Knight 27, Snow 0)
               (4) A. 50 for 0 (Lawry 25, Redpath 24)
               Barrington retired hurt at 271 for 5, resumed at 330 for 6
               Jarman retired hurt at 78 for 8

MATCH DRAWN

The next two Tests were also drawn, Cowdrey marking his 100th Test with a century at Edgbaston before sustaining an injury that kept him out of the side at Headingley. Lawry (fractured finger) missed this match too, the sides being led by Graveney and Jarman. Australia retained the Ashes, even though England squared the series with a memorable win at The Oval, where Underwood's 7 for 50 bowled England to victory with just three minutes to spare. Edrich (164) and D'Oliveira (158) had earlier been the main contributors to England's 494.

1969i

Back for their third visit in seven summers, the West Indian tourists of 1969 were not quite the all-powerful combination of recent years. Gone were Hall, Griffith, Hunte, Kanhai (temporarily) and Nurse, while skipper Sobers was feeling the effects of continuous cricket and had the least-productive series of his career.

England, too, had problems. Illingworth, in his first season as a county captain, had taken over the leadership of his country after an Achilles-tendon injury ruled out Cowdrey. Barrington (heart attack) and Milburn (lost eye in car crash) were also out of the picture, while Graveney's Test career was effectively ended by his decision to play in a benefit match on the rest day of the first Test at Old Trafford, which England had won by 10 wickets, Boycott scoring 128. Graveney's replacement at Lord's was the Yorkshire batsman John Hampshire, who was to mark his Test debut (and only Lord's Test) with a century.

West Indies won the toss and batted against an England attack from which Underwood had rather surprisingly been omitted. Left-hander Fredericks made good use of the hook shot as he and Camacho (later the secretary of the West Indian Cricket Board) shared a century opening partnership. Fredericks eventually went for 63, caught off his pads by Hampshire at leg slip, but Camacho stayed for another 75 minutes before a careless hook caused his downfall for 67.

Butcher went cheaply, but Davis and Sobers put on 50 before a misunderstanding over a leg-bye saw Boycott race in from midwicket to run out the West Indian captain. Davis, probably shocked, went into his shell, but managed to survive until the close.

Snow, who shrugged off two warnings for running down the pitch, took four wickets on the second day to finish with 5 for 114 in West Indies' total of 380. The slim Davis extended his resistance, batting in all for 372 minutes for 103, his first Test century. The value of his innings was shown when England, after the openers compiled a careful 19 in the first hour, slumped to 46 for 4 by stumps in the face of some decidedly quick bowling from Sobers. The great allrounder's first spell brought him figures of 8-6-9-2, both wickets coming in the same over.

The gates were closed on the third morning, the capacity crowd soon seeing Sharpe bowled by Holder, reducing England to 61 for 5. Knott, who scored 53 in his inimitable style, now joined Hampshire in a vital stand of 128, and when the wicketkeeper fell to the debutant Shillingford, the England captain Illingworth took up the fight. Holder twice struck Hampshire painful blows on the left arm, but the tough Yorkshireman made light of the discomfort, reaching a characterful century before falling to Shepherd for 107, his innings having contained 15 fours. Although Knight and Brown went cheaply, Snow defended stoutly, scoring just two runs in a last-wicket stand worth 72 by stumps. Especially strong on the front foot, Illingworth sailed past the highest score of his previous 31 Tests – 50 – and had reached 97 by the close. During the latter part of the day West Indies' vice-captain Gibbs had directed affairs, Sobers having left the field with a thigh strain.

Illingworth reached a richly-deserved century early on the fourth day, finally giving a return catch to Gibbs at 113, after hitting 12 fours in 3½ hours at the crease.

West Indies again made a good start as they sought to build on their slender

168

West Indies captain Garry Sobers congratulates John Hampshire on becoming the only Englishman to score a century on Test debut at Lord's. In the foreground is Stephen Camacho, now the secretary of the West Indies Cricket Board, while the wicketkeeper is Michael Findlay

lead of 36. The openers put on 73 before D'Oliveira removed Camacho and Butcher at the same score, but careless batting saw wickets tumble with some regularity before Lloyd, whose innings included eight fours and two sixes, made 70 in 100 minutes. Sobers, batting with a runner (Camacho), saw the score to 247 for 6 by the close, and he continued to reach his only half-century of the series on the final morning before declaring, leaving England 332 to win in four hours plus the now-mandatory 20 overs.

Modern observers may find it hard to believe, but West Indies, with offspinner Gibbs bowling 40 consecutive overs at the Pavilion end, rattled through 21 overs an hour throughout the day. Despite his earlier use of a runner, Sobers wheeled down 29 overs without any apparent comment from Illingworth.

England made a slow start, Parfitt taking two hours over his 39 after Edrich had gone for 1. Boycott reached 50 in 2½ hours, but it was not until Sharpe joined the opener that any interest was shown in the victory target, a partnership of 126 being posted in only 90 minutes. Just as England seemed to be gaining the upper hand, Sharpe was well caught on the boundary by Davis for a splendid 86. Boycott also fell, soon after becoming the third Yorkshireman in the match to reach three figures, and England needed 61 from the last 10 overs: in the end Illingworth and Knight batted out time to earn the draw. Most observers felt that England would have won had more urgency been shown earlier in the day.

169

ENGLAND v WEST INDIES
June 26, 27, 28, 30, July 1, 1969

WEST INDIES

R.C. Fredericks	c Hampshire b Knight	63	c Hampshire b Illingworth	60
G.S. Camacho	c Sharpe b Snow	67	b D'Oliveira	45
C.A. Davis	c Knott b Brown	103	c Illingworth b D'Oliveira	0
B.F. Butcher	c Hampshire b Brown	9	b Illingworth	24
* G.S. Sobers	run out	29	(7) not out	50
C.H. Lloyd	c Illingworth b Brown	18	(5) c Knott b Snow	70
J.N. Shepherd	c Edrich b Snow	32	(6) c Sharpe b Illingworth	11
† T.M. Findlay	b Snow	23	c Sharpe b Knight	11
V.A. Holder	lbw b Snow	6	run out	7
L.R. Gibbs	not out	18	b Knight	5
G.C. Shillingford	c Knott b Snow	3		
Extras	(b5, lb4)	9	(b4, lb7, nb1)	12
	(158 overs)	380	(9 wkts dec) (100.5 overs)	295

Fall: 106,151,167,217,247,324,336,343,376.   73,73,128,135,191,232,263,280,295.

Bowling: Snow 39-5-114-5, Brown 38-8-99-3, Knight 38-11-65-1,
D'Oliveira 26-10-46-0, Illingworth 16-4-39-0, Parfitt 1-0-8-0.
Second innings: Snow 22-4-69-1, Brown 9-3-25-0, Knight 27.5-6-78-2,
Illingworth 27-9-66-3, D'Oliveira 15-2-45-2.

ENGLAND

G. Boycott	c Findlay b Shepherd	23	c Butcher b Shillingford	106
J.H. Edrich	c Fredericks b Holder	7	c Camacho b Holder	1
P.H. Parfitt	c Davis b Sobers	4	c Findlay b Shepherd	39
B.L. D'Oliveira	c Shepherd b Sobers	0	c Fredericks b Gibbs	18
P.J. Sharpe	b Holder	11	c Davis b Sobers	86
J.H. Hampshire	lbw b Shepherd	107	run out	5
† A.P.E. Knott	b Shillingford	53	(8) b Shillingford	11
* R. Illingworth	c and b Gibbs	113	(7) not out	9
B.R. Knight	lbw b Shillingford	0	not out	1
D.J. Brown	c Findlay b Shepherd	1		
J.A. Snow	not out	9		
Extras	(b1, lb5, nb10)	16	(b9, lb5, nb5)	19
	(157.4 overs)	344	(7 wkts) (106 overs)	295

Fall: 19,37,37,37,61,189,249,250,261.   1,94,137,263,271,272,292.

Bowling: Sobers 26-12-57-2, Holder 38-16-83-2, Shillingford 19-4-53-2,
Shepherd 43-14-74-3, Gibbs 27.4-9-53-1, Davis 1-0-2-0, Butcher 3-1-6-0.
Second innings: Holder 11-4-36-1, Shillingford 13-4-30-2, Shepherd 12-3-45-1,
Gibbs 41-14-93-1, Sobers 29-8-72-1.

Toss: West Indies   Umpires: J.S. Buller and A.E. Fagg
Close of play: (1) W.I. 246 for 4 (Davis 57, Lloyd 17)
                   (2) E. 46 for 4 (Sharpe 6, Hampshire 3)
                   (3) E. 321 for 9 (Illingworth 97, Snow 2)
                   (4) W.I. 247 for 6 (Sobers 26, Findlay 1)

MATCH DRAWN

*England took the series 2-0 with a 30-run victory in a close-run third Test at
Headingley. Chasing 303 in the final innings, West Indies were 219 for 3, but
slumped to 272 all out despite Butcher's 91, the highest score of the match.*

1969ii

Lord's provided what *Wisden* described as a 'curious, mottled pitch' for their second Test of the summer, and in the end the conditions proved too much for the promising but inexperienced New Zealand tourists. Underwood took advantage of the conditions to return figures of 7 for 32 in the second innings, at the time his best Test bowling analysis.

England's selectors sprang a surprise by dropping Hampshire, a centurymaker at Lord's a month previously, in favour of Fletcher. Snow was rested, a first cap being given to the raw Derbyshire fast bowler Alan Ward.

New Zealand lost the toss, but had a marvellous first session, reducing England to 68 for 5 by lunch. Before a run had been scored Boycott had gone, well caught by Congdon, diving forward at slip, in the third over of the innings. It was Boycott's second successive Test duck. Edrich and Sharpe fell to Taylor, Motz yorked Fletcher, then Dayle Hadlee, in his first Test, pulled off a remarkable one-handed return catch to send back Knott.

England's sorry position was rescued somewhat by sensible batting from D'Oliveira, who reached 37 before Pollard ran him out, and Illingworth, whose 53 extended his run of good Test form. A handy 29 from Knight also helped to lift the total to 190. Bad light interrupted the Kiwis' reply: they reached 5 without loss in the two brief sessions of play possible.

New Zealand flattered to deceive on the third morning, going in to lunch at 71 for the loss of Turner, caught behind early on to provide the pacey Ward with his first Test wicket. Congdon had worried the purists by overdoing the sweep-shot against Underwood, but it was the speed of Ward that proved his undoing for 41. Now the spinners took over, five further wickets falling before the tea interval, and although Motz once lofted Underwood for a satisfying six, the eventual total of 169 was a grave disappointment to the tourists. Illingworth and Underwood finished with four wickets apiece.

Motz gave Boycott a torrid time as the apprehensive Yorkshireman sought to avoid the indignity of a 'pair'. Boycott remained scoreless for 28 minutes before he pushed two runs in Motz's fifth over. England had reached 21 without loss by the close.

Boycott's safety-first approach spilled over to the third morning, his eventual 47 occupying 3½ hours. Edrich had a lucky escape at 15 when Congdon, close in on the leg side, could not hold on to a sharp chance off Howarth. The Surrey man made the most of his let-off, dominating the opening stand of 125 and then sharing a partnership of 74 with Sharpe, who hit eight fours in his 46. In due course Edrich moved to his seventh Test century, his eventual 115 lasting almost five hours and containing 20 fours. From 234 for 2, England declined to 259 for 7, the impressive left-arm spinner Hedley Howarth profiting with three quick wickets on his Test debut as belated efforts to push up the scoring rate took their toll. Knight struck out boldly towards the end, one of his shots removing Dowling temporarily from the scene when the tourists' captain was hit in the face while fielding at short leg. Rather unwisely, he stayed for a while, but left the field shortly before stumps for treatment.

Knight and Ward enjoyed themselves on the fourth morning, adding 39 further

A remarkable return catch by New Zealand's Dayle Hadlee sends back Alan Knott as England subside to 63 for 5 on the first morning in 1969

runs in 37 minutes to stretch England's total to 340. New Zealand, chasing 362, needed a good start but Dowling soon fell to Ward.

Now Underwood took over. The youthful Turner was solid at one end, but he was not experienced enough to farm the bowling and the Kent left-armer ripped out the heart of New Zealand's batting in a matchwinning 6 for 14 spell. Congdon made 17, but Hastings, Pollard and Taylor all failed to score as the total dipped to 73 for 7. The determined Motz now joined Turner, and they defended stoutly, Motz scoring all but five of the 28 runs they added. It took England three hours to winkle out the last three wickets, Underwood finishing with the splendid figures of 31-18-32-7.

Turner, described by New Zealand writer Dick Brittenden as 'very much the boy left on the burning deck', became, at 22 years 63 days, the youngest player to carry his bat through a Test innings: it was the fourth time the feat had been achieved at Lord's, Australians Barrett, Bardsley and Brown being the other batsmen concerned.

England wrapped up the match at six o'clock on the fourth day, a comfortable enough victory on paper, but in fact New Zealand had come within half an hour of forcing a draw, as persistent rain throughout the next day would not have allowed any play.

ENGLAND v NEW ZEALAND
July 24, 25, 26, 28, 1969

ENGLAND

G. Boycott	c Congdon b Motz	0	c Turner b Pollard	47
J.H. Edrich	c Motz b Taylor	16	c Wadsworth b Hadlee	115
P.J. Sharpe	c Turner b Taylor	20	c Congdon b Howarth	46
K.W.R. Fletcher	b Motz	9	b Howarth	7
B.L. D'Oliveira	run out	37	c Wadsworth b Taylor	12
† A.P.E. Knott	c and b Hadlee	8	lbw b Howarth	10
* R. Illingworth	c Wadsworth b Howarth	53	c Wadsworth b Taylor	0
B.R. Knight	c Hadlee b Pollard	29	b Motz	49
D.J. Brown	not out	11	c Wadsworth b Taylor	7
D.L. Underwood	c Pollard b Howarth	1	b Motz	4
A. Ward	b Taylor	0	not out	19
Extras	(b1, lb3, w1, nb1)	6	(b4, lb15, nb5)	24
	(74.5 overs)	190	(140.4 overs)	340

Fall: 0,27,47,47,63,113,158,186,188.   125,199,234,243,259,259,259,284,300.

Bowling: Motz 19-5-46-2, Hadlee 14-2-48-1, Taylor 13.5-4-35-3, Howarth 19-9-24-2, Pollard 9-1-31-1.

Second innings: Motz 39.4-17-78-2, Hadlee 16-5-43-1, Howarth 49-20-102-3, Taylor 25-4-62-3, Pollard 8-2-20-1, Burgess 3-0-11-0.

NEW ZEALAND

* G.T. Dowling	c Illingworth b Underwood	41	c Knott b Ward	4
G.M. Turner	c Knott b Ward	5	not out	43
B.E. Congdon	c Sharpe b Ward	41	c Fletcher b Underwood	17
B.F. Hastings	c Ward b Illingworth	23	c Knott b Underwood	0
V. Pollard	c Ward b Underwood	8	lbw b Underwood	0
M.G. Burgess	lbw b Illingworth	10	lbw b Underwood	6
† K.J. Wadsworth	lbw b Illingworth	14	(8) b Underwood	5
B.R. Taylor	c Brown b Illingworth	3	(7) b Underwood	0
R.C. Motz	b Underwood	15	c Knott b Underwood	23
D.R. Hadlee	c Illingworth b Underwood	1	c Sharpe b D'Oliveira	19
H.J. Howarth	not out	0	b Ward	4
Extras	(b4, lb4)	8	(b5, lb4, nb1)	10
	(87.3 overs)	169	(75.5 overs)	131

Fall: 14,76,92,101,126,137,146,150,168.   5,27,45,45,67,67,73,101,126.

Bowling: Brown 12-5-17-0, Ward 14-2-49-2, Underwood 29.3-16-38-4, Knight 10-3-20-0, Illingworth 22-8-37-4.

Second innings: Brown 5-3-6-0, Ward 10.5-0-48-2, Underwood 31-18-32-7, Knight 3-1-5-0, Illingworth 18-9-24-0, D'Oliveira 8-3-6-1.

Toss: England   Umpires: J.S. Buller and A. Jepson
Close of play: (1) N.Z. 5 for 0 (Dowling 4, Turner 1)
(2) E. 21 for 0 (Boycott 12, Edrich 8)
(3) E. 301 for 9 (Knight 31, Ward 0)

ENGLAND WON BY 230 RUNS

Rain ruined the second Test at Trent Bridge, where Edrich and Sharpe scored centuries, but England took the series 2-0 with an eight-wicket win at The Oval, Underwood taking 12 more wickets as New Zealand were shot out for 150 and 229.

1971i

For the first time since 1927 (excluding the war years) the 1970 summer saw no official Lord's Test, in the wake of the cancellation of the proposed South African tour. Instead, a series of five unofficial 'Tests' was played between England and the Rest of the World, captained by Sobers. The Lord's match, which unusually started on a Wednesday (the traditional Thursday saw a General Election), found the home side overwhelmed by the strong World XI, for whom the remarkable Sobers took 6 for 21 and later scored 183.

The first visitors the following year, another twin-tour summer, were Pakistan, captained by legspinner Intikhab Alam. A rather complacent England, fresh from a successful tour of Australia, were jolted in the first Test at Edgbaston, where the almost unknown Zaheer Abbas stroked a marvellous 274 for the tourists. Mushtaq and Asif also reached three figures as Pakistan amassed 608 for 7. England followed on despite Illingworth's 116, but were saved from probable defeat by the loss of most of the fifth day's play.

Expectation was therefore high for the Lord's Test, but once again the weather ruined the match, allowing less than 13 of the scheduled 30 hours' play. Although many a Lord's Test had been sorely affected by dismal weather over the years, this 1971 match suffered more than any since Pakistan's first match at HQ, in 1954, when play had finally begun at 3.45 on the scheduled fourth day.

Four inches of rain had fallen on the ground in the week preceding this match, and a wet outfield delayed the start of play on Day 1 until 3.30. On a painfully slow pitch, Boycott and Luckhurst shared an untroubled stand of 118 in the 160 minutes possible. Rain on the second day, however, limited play to just 23 minutes, time enough, however, for Salim to send Luckhurst back to the pavilion.

Any slight hope of an exciting match disappeared when yet more rain washed out play completely on the Saturday, provoking gloomy predictions that the match would make a loss of some £25,000.

The fourth day saw a resumption at 2.30, and when the declaration came at 241 for 2 Boycott was still there, having batted for 310 minutes for his 121. By the close Pakistan had reached 49, both openers escaping when close catches were grassed.

D'Oliveira dismissed Sadiq before the opener had added to his score on the fifth morning, and soon afterwards Hutton took his first Test wicket, Knott's catch to remove Aftab being his 100th dismissal at this level. Only Zaheer, with an accomplished 40, mastered the conditions. Price ended the innings with the wickets of Wasim Bari and Asif Masood with successive balls, but was denied the opportunity of a hat-trick by Pervez's inability to bat (the spinner was suffering from swollen feet and ankles).

With a draw the only possible result Illingworth sent out Hutton to open the second innings with Luckhurst, and both batsmen made studied half-centuries against some rather varied bowling before the match ended. Hutton, with 58 not out, had started his Test career more promisingly than his father, who managed just 0 and 1 on his debut, at Lord's in 1937. However, 1971 proved to be Richard Hutton's only summer of Test cricket and, indeed, he drifted out of county cricket a few years later.

ENGLAND v PAKISTAN
June 17, 18, 19 (no play), 21, 22, 1971

ENGLAND

G. Boycott	not out	121		
B.W. Luckhurst	c Wasim b Salim	46	(1) not out	53
J.H. Edrich	c Asif Masood b Pervez	37		
D.L. Amiss	not out	19		
R.A. Hutton			(2) not out	58
B.L. D'Oliveira				
* R. Illingworth				
† A.P.E. Knott	did not bat			
P. Lever				
N. Gifford				
J.S.E. Price				
Extras	(b6, lb2, w5, nb5)	18	(b1, lb1, nb4)	6
	(2 wkts dec) (83 overs)	241	(0 wkt) (45 overs)	117

Fall: 124,205.

Bowling: Asif Masood 21-3-60-0, Salim 19-5-42-1, Asif Iqbal 13-2-24-0, Majid 4-0-16-0, Intikhab 20-2-64-0, Pervez 6-2-17-1.

Second innings: Salim 5-2-11-0, Asif Masood 3-1-3-0, Asif Iqbal 4-1-11-0, Mushtaq 11-3-31-0, Intikhab 9-1-26-0, Sadiq 5-1-17-0, Majid 6-2-7-0, Aftab 1-0-4-0, Zaheer 1-0-1-0.

PAKISTAN

Aftab Gul	c Knott b Hutton	33	Bowling:	
Sadiq Mohammad	c Knott b D'Oliveira	28	Price 11.4-5-29-3,	
Zaheer Abbas	c Hutton b Lever	40	Lever 16-3-38-2,	
Mushtaq Mohammad	c Amiss b Hutton	2	Gifford 12-6-13-1,	
Asif Iqbal	c Knott b Gifford	9	Illingworth 7-6-1-0,	
Majid Jahangir Khan	c Edrich b Price	9	Hutton 16-5-36-2,	
* Intikhab Alam	c Gifford b Lever	18	D'Oliveira 10-5-22-1.	
† Wasim Bari	c Knott b Price	0		
Salim Altaf	not out	0		
Asif Masood	b Price	0		
Pervez Sajjad	absent ill	–		
Extras	(lb5, w1, nb3)	9		
	(72.4 overs)	148		

Fall: 57,66,97,117,119,146,148,148,148.

Toss: England   Umpires: A.E. Fagg and A.E.G. Rhodes
Close of play: (1) E. 118 for 0 (Boycott 61, Luckhurst 46)
(2) E. 133 for 1 (Boycott 72, Edrich 0)
(4) P. 49 for 0 (Aftab 20, Sadiq 28)

MATCH DRAWN

England stole the series 1-0 with an exciting 25-run victory at Headingley. Set 231 to win, Pakistan seemed set for success at 160 for 4, but lost their last six wickets for 45, Peter Lever ending the match with three wickets in four balls.

1971ii

The confounded weather also had the final say in the other Lord's Test of 1971, washing out what promised to be an exciting final session of play. India, fresh from an historic series win in West Indies, were confident of recording a maiden victory on English soil, but both sides were in with a chance when rain set in, India needing another 38 runs and England just two wickets. The Indians, however, were adamant that their batting tactics would have been different had the weather not been threatening.

On a grey, misty morning, India made a dream start to the match after England had won the toss, Boycott having made only 3 when he touched a catch behind off the enthusiastic Abid Ali. After this initial breakthrough the Indian spinners took over, their rare skills being abetted by the pack of prehensile close fielders led by Solkar. England drooped to 71 for 5, and might have subsided completely had Solkar been able to cling on to a difficult chance off Chandrasekar's googly when Knott had made 9. Knott once swung Bedi for six, and also collected nine fours in his 67. He shared a partnership of 90 in 98 minutes with Illingworth, who early on seemed lucky to escape when Chandrasekhar's topspinner rapped him on the pad. With the spinners tiring, Snow cashed in, reaching a valuable half-century just before the close, by which time England had recovered to 252 for 8.

Snow, who hit six fours, moved to 73, his highest first-class score at the time, on the second morning as the total rose to 304. No doubt encouraged by his batting success, Snow was soon seen to advantage in his more usual role as strike bowler, having Mankad caught by Gifford. There was a suspicion that Mankad might have been distracted by a shout of 'no-ball' from the crowd. Gavaskar lingered 48 minutes for 4, but the major innings for India came from Wadekar. The Indian captain hooked his first ball, a bouncer from Snow, for four, and went on to score 40 of the first 50 runs: in all he batted for 196 minutes, hitting 11 fours in his assured 85. Later Viswanath and Engineer put on 50 in even time, the wicketkeeper falling just before stumps, which found India 125 behind at 179 for 5.

Viswanath and his new partner Solkar took their partnership slowly to 92 on Day 3, England not breaking the stand until after the tea interval. The pair slowed down the longer they were together, Viswanath eventually falling to Hutton for 68 after 4½ hours, while Solkar managed only three boundaries in his 310-minute stay for 67. The tourists edged into the lead with the ninth pair at the crease, causing ecstatic Indian journalists in the Lord's press-box to hand round a specially-prepared tray of mouthwatering delicacies from the subcontinent. The innings closed at 313 – a lead of nine – and a light drizzle prevented England from starting their second innings that evening.

Showers delayed the start of the fourth day until 2.45, and England took six overs to clear off the modest nine-run deficit. Luckhurst fell to Solkar for 1, and after Boycott had made a studious 33 Amiss was tied down for some time without scoring. Frustrated, he finally tried for a suicidal single and was run out by Solkar from short cover. More high-class spin threatened to put India on top, and only a disciplined 62 from Edrich – who fell after 190 minutes to Bedi's last ball of the

Tempers flared as India pushed for victory on the last day in 1971, and England fast bowler John Snow later received a one-Test suspension for this 'bodycheck' on India's diminutive opener Sunil Gavaskar

day – staved off total collapse.

The last five wickets went down for 46 runs in 90 minutes on the final morning, as England lurched to 191 all out. Chandrasekhar removed Knott (caught by Wadekar via Solkar's leg) in his second over and Hutton in his third, then Venkataraghavan took 3 for 10 in nearly 13 overs.

India's target was a modest 183 in 260 minutes, and although two wickets went down cheaply Gavaskar and the promoted Engineer raised a stand of 66 in 50 minutes before the latter rashly went down the wicket to Gifford and was stumped. Just before lunch Snow, trying to cut off the ball, barged into Gavaskar as he ran through for a quick single, sending the little opener flying: the bowler then tossed Gavaskar's bat back to him. Although he apologised later, Snow's action won him few friends and he was excluded from the next Test as a disciplinary measure.

Now the weather took a hand, with India anxious to finish the job before the threatening clouds did their worst. This anxiety might explain the dreadful stroke that cost Sardesai his wicket. At 114 India suffered a cruel blow when Gavaskar, having reached 53, could not avoid a flyer from Gifford and gave a catch to Edrich. Abid Ali and Venkataraghavan also succumbed to the spinners before tea, and the interval was reached with the match delicately poised. Rain, though, did its worst, and the players did not emerge for the final session.

ENGLAND v INDIA
July 22, 23, 24, 26, 27, 1971

ENGLAND

G. Boycott	c Engineer b Abid Ali	3	c Wadekar b Venkataraghavan	33
B.W. Luckhurst	c Solkar b Chandrasekhar	30	b Solkar	1
J.H. Edrich	c Venkataraghavan b Bedi	18	c Engineer b Bedi	62
D.L. Amiss	c Engineer b Bedi	9	run out	0
B.L. D'Oliveira	c Solkar b Chandrasekhar	4	b Bedi	30
† A.P.E. Knott	c Wadekar b Venkataraghavan	67	c Wadekar b Chandrasekhar	24
* R. Illingworth	c Engineer b Bedi	33	c Wadekar b Venkataraghavan	20
R.A. Hutton	b Venkataraghavan	20	b Chandrasekhar	0
J.A. Snow	c Abid Ali b Chandrasekhar	73	c Chandrasekhar b Venkataraghavan	9
N. Gifford	b Bedi	17	not out	7
J.S.E. Price	not out	5	c Abid Ali b Venkataraghavan	0
Extras	(b8, lb12, nb5)	25	(lb5)	5
	(139.3 overs)	304	(98.5 overs)	191

Fall: 18,46,56,61,71,161,183,223,294. 4,65,70,117,145,153,153,174,189.

Bowling: Abid Ali 15-3-38-1, Solkar 8-3-17-0, Venkataraghavan 28-8-44-2, Chandrasekhar 49-10-110-3, Bedi 39.3-18-70-4.

Second innings: Abid Ali 9-1-20-0, Solkar 6-3-13-1, Bedi 30-13-41-2, Chandrasekhar 23-7-60-2, Venkataraghavan 30.5-11-52-4.

INDIA

A.V. Mankad	c Gifford b Snow	1	c Knott b Snow	5
S.M. Gavaskar	c Amiss b Price	4	c Edrich b Gifford	53
* A.L. Wadekar	c Illingworth b Gifford	85	c Boycott b Price	5
D.N. Sardesai	c Illingworth b Gifford	25	(6) b Illingworth	1
G.R. Viswanath	c Knott b Hutton	68	c Amiss b Gifford	9
† F.M. Engineer	c Illingworth b Hutton	28	(4) st Knott b Gifford	35
E.D. Solkar	c Knott b Gifford	67	not out	6
S. Abid Ali	c Luckhurst b Snow	6	c Snow b Illingworth	14
S. Venkataraghavan	c Hutton b Price	11	c Hutton b Gifford	7
B.S. Bedi	c Price b Gifford	0	not out	2
B.S. Chandrasekhar	not out	0		
Extras	(b7, lb9, nb2)	18	(lb7, nb1)	8
	(165.3 overs)	313	(8 wkts) (50 overs)	145

Fall: 1,29,108,125,175,267,279,302,311. 8,21,87,101,108,114,135,142.

Bowling: Price 25-9-46-2, Snow 31-9-64-2, Hutton 24-8-38-2, Gifford 45.3-14-84-4, D'Oliveira 15-7-20-0, Illingworth 25-12-43-0.

Second innings: Snow 8-0-23-1, Price 4-0-26-1, Hutton 3-0-12-0, Gifford 19-4-43-4, Illingworth 16-2-33-2.

Toss: England   Umpires: D.J. Constant and C.S. Elliott
Close of play: (1) E. 252 for 8 (Snow 51, Gifford 4)
                  (2) I. 179 for 5 (Viswanath 24, Solkar 0)
                  (3) I. 313 all out
                  (4) E. 145 for 5 (Knott 17)

MATCH DRAWN

Rain saved India in the second Test, the final day's play at Old Trafford being washed out with England well on top after centuries from Illingworth and Luckhurst. The final Test at The Oval, however, saw a famous win for India, who thus took the series 1-0: Chandrasekhar took 6 for 38 as England collapsed for 101.

1972

Very rarely does an individual player perform well enough to have a match 'named' after him. One such game, however, was 'Massie's Match' – the second Test of the 1972 Ashes series, when Bob Massie, making his Test debut, took 16 wickets – eight in each innings. Swinging the ball both ways, often bowling round the wicket, the 25-year-old bank clerk from Perth bamboozled the England batsmen, of whom only Greig managed a half-century.

England went into this match one-up, having enjoyed a comfortable 89-run victory at Old Trafford. Massie had been unfit for that match, but came into the Australian side at Lord's for his first Test. England, on the other hand, were without Arnold (hamstring injury), who had taken five wickets at Manchester.

England, after Illingworth had won the toss, were soon in trouble, Boycott swinging across a Massie yorker and Edrich and Luckhurst being defeated by Lillee's extreme pace. The veterans Smith and D'Oliveira, aged 38 and 40 respectively and both playing in their last Lord's Tests, took the score to 84, but then Massie struck again. The pressure inevitably eased when Lillee and Massie had to rest, and Greig – who compiled his third half-century in his first three Test innings – and Knott put on 96, the wicketkeeper taking advantage of a simple dropped catch which Francis grassed off Gleeson. It was left to Massie to end the stand, and by the end of the first day he had taken 5 for 75 in England's 249 for 7.

The last three wickets put up little resistance on the second morning, the eventual total being 272. Massie cleaned up the tail to finish with 8 for 84, debut figures bettered only by Albert Trott, who took 8 for 43 for Australia against England at Adelaide in 1894-95 (Trott later settled in England, and in 1899 became the only player to hit a ball over the pavilion at Lord's).

Australia, like England, made a poor start, losing both openers before double figures were posted, but then Ian and Greg Chappell put on 75 before the captain fell to a fine running catch at long leg, the sprightly Smith seeing the ball late but clinging on to the chance. Snow soon removed Walters, picked up by one of the two specially-positioned gully fielders, but the younger Chappell and Edwards, another debutant, shared a century partnership, Edwards making a patient 28 before falling to another well-judged catch by Smith.

Greg Chappell reached his century, his second in Tests, just before the close; he continued elegantly to 131 in front of a capacity crowd on the third morning. He hit 14 fours, the first of them after he had been at the crease for more than three hours. Australia reached 308, a lead of 36, with Marsh contributing a brisk 50, which included six fours and two sixes.

The slender lead assumed more impressive proportions as England lost five wickets in clearing the arrears. Once again it was the Western Australian opening pair who did the damage: Lillee bowled Boycott, off his body, and had Luckhurst caught behind, and then Massie – who was to bowl unchanged through this innings – resumed control. Again the batsmen seemed at a loss to fathom the direction of Massie's swing, and seven of the last eight batsmen fell to catches behind the wicket or in the slips. The exception was Smith, whose second grafting innings of the match was ended by a rather inelegant hoick to square leg, where he was caught by Edwards. Massie wrapped up the innings on the fourth morning,

Watched by umpire David Constant, Australia's Bob Massie unveils the action which brought him a stunning 16 wickets – eight in each innings – in his first Test, at Lord's in 1972

ending a stubborn last-wicket partnership, and finished with 8 for 53, at the time the second-best innings analysis in a Lord's Test, surpassed only by Hedley Verity's 8 for 43 against Australia in 1934, in what became known as 'Verity's Match'. Ian Botham was to improve on these figures in 1978, and even Massie's debut figures were surpassed by the youthful Indian legspinner, Narendra Hirwani, who took 16 for 136 on his debut against West Indies at Madras in 1987-88. Massie's match figures, though, remain supreme at Lord's.

Stackpole made the lion's share of the runs as Australia pursued the 81 required for victory, which was duly achieved with well over a day to spare.

Nothing seemed more certain than that Bob Massie would play an important role in the emerging Australian side. Richie Benaud wrote: 'It will not be surprising if he is not really at his peak until the England side comes to Australia on the next occasion.' However, by the time of that next tour – 1974-75 – Massie was, astonishingly, no longer a regular member of his State side. His Test career amounted to a mere six matches, all of them during 1972-73, and in his other five appearances he managed just 15 wickets – one fewer than in his dramatic debut. Greg Chappell, whose elegant hundred was another feature of this 1972 match, opined: 'It just about ruined his career. He was never going to take 16 wickets in a match again.'

ENGLAND v AUSTRALIA
June 22, 23, 24, 26, 1972

ENGLAND

G. Boycott	b Massie	11	b Lillee		6
J.H. Edrich	lbw b Lillee	10	c Marsh b Massie		6
B.W. Luckhurst	b Lillee	1	c Marsh b Lillee		4
M.J.K. Smith	b Massie	34	c Edwards b Massie		30
B.L. D'Oliveira	lbw b Massie	32	c G.S. Chappell b Massie		3
A.W. Greig	c Marsh b Massie	54	c I.M. Chappell b Massie		3
† A.P.E. Knott	c Colley b Massie	43	c G.S. Chappell b Massie		12
* R. Illingworth	lbw b Massie	30	c Stackpole b Massie		12
J.A. Snow	b Massie	37	c Marsh b Massie		0
N. Gifford	c Marsh b Massie	3	not out		16
J.S.E. Price	not out	4	c G. S. Chappell b Massie		19
Extras	(lb6, w1, nb6)	13	(w1, nb4)		5
	(91.5 overs)	272	(55.2 overs)		116

Fall: 22,23,28,84,97,193,200,260,265. 12,16,18,25,31,52,74,74,81.

Bowling: Lillee 28-3-90-2, Massie 32.5-7-84-8, Colley 16-2-42-0,
G.S. Chappell 6-1-18-0, Gleeson 9-1-25-0.
Second innings: Lillee 21-6-50-2, Massie 27.2-9-53-8, Colley 7-1-8-0.

AUSTRALIA

K.R. Stackpole	c Gifford b Price	5	not out		57
B.C. Francis	b Snow	0	c Knott b Price		9
* I.M. Chappell	c Smith b Snow	56	c Luckhurst b D'Oliveira		6
G.S. Chappell	b D'Oliveira	131	not out		7
K.D. Walters	c Illingworth b Snow	1			
R. Edwards	c Smith b Illingworth	28			
J.W. Gleeson	c Knott b Greig	1			
† R.W. Marsh	c Greig b Snow	50			
D.J. Colley	c Greig b Price	25			
R.A.L. Massie	c Knott b Snow	0			
D.K. Lillee	not out	2			
Extras	(lb7, nb2)	9	(lb2)		2
	(122.1 overs)	308	(2 wkts) (26.5 overs)		81

Fall: 1,7,82,84,190,212,250,290,290. 20,51.

Bowling: Snow 32-13-57-5, Price 26.1-5-87-2, Greig 29-6-74-1,
D'Oliveira 17-5-48-1, Gifford 11-4-20-0, Illingworth 7-2-13-1.
Second innings: Snow 8-2-15-0, Price 7-0-28-1, Greig 3-0-17-0, D'Oliveira 8-3-14-1,
Luckhurst 0.5-0-5-0.

Toss: England Umpires: D.J. Constant and A.E. Fagg
Close of play: (1) E. 249 for 7 (Illingworth 23, Snow 28)
(2) A. 201 for 5 (G.S. Chappell 105, Gleeson 0)
(3) E. 86 for 9 (Gifford 3, Price 2)

AUSTRALIA WON BY 8 WICKETS

*Australia's success left the rubber tied at one-all, and an absorbing series continued
with a draw at Trent Bridge and a three-day England victory at Headingley, where
the recalled Derek Underwood took 10 for 82 on a pitch later found to be infected
with fuserium, a fungus. Australia squared the series at The Oval, where both
Chappell brothers scored centuries and Lillee took 10 wickets in the tourists' five-
wicket victory in a six-day match.*

1973i

New Zealand had never beaten England in nearly 44 years of trying when they arrived for the 1973 tour, but the tourists' performances leading up to the series – opener Turner reached 1000 runs before the end of May – and a sterling show in the first Test gave hope that the duck might be broken. At Trent Bridge New Zealand, set 479 to win, fell only 39 runs short, captain Congdon making 176 and Pollard, like his captain a third-time tourist, scoring 116.

England, though, were one-up when the teams arrived at Lord's, where Congdon won the toss for the first time in eight attempts as a Test captain. On a hazy, humid day, he put England in, a decision that soon paid off when Dayle Hadlee had Amiss caught by Howarth, who had replaced the young Richard Hadlee from the side which had done so well at Nottingham.

Boycott and Roope shared a sedate stand of 92, but England were well placed at 148 for 2 soon before tea when Boycott, looking for his third six, was caught at square leg for 61. Six more wickets went down before the 200 was posted, the only batsman to survive for long being Greig, who led a charmed life in reaching 53.

Collinge wrapped up the innings for 253 early on the second morning, but New Zealand were soon in trouble, both openers falling inside half an hour. Making light of some early hesitation against the moving ball, the third-wicket pair carried out an excellent repair job, although their understandably sluggish progress and a slow over rate made for one of the less sparkling days of Test cricket at Lord's. Hastings, when 21, was badly missed by Fletcher off Illingworth, but otherwise he and his captain battled throughout the day, establishing a record stand for their country, which ended five minutes before the close when, just after Congdon had reached his second successive Test century, Hastings was lbw to Snow.

New Zealand went patiently on to a formidable score on Day 3, England managing to take only three wickets all day, one of those being nightwatchman Howarth, who hit his own wicket after 92 minutes of defiance for 17. Congdon rolled on, reaching 175 in 515 minutes before Old had him caught behind. Burgess, who had escaped before opening his account when Old put down a difficult return catch, now took control: like his captain, he hit 12 fours, his 105 coming up in 228 minutes. Burgess put on 117 for the sixth wicket with Pollard, who made a slow start but later played some remarkable shots against the new ball – frequently he advanced down the wicket to Arnold and Snow and carted them to all parts. The last session saw 130 runs added in less than two hours.

Pollard, who lasted for 230 minutes in all, swept to his hundred on the fourth morning as the Kiwis batted on for 80 minutes to reach 551 for 9, their highest total in all Tests: it was the first time that a New Zealand Test innings had included three individual centuries.

Undaunted by the huge deficit of 298, Boycott and Amiss were untroubled in adding 112 for England's first wicket, although both eventually perished in the same unlikely way, pushing a Howarth full-toss back to the bowler. By stumps England had advanced to 224 for 2, st.'ı 74 in arrears.

A fine innings and a vital miss denied New Zealand victory on the final day. The innings came from Fletcher, who batted almost throughout the day for 178:

183

A vital miss: wicketkeeper Ken Wadsworth drops a fine edge from England tailender Geoff Arnold as New Zealand push for victory in 1973. Arnold survived for more than an hour, and England escaped with a draw. The frustrated fieldsmen are (l-r) Hedley Howarth, Glenn Turner and skipper Bevan Congdon, whose 175 had earlier set up his side's imposing total of 551 for 9

in all he lasted 379 minutes, hitting 21 fours and two sixes, before falling to a catch on the boundary five minutes before the close, with England safe. The slender Essex batsman far surpassed his previous-highest score of 31 in 13 Test innings in England.

Fletcher shared an important stand with Illingworth which produced 61 runs but, more importantly, used up nearly two hours, but after two more wickets from the impressive Howarth – the left-arm spinner toiled through 70 overs in England's second innings – England were only 70 ahead with two hours remaining when Arnold came in. The No. 10's first ball, from offspinner Pollard, may have shaved the bat, but his third ball certainly took the edge: sadly for New Zealand, wicketkeeper Wadsworth could not hold on to either chance. Arnold kept his head down, and with Fletcher opening out (he took 16 off one Pollard over) the pair put on 92 in 87 minutes. Fletcher's last-gasp dismissal came too late for New Zealand. Poor Wadsworth did not have a chance to make amends, and he never saw his country beat England in a Test (they managed it for the first time at home early in 1978): the popular wicketkeeper died of cancer in 1976, aged only 29.

ENGLAND v NEW ZEALAND
June 21, 22, 23, 25, 26, 1973

ENGLAND

G. Boycott	c Parker b Collinge	61	c and b Howarth		92
D.L. Amiss	c Howarth b Hadlee	9	c and b Howarth		53
G.R.J. Roope	lbw b Howarth	56	c Parker b Taylor		51
K.W.R. Fletcher	c Hastings b Howarth	25	c Taylor b Collinge		178
A.W. Greig	c Howarth b Collinge	63	c Wadsworth b Hadlee		12
* R. Illingworth	c Collinge b Hadlee	3	c Turner b Howarth		22
† A.P.E. Knott	b Hadlee	0	c Congdon b Howarth		0
C.M. Old	b Howarth	7	c Congdon b Pollard		7
J.A. Snow	b Taylor	2	c Hastings b Pollard		0
G.G. Arnold	not out	8	not out		23
N. Gifford	c Wadsworth b Collinge	8	not out		2
Extras	(lb1, w1, nb9)	11	(b8, lb3, nb12)		23
	(106 overs)	253	(9 wkts) (196 overs)		463

Fall:	24,116,148,165,171,175,195,217,237.	112,185,250,274,335,339,352,368,460.

Bowling: Collinge 31-8-69-3, Taylor 19-1-54-1, Hadlee 26-4-70-3, Congdon 5-2-7-0, Howarth 25-6-42-3.

Second innings: Collinge 19-4-41-1, Taylor 34-10-90-1. Howarth 70-24-144-4, Hadlee 25-2-79-1, Congdon 8-3-22-0, Pollard 39-11-61-2, Hastings 1-0-3-0.

NEW ZEALAND

G.M. Turner	c Greig b Arnold	4	Bowling:
J.M. Parker	c Knott b Snow	3	Snow 38-4-109-3,
* B.E. Congdon	c Knott b Old	175	Arnold 41-6-108-1,
B.F. Hastings	lbw b Snow	86	Old 41.5-7-113-5,
H.J. Howarth	hit wkt b Old	17	Roope 6-1-15-0,
M.G. Burgess	b Snow	105	Gifford 39-6-107-0,
V. Pollard	not out	105	Illingworth 39-12-87-0.
† K.J. Wadsworth	c Knott b Old	27	
B.R. Taylor	b Old	11	
D.R. Hadlee	c Fletcher b Old	6	
R.O. Collinge	did not bat		
Extras	(lb5, nb7)	12	
	(9 wkts dec) (204.5 overs)	551	

Fall:	5,10,200,249,330,447,523,535,551.

Toss: New Zealand   Umpires: A.E. Fagg and T.W. Spencer
Close of play: (1) E. 240 for 9 (Arnold 2, Gifford 2)
                         (2) N.Z. 200 for 3 (Congdon 100, Howarth 0)
                         (3) N.Z. 492 for 6 (Pollard 77, Wadsworth 14)
                         (4) E. 224 for 2 (Roope 41, Fletcher 28)

MATCH DRAWN

New Zealand's best chance of success had gone, and England wrapped up the series 2-0 with an innings victory at Headingley, where Boycott scored 115 and Arnold took eight wickets.

1973ii

Before the 1973 series started, West Indies had gone 20 Tests without a victory, but a glance at the tourists' batting order showed that England were in for a tough time: Fredericks, Kanhai, Lloyd, Kallicharran . . . and the great Sobers, making the last of his five Test tours to this country: he was to mark his last appearance at Lord's with one of his finest innings.

West Indies ended their winless streak in the first Test, at The Oval, emerging successful by 158 runs despite Hayes's debut century for England. Boyce took 11 wickets for the visitors. The second Test, a rather bad-tempered affair at Edgbaston, was drawn, Fredericks making 150 in a match best remembered for the clash between the West Indian captain Kanhai and umpire Arthur Fagg, who had turned down a vociferous caught-behind appeal against Boycott.

After losing the toss in his 11th (and last) Lord's Test, Illingworth had the satisfaction of seeing Willis, who bowled with great pace and fire throughout, remove makeshift opener Murray for 4. Further England successes, though, were few and far between on a quick, bouncy pitch that suited the West Indian strokemakers. It was a good day for Guyana: Fredericks contributed a brisk 51, then Kanhai and Lloyd shared a stand of 138 in even time, Kanhai reaching his 15th Test century and becoming the second West Indian to reach 6000 runs at this level. The first to do so, Sobers, was his partner in the later stages of a day that saw 335 runs scored.

The second day had a sedate start. Kanhai added only a single to his overnight score, and Foster struggled before falling for 9. Sobers, meanwhile, was playing himself in carefully: he later revealed that he had not gone to bed the night before! Julien, the new batsman, announced himself with two sizzling boundaries, then was dropped by Fletcher, on the long-leg boundary, off Greig. It was an expensive miss, as the young Trinidadian raced to his maiden first-class century in 2½ hours.

Sobers also reached three figures, to the delight of his many admirers, but when his partnership with Julien had produced 155 runs in only 113 minutes the great man had to leave the field with a stomach upset – no doubt not unconnected with his previous night's escapade. Kanhai instructed the 12th man to administer two brandy-and-ports to the former captain, and he was ready to resume when the next wicket fell. The sight of Sobers entering the arena with 604 for 7 on the board cannot have done much for the morale of the England bowlers, all of whom were to concede more than 100 runs during this innings (Greig, who had been a doubtful starter for this match as he was 1½-stone underweight and generally run-down, took 3 for 180 in 33 overs).

Kanhai called a halt to the slaughter at 652 for 8 when Sobers reached 150, having faced 227 balls in 288 minutes. He hit 19 fours in his 26th and last Test century.

England made a disastrous start in reply, losing three wickets for 29, Boycott contriving to get himself caught at slip playing an awkward hook shot at a rising ball. Amiss and Fletcher saw England to 88 for 3 by the close, but an overwhelming West Indian victory already seemed a certainty.

Amiss departed almost immediately on the third morning, whereupon Fletcher

The last hurrah: watched by Alan Knott, Garry Sobers hits out during his last major Test innings, a majestic unbeaten 150 at Lord's in 1973. West Indies, for whom captain Kanhai and allrounder Julien also made centuries, ran up 652 for 8 and won by an innings

and Greig shared a stand of 79. England's hopes were rocked when Fletcher and Illingworth went to successive balls from Gibbs just before lunch. Both fell to catches at backward short leg by the eagle-eyed Sobers, who went on to take six catches in the match, equalling Colin Cowdrey's record for a fielder in a Lord's Test, set in 1963 (Allan Lamb also equalled the record, in 1983).

Only Knott of the later batsmen delayed West Indies for long, but there was a unique hold-up at 2.42, when it was decided to evacuate the ground after a bomb warning. The stands were cleared, although many spectators ignored appeals to leave the ground and moved onto the playing area, where that diligent umpire 'Dickie' Bird remained to guard the pitch. After 89 minutes, play resumed (arrangements were made to make up some of the lost time later) and England were soon all out for 233. Following on, the openers survived until 20 minutes before the close, at which point three quick strikes from the lively Boyce virtually settled the match. Amiss gave another catch to Sobers and Knott was caught behind, then the last ball of the day saw Boycott, almost unbelievably, hook a bouncer straight to deep square leg, where Kallicharran had been specially posted for that shot. Boycott was jostled by ecstatic West Indian supporters as he left the field, almost in tears.

A dogged innings from Fletcher, who was unlucky to miss another century, was the only barrier to West Indies on the final day. England dipped to 87 for 6, and later still were 146 for 9 before Fletcher and Underwood prolonged matters until nearly three o'clock with a stand of 47.

Speaking afterwards about England's crushing defeat, Illingworth admitted: 'We were outbatted, outbowled and outfielded. There are no excuses.' This was Illingworth's final pronouncement as England captain: he was replaced for the winter tour of West Indies, and never represented his country again.

187

ENGLAND v WEST INDIES
August 23, 24, 25, 27, 1973

WEST INDIES

R.C. Fredericks	c Underwood b Willis	51	Bowling:
† D.L. Murray	b Willis	4	Arnold 35-6-111-0,
* R.B. Kanhai	c Greig b Willis	157	Willis 35-3-118-4,
C.H. Lloyd	c and b Willis	63	Greig 33-2-180-3,
A.I. Kallicharran	c Arnold b Illingworth	14	Underwood 34-6-105-0,
G.S. Sobers	not out	150	Illingworth 31.4-3-114-1.
M.L.C. Foster	c Willis b Greig	9	
B.D. Julien	c and b Greig	121	
K.D. Boyce	c Amiss b Greig	36	
V.A. Holder	not out	23	
L.R. Gibbs	did not bat		
Extras	(b1, lb14, w1, nb8)	24	
	(8 wkts dec) (168.4 overs)	652	

Fall: 8,87,225,256,339,373,604,610.

ENGLAND

G. Boycott	c Kanhai b Holder	4	c Kallicharran b Boyce	15
D.L. Amiss	c Sobers b Holder	35	c Sobers b Boyce	10
B.W. Luckhurst	c Murray b Boyce	1	(4) c Sobers b Julien	12
F.C. Hayes	c Fredericks b Holder	8	(5) c Holder b Boyce	0
K.W.R. Fletcher	c Sobers b Gibbs	68	(6) not out	86
A.W. Greig	c Sobers b Boyce	44	(7) lbw b Julien	13
* R. Illingworth	c Sobers b Gibbs	0	(8) c Kanhai b Gibbs	13
† A.P.E. Knott	c Murray b Boyce	21	(3) c Murray b Boyce	5
G.G. Arnold	c Murray b Boyce	5	c Fredericks b Gibbs	1
R.G.D. Willis	not out	5	c Fredericks b Julien	0
D.L. Underwood	c Gibbs b Holder	12	b Gibbs	14
Extras	(b6, lb4, w3, nb17)	30	(b9, w1, nb14)	24
	(73 overs)	233	(65.3 overs)	193

Fall: 5,7,29,97,176,176,187,205,213.   32,38,42,49,63,87,132,143,146.

Bowling: Holder 15-3-56-4, Boyce 20-7-50-4, Julien 11-4-26-0, Gibbs 18-3-39-2, Sobers 8-0-30-0, Foster 1-0-2-0.

Second innings: Holder 14-4-18-0, Julien 18-2-69-3, Sobers 4-1-7-0, Boyce 16-5-49-4, Gibbs 13.3-3-26-3.

Toss: West Indies   Umpires: H.D. Bird and C.S. Elliott
Close of play: (1) W.I. 335 for 4 (Kanhai 156, Sobers 31)
                 (2) E. 88 for 3 (Amiss 32, Fletcher 30)
                 (3) E. 42 for 3 (Luckhurst 2)
                 Sobers retired ill at 528 for 6, resumed at 604 for 7

WEST INDIES WON BY AN INNINGS AND 226 RUNS

1974i

India had enjoyed unprecedented success at Test level since taking the 1970-71 rubber in West Indies, winning a series in England for the first time in 1971, and repeating the dose at home in 1972-73. In 1974, though, largely the same combination of players was humbled by a resurgent England side which, now captained by the Scot Mike Denness, had halved the winter series in West Indies against all the odds.

The first Test of 1974, at a wintry Old Trafford, saw England emerge victorious by 113 runs, with both Fletcher and Edrich (returning to Test cricket after two years) making centuries. After that match Boycott, who had been dismissed twice for low scores by India's friendly opening bowlers, asked to be rested from the England side: his self-imposed exile was to last more than three years.

Boycott's replacement for what turned out to be a remarkable, record-breaking match was the Lancashire left-hander David Lloyd, and he started his Test career well, sharing an opening stand of 116 after Denness won the toss. Lloyd scored 46 before he fell to a good catch by the diving Solkar at short leg: this turned out to be the only success of a tiring day for an Indian side deprived early on of the services of legspinner Chandrasekhar, who injured his right thumb in trying to stop a drive which Amiss had belted back at him. Amiss went on to reach his century – his seventh in Tests in 15 months – and had taken his score to 187 by the close, having already put on 218 with Edrich, who himself had advanced into the nineties.

India had some early encouragement on the third morning, Edrich adding three and Amiss only one to their overnight scores before both fell lbw to the spinners. Their 226-minute second-wicket stand was worth 221, an England record in Lord's Tests. Fletcher also went cheaply, but then Denness and his vice-captain Greig combined in another big stand, both reaching three figures in adding 202. Denness's century was his first in Tests, Greig's his third in his last seven innings.

After reaching 571 for 4, England's last six wickets went down for just 58, but even so the eventual total of 629 remains England's highest at Lord's. Bedi, whose main spell on the second day stretched from the start to just before tea, finished with six wickets, but the Sikh conceded 226 runs, another Lord's Test record. The spinners carried the attack almost throughout the day – Solkar did not bowl at all, and Abid Ali sent down only eight overs, taking two wickets when he did appear. Sunil Gavaskar was critical of Bedi's approach, suggesting that the left-arm spinner should have pushed the ball through more, rather than continuing to toss it up.

India had an hour to survive before the close, which they did. Engineer, who had kept wicket throughout England's big innings, lived dangerously at first, but survived to the close, scoring comfortably more than half the 51 runs his side made before stumps.

The opening stand swelled to 131 on the third morning before Gavaskar was caught behind for 49, Engineer having refused three sharp singles, any one of which would have given the little man his half-century. From this high point India

Geoff Arnold (left) and Chris Old toast their success in bowling out India for 42, the lowest-ever total in a Lord's Test

went into a terminal decline that saw them lose all 19 wickets for another 213 runs. Engineer went on to 86, and although skipper Wadekar and Patel fell cheaply another useful stand between Viswanath and the tenacious Solkar took the score to 250 for 4. Now the swing bowlers took over, India's last six wickets going down for 52: Old finished with four wickets and Hendrick three.

Following on a daunting 327 behind, India scored two runs in the two overs possible before the close.

Although England were favourites as the teams regrouped after the rest day, no-one was prepared for the speed of India's collapse. In 69 minutes on the fourth morning, nine wickets fell (Chandrasekhar was absent hurt) as the tourists slumped to 42 all out, the lowest-ever total in a Lord's Test. Under grey, threatening skies Arnold found he could move the ball either way, and he soon sent back Engineer (for a duck), Gavaskar, Viswanath and Patel. Ironically, Arnold would not have played in the match had Willis not reported unfit with a back injury.

Old took over, five wickets coming his way as the Indians gave up the ghost. Only Solkar, who remained undefeated with 18, reached double figures, and even his stay at the crease was an eventful one. The left-hander was hit on the head by an Old bouncer, then hooked the next ball for six.

In all, India's miserable second innings, their lowest-ever Test total, lasted a paltry 77 minutes. After the loss of this match and the other two Tests in the series, captain Wadekar correctly assessed the reaction of his countrymen and delayed his return to India, where a statue commemorating the deeds of his earlier successful teams was vandalised. After the tour the Nawab of Pataudi returned as India's captain, and the elegant left-hander Wadekar never appeared in another Test match.

ENGLAND v INDIA
June 20, 21, 22, 24, 1974

ENGLAND

D.L. Amiss	lbw b Prasanna	188	Bowling:
D. Lloyd	c Solkar b Prasanna	46	Abid Ali 22-2-79-2,
J.H. Edrich	lbw b Bedi	96	Solkar 6-2-16-0,
* M.H. Denness	c sub (S. Venkataraghavan) b Bedi	118	Madan Lal 30-6-93-0,
K.W.R. Fletcher	c Solkar b Bedi	15	Bedi 64.2-8-226-6,
A.W. Greig	c and b Abid Ali	106	Chandrasekhar 9.3-1-33-0,
† A.P.E. Knott	c and b Bedi	26	Prasanna 51-6-166-2.
C.M. Old	b Abid Ali	3	
G.G. Arnold	b Bedi	5	
D.L. Underwood	c Solkar b Bedi	9	
M. Hendrick	not out	1	
Extras	(b8, lb4, w2, nb2)	16	
	(182.5 overs)	629	

Fall: 116,337,339,369,571,591,604,611,624.

INDIA

S.M. Gavaskar	c Knott b Old	49	lbw b Arnold	5	
† F.M. Engineer	c Denness b Old	86	lbw b Arnold	0	
* A.L. Wadekar	c Underwood b Hendrick	18	b Old	3	
G.R. Viswanath	b Underwood	52	c Knott b Arnold	5	
B.P. Patel	c Fletcher b Greig	1	c Knott b Arnold	1	
E.D. Solkar	c Underwood b Hendrick	43	not out	18	
S. Abid Ali	c Arnold b Old	14	c Knott b Old	3	
S. Madan Lal	c Knott b Old	0	c Hendrick b Old	2	
E.A.S. Prasanna	c Denness b Hendrick	0	b Old	5	
B.S. Bedi	b Arnold	14	b Old	0	
B.S. Chandrasekhar	not out	2	absent hurt	–	
Extras	(b4, lb7, nb12)	23		0	
	(101.5 overs)	302	(17 overs)	42	

Fall: 131,149,183,188,250,280,281,286,286.   2,5,12,14,25,28,30,42,42.

Bowling: Arnold 24.5-6-81-1, Old 21-6-67-4, Hendrick 18-4-46-3, Greig 21-4-63-1, Underwood 15-10-18-1, Lloyd 2-0-4-0.

Second innings: Hendrick 1-0-2-0, Arnold 8-1-19-4, Old 8-3-21-5.

Toss: England   Umpires: A.E. Fagg and T.W. Spencer
Close of play: (1) E. 334 for 1 (Amiss 187, Edrich 93)
(2) I. 51 for 0 (Gavaskar 17, Engineer 33)
(3) I. 2 for 0 (Gavaskar 2, Engineer 0)

ENGLAND WON BY AN INNINGS AND 285 RUNS

England wrapped up a 3-0 clean sweep with a straightforward innings win at Edgbaston, losing only two wickets in the match. After India were bowled out for 165, England ran up 459 for 2 dec, Lloyd scoring 214 not out in his second Test and Denness making another century. India fared a little better second time around, totalling 216 (Naik 77).

191

1974ii

The 1974 Pakistanis, captained once again by the genial Intikhab Alam and containing many other players with county experience, were expected to extend England to a greater degree than the disappointing Indians had managed, and so it proved. The absorbing first Test, at Headingley, was left drawn when rain washed out the final day's play, which would have seen England trying to score 44 more runs for victory with four wickets in hand.

Unfortunately, rain made most of the headlines during the Lord's Test as well, mainly for the wrong reasons as the Lord's covers proved inadequate to the task of coping with a storm on the Sunday night. Even before this, though, bad weather had affected the course of the match.

Pakistan, after winning the toss, had made a good start, Sadiq and the fluent Majid putting on 51 in an hour before the heavens opened. No play was possible for some five hours, but soon after the resumption Hendrick ended the stand by trapping Sadiq lbw and then Greig removed Majid. Now Underwood, on his favourite type of drying pitch, took over, decimating the middle order and finishing with 5 for 20 from 14 overs. Only Wasim Raja, who made 24, resisted for long, and he too perished to Underwood in the end, albeit in spectacular fashion. The angular left-hander lofted Underwood high out towards the Nursery-end boundary, his hit looking for all the world like a six before the running Greig propelled his 6ft 7½ins frame high into the air in front of the sightscreen to grasp a sensational one-handed catch.

Two late wickets from Greig reduced Pakistan to 130 for 9, at which point Intikhab declared, giving England a potentially tricky 50 minutes' batting before the close, which, in accordance with a recently-introduced special regulation, was delayed until 7.30 (bad weather meant that this regulation was invoked on the first, second and fourth days of this match). A smart close catch by Sadiq accounted for Amiss, but otherwise England were untroubled in reaching 42 by the end.

England were rescued by the tailenders on the second day, after undistinguished efforts from the specialist batsmen saw the score decline to 118 for 6 when Asif Iqbal's throw from cover ran out Greig. Edrich grafted his way to 40 before his Surrey team-mate Intikhab had him caught at short leg, but otherwise Lloyd's 23 was the best effort before the dependable Knott organised the last four wickets so well that 152 runs were produced. Old, who hit out for 41, helped the wicketkeeper add 69, then Knott took the initiative himself in a stand of 44 with Arnold, who made 10. Neatly, England's innings ended right on close of play at 270, a lead of 140.

The crowd for the Saturday of the Lord's Test once again had to put up with indifferent weather, frequent showers interrupting play as Pakistan progressed to 173 for 3. Sadiq took the breaks in his stride to score an accomplished 43, but with Underwood snapping up the wickets of Majid and Zaheer, Pakistan were teetering at 77 for 3 before a responsible innings from Mushtaq and another impressive display from Wasim Raja took them into the black. When rain stopped play for the last time soon after six o'clock, Pakistan were 33 in front with seven wickets standing.

Water seeped under the covers in 1974 to provide Kent left-armer Derek Underwood with his favourite type of rain-affected pitch. Result: Underwood 5 for 20 and 8 for 51 – but rain returned on the final day to wash out a certain victory for England. Here 'Deadly' Underwood deceives Pakistan's captain Intikhab Alam

A storm on the evening of the rest day was the villain of the piece when the teams assembled for the fourth day's play. Water had seeped under the covers, affecting the pitch, evoking a plaintive, if predictable response from the tourists' manager Omar Kureishi, who accused MCC of 'an appalling show of negligence and incompetence in not covering the wicket adequately'. It was a thorny problem for Jack Bailey, in his first year as MCC secretary, but he penned a reasoned reply to Pakistan's allegations.

It was an eventful day off the field too: in the pavilion, England bowler Hendrick and physiotherapist 'Nick' Nicholas were slightly injured when part of the ceiling in the treatment-room collapsed.

Extensive mopping-up operations allowed play to resume at 5.15, whereupon the overnight pair took their stand to 115. After half an hour, though, Underwood struck, as Raja was smartly held at short leg after 3¾ hours of resistance. Soon afterwards Mushtaq fell to Greig, his 4¼-hour innings of 76 having contained nine fours. The other batsmen were easy prey for 'Deadly' Underwood, the innings folding for 226 after Mushtaq and Raja had taken the score to 192 for 3. Underwood, operating from the Nursery end, was virtually unplayable, his last six wickets costing him just two runs in a 51-ball spell. Overall he finished with Test-best figures of 8 for 51, the best analysis in a Lord's Test since Verity's 8 for 43 in 1934.

England's target was a lowly 87, and they had scored 27 of these by the 7.30 close. It seemed that the home side would complete a leisurely, if controversial, victory early on the final day, but it was not to be: for the second Test running rain washed out any possibility of play on the final day, allowing Pakistan to escape with a draw. Most observers agreed that justice had been done, the tourists having been unlucky enough to be caught twice on a drying pitch. The abandonment also spared England the embarrassment of a win which would have owed much to the unfortunate shortcomings of the Lord's covers.

193

ENGLAND v PAKISTAN
August 8, 9, 10, 12, 13 (no play), 1974

PAKISTAN

Sadiq Mohammad	lbw b Hendrick	40	lbw b Arnold	43
Majid Jahangir Khan	c Old b Greig	48	lbw b Underwood	19
Zaheer Abbas	c Hendrick b Underwood	1	c Greig b Underwood	1
Mushtaq Mohammad	c Greig b Underwood	0	c Denness b Greig	76
Wasim Raja	c Greig b Underwood	24	c Lloyd b Underwood	53
Asif Iqbal	c Amiss b Underwood	2	c Greig b Underwood	0
* Intikhab Alam	b Underwood	5	(8) b Underwood	0
Imran Khan	c Hendrick b Greig	4	(7) c Lloyd b Underwood	0
† Wasim Bari	lbw b Greig	4	(10) lbw b Underwood	1
Sarfraz Nawaz	not out	0	(9) c Lloyd b Underwood	1
Asif Masood	did not bat		not out	17
Extras	(nb2)	2	(lb8, nb7)	15
	(9 wkts dec) (44.5 overs)	130	(97.5 overs)	226

Fall: 71,91,91,91,103,111,116,130,130.   55,61,77,192,192,200,200,206,208.

Bowling: Arnold 8-1-32-0, Old 5-0-17-0, Hendrick 9-2-36-1, Underwood 14-8-20-5, Greig 8.5-4-23-3.

Second innings: Arnold 15-3-37-1, Old 14-1-39-0, Hendrick 15-4-29-0, Underwood 34.5-17-51-8, Greig 19-6-55-1.

ENGLAND

D.L. Amiss	c Sadiq b Asif Masood	2	not out	14
D. Lloyd	c Zaheer b Sarfraz	23	not out	12
J.H. Edrich	c Sadiq b Intikhab	40		
* M.H. Denness	b Imran	20		
K.W.R. Fletcher	lbw b Imran	8		
A.W. Greig	run out	9		
† A.P.E. Knott	c Wasim Bari b Asif Masood	83		
C.M. Old	c Wasim Bari b Mushtaq	41		
G.G. Arnold	c Wasim Bari b Asif Masood	10		
D.L. Underwood	not out	12		
M. Hendrick	c Imran b Intikhab	6		
Extras	(lb14, w1, nb1)	16	(nb1)	1
	(105 overs)	270	(0 wkt) (10 overs)	27

Fall: 2,52,90,94,100,118,187,231,254.

Bowling: Asif Masood 25-10-47-3, Sarfraz 22-8-42-1, Intikhab 26-4-80-2, Wasim Raja 2-0-8-0, Mushtaq 7-3-16-1, Imran 18-2-48-2, Asif Iqbal 5-0-13-0.

Second innings: Sarfraz 3-0-7-0, Majid 2-0-10-0, Asif Masood 4-0-9-0, Intikhab 1-1-0-0.

Toss: Pakistan   Umpires: D.J. Constant and C.S. Elliott
Close of play: (1) E. 42 for 1 (Lloyd 18, Edrich 22)
                 (2) E. 270 all out
                 (3) P. 173 for 3 (Mushtaq 55, Wasim Raja 44)
                 (4) E. 27 for 0 (Amiss 14, Lloyd 12)

MATCH DRAWN

A high-scoring third Test saw the series shared, the Pakistanis going through the entire tour undefeated, a rare feat. At The Oval Zaheer scored 240 as Pakistan ran up 600 for 7: England replied with 545, Amiss making 183 and Fletcher 122, his 458-minute century being the slowest ever recorded in England.

1975

For the first time since the halcyon days of the Varsity or Gentlemen v Players matches, the Test in 1975 arguably was not the highlight of the Lord's season. On the Saturday which usually staged the Lord's Test – June 21 – West Indies met Australia in the first-ever one-day World Cup final, a pulsating affair in which the favourites scraped home by 17 runs despite a late rally from the Australians.

Almost inevitably, the four-Test series that followed the World Cup was rather a low-key affair, even though (or perhaps because) England's opposition was Ian Chappell's Australians who, with Lillee and Thomson to the fore, had steamrollered Denness's tourists the previous winter.

Australia took the first Test, at Edgbaston, Denness's gamble to field first costing him both the match and the captaincy. Lillee, Walker and Thomson shared all but one of the wickets as England stumbled to 101 and 173, the luckless Graham Gooch collecting a 'pair' on his debut.

England's new captain at Lord's was the charismatic South African-born allrounder Tony Greig, whose side included two new caps in Kent allrounder Woolmer and Northants batsman David Steele, who was to become something of a folk hero over the summer. Greig won the toss, and looked on in dismay as Lillee ripped out four quick wickets as England slid to 49 for 4. Greig strode to the crease to join the grey-haired Steele, whose Test baptism was briefly delayed when he went down one flight of stairs too many in the pavilion and found himself in the lavatories. He quickly made his way to the middle, where Thomson jokingly mistook him for Father Christmas (Steele, however, recalls that he was described as 'Groucho Marx'). It was one bright moment in a disappointing day for Thomson, who struggled for rhythm and delivered 22 no-balls and a wide that sped to the boundary.

Steele, plunging resolutely forward, took two quick fours off Lillee, and shared an important stand of 96 with Greig before dragging a ball from Thomson onto his stumps. In all, he hit nine fours in his 163-minute half-century. Greig continued the rescue act, falling an agonising four runs short of a century in his first match as captain when, after 160 minutes, he edged Walker to first slip, having hit 15 fours. Kent colleagues Knott and Woolmer shared another useful partnership before the wicketkeeper, on 69, was lbw to a well-pitched-up ball from Thomson. By the close England had advanced to 313 for 9: Walker wrapped up the innings next morning with just two runs added.

Like England, Australia made a hesitant start, in the face of a fine spell from Snow. The 33-year-old Sussex paceman, the scourge of Australia in 1970-71, trapped Turner and Greg Chappell lbw and also had Ian Chappell caught behind. Lever hung on to a fine return catch to dispose of McCosker, and with Walters, Marsh and Walker all failing to reach double figures Australia were facing humiliation at 81 for 7. Edwards, though, had other ideas, and he averted the follow-on in a stand of 52 with Thomson, then put on 66 more with Lillee before, with his score at 99 and the total 199, he played across the line at Woolmer and was lbw, giving the Kent man his first Test wicket. Edwards, who batted for 201 minutes and hit 15 fours, was the fourth and last batsman to be dismissed for 99 in a Lord's Test, Macartney (1912), Paynter (1938) and Mike Smith (1960) being the others.

195

David Steele, an unlikely hero who had difficulty in finding his way out of the pavilion to start his maiden Test innings, exhibits the style that made him something of a national hero during the summer of 1975. Wicketkeeper Rod Marsh looks on

Even now the Australian resistance was not over, as Lillee hit out to reach 73 not out, his highest score. He clubbed three sixes and eight fours, adding 69 for the last wicket with Mallett to take his side to within 47 of England's total. Steele ended the fun with the wicket of Mallett with his fourth ball in Tests. One over from Lillee that night saw Wood increase the lead by five.

A patient innings from Edrich, the last of his 12 Test centuries and his third at Lord's, was the feature of Day 3, on which England accumulated 225 runs in 95 overs for the loss of only two wickets. Wood made 52 before Thomson had him caught behind, and Steele played another staunch innings, reaching 45 before stabbing a full-toss back to the bowler Walters, who had been given the new ball in an inspirational move by Ian Chappell.

Making the most of an easy-paced pitch, whose occasional unpredictable bounce was its only vice, Edrich moved to 175 on the fourth day, the highest of his seven centuries against Australia. In all he batted for 538 minutes: he hit 21 fours. Lillee, usually operating off his shortened run, bowled unchanged before lunch, and sent down 33 overs in all. Not long before Greig's declaration, which left Australia to score 484 in 500 minutes, the crowd was enlivened by another Lord's 'first', when 24-year-old ship's cook Michael Angelow shed his clothes and ran naked across the pitch, hurdling the stumps. The first streaker (or 'freaker' as John Arlott memorably described him on the radio) made his dash for a £20 bet: he was later fined the same amount in court.

Another Australian collapse on the fourth evening would have helped England's cause, but Turner's was the only wicket to fall as the tourists reached 97 by stumps. The changeable weather was a possible England ally: if rain provided Underwood with another helpful pitch, Australia might have struggled on the last day, but in the event the rain came too early, with the pitch fully covered before the start of play (rain after play had started would have left most of the strip open to the elements).

Play started an hour late on the final day, and Australia had little difficulty in surviving and scoring reasonably quickly against Greig's close-set fields. McCosker lasted 262 minutes for his 79, hitting eight fours, while Ian Chappell struck 13 boundaries in his 86. Towards the end, with a draw inevitable, Greg Chappell, who hit the first ball he received (from Steele) for six, played his only substantial innings of the Test series, sharing an unbeaten century partnership with Edwards.

ENGLAND v AUSTRALIA
July 31, August 1, 2, 4, 5, 1975

ENGLAND

B. Wood	lbw b Lillee	6	c Marsh b Thomson	52
J.H. Edrich	lbw b Lillee	9	c Thomson b Mallett	175
D.S. Steele	b Thomson	50	c and b Walters	45
D.L. Amiss	lbw b Lillee	0	c G.S. Chappell b Lillee	10
G.A. Gooch	c Marsh b Lillee	6	b Mallett	31
* A.W. Greig	c I.M. Chappell b Walker	96	c Walters b I.M. Chappell	41
† A.P.E. Knott	lbw b Thomson	69	not out	22
R.A. Woolmer	c Turner b Mallett	33	b Mallett	31
J.A. Snow	c Walker b Mallett	11		
D.L. Underwood	not out	0		
P. Lever	lbw b Walker	4		
Extras	(b3, lb1, w4, nb23)	31	(lb18, w2, nb9)	29
	(87.4 overs)	315	(7 wkts dec) (147.4 overs)	436

Fall: 10,29,31,49,145,222,288,309,310. 111,215,249,315,380,387,436.

Bowling: Lillee 20-4-84-4, Thomson 24-7-92-2, Walker 21.4-7-52-2, Mallett 22-4-56-2.

Second innings: Lillee 33-10-80-1, Walker 37-8-95-0, Thomson 29-8-73-1, Mallett 36.4-10-127-3, I.M. Chappell 10-2-26-1, Walters 2-0-6-1.

AUSTRALIA

R.B. McCosker	c and b Lever	29	lbw b Steele	79
A. Turner	lbw b Snow	9	c Gooch b Greig	21
* I.M. Chappell	c Knott b Snow	2	lbw b Greig	86
G.S. Chappell	lbw b Snow	4	not out	73
R. Edwards	lbw b Woolmer	99	not out	52
K.D. Walters	c Greig b Lever	2		
† R.W. Marsh	c Amiss b Greig	3		
M.H.N. Walker	b Snow	5		
J.R. Thomson	b Underwood	17		
D.K. Lillee	not out	73		
A.A. Mallett	lbw b Steele	14		
Extras	(lb5, nb6)	11	(b4, nb14)	18
	(77.4 overs)	268	(3 wkts) (109 overs)	329

Fall: 21,29,37,54,56,64,81,133,199. 50,169,222.

Bowling: Snow 21-4-66-4, Lever 15-0-83-2, Woolmer 13-5-31-1, Greig 15-5-47-1, Underwood 13-5-29-1, Steele 0.4-0-1-1.

Second innings: Snow 19-3-82-0, Lever 20-5-55-0, Greig 26-6-82-2, Underwood 31-14-64-0, Woolmer 3-1-3-0, Steele 9-4-19-1, Wood 1-0-6-0.

Toss: England Umpires: W.E. Alley and T.W. Spencer

Close of play: (1) E. 313 for 9 (Underwood 0, Lever 2)
(2) E. 5 for 0 (Wood 5, Edrich 0)
(3) E. 230 for 2 (Edrich 104, Amiss 6)
(4) A. 97 for 1 (McCosker 46, I.M. Chappell 25)

MATCH DRAWN

The final two Tests were also drawn, giving Australia the series 1-0. The Headingley Test was evenly poised when the last day's play was abandoned after vandals spoiled the pitch, while at The Oval six days were not enough to ensure a result. Australia made 532 for 9, Ian Chappell scoring 192 and McCosker (who had been denied a century at Headingley by the vandals) 127. England made only 191 first time around but did better in the follow-on, Woolmer scoring a painstaking 149.

1976

Ironically, in the middle of one of the hottest, driest summers on record, rain – the scourge of so many Lord's Tests in the 1970s – returned to wash out the whole of the third day of a match in which England held a slight advantage. Despite the interruption the match came tantalisingly close to providing an exciting finish.

The teams arrived at Lord's all square, although West Indies had the better of the first Test, at Trent Bridge, where Viv Richards scored a splendid 232. Richards, though, fell ill and missed the Lord's Test, where Clive Lloyd, in the first of his three tours to England as captain, continued his recently-conceived plan of playing four fast bowlers – in this case Roberts, Holding, Julien and Holder.

Greig, who had raised West Indian hackles before the tour with his remarks about making the visitors 'grovel', won the toss but saw Roberts strike two early blows by dismissing Wood and Steele. The Middlesex captain Brearley, in his first Lord's Test, combined with the 45-year-old Close in lifting the score to 115, at which point Brearley fell for 40, again to Roberts. Close, however, went on to a brave 60, striking six fours in 205 minutes before he hit a full-toss from left-arm spinner Jumadeen to a diving Holder at extra cover. The remainder of the English batting was undistinguished, Woolmer's 38 being the best effort as the score drifted to 197 for 8 by the close, with the impressive Roberts taking five wickets.

A stirring partnership of 52 between Old·and Underwood enlivened the second morning, the fun ending when Holder plucked out Old's off stump. Chasing 250, West Indies had an immediate setback when Old had Fredericks well caught for a duck, then catcher Snow returned to the bowling crease to dispose of Gomes and Kallicharran in an impressive spell.

Greenidge and Lloyd now hit out, the opener's half-century including 10 fours and a six, but Underwood eventually removed both, Greenidge going to another good catch by Snow at deep mid-on. The Barbadian had hooked both Snow and Old for six in his 84, which also included 14 fours. Lloyd was caught behind for 50, and three more wickets from Underwood, giving him 5 for 39 in all, ended the innings at 182, giving England a surprise lead of 68. The last seven wickets went down for 43 in 69 minutes, and at the end of the day a delighted crowd sang *Rule Britannia* and *God Save the Queen*!

England had a late setback on an otherwise excellent day when Wood (10) was forced to retire hurt after twice being hit on the hand by Roberts. Brearley and nightwatchman Pocock survived to stumps, by which time the lead had grown to 95.

If the second day had been a delight for England followers, the third day was a terrible anticlimax. Light drizzle started minutes after the gates had been closed on a capacity crowd, and rain fell ever harder throughout the day, leading to play being abandoned at five o'clock.

The fourth day saw England consolidate their position with, perhaps, too much caution. Only 196 runs came in the full day's play: top-scorer Steele grafted for 266 minutes for his 64 (seven boundaries) before mishooking to square leg. Close played another defiant innings, hitting four fours and a six off Jumadeen in his 46 before, for the second time in the match, he perished to good fielding from

All England's fielders crowd round the bat as optimistic skipper Tony Greig pushes for an unlikely victory on the last afternoon of the 1976 Lord's Test. The fieldsmen hemming in batsman Deryck Murray are (l-r) Old, Willis, Steele, wicketkeeper Knott, Brearley, Barlow (sub), Greig, Close, Woolmer and Radley (another sub)

Holder, who this time held on acrobatically to a high return catch.

Already 291 in front, England extended the lead on the final morning, with Wood (who had returned at the fall of the sixth wicket) making 30. Roberts ended the innings by bowling Underwood: it was his 10th wicket of the match, a fitting reward for a sustained display of high-class fast bowling.

Facing a target of 323 in 294 minutes, West Indies made a slow start and were never really on terms. After Greenidge went for 22, Kallicharran batted 2½ hours for 34, and although no further wickets fell the tourists' progress was still leisurely. When the last 20 overs were signalled, West Indies needed a further 154. The two Guyanese left-handers, Fredericks and Lloyd, mounted an attack, but it was too late. Fredericks eventually perished at ten-to-six for 138, having hit 14 fours and a six off Greig in his 282-minute innings: he had become the fifth (and last) player to score a century and a duck in the same Lord's Test, the others being Harry Trott (1896), Sid Barnes (1948), Peter May (1955) and Charlie Davis (1969). The innings rounded off a splendid Lord's Test career for Fredericks, whose five innings at the ground produced scores of 63, 60, 51, 0 and 138.

Scenting victory, Lloyd claimed the last half-hour, but when he was out he signalled that he wanted to call off the match: Greig, however, had other ideas, and crowded the batsmen. England grabbed two more wickets, but there was never much chance of a total collapse, and the England captain accepted the inevitable draw with three balls left and four wickets still to fall.

199

ENGLAND v WEST INDIES
June 17, 18, 19 (no play), 21, 22, 1976

ENGLAND

B. Wood	c Murray b Roberts	6	c Murray b Holding	30
J.M. Brearley	b Roberts	40	b Holding	13
D.S. Steele	lbw b Roberts	7	(4) c Jumadeen b Roberts	64
D.B. Close	c Holder b Jumadeen	60	(5) c and b Holder	46
R.A. Woolmer	c Murray b Holding	38	(6) c Murray b Roberts	29
* A.W. Greig	c Lloyd b Roberts	6	(7) c Gomes b Holder	20
† A.P.E. Knott	b Holder	17	(8) lbw b Roberts	4
C.M. Old	b Holder	19	(9) run out	13
J.A. Snow	b Roberts	0	(10) not out	6
D.L. Underwood	b Holder	31	(11) b Roberts	2
P.I. Pocock	not out	0	(3) c Jumadeen b Roberts	3
Extras	(b7, lb5, w5, nb9)	26	(b7, lb7, nb10)	24
	(95.4 overs)	250	(104.5 overs)	254

Fall: 15,31,115,153,161,188,196,197,249. 29,29,112,169,186,207,215,245,249.

Bowling: Roberts 23-6-60-5, Holding 19-4-52-1, Julien 23-6-54-0, Holder 18.4-7-35-3, Jumadeen 12-4-23-1.
Second innings: Roberts 29.5-10-63-5, Holding 27-10-56-2, Julien 13-5-20-0, Jumadeen 16-4-41-0, Holder 19-2-50-2.

WEST INDIES

R.C. Fredericks	c Snow b Old	0	c Greig b Old	138
C.G. Greenidge	c Snow b Underwood	84	c Close b Pocock	22
H.A. Gomes	c Woolmer b Snow	11	(7) b Underwood	0
A.I. Kallicharran	c Old b Snow	0	(3) b Greig	34
* C.H. Lloyd	c Knott b Underwood	50	(4) b Greig	33
† D.L. Murray	b Snow	2	not out	7
B.D. Julien	lbw b Snow	3	(5) b Underwood	1
M.A. Holding	b Underwood	0		
V.A. Holder	c Woolmer b Underwood	12	(8) not out	0
A.M.E. Roberts	b Underwood	16		
R.R. Jumadeen	not out	0		
Extras	(b2, nb2)	4	(b3, lb2, nb1)	6
	(50.4 overs)	182	(6 wkts) (86.3 overs)	241

Fall: 0,28,40,139,141,145,146,153,178. 41,154,230,233,238,238.

Bowling: Old 10-0-58-1, Snow 19-3-68-4, Underwood 18.4-7-39-5, Pocock 3-0-13-0.
Second innings: Old 14-4-46-1, Snow 7-2-22-0, Underwood 24.3-8-73-2, Pocock 27-9-52-1, Greig 14-3-42-2.

Toss: England   Umpires: H.D. Bird and D.J. Constant
Close of play: (1) E. 197 for 8 (Old 0)
(2) E. 27 for 0 (Brearley 12, Pocock 2)
(4) E. 223 for 7 (Wood 14, Old 7)
Wood retired hurt at 19 for 0, resumed at 207 for 6

MATCH DRAWN

West Indies' superiority told with victories in the remaining three Tests. Greenidge hit twin centuries and Richards another at Old Trafford, where England collapsed embarrassingly for 71 and 126, extras (44) being the chief contributor to the combined totals. At Headingley, Fredericks and Greenidge reached three figures again, and scores of 116 from Greig and Knott were not enough to save England. At The Oval, even 203 from Amiss was insufficient after Richards's brilliant 291 dominated the tourists' huge total of 687 for 8.

1977

The 1977 season was a turbulent one for cricket in general and Lord's in particular. The announcement of Australian TV magnate Kerry Packer's ambitious plans for 'Super Tests' had stunned the authorities, and can have done little for the morale of Greg Chappell's touring party, some of whom were not privy to the secret. Chappell, who had assumed the captaincy from his brother Ian after the 1975 tour, faced a new opponent in Brearley, who had been appointed after Greig (Packer's chief recruitment officer) was sacked as captain for his part in the machinations.

All these complications lay in the future when it was decided, against normal practice, to make the 1977 Lord's Test the first of the five-match series. It was designated the 'Jubilee Test', to mark the Queen's 25 years on the throne: however, the Monarch was not able to mark the occasion with her usual visit to the ground.

Brearley won the toss, but England made a poor start, the openers finding Thomson's speed too much for them. The tearaway fast bowler had not had much success on the tour before this match, and fears had been growing that his terrible shoulder injury the previous winter (he collided with a fieldsman while attempting a catch at Adelaide) might curtail his career. Thomson's pace proved too much, though, for Amiss, who is recorded as having been bowled for 4, although Brearley, the non-striker at the time, says that the batsman chopped the top of his stumps with his bat, and should have been given out 'hit wicket'. Brearley himself did not last much longer, giving a chance to short leg, where Robinson – one of three Australian debutants, the others being Serjeant and Pascoe – held on to a sharp catch.

With Walker bowling well and Thomson and Pascoe working up impressive pace, England's third-wicket pair did well to weather the storm. Woolmer batted calmly, while Randall, the hero of the Centenary Test in Melbourne three months previously, played a typically impish innings of 53, which included four fours and an all-run five, which eventuated when Walker, labouring after an on-drive, overshot the ball into the crowd and had to disentangle himself.

After Randall was well caught by Chappell at slip off an attempted cut, Woolmer was left high and dry as five men came and went without reaching double figures. The Kent man had reached 79 in 269 minutes (seven fours) when he attempted a quick single to cover and was beaten by Walters's direct hit. A brief last-wicket flurry was ended by Thomson, whose timing was much appreciated by his opening batsmen: with only eight minutes remaining, there was no time for the Australian reply to England's 216 to start that night.

Rain, that frequent Lord's Test visitor, returned to haunt the second day. After a delayed start, only 102 minutes' play was possible. Robinson, the team's reserve wicketkeeper who had been pressed into service as an opener, fell to Lever for 11, but McCosker and Chappell hung on until a brisk bouncer from Willis to McCosker persuaded the umpires – perhaps mindful of the broken jaw inflicted by an identical ball at the Centenary Test – that the light was too bad for play to continue. A brief resumption later saw Australia take their score to 51 for 1 before the final interruption.

Craig Serjeant, who started his surprisingly brief Test career with a sterling innings of 81 for Australia in the 1977 Jubilee Test

England made a bright start on the third day, McCosker falling to the seventh ball without addition, but a partnership of 84 between Chappell and the debutant Serjeant steadied matters, then a century stand between Serjeant and Walters – dropped early on by Brearley at slip – took Australia into the lead. Chappell, reprieved at 13 when Underwood missed a testing return catch, batted watchfully for his 66 and, as in his 1972 Lord's Test century, did not manage the first of his four boundaries until he had batted for more than three hours.

Serjeant made a jittery start, remaining scoreless for 39 minutes and once being trapped plumb in front of his stumps by an Old no-ball, but he went on to an impressive 255-minute innings of 81, which included 10 fours. Like Chappell, he finally fell to Willis, whose final figures of 7 for 78 bore testimony to the excellence of his bowling.

After Walters had gone for a bright 53 – the highest score of his four Lord's Tests – the tourists rather lost their way, both Hookes and Marsh falling before the close, and on the fourth morning three more wickets from Willis brought the innings to an end at 296, giving Australia a lead of 80.

England made the worst of starts, Amiss falling to Thomson fourth ball for a duck, but Brearley and Woolmer repaired the damage with a stand of 132. An irate Pascoe, unimpressed with Ted Dexter's newspaper allegations that he was a thrower, worked up a fair pace, and both batsmen had some luck early on: Brearley survived a confident caught-behind appeal and a hard chance to Robinson at short leg, while Woolmer (20) saw Serjeant in the gully put down a stinging chance off Walker. Brearley was eventually caught by Robinson for 49, but the Kent man went serenely on, reaching three figures in 217 minutes, and he was still there at the close, which found England 109 in front.

Woolmer departed early on the final morning, having batted for a minute over five hours, hitting 13 boundaries. It was left to Greig, whose place in the side was by no means secure, to hit a defiant 91, with 11 rasping fours. The former captain had also fallen just short of a century against Australia at Lord's in 1975.

Any thoughts Brearley may have been harbouring about a declaration were rudely interrupted when four wickets tumbled with the score at 286, and when the innings ended at 305 – the last six wickets went down for 19 in 40 minutes – the target of 226 in 165 minutes was certainly attainable. Australia, however, slumped to 5 for 2, with Robinson becoming Old's 100th Test wicket, and when Chappell and Walters went cheaply an England victory suddenly seemed a possibility, with five wickets wanted in 21 overs. A steady 50 from Hookes, however, spared Australia's blushes, and bad light brought proceedings to an end five overs early.

ENGLAND v AUSTRALIA
June 16, 17, 18, 20, 21, 1977

ENGLAND

D.L. Amiss	b Thomson	4	b Thomson		0
* J.M. Brearley	c Robinson b Thomson	9	c Robinson b O'Keeffe		49
R.A. Woolmer	run out	79	c Chappell b Pascoe		120
D.W. Randall	c Chappell b Walker	53	(7) c McCosker b Thomson		0
A.W. Greig	b Pascoe	5	(4) c O'Keeffe b Pascoe		91
G.D. Barlow	c McCosker b Walker	1	(5) lbw b Pascoe		5
† A.P.E. Knott	c Walters b Thomson	8	(6) c Walters b Walker		8
C.M. Old	c Marsh b Walker	9	c Walters b Walker		0
J.K. Lever	b Pascoe	8	c Marsh b Thomson		3
D.L. Underwood	not out	11	not out		12
R.G.D. Willis	b Thomson	17	c Marsh b Thomson		0
Extras	(b1, lb3, w1, nb7)	12	(b5, lb9, w1, nb2)		17
	(86.5 overs)	216	(112.4 overs)		305

Fall: 12,13,111,121,134,155,171,183,189. 0,132,224,263,286,286,286,286,305.

Bowling: Thomson 20.5-5-41-4, Pascoe 23-7-53-2, Walker 30-6-66-3,
O'Keeffe 10-3-32-0, Chappell 3-0-12-0.
Second innings: Thomson 24.4-3-86-4, Pascoe 26-2-96-3, Walker 35-13-56-2,
Chappell 12-2-24-0, O'Keeffe 15-7-26-1.

AUSTRALIA

R.D. Robinson	b Lever	11	c Woolmer b Old		4
R.B. McCosker	b Old	23	b Willis		1
* G.S. Chappell	c Old b Willis	66	c Lever b Old		24
C.S. Serjeant	c Knott b Willis	81	(6) c Amiss b Underwood		3
K.D. Walters	c Brearley b Willis	53	c sub (A.G.E. Ealham) b Underwood	10
D.W. Hookes	c Brearley b Old	11	(4) c and b Willis		50
† R.W. Marsh	lbw b Willis	1	not out		6
K.J. O'Keeffe	c sub (A.G.E. Ealham) b Willis	12	not out		8
M.H.N. Walker	c Knott b Willis	4			
J.R. Thomson	b Willis	6			
L.S. Pascoe	not out	3			
Extras	(lb7, w1, nb17)	25	(nb8)		8
	(114.1 overs)	296	(6 wkts) (39 overs)		114

Fall: 25,51,135,238,256,264,265,284,290. 5,5,48,64,71,102.

Bowling: Willis 30.1-7-78-7, Lever 19-5-61-1, Underwood 25-6-42-0, Old 35-10-70-2,
Woolmer 5-1-20-0.
Second innings: Willis 10-1-40-2, Old 14-0-46-2, Underwood 10-3-16-2, Lever 5-2-4-0.

Toss: England Umpires: H.D. Bird and W.L. Budd
Close of play: (1) E. 216 all out
(2) A. 51 for 1 (McCosker 23, Chappell 11)
(3) A. 278 for 7 (O'Keeffe 8, Walker 1)
(4) E. 189 for 2 (Woolmer 114, Greig 18)

MATCH DRAWN

*England clinched the series – and regained the Ashes – with victories in the next
three Tests. At Old Trafford, Woolmer made another century, and Amiss hit the
winning runs in what turned out to be his final Test innings; Trent Bridge saw
Boycott mark his return to Test cricket with 107, while Knott scored 135. Botham,
on his debut, took five wickets, a feat he repeated at Headingley, where Boycott's
191 – his 100th hundred – set up a win by an innings. The final Test at The Oval
was drawn after rain intervened.*

1978i

After the first season of Kerry Packer's disapproved World Series Cricket in Australia, Pakistan were obliged to send a weakened team to England in 1978. Lacking five senior players who had been banned for their involvement with Packer – Mushtaq, Majid, Zaheer, Asif and Imran – the young side under veteran wicketkeeper Wasim Bari's captaincy always looked likely to struggle. England too had lost players to Packer, but the performances of Gower, Taylor and, most particularly, Botham meant that the defections of Underwood, Knott and Greig were barely noticed. Botham, indeed, turned in a recordbreaking performance in this, his first Test at the ground where he had spent two seasons as a young member of the MCC cricket staff before joining Somerset.

With Brearley back in charge after breaking an arm on the winter tour of Pakistan (where the series had been drawn 0-0), England won the first Test, at Edgbaston, by an innings with more than a day to spare. Radley and Botham scored centuries, while Old took four wickets in five deliveries on the way to Test-best figures of 7 for 50.

At Lord's England, still without the injured Boycott, recalled Gooch for his first Test since Lord's 1975. Persistent rain, however, led to the first day being abandoned: the teams were presented to the Queen in the Long Room during the scheduled tea interval.

A start was made, albeit 45 minutes late, on the Friday, when the left-arm medium-pacer Liaquat had two early strikes to send back the Middlesex pair of Brearley and Radley. Gooch and Gower, two of England's brightest prospects, combined in an entertaining stand of 101 in 97 minutes. Gooch, cutting and driving well, made 54 before falling to Raja's legspin, and Gower also passed a half-century in his first Lord's Test before swiping at left-arm spinner Qasim.

Miller failed to score, but Roope and Botham now shared another century partnership, Roope once despatching a Raja long-hop for six on his way to his third half-century in three Test innings at Lord's (he never played there again, and his record is unique). Botham was his usual attacking self: his second scoring shot was a six into the Mound Stand off Qasim, and he also hit 11 fours as he hurried to his century from only 104 balls.

Botham, 102 overnight, hit one more boundary on Saturday morning before playing on, but Edmonds hit out well, once driving Sikander into the pavilion for six during an entertaining last-wicket stand of 40 with Willis.

Encouraged by his batting, Willis tore into the Pakistanis with vigour, soon removing both openers. Mohsin and Wasim Raja batted sensibly in taking the score from a precarious 41 for 4 to 84, but then the innings crumbled for 105, four wickets going down in the nineties: the hostile Willis finished with 5 for 47. Left-arm spinner Edmonds conceded just two scoring shots in his eight-over spell, which brought him the startling figures of 4 for 6.

Following on, Sadiq and Mudassar again went cheaply, but the stylish Mohsin, now in concert with Talaat, impressed again as the tourists moved to 96 without further loss by stumps.

A phenomenal spell from Botham brought the match to a sudden end on the fourth morning. The overnight pair raised three figures, but from that high point

Pakistan's Haroon Rashid is beaten and bowled by an unplayable delivery from
Ian Botham, whose second-innings figures of 8 for 34 in 1978 are the best-ever in a
Lord's Test. Earlier Botham had scored a brisk 108

the last eight wickets tumbled for 39, with only Miandad – last out for 22 in 80
minutes – resisting for long. The next-best score on the fateful fourth day was
Haroon's 4, and he was undone by an unplayable ball from Botham that shattered
his stumps. Botham later rated this as one of his best two balls to claim a Test
wicket (the other was 'wasted' on Jeff Thomson).

On a cloudless day, Botham – who came on to bowl only because Willis
wanted to change ends – swung the ball remarkably, his early difficulty in
controlling the swing being instanced by a wild delivery that eluded Taylor and
went for four wides. The ball in use was a replacement, the original having gone
out of shape late on the third evening. Botham's fourth-day spell brought him 7
for 14, and his overall figures of 8 for 34 are the best-ever in a Lord's Test,
surpassing Verity's 8 for 43 in 1934. Botham remains the only player to score a
century and take eight wickets in an innings in the same Test.

Botham's astonishing spell brought the match to an end a few minutes before
lunch, the actual playing time in the game amounting to 12 hours 42 minutes.

ENGLAND v PAKISTAN
June 15 (no play), 16, 17, 19, 1978

ENGLAND

* J.M. Brearley	lbw b Liaquat	2
G.A. Gooch	lbw b Wasim Raja	54
C.T. Radley	c Mohsin b Liaquat	8
D.I. Gower	b Qasim	56
G.R.J. Roope	c Mohsin b Qasim	69
G. Miller	c Miandad b Qasim	0
I.T. Botham	b Liaquat	108
† R.W. Taylor	c Mudassar b Sikander	10
C.M. Old	c Mohsin b Sikander	0
P.H. Edmonds	not out	36
R.G.D. Willis	b Mudassar	18
Extras	(lb2, nb1)	3
	(91.2 overs)	364

Fall: 5,19,120,120,134,252,290,290,324.

Bowling:
Sikander 27-3-115-2, Liaquat 18-1-80-3, Mudassar 4.2-0-16-1, Qasim 30-5-101-3, Wasim Raja 12-3-49-1.

PAKISTAN

Mudassar Nazar	c Edmonds b Willis	1	c Taylor b Botham	10
Sadiq Mohammad	c Botham b Willis	11	c Taylor b Willis	0
Mohsin Khan	c Willis b Edmonds	31	c Roope b Willis	46
Haroon Rashid	b Old	15	(5) b Botham	4
Javed Miandad	c Taylor b Willis	0	(6) c Gooch b Botham	22
Wasim Raja	b Edmonds	28	(7) c and b Botham	1
Talaat Ali	c Radley b Edmonds	2	(4) c Roope b Botham	40
*† Wasim Bari	c Brearley b Willis	0	c Taylor b Botham	2
Iqbal Qasim	b Willis	0	(10) b Botham	0
Sikander Bakht	c Brearley b Edmonds	4	(9) c Roope b Botham	1
Liaquat Ali	not out	4	not out	0
Extras	(nb9)	9	(b1, lb3, w5, nb4)	13
	(36 overs)	105	(66.5 overs)	139

Fall: 11,22,40,41,84,96,97,97,97.
1,45,100,108,114,119,121,130,130.

Bowling: Willis 13-1-47-5, Old 10-3-26-1, Botham 5-2-17-0, Edmonds 8-6-6-4.
Second innings: Willis 10-2-26-2, Old 15-4-36-0, Botham 20.5-8-34-8, Edmonds 12-4-21-0, Miller 9-3-9-0.

Toss: England
Umpires: W.L. Budd and D.J. Constant
Close of play: (2) E. 309 for 8 (Botham 102, Edmonds 6)
(3) P. 96 for 2 (Mohsin 45, Talaat 36)

ENGLAND WON BY AN INNINGS AND 120 RUNS

Rain ruined the final Test, with 19½ hours out of a possible 30 being washed out. England reached 119 for 7 in reply to Pakistan's 201 in the time available.

1978ii

New Zealand had shared their home series 1-1 against England in the 1977-78 winter, their victory at Wellington being their first against the Mother Country after 47 unsuccessful attempts. However, Mark Burgess's 1978 tourists were outgunned by an England side for whom the irrepressible Botham was in magnificent form.

Planned rebuilding at The Oval meant that the first of the three Tests was played there, with Lord's staging the final match. England won the first two encounters comfortably: Gower hit his first Test century at The Oval, while Boycott, in his first Test of the summer, marked his return with 131 at Trent Bridge, where New Zealand managed only 120 and 190: Botham took nine wickets as England won by an innings.

Looking for a clean sweep at Lord's, England included Middlesex offspinner Emburey for the first time. New Zealand recalled veteran fast bowler Collinge, for what turned out to be his final Test. It was the swansong, too, for 40-year-old former captain Congdon. At the time, Congdon and Collinge were New Zealand's leading Test runscorer and wicket-taker respectively: in time, their records would be surpassed by two other players from this match, Wright and Hadlee.

New Zealand batted competently through the first day. Wright, slow at first, and fellow left-hander Edgar put on 65 for the first wicket before Wright fell for a sedate 17: his partner soon followed for 39 (seven fours), Emburey's fourth ball in Tests inducing a catch to Edmonds. It was an impressive innings from the 21-year-old Edgar, who had a lot on his mind: having not kept wicket since his schooldays, he had been entrusted with the gloves for this match after the indifferent performances of the team's only specialist stumper, 'Jock' Edwards.

Geoff Howarth, struggling against the effects of influenza, shared a century partnership with his captain, Burgess, who hit eight fours in his 68. Howarth battled on, although he was lucky to survive three chances off the little-used bowling of Gooch. The normally-reliable trio of Hendrick, Botham and Brearley were the culprits, two of the catches going down in one over with Howarth marooned on 45. Towards the close Botham struck back with the wickets of Burgess and Congdon, but Howarth would not be denied, reaching his century with his 12th four, five minutes before stumps.

Botham snapped up two more wickets in his first three overs on the second morning, and he eventually claimed his sixth victim when Howarth succumbed after 340 minutes for 123, having found the boundary 14 times.

New Zealand's total of 339 looked more imposing when Gooch fell to the second ball of the innings. Boycott and Radley had to be at their most watchful to keep out Hadlee and Collinge, but ironically it was the 18-year-old fast bowler Bracewell who eventually ended the stand by removing Boycott for an adhesive 24. Radley and Gower were more adventurous, and brought up a century stand before the close, the last hour producing 75 runs.

Radley, anxious for a century on his second and last Test appearance at his home ground, fell to a lifter from Hadlee early on the third morning, and Gower lasted but a little longer in reaching 71 before misjudging a sweep against Boock.

Geoff Howarth sweeps during his elegant century in 1978, watched by close
fielders Clive Radley (in helmet) and Ian Botham. Once again, Botham was
England's destroyer with the ball, following his first-innings 6 for 101 with 5 for 39
as New Zealand subsided to a dismal 67 all out second time around

Only 67 runs came in the morning session, and indeed the day's ration of 151
remains the lowest-ever for a full day's play in a Test in England. England's
remaining batting was disappointing, Hadlee scotching any hopes of a middle-
order revival with a new-ball spell of 3 for 8 in eight overs. England's eventual
total of 289 conceded a first-innings lead of 50 to the happy Kiwis, but their
pleasure was shortlived.

An hour and a half remained for play when New Zealand batted again, and in
that time they contrived to lose seven wickets – including two nightwatchmen –
for just 37 runs. It seemed that the Lord's 'ridge' had suddenly reappeared as
Willis obtained surprising lift from a good length, and the big fast bowler picked
up four wickets as the tourists' disastrous collapse took shape. Botham, though,
was the real architect of New Zealand's downfall, bowling both openers (Wright
fell to a prodigious inswinging yorker) and having Parker caught behind.
Bracewell fell to Willis's last ball of the day, Hendrick at slip bringing off a
magnificent catch, a feat he repeated to send back Burgess for 14 off Botham's
11th ball of the fourth morning.

The 'flu-stricken Howarth, who had been unable to bat on Saturday, came to
the crease first thing on Day 4, Bank Holiday Monday, and he was to become one
of only three batsmen to reach double figures in New Zealand's miserable total of
67. Botham wrapped up the innings by bowling Collinge, having earlier run out
Hadlee as Howarth tried to manipulate the strike: Botham finished with 5 for 39,
the eighth time he had taken five or more wickets in an innings in his 11 Tests.

England, needing 118 to win, had an early jolt when Hadlee, working up a fair
head of steam, produced two fast, induckers which shattered the stumps of
Boycott and Radley in successive deliveries, reducing the home side to 14 for 2.
Gooch and Gower retrieved the situation with a stand of 70, Gower taking a six
off Collinge before falling to Bracewell for 46. No further hitches upset England,
who completed a four-day victory by seven wickets when Hadlee sent down a no-
ball at half-past-three.

England thus rounded off a successful summer with their fifth win in six Tests,
the other match having been drawn.

ENGLAND v NEW ZEALAND
August 24, 25, 26, 28, 1978

NEW ZEALAND

J.G. Wright	c Edmonds b Botham	17	b Botham	12
† B.A. Edgar	c Edmonds b Emburey	39	b Botham	4
G.P. Howarth	c Taylor b Botham	123	(9) not out	14
J.M. Parker	lbw b Hendrick	14	c Taylor b Botham	3
* M.G. Burgess	lbw b Botham	68	c Hendrick b Botham	14
B.E. Congdon	c Emburey b Botham	2	c Taylor b Willis	3
R.W. Anderson	b Botham	16	(3) c Taylor b Willis	1
R.J. Hadlee	c Brearley b Botham	0	(10) run out	5
R.O. Collinge	c Emburey b Willis	19	(11) b Botham	0
S.L. Boock	not out	4	(7) c Radley b Willis	0
B.P. Bracewell	st Taylor b Emburey	4	(8) c Hendrick b Willis	0
Extras	(b4, lb18, w4, nb7)	33	(lb3, nb8)	11
	(143.1 overs)	339	(37.1 overs)	67

Fall: 65,70,117,247,253,290,290,321,333.

10,14,20,29,33,37,37,43,57.

Bowling: Willis 29-9-79-1, Hendrick 28-14-39-1, Botham 38-13-101-6, Edmonds 12-3-19-0, Emburey 26.1-12-39-2, Gooch 10-0-29-0.

Second innings: Willis 16-8-16-4, Botham 18.1-4-39-5, Emburey 3-2-1-0.

ENGLAND

G.A. Gooch	c Boock b Hadlee	2	not out	42
G. Boycott	c Hadlee b Bracewell	24	b Hadlee	4
C.T. Radley	c Congdon b Hadlee	77	b Hadlee	0
D.I. Gower	c Wright b Boock	71	c Congdon b Bracewell	46
* J.M. Brearley	c Edgar b Hadlee	33	not out	8
I.T. Botham	c Edgar b Collinge	21		
† R.W. Taylor	lbw b Hadlee	1		
P.H. Edmonds	c Edgar b Hadlee	5		
J.E. Emburey	b Collinge	2		
M. Hendrick	b Bracewell	12		
R.G.D. Willis	not out	7		
Extras	(b7, lb5, nb22)	34	(lb3, w4, nb11)	18
	(112.3 overs)	289	(3 wkts) (30.5 overs)	118

Fall: 2,66,180,211,249,255,258,263,274.

14,14,84.

Bowling: Hadlee 32-9-84-5, Collinge 30-9-58-2, Bracewell 19.3-1-68-2, Boock 25-10-33-1, Congdon 6-1-12-0.

Second innings: Hadlee 13.5-2-31-2, Collinge 6-1-26-0, Boock 5-1-11-0, Bracewell 6-0-32-1.

Toss: New Zealand   Umpires: H.D. Bird and B.J. Meyer

Close of play: (1) N.Z. 280 for 5 (Howarth 105, Anderson 8)
(2) E. 175 for 2 (Radley 75, Gower 55)
(3) N.Z. 37 for 7 (Burgess 8)

ENGLAND WON BY 7 WICKETS

1979

As had been the case four years previously, the 1979 Lord's Test was played later in the season than usual, a four-Test rubber against India being contested after the second World Cup competition. West Indies retained the Prudential Cup at Lord's on June 23, defeating England by 92 runs in a rather one-sided final.

India, making their first Test tour of England for five years, had undergone one of their frequent captaincy changes just before the tour, with Gavaskar being relieved of the leadership in favour of offspinner Venkataraghavan. Although India at last had a fast bowler worth the name in Kapil Dev, the signs were that the spinners who had served their country well for so long were nearing the end of the road, and so it proved. The batting, however, looked good on paper, with the run-hungry Gavaskar leading the way.

England, whose crushing 5-1 series win in Australia the previous winter was still fresh in the memory, took an early lead in the Test series with an innings victory at Edgbaston, Gower scoring 200 not out and Boycott 155 as England ran up the imposing total of 633 for 5. India could muster only 297 and 253 in reply, although Gavaskar and Viswanath both passed 50 in each innings.

For the second match, England brought in Essex's John Lever in place of the injured Willis. India were forced to replace the injured Amarnath with debutant Yashpal Sharma. The match had an unusual start, with both captains, Brearley and Venkataraghavan, claiming they had won the toss. With India wanting to bat and England hoping to field, the actual result was immaterial, but Venkataraghavan was adamant that he had called correctly, and finally an exasperated Brearley gave in, saying 'Let him have the toss – it's the only f***ing thing he'll win in this Test!'

Bad weather frequently interrupted proceedings on the first morning. Play was halted three times in the first 70 minutes, and Gavaskar had to restart his innings five times in all. His 42 was the one sizable contribution to a disappointing innings of 96, the others having no answer to the lively Botham (5 for 35) and the nagging Hendrick (2 for 15 from 15 overs). The last four wickets all fell at 96, Venkataraghavan perishing to an exceptional piece of fielding from Gower.

India's rapid decline left England with 80 minutes to bat, and they reduced the arrears by 53 for the loss of Brearley, who gave a catch behind off Kapil Dev.

The score was advanced by just 19 runs on the second day, Boycott and Gooch both coming to grief in the 40 minutes' play possible. A midday cloudburst left the groundstaff frantically clearing away the moisture, and just as play seemed likely to resume another, even heavier storm flooded the ground in the afternoon, forming a lake of impressive proportions down the slope towards the Tavern. Some well-lubricated spectators enjoyed themselves by diving into the ground's new amenity.

Trojan work by the hard-pressed groundsmen meant that play could start only 45 minutes late on the third morning, and the crowd were treated to a beautiful cameo from Gower, who took sixes off Bedi and Venkataraghavan and also stroked 10 fours in reaching 82 in 95 balls. Then, incomprehensibly, he played no shot at left-arm seamer Ghavri and lost his off stump. Randall, although overshadowed by Gower, made a useful 57 (eight fours) before being run out by

The diminutive Indian Gundappa
Viswanath shared a matchsaving
stand of 210 with his
fellow-centurion Dilip Vengsarkar
in 1979

Chauhan from mid-on.

The scoring rate slowed as Miller and Edmonds ground out a stand of 38, and although the Middlesex man fell to Kapil Dev's new-ball burst, the Derbyshire pair of Miller and Taylor survived until the close. They extended their stand past three figures on the fourth morning, a much-needed injection of pace seeing 62 runs added in 11 overs before the declaration came at 419 for 9, giving England a lead of 323.

India's openers were undaunted by such a huge deficit, 52 being posted by lunch. After the interval, though, Chauhan went for 31 and Gavaskar – dropped by Randall at cover four balls previously – fell for 59, Brearley's good low left-handed catch at first slip providing Botham with his 100th wicket, in his 19th Test, in the then-record time of two years nine days (this mark was beaten a few months later by Kapil Dev). Twenty-five of Botham's wickets had come in his three Lord's Tests.

The third-wicket pair, Vengsarkar and Viswanath, were unimpressed by the general view that England's victory was purely a matter of time. They resisted a long spell from Edmonds, who bowled unchanged between lunch and tea, and survived until bad light brought forward the close by 15 minutes, India having reached 196 for 2, still 127 behind.

Memories of the epic Watson-Bailey stand of 1953 were rekindled by the Indian batsmen on the final day, from which nearly two hours were trimmed by bad weather. The tall Vengsarkar's pencil-slim figure contrasted with the small, rotund frame of Viswanath, at 30 the senior partner by seven years. The pair survived until after the tea interval, by which time India were all but safe. Both made richly-deserved centuries as the partnership swelled to 210 in 326 minutes, and both perished within three runs of each other as a draw beckoned. The figures of their innings are strikingly similar: Vengsarkar hit 13 fours in his 353 minutes at the crease, while Viswanath, for once outshining his equally-diminutive brother-in-law Gavaskar (who never managed a century in five Lord's Tests), batted for 351 minutes and hit 14 fours. Among Indians, only Vinoo Mankad, with 184 in 1952, had previously reached three figures in a Lord's Test.

211

ENGLAND v INDIA
August 2, 3, 4, 6, 7, 1979

INDIA

S.M. Gavaskar	c Taylor b Gooch	42	c Brearley b Botham		59
C.P.S. Chauhan	c Randall b Botham	2	c Randall b Edmonds		31
D.B. Vengsarkar	c Botham b Hendrick	0	c Boycott b Edmonds		103
G.R. Viswanath	c Brearley b Hendrick	21	c Gower b Lever		113
A.D. Gaekwad	c Taylor b Botham	13	not out		1
Yashpal Sharma	c Taylor b Botham	11	not out		5
Kapil Dev	c Miller b Botham	4			
K.D. Ghavri	not out	3			
† B. Reddy	lbw b Botham	0			
* S. Venkataraghavan	run out	0			
B.S. Bedi	b Lever	0			
Extras		0	(b2, lb2, w1, nb1)		6
	(55.5 overs)	96	(4 wkts) (148 overs)		318

Fall: 12,23,51,75,79,89,96,96,96. 79,99,309,312.

Bowling: Lever 9.5-3-29-1, Botham 19-9-35-5, Hendrick 15-7-15-2, Edmonds 2-1-1-0, Gooch 10-5-16-1.

Second innings: Botham 35-13-80-1, Hendrick 25-12-56-0, Lever 24-7-69-1, Edmonds 45-18-62-2, Miller 17-6-37-0, Gooch 2-0-8-0.

ENGLAND

* J.M. Brearley	c Reddy b Kapil Dev	12	Bowling:
G. Boycott	c Gavaskar b Ghavri	32	Kapil Dev 38-11-93-3,
G.A. Gooch	b Kapil Dev	10	Ghavri 31-2-122-2,
D.I. Gower	b Ghavri	82	Bedi 38.5-13-87-2,
D.W. Randall	run out	57	Venkataraghavan 22-2-79-1.
I.T. Botham	b Venkataraghavan	36	
G. Miller	st Reddy b Bedi	62	
P.H. Edmonds	c Reddy b Kapil Dev	20	
† R.W. Taylor	c Vengsarkar b Bedi	64	
J.K. Lever	not out	6	
M. Hendrick	did not bat		
Extras	(b11, lb21, w2, nb4)	38	
	(9 wkts dec) (129.5 overs)	419	

Fall: 21,60,71,185,226,253,291,394,419.

Toss: India Umpires: H.D. Bird and K.E. Palmer

Close of play: (1) E. 53 for 1 (Boycott 26, Gooch 8)
(2) E. 72 for 3 (Gower 9, Randall 0)
(3) E. 357 for 7 (Miller 52, Taylor 25)
(4) I. 196 for 2 (Vengsarkar 66, Viswanath 35)

MATCH DRAWN

Rain returned to spoil the third Test at Headingley, nearly 18 hours' play being lost in a match enlivened by Botham's 137, 99 of which came before lunch on the fourth day. The final Test at The Oval, however, was a magnificent match, Boycott's 125 setting up an Indian target of 438 in the fourth innings. Gavaskar's superb 221 took them agonisingly close to the victory which would have squared the series, but the tourists ended up nine runs short, with two wickets standing.

1980i

With rain having seriously interfered with seven Tests at Lord's during the 1970s, it was hoped that the new decade would bring better luck with the weather. Unfortunately, it was not to be: nearly 10 hours were lost from the first Lord's Test of a generally miserable summer, which earlier had been illuminated by a splendid century from Vivian Richards, making his first Test appearance at HQ, having missed the 1976 Test through illness.

The West Indians went into the match one-up, having scraped home in the first Test, at Trent Bridge, by just two wickets: of the now-familiar four-man pace battery, Roberts took eight wickets and Garner seven. For England, Boycott made 75 and Botham, in his first match as captain, 57.

England won the toss, but lost Boycott soon after a short break for rain. Gooch, though, was in magnificent form, dominating a second-wicket stand of 145 with Tavaré, whose defensive innings matched anything produced by Trevor Bailey in years gone by. Gooch took on the fast bowlers in grand style, reaching a fine century – his first in Tests – and going on to 123, the runs coming in 211 minutes, from 162 balls, with 17 fours and a six. When he was out, the score was 165, Tavaré having been almost strokeless: in all he batted 294 minutes for 42, hitting a solitary boundary. Criticism of Tavaré's defensive innings, however, takes little account of England's later collapse: the next-best score was Gatting's 18. The later batting was disappointing, loose shots accounting for Gatting and Botham, the captain falling to the last ball of the day.

An entertaining last-wicket flourish from Willis and Hendrick, which earned them some bouncers from the unamused bowlers, lifted the total to 269 on the second morning. Holding, who had removed the first three in the order, finished with 6 for 67, while Garner snapped up the other four wickets.

Greenidge got the West Indian innings off to a rousing start, hitting Willis's first three balls for four, but he fell lbw to Botham immediately after lunch. Haynes was now joined by Richards, who took on the bowlers from his first ball, which yielded the runs that took him to 3000 in Tests. Richards soon overhauled Haynes, and played some memorable strokes as he raced to his century in 125 minutes. Underwood – one of three former Packer players restored to the England side – was despatched for four fours in one over, while Botham saw five crisp drives penetrate his well-stocked off-side field. Richards passed 1000 runs against England in only his sixth Test (only Bradman has done it quicker, in five), but perished a few minutes before the close, having hit 25 fours and a six from 159 balls. His stand with Haynes realised 223 in 196 minutes.

Nightwatchman Croft negotiated some retaliatory bouncers from Willis, but was soon run out, backing up too far, by Gatting. Willis, displaying an impressive turn of speed, quickly disposed of Kallicharran and Bacchus, but Lloyd made light of an injured right hand to score 56, with seven fours and a muscular six, before Willey penetrated his defences. Haynes's long innings had earlier come to an end at 184, the highest by a West Indian at Lord's at the time, the opener having struck 27 fours and a six in his 490-minute marathon.

Murray (34) and Roberts (24) prolonged England's agony, lifting the final score to 518, a lead of 249. England, left with a potentially difficult 40 minutes'

An imperious innings of 145 from Vivian Richards set West Indies on their way to a big total in 1980. Desmond Haynes added 184 as the visitors ran up 518

batting, survived unscathed to the close.

England added 18 more runs in 36 minutes on the fourth morning, at which point bad light intervened: deteriorating weather meant that no further play was possible. Only a dramatic England collapse on the final day could have produced a result, and in threatening conditions Gooch and Boycott took their stand to 71 before Garner struck. The lanky Barbadian also removed Tavaré, but Boycott, whose undefeated 49 occupied 3½ hours, and Woolmer survived until gathering clouds forced the players off at 2.05. Play was finally abandoned 1½ hours later, a thunderstorm having put paid to hopes of a restart.

214

ENGLAND v WEST INDIES
June 19, 20, 21, 23, 24, 1980

ENGLAND

G.A. Gooch	lbw b Holding	123	b Garner	47
G. Boycott	c Murray b Holding	8	not out	49
C.J. Tavaré	c Greenidge b Holding	42	lbw b Garner	6
R.A. Woolmer	c Kallicharran b Garner	15	not out	19
M.W. Gatting	b Holding	18		
* I.T. Botham	lbw b Garner	8		
D.L. Underwood	lbw b Garner	3		
P. Willey	b Holding	4		
† A.P.E. Knott	c Garner b Holding	9		
R.G.D. Willis	b Garner	14		
M. Hendrick	not out	10		
Extras	(b4, lb1, w4, nb6)	15	(lb1, nb11)	12
	(95.3 overs)	269	(2 wkts) (52 overs)	133

Fall: 20,165,190,219,220,231,232,244,245. 71,96.

Bowling: Roberts 18-3-50-0, Holding 28-11-67-6, Garner 24.3-8-36-4, Croft 20-3-77-0, Richards 5-1-24-0.

Second innings: Roberts 13-3-24-0, Holding 15-5-51-0, Garner 15-6-21-2, Croft 8-2-24-0, Richards 1-0-1-0.

WEST INDIES

C.G. Greenidge	lbw b Botham	25	Bowling:
D.L. Haynes	lbw b Botham	184	Willis 31-12-103-3,
I.V.A. Richards	c sub (G.R. Dilley) b Willey	145	Botham 37-7-145-3,
C.E.H. Croft	run out	0	Underwood 29.2-7-108-1,
A.I. Kallicharran	c Knott b Willis	15	Hendrick 11-2-32-0,
S.F.A.F. Bacchus	c Gooch b Willis	0	Gooch 7-1-26-0,
* C.H. Lloyd	b Willey	56	Willey 25-8-73-2,
† D.L. Murray	c Tavaré b Botham	34	Boycott 7-2-11-0.
A.M.E. Roberts	b Underwood	24	
J. Garner	c Gooch b Willis	15	
M.A. Holding	not out	0	
Extras	(b1, lb9, w1, nb9)	20	
	(147.2 overs)	518	

Fall: 37,260,275,326,330,437,469,486,518.

Toss: England   Umpires: W.E. Alley and B.J. Meyer
Close of play: (1) E. 232 for 7 (Willey 1)
                 (2) W.I. 265 for 2 (Haynes 92, Croft 0)
                 (3) E. 33 for 0 (Gooch 21, Boycott 10)
                 (4) E. 51 for 0 (Gooch 32, Boycott 13)

MATCH DRAWN

The three remaining Tests were all drawn, leaving West Indies 1-0 winners of the series. Rain interfered with all the games, washing out the third days at Old Trafford and The Oval and the first and fourth days at Headingley. Lloyd made a popular century at his adopted home ground in Manchester, while a stubborn century from Willey, who shared a 10th-wicket stand of 117 with Willis, saved England's bacon at The Oval.

215

1980ii

Despite the wet summer, hopes were high that the showpiece of the 1980 season, a special match to celebrate the centenary of Test cricket in England, would be spared. Alas, the weather did not relent, and a combination of inadequate covers, fussy umpires and overcautious captains led to long delays on the third day, culminating in an incident which saw the umpires manhandled by some furious MCC members in front of the pavilion. Perhaps it was foolish to have tried to recreate the unique atmosphere of the Centenary Test at Melbourne in 1977, an event helped no end by beautiful weather throughout.

The Australians had displayed indifferent form in their warm-up matches, but after Greg Chappell, in his fourth and last Lord's Test, had won the toss his side rarely looked back. Ominously, the start was delayed by 50 minutes, but Wood and Laird got the innings off to a sound start with a stand of 64. Chappell, one of only four survivors from Melbourne's Centenary Test (the others were Marsh, Lillee and Old), hit nine fours in his 47, looking untroubled before Old took his second wicket. Wood, whose stand with Chappell was worth 86, was now joined by his Western Australian team-mate Hughes, and they took the score to 227 for 2 by the close, the patient left-hander reaching a deserved century just before the end.

Only 1¼ hours' play was possible on the second day, in which time Australia lost Wood for 112 (10 fours), brilliantly stumped by Bairstow off Emburey. It was a sweet moment for the Yorkshire wicketkeeper, who was playing in his only Lord's Test: on the eve of the match a burglar stole £120 and a coat from his hotel room. Yallop also went cheaply, but Hughes had moved to 82 by the time bad light brought matters to an end at 12.45: rain ensured that no more play would be possible.

Heavy overnight rain meant that a prompt start on Saturday was unlikely, but few were prepared for the long delays which eventuated. The harassed umpires made no fewer than five inspections, their main concern being two old pitches on the Tavern (lower) side of the square, which were wet after being left uncovered. The crowd grew more and more impatient with each lengthy pitch-inspection, especially when it became common knowledge that the groundsmen considered conditions playable. With Australia having the upper hand, England's captain Botham was not particularly keen to see play starting, which left the umpires in an awkward position, but despite this the match should have restarted some time before it eventually got under way at 3.45, the umpires being escorted through the Long Room and down the pavilion steps after the unseemly behaviour of a number of exasperated MCC members.

Hughes soon took charge when play began at last, rushing to his century with a pulled six off Old. With quick runs the requirement, Hughes perished for 117, having hit 14 fours and three sixes in his 205-minute stay at the crease. Border took up the cudgels, taking 14 off a Hendrick over on his way to a quick half-century. The declaration came at 385 for 5, but bad light halted England's reply after two deliveries from Lillee, one of which was a no-ball.

Australia were batting again well before the end of the fourth day, which like the fifth was extended by an hour. Gooch and the debutant Athey failed to reach

A rare inelegant moment for Australia's Kim Hughes, undoubted star of the otherwise disappointing Centenary Test at Lord's in 1980. Hughes made 117 and 84, one of his drives ending up in the top tier of the pavilion

double figures, and only a stand of 96 between Gower and the obdurate Boycott held up the tourists for long. Gower, restored to the team after missing the previous four Tests, looked in good form, stroking seven fours in his two-hour innings: he also received a five-run bonus when his inside edge off Lillee eluded Marsh and struck a fielder's helmet 'parked' on the ground (this was the first such occurrence in a Test).

Boycott moved to 62 in 193 minutes before Lillee struck again; then it was the turn of Pascoe, matching his more famous partner for speed, to destroy England's middle order with a spell of 5 for 10 in 32 balls. In all, England lost eight wickets for 68, and it was left to Old to save the follow-on, which he did in the grand manner, lofting Bright for one of his two sixes.

Looking for quick runs to augment their lead of 180, Australia instead lost two quick wickets, Wood and Laird falling to the persistent Old. Chappell and Hughes, however, would not be subdued, and they took the score to 106 by stumps, Hughes producing the shot of the match near the end when he shimmied

217

down the pitch and drove Old – not the slowest of bowlers – high into the top tier of the pavilion.

Hughes impressed again on the fifth morning as Australia piled on 83 runs in less than an hour. Chappell departed for 59, but Hughes went on to 84, hitting 11 fours and two sixes in 141 minutes before Botham ended his hopes of making twin centuries on such a notable occasion.

The declaration came with Hughes's wicket, leaving England a target of 370 in 350 minutes, but the home side showed little interest in chasing such a score, especially after the early loss of Gooch and Athey. Boycott and Gower shared another useful stand, but the match petered out as the Yorkshireman and Gatting notched up a century partnership. Boycott hit his 19th Test century, passing 7000 runs and eclipsing the run aggregates of Hutton and Bradman in the process, but his efforts were not universally appreciated by the long-suffering crowd, who greeted the end of the match with slow handclaps and catcalls after England's rather timid performance.

The match that celebrated the end of the first century of Test cricket in England also marked the end of John Arlott's peerless 35-year career as a cricket commentator. After this match he withdrew to his retirement home on the Channel island of Alderney.

A long investigation by MCC into the behaviour of some of its members on 'Black Saturday' did not bring the expected expulsions from the club. Geoffrey Moorhouse, in his book *Lord's*, revealed that the man singled out as the main offender was sent a stiff letter warning him about his future behaviour: not for the last time, the club's committee seemed to be strangely fearful of applying what many saw as the ultimate sanction.

ENGLAND v AUSTRALIA
August 28, 29, 30, September 1, 2, 1980

AUSTRALIA

G.M. Wood	st Bairstow b Emburey	112	lbw b Old	8
B.M. Laird	c Bairstow b Old	24	c Bairstow b Old	6
* G.S. Chappell	c Gatting b Old	47	b Old	59
K.J. Hughes	c Athey b Old	117	lbw b Botham	84
G.N. Yallop	lbw b Hendrick	2		
A.R. Border	not out	56	(5) not out	21
† R.W. Marsh	not out	16		
R.J. Bright				
D.K. Lillee	did not bat			
A.A. Mallett				
L.S. Pascoe				
Extras	(b1, lb8, nb2)	11	(b1, lb8, nb2)	11
	(5 wkts dec) (134 overs)	385	(4 wkts dec) (53.2 overs)	189

Fall: 64,150,260,267,320.   15,28,139,189.

Bowling: Old 35-9-91-3, Hendrick 30-6-67-1, Botham 22-2-89-0, Emburey 38-9-104-1, Gooch 8-3-16-0, Willey 1-0-7-0.

Second innings: Old 20-6-47-3, Hendrick 15-4-53-0, Emburey 9-2-35-0, Botham 9.2-1-43-1.

ENGLAND

G.A. Gooch	c Bright b Lillee	8	lbw b Lillee	16
G. Boycott	c Marsh b Lillee	62	not out	128
C.W.J. Athey	b Lillee	9	c Laird b Pascoe	1
D.I. Gower	b Lillee	45	b Mallett	35
M.W. Gatting	lbw b Pascoe	12	not out	51
* I.T. Botham	c Wood b Pascoe	0		
P. Willey	lbw b Pascoe	5		
† D.L. Bairstow	lbw b Pascoe	6		
J.E. Emburey	lbw b Pascoe	3		
C.M. Old	not out	24		
M. Hendrick	c Border b Mallett	5		
Extras	(b6, lb8, nb12)	26	(b3, lb2, nb8)	13
	(63.2 overs)	205	(3 wkts) (82 overs)	244

Fall: 10,41,137,151,158,163,164,173,200.   19,43,124.

Bowling: Lillee 15-4-43-4, Pascoe 18-5-59-5, Chappell 2-0-2-0, Bright 21-6-50-0, Mallett 7.2-3-25-1.

Second innings: Lillee 19-5-53-1, Pascoe 17-1-73-1, Bright 25-9-44-0, Mallett 21-2-61-1.

Toss: Australia   Umpires: H.D. Bird and D.J. Constant
Close of play: (1) A. 227 for 2 (Wood 100, Hughes 47)
(2) A. 278 for 4 (Hughes 82, Border 2)
(3) E. 1 for 0 (Gooch 0, Boycott 0)
(4) A. 106 for 2 (Chappell 47, Hughes 38)

MATCH DRAWN

1981

Kim Hughes, the freshfaced batting hero of the Centenary Test, returned in 1981 as Australia's captain for the first-ever six-Test series in England. Although the tourists were without Greg Chappell, the famous surname was not absent from the team lists, as Trevor, the youngest of the three brothers, made the trip. He made his Test debut in the first match at Trent Bridge, which Australia won by four wickets, opening bowler Alderman (another debutant) taking nine wickets and his partner Lillee – recently recovered from a debilitating bronchial virus – managing eight.

England's captain was Botham, whose position was under threat after 11 successive matches without a win. The Lord's Test, yet again marred by bad weather and unimaginative umpiring, was to be the allrounder's last match in charge. Boycott was playing in his 100th Test, the second to do this after Colin Cowdrey, and this match, his last at Lord's, was his 16th Test there, a record equalled by Gower in 1989.

Hughes won the toss and, rather surprisingly, elected to field. Apart from Gooch, who made a robust 44 in 75 minutes, England made slow progress on a dry pitch which occasionally displayed uneven bounce. Boycott grafted 98 minutes for 17 before edging Lawson to second slip, where Border fluffed the catch but knocked it on to his first-slip neighbour Alderman. Woolmer had to retire hurt at 13 after being hit on the left arm by the rampant Lawson.

Gower, although not at his best, managed one unusual feat, taking successive fours in the same over from different bowlers when Lillee completed an over after Alderman limped off with a damaged hamstring. Lawson, however, ended Gower's resistance at 27. Gatting struck nine meaty fours in his 59 before falling to Bright just before the close, by which time England had advanced to 191 for 4 in a day shortened by a 31-minute bad-light stoppage in mid-afternoon.

Four runs were added on the second morning before rain held up proceedings for 2¼ hours, but when play resumed Willey and nightwatchman Emburey took their partnership to 97. Willey hit 12 fours and two sixes before edging Alderman to slip, while Emburey's adhesive 171-minute innings came to an end when he underestimated the power of Lillee's return to Marsh from fine leg. With Botham (third ball) and Taylor falling for ducks, the last six wickets tumbled for 27 inside an hour, with the impressively quick Lawson finishing with 7 for 81, the best figures for Australia in a Lord's Test apart from Massie's 1972 efforts.

Australia had made 10 in reply when bad light stopped play during the extra hour, which the regulations now permitted to be added to any of the first four days of a Test in the event of weather interference on the day in question. The umpires, though, interpreted the rather loose wording of the new regulation to mean that play could not resume once it had been suspended in that final hour, and therefore abandoned play for the day minutes before the sun returned to make conditions playable again. The put-upon crowd, whose memories of the events of the Centenary Test were fresh, hooted their disapproval and rained seat-cushions onto the ground. Next day the regulations were tightened up.

Australia, too, tightened up on the third day, reaching 253 for 6 after early setbacks. With the aid of frequent no-balls – Willis alone bowled 28 in the innings

The 1981 Lord's Test was Geoffrey Boycott's 100th overall and his last at HQ: he ended his Lord's Test career with 16 appearances (a number equalled by David Gower in 1989) and a record 1189 runs

– the openers added 62, of which Dyson's share was 7. Wood, who earlier had been 'caught' by Woolmer at short leg off a Willis no-ball, inside-edged the same bowler but saw a diving Taylor cling on to a right-handed catch. Dyson went at the same score, and when Dilley struck to remove Yallop and Chappell, Australia had slipped to 81 for 4. Hughes and Border more than doubled the score before the captain perished to Emburey, and near the close Border was brilliantly caught by Gatting at second slip after a valuable 64, which included eight fours and a six off Botham.

Marsh added four to his overnight 43 before offering no stroke to an inswinger in Dilley's first over with the new ball, but English hopes of a first-innings lead were dashed by Bright, who survived more than two hours for 33, and Lillee, whose unbeaten 40 occupied 107 minutes as Australia contrived a lead of 34. The total included 55 extras, a record for any Lord's Test.

Before moving back in front England lost Gooch, lbw to Lawson's second ball, while Woolmer – in what turned out to be his final Test – also went cheaply, the fifth lbw victim of the six wickets to fall on this fourth day.

Boycott and Gower safely negotiated the remaining 1¾ hours, adding 74, and they extended their partnership to 123 on the final morning. The rate of progress, though, was too sluggish for a declaration to be considered: only 68 came in two hours in the pre-lunch session (68 came in *one* hour after the interval), Boycott taking an hour to move from his overnight 47 to his half-century. He then took 10 off a Lawson over, but after 279 minutes Boycott's hopes of marking his 100th Test with a century were dashed by the 'old firm' of Marsh and Lillee.

Gower, having survived a stumping chance at 43, looked set for a century before he too fell to Lillee, having hit 11 fours and a pulled six off Bright in his 89. In the search for quick runs Gatting, Willey and Taylor all managed a six in their brief innings, Willey's being a remarkable sliced shot over cover point off an unamused Lillee. Botham's own effort to raise the run rate was singularly unsuccessful: sweeping at Bright, he was bowled behind his legs first ball, completing a 'pair' which was received in stony silence by the crowd.

The eventual declaration set Australia an unlikely 232 in 170 minutes. The sensational happenings of the next two Tests were foreshadowed when Australia slumped to 17 for 3, but defiant innings from Wood and Chappell (66 minutes for 5) saved the day.

After the match Botham informed the selectors – who had been about to sack him anyway – that he did not wish to continue as captain on the match-by-match basis that had been in force for the first two Tests. Brearley was recalled as captain, with remarkable results.

ENGLAND v AUSTRALIA
July 2, 3, 4, 6, 7, 1981

ENGLAND

G.A. Gooch	c Yallop b Lawson	44	lbw b Lawson	20
G. Boycott	c Alderman b Lawson	17	c Marsh b Lillee	60
R.A. Woolmer	c Marsh b Lawson	21	lbw b Alderman	9
D.I. Gower	c Marsh b Lawson	27	c Alderman b Lillee	89
M.W. Gatting	lbw b Bright	59	c Wood b Bright	16
P. Willey	c Border b Alderman	82	(7) c Chappell b Bright	12
J.E. Emburey	run out	31		
* I.T. Botham	lbw b Lawson	0	(6) b Bright	0
† R.W. Taylor	c Hughes b Lawson	0	b Lillee	9
G.R. Dilley	not out	7	(8) not out	27
R.G.D. Willis	c Wood b Lawson	5		
Extras	(b2, lb3, w3, nb10)	18	(b2, lb8, nb13)	23
	(124.1 overs)	311	(8 wkts dec) (98.4 overs)	265

Fall: 60,65,134,187,284,293,293,293,298.   31,55,178,217,217,217,242,265.

Bowling: Lillee 35.4-7-102-0, Alderman 30.2-7-79-1, Lawson 43.1-14-81-7, Bright 15-7-31-1.

Second innings: Lillee 26.4-8-82-3, Alderman 17-2-42-1, Lawson 19-6-51-1, Bright 36-18-67-3.

AUSTRALIA

G.M. Wood	c Taylor b Willis	44	not out	62
J. Dyson	c Gower b Botham	7	lbw b Dilley	1
G.N. Yallop	b Dilley	1	c Botham b Willis	3
* K.J. Hughes	c Willis b Emburey	42	lbw b Dilley	4
T.M. Chappell	c Taylor b Dilley	2	c Taylor b Botham	5
A.R. Border	c Gatting b Botham	64	not out	12
† R.W. Marsh	lbw b Dilley	47		
R.J. Bright	lbw b Emburey	33		
G.F. Lawson	lbw b Willis	5		
D.K. Lillee	not out	40		
T.M. Alderman	c Taylor b Willis	5		
Extras	(b6, lb11, w6, nb32)	55	(w1, nb2)	3
	(118.4 overs)	345	(4 wkts) (48.5 overs)	90

Fall: 62,62,69,81,167,244,257,268,314.   2,11,17,62.

Bowling: Willis 27.4-9-50-3, Dilley 30-8-106-3, Botham 26-8-71-2, Gooch 10-4-28-0, Emburey 25-12-35-2.

Second innings: Willis 12-3-35-1, Dilley 7.5-1-18-2, Emburey 21-10-24-0, Botham 8-3-10-1.

Toss: Australia   Umpires: D.O. Oslear and K.E. Palmer
Close of play: (1) E. 191 for 4 (Willey 23, Emburey 0)
(2) A. 10 for 0 (Wood 5, Dyson 3)
(3) A. 253 for 6 (Marsh 43, Bright 3)
(4) E. 129 for 2 (Boycott 47, Gower 38)
Woolmer retired hurt at 83 for 2, resumed at 284 for 5

MATCH DRAWN

A rejuvenated Botham performed well-chronicled wonders in the next three Tests, all of which were won by England. Centuries at Headingley and Old Trafford, and a 5 for 1 spell at Edgbaston set up victories, the first two of which were little short of miraculous. Willis's 8 for 34 spell at Headingley was another exceptional performance. The final Test was drawn, leaving England 3-1 winners of a pulsating series.

1982i

During the 1981-82 winter, England had lost a six-Test series in India 1-0, the tempo of the matches after India's first-Test win being, by and large, dreadfully boring. At times the Indian over rate, with two spinners operating, drooped below 10 an hour, and England's new skipper, Keith Fletcher, allowed his team to be dragged down to the same level, one of a few minor 'offences' which had cost him the captaincy by the time the teams reassembled for a three-Test rubber in England in 1982.

The stultifying nature of the winter's cricket had other effects as well: a number of England players, disillusioned with the pace of Test cricket, accepted lucrative offers to make an unauthorised tour of South Africa, and received three-year Test bans for their trouble. Thus did Boycott and Underwood end their Test careers, while Gooch, Lever, Emburey and others were temporarily lost to the England team.

Lord's staged the first Test of the 1982 summer, the match having been chosen to mark the Golden Jubilee of England-India Test cricket, which began at Lord's in 1932. England, captained by Willis, included two interesting debutants: the South African-born Lamb, having recently completed his qualification period, was immediately called up, while the Cambridge University captain Pringle became the first undergraduate to play for England since Peter May – coincidentally the new chairman of selectors – in 1951. India's side included one newcomer, opener Ghulam Parkar, while wicketkeeper Kirmani made his first appearance in England after playing 54 Tests overseas.

Willis won the toss, and must have been alarmed by the start his team made. In India's first Test, at Lord's in 1932, England had slumped to 19 for 3: this time Kapil Dev took three quick wickets to reduce the home side to 37 for 3, Viswanath's stinging slip catch to remove Tavaré providing the 'Haryana Hurricane' with his 150th Test wicket. Gower and the promoted Botham took the score to 96, Botham lofting Doshi's first ball for six, but both fell to good catches, Viswanath's second sharp effort in the slips sending back Gower. Botham went on to 67, but when he and Pringle left in quick succession England were languishing at 166 for 6. Randall and Edmonds, however, stayed to the end of the day, Randall emulating Botham in despatching the toiling Doshi for a six. By stumps the seventh-wicket stand was worth 112, a figure extended by 13 on the second morning before Edmonds fell for 64, his highest Test score. Randall continued to his third Test century (first in England), and eventually became Kapil Dev's fifth victim of the innings after 354 minutes, having hit 11 fours and a six in his 126.

The resistance was not over, however, as Taylor survived for two hours for 31, then Allott and Willis combined in an unorthodox partnership of 70 for the last wicket, like the Randall/Edmonds association an England record against India. Willis displayed a liking for the Indian bowlers, whom he had struck for a career-best 72 during Warwickshire's match with the tourists.

England's last four wickets had added 267, the eventual total of 433 looking even more imposing when India lost five quick wickets for 45 in indifferent weather. Gavaskar's impeccable technique enabled him to survive, but Botham and Willis swept away the first three wickets for 22; then Pringle trapped Yashpal

India's Yashpal Sharma is lbw, providing Derek Pringle with a wicket in his first over in Tests. The England fielders are (l-r) Gower, Botham, Tavaré, wicketkeeper Taylor and Edmonds, while the non-striker is Gavaskar

lbw with his sixth delivery in Tests, and shortly afterwards Malhotra went the same way. Gavaskar and Kapil Dev piloted the tourists to 92 for 5 by the close.

Rain, that frequent visitor to Lord's Test Saturdays, allowed only 2½ hours' play on the third day, but in that time England made decisive strides towards victory, twice dismissing the Indian captain Gavaskar. The first innings was soon over, the total being a paltry 128, only Gavaskar, who survived 191 minutes for 48, and Kapil Dev reaching double figures: yet again Botham took five wickets in an innings, for the 19th time at Test level.

Following on, India soon lost Parkar for 1, but the hammer blow fell at 47, when Gavaskar could not control a Willis lifter and gave a catch to backward short leg. Vengsarkar and Shastri hung on to stumps, by which time India were still 244 in arrears.

Two fine innings on Day 4 saved India's pride and prolonged the match into the final day. First Vengsarkar, a centurymaker at Lord's in 1979, played another high-class innings, unleashing a varied range of powerful, often wristy shots in his 157, which stretched for 334 minutes and contained 21 fours. He scored 86 runs between lunch and tea. Vengsarkar and the stubborn Yashpal put on 142, but Willis, who finished with 6 for 101, broke the stand and induced a collapse, with four wickets in as many overs, including his 250th in Tests (Malhotra).

England seemed set for a four-day win, but they had reckoned without Kapil Dev, who played an explosive innings which lasted just 78 minutes (55 balls). In that time he blasted his way to 89, lashing 13 fours and three sixes to all parts of the ground. Botham went for 18 in an over, while Edmonds, after a tight spell, had his figures spoiled as two successive sixes sailed over the ropes. It could not last, although few would have begrudged the smiling batsman his century, and finally Botham stopped the rot with the total at 369.

England's target was 65, but any faint hopes that remained for an early finish were dashed by the ubiquitous Kapil Dev, whose inspired new-ball spell brought him three wickets in eight balls. England limped to 23 for 3 by the close, but a few timely boundaries from Lamb brought England victory in the 11th over of the fifth morning.

ENGLAND v INDIA
June 10, 11, 12, 14, 15, 1982

ENGLAND

G. Cook	lbw b Kapil Dev	4	lbw b Kapil Dev	10
C.J. Tavaré	c Viswanath b Kapil Dev	4	b Kapil Dev	3
A.J. Lamb	lbw b Kapil Dev	9	(4) not out	37
D.I. Gower	c Viswanath b Kapil Dev	37	(5) not out	14
I.T. Botham	c Malhotra b Madan Lal	67		
D.W. Randall	c Parkar b Kapil Dev	126		
D.R. Pringle	c Gavaskar b Doshi	7		
P.H. Edmonds	c Kirmani b Madan Lal	64		
† R.W. Taylor	c Viswanath b Doshi	31	(3) c Malhotra b Kapil Dev	1
P.J.W. Allott	not out	41		
* R.G.D. Willis	b Madan Lal	28		
Extras	(b1, lb5, nb9)	15	(lb2)	2
	(148.1 overs)	433	(3 wkts) (19 overs)	67

Fall: 5,18,37,96,149,166,291,363,363. 11,13,18.

Bowling: Kapil Dev 43-8-125-5, Madan Lal 28.1-6-99-3, Shastri 34-10-73-0, Doshi 40-7-120-2, Yashpal 3-2-1-0.

Second innings: Kapil Dev 10-1-43-3, Madan Lal 2-1-2-0, Doshi 5-3-11-0, Shastri 2-0-9-0.

INDIA

* S.M. Gavaskar	b Botham	48	c Cook b Willis	24
G.A. Parkar	lbw b Botham	6	b Willis	1
D.B. Vengsarkar	lbw b Willis	2	c Allott b Willis	157
G.R. Viswanath	b Botham	1	(5) c Taylor b Pringle	3
Yashpal Sharma	lbw b Pringle	4	(6) b Willis	37
A.O. Malhotra	lbw b Pringle	5	(7) c Taylor b Willis	0
Kapil Dev	c Cook b Willis	41	(8) c Cook b Botham	89
R.J. Shastri	c Cook b Willis	4	(4) b Allott	23
† S.M.H. Kirmani	not out	6	c Gower b Willis	3
S. Madan Lal	c Tavaré b Botham	6	lbw b Pringle	15
D.R. Doshi	c Taylor b Botham	0	not out	4
Extras	(lb1, nb4)	5	(lb2, nb11)	13
	(50.4 overs)	128	(111.5 overs)	369

Fall: 17,21,22,31,45,112,116,116,128. 6,47,107,110,252,252,254,275,341.

Bowling: Botham 19.4-3-46-5, Willis 16-2-41-3, Pringle 9-4-16-2, Edmonds 2-1-5-0, Allott 4-1-15-0.

Second innings: Botham 31.5-7-103-1, Willis 28-3-101-6, Pringle 19-4-58-2, Allott 17-3-51-1, Edmonds 15-6-39-0, Cook 1-0-4-0.

Toss: England   Umpires: D.G.L. Evans and B.J. Meyer
Close of play: (1) E. 278 for 6 (Randall 84, Edmonds 59)
(2) I. 92 for 5 (Gavaskar 41, Kapil Dev 28)
(3) I. 61 for 2 (Vengsarkar 30, Shastri 6)
(4) E. 23 for 3 (Lamb 6, Gower 2)

ENGLAND WON BY 7 WICKETS

Rain washed out the last day of the Old Trafford Test, India having reached 379 for 8 (Patil a sparkling century) in reply to England's 425 in the time available. The third Test, at The Oval, was also left drawn: Botham's 208 led England to 594, but India made 410 in reply and saved the match with ease, despite the absence of Gavaskar, whose shin had been broken by a firm shot from Botham.

1982ii

Pakistan, under a new captain in allrounder Imran Khan, were the visitors for the second half of the 1982 season. A string of impressive performances in county matches issued notice that the tourists were not to be taken lightly, and indeed Pakistan might have won the first Test, at Edgbaston, but for stout resistance from the last three batsmen in England's second innings, who added 140 to stretch Pakistan's target to a distant 313: they fell 114 short.

Willis had played his part in England's batting fightback with a defiant 28 not out, but he damaged his neck in avoiding some rapid bouncers from Imran, and was unfit to play at Lord's. Gower stepped up for his first taste of Test captaincy, but his bowling attack was one of the friendliest ever fielded by England: lacking Miller (chicken-pox) as well as Willis, the four-prong 'pace' attack comprised Botham, Jackman, Pringle and Ian Greig, with Hemmings as the only spinner. The last four had seven Test caps between them before this match.

Pakistan won the toss and Mohsin gave a taste of things to come by straight-driving the first ball of the match, from Botham, to the boundary. Mohsin, slim, calm and correct, shared an opening stand of 53 with Mudassar then, in concert with Mansoor, steered Pakistan to 107 by lunch. Their stand swelled to 144 before Botham struck, and England had a bonus shortly afterwards when Miandad backed his speed against Tavaré's return and lost.

By now Mohsin had completed his century: although he had occasionally played and missed, he had offered only one definite chance, at 72, an edge off Botham which eluded Pringle at first slip. Soon after reaching three figures, Mohsin drove a hard chance back at bowler Jackman, but again it went down.

Mohsin and the equally elegant Zaheer took the score to 295 for 3 by the close, Zaheer escaping when a chance went begging from Pringle's third delivery with the new ball. On the second morning the partnership grew to 153, equalling Pakistan's record against England. Zaheer eventually fell to Jackman for 75 (eight fours) but Mohsin, who once took 14 off a Pringle over, had reached 199 when rain set in and drove the players from the field. Four hours later play restarted, and a relieved Mohsin finally reached his double-century – the eighth in a Lord's Test – at six o'clock. Three balls later he was gone, happy with his 496-minute innings, which contained 23 fours. Pakistan's middle-order batting disappointed, and by stumps the total was 428 for 8. Jackman, on his 37th birthday, ended up with 4 for 110.

Imran declared at the overnight total, and soon was celebrating Sarfraz's dismissal of Tavaré, who played on. Enterprising batting from Randall and Lamb saw 50 up in 10 overs, but soon Randall, never the most convincing of openers, became another Sarfraz victim. Lamb, too, was soon gone, and it was left to Botham and a subdued Gower to save the day. They shared a stand of 68 before Gower fell to his rival captain for 29. Botham survived 124 minutes for 31, an exasperated Qadir earning a rebuke from umpire Constant after performing a war-dance on a good length after an lbw appeal was rejected. Qadir eventually got his man, and soon added Pringle, Greig and Taylor to his bag, the two allrounders' efforts to counter the legspinner's wiles proving almost comical to behold.

The stylish Mohsin Khan collects more runs on the way to his memorable 200 in 1982, which set up Pakistan's only victory in a Lord's Test

Gatting fought on, guiding the score to 226 for 9 – within three of avoiding the follow-on – before rather surprisingly accepting the umpires' bad-light offer.

Refreshed by a night's rest, Imran trapped last man Jackman lbw in the first over of the fourth morning – the first and only day of Sunday play in a Lord's Test – with England still two short of the magic figure which would have saved the follow-on and, almost certainly, the match. Extras, with 46, were the highest contributor to England's modest 227, the 13 wides being a Test record.

As it was, England had to bat again, and they were soon reduced to 9 for 3, the wrecker being the gentle medium-pacer Mudassar, bowling only because Sarfraz and Tahir were nursing injuries. In what became known as his 'Golden Arm' spell, Mudassar shot out Randall, Lamb and Gower in the space of 10 scoreless balls. Rain wiped out the afternoon session, and when play resumed after tea England recovered to reach 95 for 3 by the close, still 106 behind.

Tavaré and Botham continued their partnership on the fifth morning as England inched towards safety. At one point Tavaré, who had waited 67 minutes before opening his account the day before, completed a unique slow-scoring double by spending an hour on 24: eventually he completed his half-century in 350 minutes, the second-slowest in first-class cricket. Tavaré speeded up towards the end, reaching 82 in 406 minutes before falling to Imran, who sent down 29 consecutive overs in one spell. By now Botham's responsible 199-minute 69 had been ended by Mudassar, who also removed Gatting and Greig: Qadir returned to dispose of Pringle.

When the ninth wicket fell, England were only 34 to the good, but time became a factor as Taylor and Jackman eked out 41 runs in a last-wicket stand that lasted for an hour. In desperation, Imran took the new ball, and after an over from Mudassar (who finished with 6 for 32) Qadir returned and immediately the Surrey man was adjudged caught off bat and pad.

The last hour of the match loomed, with Pakistan needing 76 in 18 overs to square the series with only their second win in England, the other having come at The Oval in 1954. With heavy clouds threatening, tension was high, but Mohsin and Miandad soon put the issue beyond doubt, the winning run coming with 29 balls to spare.

Fittingly, Mohsin Khan was still there at the end of Pakistan's first-ever victory in a Lord's Test: he ignored the invading spectators and knelt down to kiss the hallowed Lord's turf before joining the mad rush to the pavilion.

ENGLAND v PAKISTAN
August 12, 13, 14, 15, 16, 1982

PAKISTAN

Mohsin Khan	c Tavaré b Jackman	200	not out	39
Mudassar Nazar	c Taylor b Jackman	20		
Mansoor Akhtar	c Lamb b Botham	57		
Javed Miandad	run out	6	(2) not out	26
Zaheer Abbas	b Jackman	75		
Haroon Rashid	lbw b Botham	1		
* Imran Khan	c Taylor b Botham	12		
Tahir Naqqash	c Gatting b Jackman	2		
† Wasim Bari	not out	24		
Abdul Qadir	not out	18		
Sarfraz Nawaz	did not bat			
Extras	(b3, lb8, nb2)	13	(b1, lb10, w1)	12
	(8 wkts dec) (139 overs)	428	(0 wkt) (13.1 overs)	77

Fall: 53,197,208,361,364,380,382,401.

Bowling: Botham 44-8-148-3, Jackman 36-5-110-4, Pringle 26-9-62-0, Greig 13-2-42-0, Hemmings 20-3-53-0.

Second innings: Botham 7-0-30-0, Jackman 4-0-22-0, Hemmings 2.1-0-13-0.

ENGLAND

D.W. Randall	b Sarfraz	29	b Mudassar	9
C.J. Tavaré	b Sarfraz	8	c Miandad b Imran	82
A.J. Lamb	c Haroon b Tahir	33	lbw b Mudassar	0
* D.I. Gower	c Mansoor b Imran	29	c Wasim b Mudassar	0
I.T. Botham	c Mohsin b Qadir	31	c Sarfraz b Mudassar	69
M.W. Gatting	not out	32	c Wasim b Mudassar	7
D.R. Pringle	c Haroon b Qadir	5	c Miandad b Qadir	14
I.A. Greig	lbw b Qadir	3	lbw b Mudassar	2
E.E. Hemmings	b Sarfraz	6	c Wasim b Imran	14
† R.W. Taylor	lbw b Qadir	5	not out	24
R.D. Jackman	lbw b Imran	0	c Haroon b Qadir	17
Extras	(b11, lb12, w13, nb10)	46	(b10, lb19, w5, nb4)	38
	(86 overs)	227	(119.5 overs)	276

Fall: 16,69,89,157,173,187,197,217,226.   9,9,9,121,132,171,180,224,235.

Bowling: Imran 23-4-55-2, Sarfraz 23-4-56-3, Tahir 12-4-25-1, Qadir 24-9-39-4, Mudassar 4-1-6-0.

Second innings: Imran 42-13-84-2, Sarfraz 14-5-22-0, Qadir 37.5-15-94-2, Mudassar 19-7-32-6, Tahir 7-5-6-0.

Toss: Pakistan   Umpires: H.D. Bird and D.J. Constant
Close of play: (1) P. 295 for 3 (Mohsin 159, Zaheer 44)
(2) P. 428 for 8 (Wasim 24, Qadir 18)
(3) E. 226 for 9 (Gatting 31, Jackman 0)
(4) E. 95 for 3 (Tavaré 24, Botham 55)

PAKISTAN WON BY 10 WICKETS

England won the third Test, at Headingley, to take an absorbing series 2-1. Again, it was a close-run thing, England scraping home by three wickets after a controversial umpiring decision hastened the end of Pakistan's second innings.

1983

The 1983 season saw the third World Cup, the last to date to have been held in England. The final, played at Lord's on June 25, produced one of cricket's greatest upsets, outsiders India defeating mighty West Indies by 43 runs. After the one-day excitement England and New Zealand regrouped to contest a four-Test series. Willis still led England, despite losing the Ashes the previous winter, while New Zealand's captain was Howarth – an old friend of Willis's from their early Surrey days – who had scored an attractive century in the 1978 Lord's Test.

The teams came to Lord's for the third Test all-square at 1-1. England won the opening encounter, at The Oval, by 189 runs, Fowler, Tavaré and Lamb all scoring second-innings centuries. The second Test, at Headingley, saw New Zealand register their first victory in England, the hero being Cairns, with match figures of 10 for 144.

At Lord's, though, the unfortunate Cairns came back down to earth when he dropped the simplest of chances at square leg when Gower had made 21. The elegant left-hander went on to 108, benefiting from another let-off from Cairns, now at third slip, when he had reached 25. Cairns later wrote: 'I could have dug a hole right in the middle of Lord's and buried myself.'

Earlier, Howarth had won the toss for the eighth time in Tests, and for the eighth time he had sent the opposition in. His action paid early dividends on a dry, cracked pitch when Chris Smith, one of three England debutants in the match, fell lbw to his first ball, from Hadlee.

Gower made the most of his double escape, reaching his seventh Test century from only 93 balls after being becalmed on 0 for 20 minutes. He shared a stand of 149 with Tavaré, whose only four brought up his half-century soon after lunch. After 227 minutes (16 fours), Gower's pleasant innings was ended when a ball from medium-pacer Crowe kept low, and it seemed the infamous Lord's 'ridge' had reared its head again when Lamb fell almost immediately, fending off a Chatfield lifter. Botham also went cheaply, but Gatting – who had to duck an unintentional beamer from Crowe before he had scored – hit out boldly, taking nine fours in his half-century: by the close the solidly-built Middlesex captain looked set for his elusive first Test century, having reached 74 out of England's 279 for 5.

An ill-judged hook at Hadlee cost Gatting his wicket and his century early on the second morning. The great fast bowler took three more wickets to mop up the tail, finishing with 5 for 93, thus making up for his unusual barren spell during his side's win at Leeds, where he had failed to take a wicket.

New Zealand soon lost Wright, to a lifter from Willis, but Edgar and Howarth took the score to 49 before the captain became the first victim in Tests for left-arm spinner Cook, who owed his place in the side to a freak injury to Edmonds, who ricked his back getting out of his car the day before the match. Cook was withdrawn from his county's Championship match at Chelmsford and rushed to Lord's.

The talented Crowe, who spent a year on the MCC cricket staff in 1981, made a polished 46, and Edgar lasted nearly four hours for his 70, which contained eight fours. Nearing the close, New Zealand were 159 for 3, but the first ball of

Short-leg fielder Martin Crowe puts safety first as David Gower hits to leg during his century at Lord's in 1983. By 1989, Gower had amassed 1169 Test runs at Lord's, only 20 behind recordholder Geoffrey Boycott

Cook's second spell accounted for Edgar, and shortly afterwards Coney and Bracewell fell in the space of three balls.

The Kiwis' tail refused to wag on the third morning, Hadlee falling to the fourth ball of the day, and the eventual total of 191 conceded a lead of 135: Cook, whose flight and spin impressed, finished with 5 for 35, while Botham took 4 for 50.

The nervous Smith took 19 minutes to avoid the possibility of a 'pair', but once he broke his duck he looked solid enough. Tavaré went to Hadlee for 16, and after Smith and Gower shared a bright half-century stand the left-arm spinner Gray, another debutant, took three quick wickets, Gower falling to a low short-leg catch by the predatory Crowe.

Smith's doughty 43 was ended by Hadlee after 204 minutes, but a breezy 61 from Botham – reprieved early on by wicketkeeper Ian Smith – took the lead past 300. By stumps England were 206 for 7, but the innings was over within minutes of the fourth-day restart.

New Zealand's target was 347: time was not a worry, but the pitch was, and the tourists were further handicapped by a freak injury to their captain, Howarth, who had been hit near the eye in the nets that morning. When Wright provided Taylor with his 150th Test catch, Howarth came to the crease, but he too gave a catch to Taylor, without troubling the scorers.

Only Coney, who survived 2½ hours for 68, held up England's march to victory on the fourth afternoon. The lean right-hander, at his best in a crisis, hit eight fours, three of them in one Cowans over, before becoming Foster's first Test wicket. Cowans, playing in his only Lord's Test, took two wickets, and Willis returned to remove Hadlee after the allrounder had made a quick 30. Cook ended proceedings soon after five o'clock with his third wicket of the innings, juggling a return catch from Chatfield to round off a splendid debut with overall match figures of 8 for 125.

ENGLAND v NEW ZEALAND
August 11, 12, 13, 15, 1983

ENGLAND

C.J. Tavaré	b Crowe	51	c Crowe b Hadlee	16
C.L. Smith	lbw b Hadlee	0	c Coney b Hadlee	43
D.I. Gower	lbw b Crowe	108	c Crowe b Gray	34
A.J. Lamb	c sub (J.J. Crowe) b Chatfield	17	c Hadlee b Gray	4
M.W. Gatting	c Wright b Hadlee	81	b Gray	15
I.T. Botham	lbw b Cairns	8	c Coney b Chatfield	61
† R.W. Taylor	b Hadlee	16	c and b Coney	7
N.A. Foster	c Smith b Hadlee	10	c Wright b Hadlee	3
N.G.B. Cook	b Chatfield	16	c Bracewell b Chatfield	5
* R.G.D. Willis	c Smith b Hadlee	7	not out	2
N.G. Cowans	not out	1	c Smith b Chatfield	1
Extras	(b3, lb3, w2, nb3)	11	(b5, lb6, nb9)	20
	(120.3 overs)	326	(89.3 overs)	211

Fall: 3,152,174,191,218,288,290,303,318.   26,79,87,119,147,195,199,208,210.

Bowling: Hadlee 40-15-93-5, Cairns 23-8-65-1, Chatfield 36.3-8-116-2, Crowe 13-1-35-2, Coney 8-7-6-0.

Second innings: Hadlee 26-7-42-3, Chatfield 13.3-4-29-3, Cairns 3-0-9-0, Bracewell 11-4-29-0, Gray 30-8-73-3, Coney 6-4-9-1.

NEW ZEALAND

J.G. Wright	c Lamb b Willis	11	c Taylor b Botham	12
B.A. Edgar	c Willis b Cook	70	c Lamb b Cowans	27
* G.P. Howarth	b Cook	25	c Taylor b Willis	0
M.D. Crowe	b Botham	46	c Foster b Cowans	12
J.V. Coney	b Cook	7	c Gatting b Foster	68
E.J. Gray	c Lamb b Botham	11	c Lamb b Cook	17
J.G. Bracewell	c Gower b Cook	0	(8) lbw b Willis	4
R.J. Hadlee	c Botham b Cook	0	(7) b Willis	30
B.L. Cairns	c Lamb b Botham	5	b Cook	16
† I.D.S. Smith	c Lamb b Botham	3	not out	17
E.J. Chatfield	not out	5	c and b Cook	2
Extras	(lb5, nb3)	8	(b3, lb4, nb7)	14
	(84.4 overs)	191	(69.2 overs)	219

Fall: 18,49,147,159,176,176,176,183,184.   15,17,57,61,108,154,158,190,206.

Bowling: Willis 13-6-28-1, Foster 16-5-40-0, Cowans 9-1-30-0, Botham 20.4-6-50-4, Cook 26-11-35-5.

Second innings: Willis 12-5-24-3, Botham 7-2-20-1, Cowans 11-1-36-2, Cook 27.2-9-90-3, Foster 12-0-35-1.

Toss: New Zealand   Umpires: D.J. Constant and D.G.L. Evans
Close of play: (1) E. 279 for 5 (Gatting 74, Taylor 12)
                  (2) N.Z. 176 for 6 (Gray 10, Hadlee 0)
                  (3) E. 206 for 7 (Foster 2, Cook 5)

ENGLAND WON BY 127 RUNS

England completed a 3-1 series win by taking the fourth Test, at Trent Bridge, by 165 runs. Botham and Lamb scored centuries for England, while Cook took nine more wickets.

1984i

The centenary of Test cricket at Lord's was marked by the visit of one of the strongest teams ever to come to this country, the 1984 West Indians, captained once again by Clive Lloyd. His side allied a talented batting line-up to the now-customary fast-bowling quartet and – unusually for sides under Lloyd's direction – also included a spinner, in the promising Harper.

West Indies were destined to record emphatic victories in all five Tests, becoming the first side to manage a clean sweep away from home. The Lord's Test was the most evenly-contested of the five, with England being in contention throughout the first four days of the match.

Centuries from Gomes and Richards, plus a ninth-wicket stand of 150 between Baptiste and Holding, set up West Indies' winning total of 606 in the first Test at Edgbaston. England could manage only 191 and 235, with opener Andy Lloyd – making his Test debut on his home ground – receiving a blow on the temple from Marshall that put him in hospital for nine days and ended his brief international career.

Nottinghamshire opener Broad replaced Lloyd at Lord's, where England's first three batsmen uniquely were left-handers. Clive Lloyd equalled Sobers's West Indian record by playing in his fifth Lord's Test, while Milton Small (a distant relative of Gladstone Small, who later played for England) replaced the unfit Holding.

Put in, England made satisfactory progress on an overcast day often interrupted by bad light. The openers added 101, the angular Broad's 55 containing nine fours – five of them coming in the space of 11 balls – before Dujon pulled off a good legside catch. Gower soon departed, one of three lbw victims in Marshall's eventual 6 for 85, but Fowler and Lamb took the score to 167 without further loss by the close.

Lamb and Gatting were both lbw to Marshall early on Day 2, but the busy Fowler carried on to a characterful century, eventually falling for 106, made in 369 minutes and containing 13 fours. Fowler and Botham had shared a partnership of 58, but both departed within the space of five runs, and afterwards only Downton held things up for long as England slipped to 286 all out. Miller was dismissed in spectacular fashion: thinking himself safe, he was sauntering towards the crease at the bowler's end as Baptiste picked up the ball at deep fine leg nearly 100 yards away: the fielder's rocket-like flat throw removed the middle stump to run out the astonished Miller.

West Indies made a poor start in reply, Botham taking three early wickets in a good spell. Captain Lloyd and his deputy Richards prevented any further alarms, taking the score from 35 to 119 for 3 by the close, Lloyd reaching 7000 Test runs at 25.

Lloyd could add only seven runs in 59 balls on the third morning as Botham, moving his outswinger testingly during an unchanged spell from the Nursery end, continued his good form with the ball to finish with 8 for 103. West Indies could manage only 245, conceding a lead of 41. Richards hit 11 fours in his 72 before being adjudged lbw to Botham when the ball seemed to be slipping down the leg side: umpire Barrie Meyer later took the unusual step of apologising to Richards,

Gordon Greenidge, who finished with a brilliant 214 not out, takes another boundary as West Indies cruise to victory on the final day in 1984

saying that he may have made a mistake: this was Botham's 50th Test wicket at Lord's. Marshall and Baptiste got in some solid blows before Willis removed them both: Marshall had a lucky escape when he hooked Willis to the fine-leg boundary, where Don Topley of the MCC cricket staff (he later played for Essex) took a well-judged one-handed catch but put a foot over the boundary rope.

When England batted, it was their turn to lose three quick wickets, Broad falling to Garner for a duck while Small removed Fowler and Gower. Lamb and Gatting took the score to 88, at which point Gatting, for the second time in the match, played no stroke at Marshall and was lbw. His double misjudgment cost him his place in the next Test.

On a fourth day again interrupted by rain, England batted solidly to take the score to 287 for 7, a lead of 328. England's hero was Lamb, whose 110, his fourth Test century, contained 13 fours and occupied 362 minutes. Lamb's main support came in a stand of 128 with Botham, who scored a responsible 81, the highest score in his 19 matches against West Indies.

As the last hour of the fourth day started, England held the upper hand, with West Indies on the defensive for once, and the visitors were relieved when Lamb, rather surprisingly, accepted the umpires' bad-light offer and left the field. Lamb was out almost immediately on the final morning, and Gower's declaration after 20 minutes left West Indies needing 342 to become the first team to win a Lord's Test after a declaration by the other side.

It seemed a remote target – only four higher totals have ever been made to win a Test – but the confident West Indians strolled to their goal as if playing in a Sunday League match. The only setback in the victory push came when Haynes was run out by Lamb at square leg with the score at 57, but after that Greenidge and Gomes took complete charge. Greenidge was the senior partner, his precise strokeplay being a joy to watch, and he stormed to his century within 33 overs, Gomes (dropped at 5) having unselfishly given him the lion's share of the strike. Botham at slip dropped him off Willis when 110, but apart from giving a catch off a Willis no-ball Greenidge was untroubled as he raced to his first Test double-century, passing 4000 runs in Tests (a landmark also reached by Botham earlier in the match).

Remarkably, it was all over with 11.5 overs to spare, Greenidge ending up with a superlative 214 not out, made in 300 minutes and containing 29 fours and two sixes. His valiant partner Gomes – who had four unspectacular seasons with Middlesex in the 1970s – finished with 92 not out, his 236-minute innings having included 13 fours. The unbroken stand of 287 remains a West Indian second-wicket record against England.

ENGLAND v WEST INDIES
June 28, 29, 30, July 2, 3, 1984

ENGLAND

G. Fowler	c Harper b Baptiste	106	lbw b Small	11
B.C. Broad	c Dujon b Marshall	55	c Harper b Garner	0
* D.I. Gower	lbw b Marshall	3	c Lloyd b Small	21
A.J. Lamb	lbw b Marshall	23	c Dujon b Marshall	110
M.W. Gatting	lbw b Marshall	1	lbw b Marshall	29
I.T. Botham	c Richards b Baptiste	30	lbw b Garner	81
† P.R. Downton	not out	23	lbw b Small	4
G. Miller	run out	0	b Harper	9
D.R. Pringle	lbw b Garner	2	lbw b Garner	8
N.A. Foster	c Harper b Marshall	6	not out	9
R.G.D. Willis	b Marshall	2		
Extras	(b4, lb14, w2, nb15)	35	(b4, lb7, w1, nb6)	18
	(105.5 overs)	286	(9 wkts dec) (98.3 overs)	300

Fall: 101,106,183,185,243,248,251,255,264.   5,33,36,88,216,230,273,290,300.

Bowling: Garner 32-10-67-1, Small 9-0-38-0, Marshall 36.5-10-85-6,
Baptiste 20-6-36-2, Harper 8-0-25-0.
Second innings: Garner 30.3-3-91-3, Marshall 22-6-85-2, Small 12-2-40-3,
Baptiste 26-8-48-0, Harper 8-1-18-1.

WEST INDIES

C.G. Greenidge	c Miller b Botham	1	not out	214
D.L. Haynes	lbw b Botham	12	run out	17
H.A. Gomes	c Gatting b Botham	10	not out	92
I.V.A. Richards	lbw b Botham	72		
* C.H. Lloyd	lbw b Botham	39		
† P.J.L. Dujon	c Fowler b Botham	8		
M.D. Marshall	c Pringle b Willis	29		
E.A.E. Baptiste	c Downton b Willis	44		
R.A. Harper	c Gatting b Botham	8		
J. Garner	c Downton b Botham	6		
M.A. Small	not out	3		
Extras	(lb5, w1, nb7)	13	(b4, lb4, nb13)	21
	(65.4 overs)	245	(1 wkt) (66.1 overs)	344

Fall: 1,18,35,138,147,173,213,231,241.   57.

Bowling: Willis 19-5-48-2, Botham 27.4-6-103-8, Pringle 11-0-54-0, Foster 6-2-13-0,
Miller 2-0-14-0.
Second innings: Willis 15-5-48-0, Botham 20.1-2-117-0, Pringle 8-0-44-0, Foster 12-0-69-0,
Miller 11-0-45-0.

Toss: West Indies   Umpires: D.G.L. Evans and B.J. Meyer
Close of play: (1) E. 167 for 2 (Fowler 70, Lamb 13)
                  (2) W.I. 119 for 3 (Richards 60, Lloyd 32)
                  (3) E. 114 for 4 (Lamb 30, Botham 17)
                  (4) E. 287 for 7 (Lamb 109, Pringle 6)

WEST INDIES WON BY 9 WICKETS

West Indies completed what their supporters called a 'blackwash' with comfortable victories at Headingley, Old Trafford and The Oval. Only Lamb, with two more centuries, impressed for England, while Gomes, Greenidge (223 at Old Trafford), Dujon and Haynes all reached three figures for the visitors, for whom Marshall, Holding, Garner and Harper all had impressive spells with the ball.

1984ii

After their mauling at the hands of West Indies, England anticipated an easier time of it against Sri Lanka in the islanders' inaugural Test in this country, which rounded off the 1984 international season at Lord's. The most recent addition to Test-match ranks, the islanders had played their first Test at home in 1981-82, and were still without a win: furthermore, like England, they were lacking a number of players, banned after joining an unauthorised tour of South Africa.

The tourists had failed to impress during their warm-up matches, and it was a confident Gower who chose to field first after Duleep Mendis called wrongly. The start was delayed slightly by the first of two demonstrations by disaffected Sri Lankan Tamils, but when play did get under way England made two quick breakthroughs, Silva going for 5 and Madugalle, still feeling the effects of an assault by a drunk in Canterbury, falling for 8. That was the extent of English success for a while, however, Wettimuny and the elegant Dias sharing a partnership worth 101. Dias fell to Pocock for 32, but Wettimuny, calm and correct, batted on, reaching a splendid century in 219 minutes (175 balls). Now in company with the comfortably-built left-hander Ranatunga, Wettimuny survived until bad light brought an early close with the score at 226 for 3.

Sri Lanka made the most of unimaginative England bowling on the second day, losing only the wicket of Ranatunga in progressing to 434 for 4. The overnight pair swelled their stand to 148, both surviving very difficult chances to Gower in the gully. Ranatunga hit eight fours and a six (a two augmented by four overthrows) before falling for 84 to Agnew, who had had him dropped by Lamb in his previous over. Wettimuny remained, however, his classical side-on technique giving scant encouragement to England's toiling bowlers: despite suffering from cramp in the later stages of his innings, he survived throughout a day interrupted twice by bad light and rain.

Ranatunga's replacement at the crease was the rotund Sri Lankan skipper Mendis, and he caned the tiring bowlers in a delightful attacking innings. Hitting out almost from the start, he dominated yet another century partnership. He delighted in the savage cut and hard-hit drive, and when Botham, in desperation, pitched short, Mendis three times hooked him into the Mound Stand for sixes. After twice declining the umpires' bad-light offers, Mendis reached an entertaining century in just 112 balls, at which point the gloom did bring play to a halt.

Wettimuny's marathon came to an end in the 10th over of the third day, his 190 (21 fours) being Sri Lanka's highest Test score at the time. His 637-minute innings is the longest in any match at Lord's. Mendis went for 111 (11 fours and those three sixes), and after some late blows from de Mel the declaration came at 491 for 7.

England's bowling had been disappointing, but their efforts with the bat tested the patience of even the most ardent home fan, terribly heavy weather being made of a friendly bowling attack in which legspinner Somachandra de Silva, potentially the tourists' best bowler, was struggling after turning an ankle in the nets so badly that he had to go to hospital for an X-ray. He was on crutches not long before he was due to field, but somehow managed to get through 45 overs.

Slips Lamb and Tavaré watch as another pull from Duleep Mendis sails towards the Mound Stand. The tubby Sri Lankan skipper made 111 and 94: no-one has come closer to emulating George Headley's 1939 feat of scoring a century in each innings of a Lord's Test

England made a useful start, the total reaching 49 before Fowler fell to the burly opening bowler Vinothen John, another who was barely fit. The low-point for England, though, came in the painfully slow partnership between Broad and Tavaré, the Kent man's 14 taking him 2¼ hours. In 260 minutes, England faced 61 overs and crawled to 139 for 2, Broad having made 69: he went on to 86 on the fourth morning, but his laborious 339-minute innings cost him a place on England's winter tour of India, his county colleague Robinson winning selection instead.

When Botham gave a catch to substitute Marlon Vonhagt in the gully, England, at 218 for 4, were in real danger of having to follow on, but a sensible stand of 87 between Lamb (dropped by wicketkeeper Silva at 36) and Ellison at least averted that indignity. Lamb went on to his fourth Test century of the summer, a feat previously achieved only by Sutcliffe, Bradman and Compton: he hit 10 fours and a six during his 267 minutes at the crease. The last four wickets went down for 16 at the end of the day, Pocock averting a hat-trick after de Mel removed Downton and Allott with successive balls. The final total of 370 gave Sri Lanka a lead of 121.

Unsurprisingly there was to be no generous declaration on the final day, which therefore was something of an anticlimax. Left-hander Silva batted throughout the day, reaching his maiden first-class century just before the end despite cramp, which caused him to call for a runner during the later stages of his 316-minute innings. His innings was overshadowed, though, by Mendis, who fell agonisingly short of emulating Headley's unique feat of scoring a century in each innings of a Lord's Test. Mendis made 94 this time, hitting three more sixes and nine fours in two exciting hours before he fell to Botham, who by now was bowling offspin of a sort (nevertheless he managed to take six of the seven wickets to fall).

England at least escaped with a draw, which enabled them to lick the wounds caused by West Indies and look forward to their forthcoming tour of India with some optimism. Sri Lanka, on the other hand, were delighted with their strong showing, although they were disappointed at being unable to clinch their elusive first Test victory (which came two years later, against India at home). Unfortunately, the islanders' development at Test level has since been hampered by their lack of a domestic first-class competition and political problems at home.

ENGLAND v SRI LANKA

August 23, 24, 25, 27, 28, 1984

SRI LANKA

S. Wettimuny	c Downton b Allott	190	c Gower b Botham		13
† S.A.R. Silva	lbw b Botham	8	not out		102
R.S. Madugalle	b Ellison	5	b Botham		3
R.L. Dias	c Lamb b Pocock	32	lbw b Botham		38
A. Ranatunga	b Agnew	84	lbw b Botham		0
* L.R.D. Mendis	c Fowler b Pocock	111	(7) c Fowler b Botham		94
P.A. de Silva	c Downton b Agnew	16	(6) c Downton b Pocock		3
A.L.F. de Mel	not out	20	c Ellison b Botham		14
J.R. Ratnayeke	not out	5	not out		7
D.S. de Silva	) did not bat				
V.B. John	)				
Extras	(b2, lb8, w2, nb8)	20	(b5, lb4, nb11)		20
	(7 wkts dec) (166 overs)	491	(7 wkts dec) (80 overs)		294

Fall: 17,43,144,292,442,456,464.   19,27,111,115,118,256,276.

Bowling: Agnew 32-3-123-2, Botham 29-6-114-1, Ellison 28-6-70-1, Pocock 41-17-75-2, Allott 36-7-89-1.

Second innings: Agnew 11-3-54-0, Allott 1-0-2-0, Botham 27-6-90-6, Pocock 29-10-78-1, Ellison 7-0-36-0, Lamb 1-0-6-0, Tavaré 3-3-0-0, Fowler 1-0-8-0.

ENGLAND

G. Fowler	c Madugalle b John	25	Bowling:
B.C. Broad	c Silva b de Mel	86	de Mel 37-10-110-4,
C.J. Tavaré	c Ranatunga b D.S. de Silva	14	John 39.1-12-98-4,
* D.I. Gower	c Silva b de Mel	55	Ratnayeke 22-5-50-0,
A.J. Lamb	c Dias b John	107	D.S. de Silva 45-16-85-2,
I.T. Botham	c sub (D.M. Vonhagt) b John	6	Ranatunga 1-1-0-0,
R.M. Ellison	c Ratnayeke b D.S. de Silva	41	Madugalle 3-0-4-0.
† P.R. Downton	c Dias b de Mel	10	
P.J.W. Allott	b de Mel	0	
P.I. Pocock	c Silva b John	2	
J.P. Agnew	not out	1	
Extras	(b5, lb7, w5, nb6)	23	
	(147.1 overs)	370	

Fall: 49,105,190,210,218,305,354,354,369.

Toss: England   Umpires: H.D. Bird and D.G.L. Evans

Close of play: (1) S.L. 226 for 3 (Wettimuny 116, Ranatunga 54)
(2) S.L. 434 for 4 (Wettimuny 187, Mendis 100)
(3) E. 139 for 2 (Broad 69, Gower 16)
(4) E. 370 all out

MATCH DRAWN

1985

After the tribulations and humiliations of 1984, England's cricketers restored their pride by emerging victorious from the winter series in India, Gower's men coming from behind after the hosts had won the first Test. England's hopes for the 1985 Ashes series were further enhanced by the return after a three-year ban of the South African 'rebel' tourists: Gooch, Willey and Emburey earned an immediate recall.

Australia, however, had their own South African problems: three of their selected side (Alderman, McCurdy and Rixon) withdrew after agreeing to tour South Africa in a side led by Kim Hughes, who had resigned the Australian captaincy in tears the previous winter. His replacement, Allan Border, brought the team to England.

England took the first Test, at Headingley, by five wickets, Robinson's 175 setting up a total of 533, which proved too much for Australia despite Hilditch's 119 and 80.

Heavy rain before the Lord's Test gave the groundsmen plenty of work: the ground was waterlogged the day before the match, but around-the-clock efforts enabled play to start on time. Put in, England faced an impressive opening spell from the 20-year-old McDermott, who trapped both openers lbw, Gooch looking a little unlucky to be given out. Gower was soon into his stride, his feet moving well as he embarked on a charming innings of 89, many of his 12 fours coming from elegant back-foot shots.

After Gatting had gone for 14, padding up yet again and falling lbw – his third successive such dismissal in a Lord's Test – Gower's main partner was Lamb, who made 47 in 2½ hours before, like his captain, he edged a drive and was caught. Botham scored his first runs against Australia at Lord's in his fourth innings, but then was immediately caught on the cover boundary playing an extravagant drive at Lawson. Staunch play from the Middlesex trio of Downton, Emburey and Edmonds guided the score to 273 for 8 by the close, and 17 runs were added on the second morning before McDermott wrapped up the innings to finish with 6 for 70.

Australia made an indifferent start on a day in which bad light intervened five times before forcing a premature close. Both openers had gone with 24 on the board, and although Wessels and Border – Queensland left-handers both – shared a stand of 56, the South African-born Wessels struggled for 11 in 93 minutes before Botham won an lbw shout. When Boon went for 4 England entertained hopes of a first-innings lead, but Border and Ritchie (another Queenslander) took the score to 183 before the umpires earned catcalls from the crowd by deeming the light too bad for play to continue, even though England's attack was in the hands of spinners Edmonds and Emburey.

Shortly before the close Border, then 87, had an escape when he clipped Edmonds firmly off his legs, only to see Gatting at short leg apparently catch the ball. Border turned to leave, but Gatting was struggling to keep the ball under control, and eventually the ball dropped to earth, despite the despairing attempts of the fieldsman. Umpire Bird ruled that the catch had not been properly taken, and Border survived.

Border did more than survive on the third day, taking his score to 196, his highest in Tests at the time and the third-highest by an Australian at Lord's after Bradman and Brown. The captain hit 22 fours in his 450-minute stay, but was deprived of his double-century by the persistent Botham, who earlier had ended the Border/Ritchie stand at 216: unsettled by two bouncers, Ritchie fell lbw to a well-pitched-up ball for 94 (10 fours). Bright contributions from Phillips and O'Donnell lifted the score to 425, a lead of 135. Botham, making light of an injured ankle, finished with 5 for 109.

Australia strengthened their grip on the match in the closing overs, Gooch falling to McDermott again and Robinson getting in a tangle against the legspin of Holland, who was appearing in his first Test against England (and only Lord's Test) at the age of 38.

When these wickets fell, Gower sent out two nightwatchmen – Emburey and Allott – an unorthodox tactic which gave rise to fears that one of the recognised batsmen might run out of partners later in the innings, and so it proved: Gatting ended up with 75 not out. Neither nightwatchman lasted long on the fourth morning, and England declined to 98 for 6 when Gower and Lamb went cheaply, the captain's frenetic 22 including five fours, three of them coming in successive balls from Lawson.

Gatting, astonishingly enough, padded up to his first ball, but this time he survived the concerted appeal to play second fiddle in an important stand of 131 with Botham, entering at No. 8. Botham cantered to 85, hitting 12 fours and swatting McDermott into the Mound Stand for six, but after 135 minutes his exciting innings came to an end when Holland induced a false stroke, which was caught by Border at cover. Holland's next ball accounted for Downton, and although Edmonds survived 47 minutes for a single, the grey-haired legspinner took the last two wickets to finish with 5 for 68. Gatting was undefeated after 248 minutes, having hit six boundaries.

Needing 127 to win, Australia made a nervous start, Hilditch obligingly hooking Botham's fourth ball straight to Lamb. Wood soon followed, Lamb's second catch providing Botham with his 326th wicket and taking him past Bob Willis as England's leading wicket-taker. The promoted Ritchie, too, did not last long, and at 22 for 3 Australia looked shaky.

Wessels and Border took the score to 46 that night, and on to 63 on the final morning before Wessels was run out by some sleight-of-hand from Gower at silly point. Boon went for 1 (65 for 5), but with Border looking solid some clean blows from Phillips, yet another left-hander, put the result beyond doubt. Phillips, who spent a season on the MCC cricket staff in 1981 (as did Martin Crowe, a Lord's Test centurymaker the following year), struck four fours in his 29 before Edmonds took an acrobatic catch at point. Border, who finished with 41, had few problems, although he did show signs of irritation when a lengthy announcement from MCC secretary Jack Bailey, exhorting spectators not to run on to the playing area at the end of the match, briefly held up the push for victory. Australian celebrations were not long delayed, however: O'Donnell lofted Edmonds to the Nursery end for six, then ended the match with a similar hit for two, Border punching the air with delight as he ran through for the runs which won the match and squared the series.

Friendly rivalry: Ian Botham congratulates Allan Border after dismissing the
Australian captain for a decisive 196. Border's innings set up his side's only victory
in the 1985 Ashes series

ENGLAND v AUSTRALIA
June 27, 28, 29, July 1, 2, 1985

ENGLAND

G.A. Gooch	lbw b McDermott	30	c Phillips b McDermott	17
R.T. Robinson	lbw b McDermott	6	b Holland	12
* D.I. Gower	c Border b McDermott	86	(5) c Phillips b McDermott	22
M.W. Gatting	lbw b Lawson	14	(6) not out	75
A.J. Lamb	c Phillips b Lawson	47	(7) c Holland b Lawson	9
I.T. Botham	c Ritchie b Lawson	5	(8) c Border b Holland	85
† P.R. Downton	c Wessels b McDermott	21	(9) c Boon b Holland	0
J.E. Emburey	lbw b O'Donnell	33	(3) b Lawson	20
P.H. Edmonds	c Border b McDermott	21	(10) c Boon b Holland	1
N.A. Foster	c Wessels b McDermott	3	(11) c Border b Holland	0
P.J.W. Allott	not out	1	(4) b Lawson	0
Extras	(b1, lb4, w1, nb17)	23	(b1, lb12, w4, nb3)	20
	(99.2 overs)	290	(80 overs)	261

Fall: 26,51,99,179,184,211,241,273,283.   32,34,38,57,77,98,229,229,261.

Bowling: Lawson 25-2-91-3, McDermott 29.2-5-70-6, O'Donnell 22-3-82-1, Holland 23-6-42-0.

Second innings: McDermott 20-2-84-2, Lawson 23-0-86-3, Holland 32-12-68-5, O'Donnell 5-0-10-0.

AUSTRALIA

G.M. Wood	c Emburey b Allott	8	(2) c Lamb b Botham	6
A.M.J. Hilditch	b Foster	14	(1) c Lamb b Botham	0
K.C. Wessels	lbw b Botham	11	run out	28
* A.R. Border	c Gooch b Botham	196	(5) not out	41
D.C. Boon	c Downton b Botham	4	(6) b Edmonds	1
G.M. Ritchie	lbw b Botham	94	(4) b Allott	2
† W.B. Phillips	c Edmonds b Botham	21	c Edmonds b Emburey	29
S.P. O'Donnell	c Lamb b Edmonds	48	not out	9
G.F. Lawson	not out	5		
C.J. McDermott	run out	9		
R.G. Holland	b Edmonds	0		
Extras	(lb10, w1, nb4)	15	(lb11)	11
	(124.4 overs)	425	(6 wkts) (46 overs)	127

Fall: 11,24,80,101,317,347,398,414,425.   0,9,22,63,65,116.

Bowling: Foster 23-1-83-1, Allott 30-4-70-1, Botham 24-2-109-5, Edmonds 25.4-5-85-2, Gooch 3-1-11-0, Emburey 19-3-57-0.

Second innings: Botham 15-0-49-2, Allott 7-4-8-1, Edmonds 16-5-35-1, Emburey 8-4-24-1.

Toss: Australia   Umpires: H.D. Bird and D.G.L. Evans
Close of play: (1) E. 273 for 8 (Edmonds 9, Foster 0)
    (2) A. 183 for 4 (Border 92, Ritchie 46)
    (3) E. 37 for 2 (Emburey 4, Allott 0)
    (4) A. 46 for 3 (Wessels 23, Border 12)
Note: from 1985, wides and no-balls debited against the bowlers' analyses

AUSTRALIA WON BY 4 WICKETS

High scoring remained a feature of the series, five batsmen exceeding 140 in the next two matches, both draws. Further centuries from Gower (215), Robinson and Gatting set up England's innings victory in the fifth Test at Edgbaston, where Ellison took 10 wickets: he added another seven victims in another innings victory at The Oval, Gooch (196) and Gower (157) being the batting heroes. England's 3-1 series victory recovered the Ashes, lost in 1982-83.

1986i

The rival skippers for the first Test of the 1986 twin-tour summer both arrived at Lord's with their captaincy records under scrutiny. Kapil Dev had led India to a shock victory in the 1983 World Cup, but his 20 Tests in charge had produced not one victory: his opposite number Gower, after the elation of the previous season's Ashes victory, had presided over an embarrassing 5-0 defeat at the hands of West Indies in the Caribbean. It was a fair bet, therefore, that the captain losing this series would lose his job, but the axe fell sooner than that, with Gower being relieved of his responsibilities within minutes of India's victory, which ironically was sealed by Kapil Dev's mighty blow into the Grand Stand off the bowling of Edmonds.

England were at full strength for the Test, save for the absence of Botham, whose revelation that he had once smoked 'pot' had earned him a two-month ban from first-class cricket. Kapil Dev's side include Gavaskar, making his fifth and last appearance in a Lord's Test (an Indian record), while at the other end of the scale wicketkeeper Moré was making his Test debut.

On the first day things had looked rosier for Gower and England: put in on an overcast day, the only wicket to go down before lunch was that of Robinson, after an opening stand of 66 with Gooch, who was looking encouragingly solid even if he was perhaps not at his best. After lunch, though, the bustling Sharma caused a collapse, with three wickets in 11 balls to reduce England to 98 for 4. Gooch and his county colleague Pringle now combined in a saving stand of 147, which terminated five minutes before the close when Gooch, having hit 12 fours and a six (off Shastri), was bowled by Sharma for 114.

Pringle, despite looking overplaced in the order at No. 6, completed his highest Test score of 63 after a late start on the second morning, but none of the other batsmen made much impression as the innings folded for 294 in the face of steady bowling and good fielding from the Indians. Binny took three late wickets, while Sharma finished with 5 for 80.

India's reply began with fireworks from Srikkanth, who struck four quick fours before he fell to Dilley, the batsman possibly being unnerved by a half-naked lady streaker, who brightened up a cold, cheerless day by running on to the pitch brandishing a 'Bring Back Botham' scarf. No further wickets fell before the close, India reaching 83 for 1 from 50 overs, with both Gavaskar and Amarnath – playing his only Lord's Test more than 16 years after his debut – looking solid. In all, only 132 runs were scored in 83 overs during a day which bad light shortened by half an hour.

Gavaskar had looked set for that elusive Lord's Test century, but he departed in the second over of the third morning. Amarnath punished the successful bowler, Dilley, to the tune of 14 runs in one over, but after hitting 10 fours in his 69 Amarnath gave a catch to Pringle. Now Vengsarkar took control, his upright strokeplay and correct footwork rekindling memories of his fighting centuries in both his previous Lord's Tests. He added 71 in 80 minutes with Azharuddin, who himself had scored centuries in each of his previous three Tests against England. However, Dilley removed Azharuddin for 33, whereupon four more quick wickets tumbled. When No. 10 Moré came in, Vengsarkar – by now troubled by

Two appealing Indian greats: Dilip Vengsarkar (centre) became the first overseas player to score three centuries in Tests at Lord's during this match, but the great Sunil Gavaskar (right), in his fifth and last Lord's Test, failed to record that elusive maiden hundred. The other fielder is Mohinder Amarnath

cramp in his left forearm – was 81, and he had advanced to 99 when the little wicketkeeper was lbw to Pringle. Last man Maninder, a novice with the bat, somehow survived long enough to allow Vengsarkar to reach his century; then the pair enjoyed themselves, adding 38 in over an hour before Emburey ended the fun.

Vengsarkar was undefeated with 126 (16 fours) when the innings closed, having become the first overseas player to score three Test centuries at Lord's. Among England players, the feat had been achieved only by Boycott, Compton, John Edrich, Hobbs and Hutton (Gooch joined the select band later in the season, and Lamb in 1988).

In four overs before the close England scored eight without loss, but Kapil Dev, with a 19-ball spell of 3 for 1, reduced England to 35 for 3 on an overcast fourth morning (perversely, England always seemed to be batting in cloudy conditions, whereas the sun came out during India's innings). Gatting and Lamb put England into the black, their stand of 73 being the most entertaining part of another slow day, which saw England manage a meagre 172 runs from 92.4 overs despite a close-set field throughout the day – slow left-armer Maninder had the remarkable figures of 3 for 9 from 20.4 overs. After Gatting and Lamb had gone, only Downton and Ellison, who both survived for two hours, resisted for long, Downton being unlucky that his well-timed sweep flew straight to Shastri at square leg. The innings ended at 180 a few minutes before the scheduled close, leaving India all the final day to score 134 for victory.

Dilley removed both openers in a brisk opening burst, but hamstring trouble soon drove him back into the dressing-room, were he joined Emburey (injured back). Their absence eased India's task, and although three more wickets fell, the end came in grand style with Kapil Dev taking 18 from an Edmonds over, the 42nd of the innings.

India's triumph was their first in 11 Lord's Tests (England have won eight), and only their second in this country. England, on the other hand, had suffered their sixth successive defeat, in the match which marked the end of Gower's first spell of Test captaincy.

244

ENGLAND v INDIA
June 5, 6, 7, 9, 10, 1986

ENGLAND

G.A. Gooch	b Sharma	114	lbw b Kapil Dev		8
R.T. Robinson	c Azharuddin b Maninder	35	c Amarnath b Kapil Dev		11
* D.I. Gower	c Moré b Sharma	18	lbw b Kapil Dev		8
M.W. Gatting	b Sharma	0	b Sharma		40
A.J. Lamb	c Srikkanth b Sharma	6	c Moré b Shastri		39
D.R. Pringle	b Binny	63	c Moré b Kapil Dev		6
J.E. Emburey	c Amarnath b Kapil Dev	7	(9) c and b Maninder		1
† P.R. Downton	lbw b Sharma	5	(7) c Shastri b Maninder		29
R.M. Ellison	c Kapil Dev b Binny	12	(8) c Moré b Binny		19
G.R. Dilley	c Moré b Binny	4	not out		2
P.H. Edmonds	not out	7	c Binny b Maninder		7
Extras	(lb15, w1, nb7)	23	(lb6, w1, nb3)		10
	(128.2 overs)	294	(96.4 overs)		180

Fall: 66,92,92,98,245,264,269,271,287. 18,23,35,108,113,121,164,170,170.

Bowling: Kapil Dev 31-8-67-1, Binny 18.2-4-55-3, Sharma 32-10-64-5, Maninder 30-15-45-1, Amarnath 7-1-18-0, Shastri 10-3-30-0.

Second innings: Kapil Dev 22-7-52-4, Sharma 17-4-48-1, Binny 15-3-44-1, Shastri 20-8-21-1, Maninder 20.4-12-9-3, Amarnath 2-2-0-0.

INDIA

S.M. Gavaskar	c Emburey b Dilley	34	c Downton b Dilley		22
K. Srikkanth	c Gatting b Dilley	20	c Gooch b Dilley		0
M.B. Amarnath	c Pringle b Edmonds	69	lbw b Pringle		8
D.B. Vengsarkar	not out	126	b Edmonds		33
M. Azharuddin	c and b Dilley	33	run out		14
R.J. Shastri	c Edmonds b Dilley	1	not out		20
R.M.H. Binny	lbw b Pringle	9			
* Kapil Dev	c Lamb b Ellison	1	(7) not out		23
C. Sharma	b Pringle	2			
† K.S. Moré	lbw b Pringle	25			
Maninder Singh	c Lamb b Emburey	6			
Extras	(lb5, w1, nb9)	15	(b1, lb9, w1, nb5)		16
	(137 overs)	341	(5 wkts) (42 overs)		136

Fall: 31,90,161,232,238,252,253,264,303. 10,31,76,78,110.

Bowling: Dilley 34-7-146-4, Ellison 29-11-63-1, Emburey 27-13-28-1, Edmonds 22-7-41-1, Pringle 25-7-58-3.

Second innings: Dilley 10-3-28-2, Ellison 6-0-17-0, Pringle 15-5-30-1, Edmonds 11-2-51-1.

Toss: India Umpires: K.E. Palmer and D.R. Shepherd
Close of play: (1) E. 245 for 5 (Pringle 51, Emburey 0)
(2) I. 83 for 1 (Gavaskar 30, Amarnath 27)
(3) E. 8 for 0 (Gooch 5, Robinson 3)
(4) E. 180 all out

INDIA WON BY 5 WICKETS

Gower's replacement as captain, Mike Gatting, fared little better, England losing the second Test, at Headingley, by 279 runs: Vengsarkar made another century (once again reaching it with last man Maninder as his partner). Gatting scored 183 not out in the third Test at Edgbaston, an evenly-balanced affair which ended when bad light intervened with India, chasing 236, at 174 for 5.

1986ii

New Zealand, the second of 1986's touring teams, were hopeful of emulating India by recording their first Lord's Test win against the dispirited England side. Shrewdly led by Jeremy Coney, the New Zealanders boasted two players of undoubted world class in batsman Martin Crowe and champion allrounder Richard Hadlee. The tourists called upon Hadlee's services only in the Tests: for the rest of the season, with the TCCB's permission, he concentrated on his benefit with Nottinghamshire and turned out for them.

An injury to Hadlee's longtime partner Ewen Chatfield meant that New Zealand were forced to give a first cap to 20-year-old Aucklander Willie Watson, who made an inauspicious start to his Test career by splitting his trousers soon after play began (his substitute, Tony Blain, unwittingly emulated David Steele in 1975 by losing his way inside the pavilion: he eventually appeared through the wrong door and had to jump over the fence). For England, Yorkshire opener Martyn Moxon made his Test debut, two years late: but for a rib injury, he would have played in the 1984 Lord's Test against West Indies.

Moxon was soon in action after Gatting, in his first Lord's Test as captain, won the toss. Gooch soon fell to the probing Hadlee, but the two Yorkshiremen, Moxon and Athey, combined in a stand of 75 which stretched to the lunch interval but not far beyond. Immediately after lunch, Athey edged Hadlee to slip, where Jeff Crowe dislocated his thumb in making the catch. Moxon and Gower now put on 94, Moxon's promising innings being cut short after four hours by the inevitable Hadlee. Gatting went cheaply, but Gower continued to impress, hitting 10 fours in his 62 before giving a catch off Bracewell shortly before the close, which found England 248 for 5.

Hadlee soon removed Edmonds on the second morning, then dug in a bouncer at his Notts colleague French, who turned his back on the ball. He was hit near the edge of his helmet, which dug into his head, causing a gash which needed three stitches. The dizzy French was helped off the field: he felt groggy until the fourth day, giving rise to an interesting procession of wicketkeeping substitutes when New Zealand batted. Hadlee greeted the new batsman, Dilley, with a snorting bouncer that shot past his head and went for four byes.

Watson ended the innings at 307 with his first two Test wickets, but Hadlee, with 6 for 80, was the main destroyer. The bowlers' good work, however, was threatened when Dilley, working up an impressive head of steam, disposed of Wright and Rutherford, both for ducks. Edgar and Martin Crowe, in their contrasting styles, saw out the rest of the day: both looked solid (Edgar remained scoreless for 50 minutes) and both ended the day unbeaten with 52.

The main talking-point of the day was the re-appearance behind the stumps of England's former wicketkeeper Bob Taylor, who had retired in 1984. With French unfit, Athey took the gloves for two overs, but, Gatting having obtained Coney's permission for the switch, Taylor was summoned from his public-relations duties with Test sponsors Cornhill: he borrowed some kit, collected his gloves from his car, and ran out to warm applause.

Taylor gave a faultless performance until shortly before lunch on the third day, when he was replaced by yet another substitute, Bobby Parks, whose county

New Zealand's Richard Hadlee, who has taken more Test wickets at Lord's than any other overseas bowler (22) celebrates the dismissal of Martyn Moxon in 1986. The fielders are (l-r) Bracewell, captain Coney, Jeff Crowe, wicketkeeper Smith and Rutherford; the non-striker is Gooch, who made his third Lord's Test century in this match

Hampshire were without a game. Both Parks's father (1960-66) and grandfather (1937) played in Test matches at Lord's.

The third morning saw Edgar and Crowe extend their third-wicket partnership to 210, a New Zealand record against England. Edgar perished to the occasional bowling of Gooch for 83, made in 357 minutes with eight fours, but Martin Crowe continued in his simple, upright style, reaching 99 by lunch. He reached a well-made century straight after the interval, but almost immediately sent a simple return catch to Edmonds, having made 106 in 339 minutes, with 11 fours.

Fine bowling from Edmonds, who removed Jeff Crowe (his 100th Test wicket), Gray and Hadlee during a long spell, brought England back into the match, but Coney, with a bright 51, made sure that his side took a first-innings lead. By the close, New Zealand were 35 runs to the good at 342 for 9.

With French back in his rightful place behind the stumps, one ball from Dilley was enough to end the innings on the fourth morning. Both Dilley and Edmonds finished with four wickets.

England, batting again on an overcast day, soon lost Moxon to Hadlee, and after Gooch and Athey had added 59 left-armer Gray took two quick wickets, both Athey and Gower leaving their stumps unguarded as they sought to attack. Rain, which allowed only half the day's ration of overs, prevented any play after 3.30, by which time England had progressed to 110 for 3.

New Zealand smelled victory when Gatting fell early on the final morning to the persistent Gray, but Gooch, 64 overnight, progressed to join the ranks of those who have scored three Test centuries at Lord's, most recently augmented by Vengsarkar earlier in the year. Gooch shared a stand of 126 with Willey, who hit 42 in his second valuable innings of the match, and when Bracewell ended the stand the match was safe. The only remaining interest was Gooch's quest for his maiden Test double-century, but at 183 he put up a catch to long-off, having batted 442 minutes and hit 22 fours.

Gatting immediately declared, leaving New Zealand to bat out 15 overs for the draw. Two smart catches by Gower at third slip sent back the first two batsmen for ducks, as in the first innings: Wright thus completed a 'pair'. When stumps were drawn the tourists had progressed quietly to 41 for 2.

The result meant that New Zealand had still not beaten England in 10 attempts at Lord's: the home side had won five, with five draws.

ENGLAND v NEW ZEALAND
July 24, 25, 26, 28, 29, 1986

ENGLAND

G.A. Gooch	c Smith b Hadlee	18	c Watson b Bracewell	183
M.D. Moxon	lbw b Hadlee	74	lbw b Hadlee	5
C.W.J. Athey	c J.J. Crowe b Hadlee	44	b Gray	16
D.I. Gower	c M.D. Crowe b Bracewell	62	b Gray	3
* M.W. Gatting	b Hadlee	2	c M.D. Crowe b Gray	26
P. Willey	lbw b Watson	44	b Bracewell	42
P.H. Edmonds	c M.D. Crowe b Hadlee	6	not out	9
† B.N. French	retired hurt	0		
G.R. Dilley	c Smith b Hadlee	17		
N.A. Foster	b Watson	8		
N.V. Radford	not out	12		
Extras	(b6, lb7, nb7)	20	(lb6, w1, nb4)	11
	(118.5 overs)	307	(6 wkts dec) (120.4 overs)	295

Fall: 27,102,196,198,237,258,271,285,307.   9,68,72,136,262,295.

Bowling: Hadlee 37.5-11-80-6, Watson 30-7-70-2, M.D. Crowe 8-1-38-0, Coney 4-0-12-0, Bracewell 26-8-65-1, Gray 13-9-29-0.

Second innings: Hadlee 27-3-78-1, Watson 17-2-50-0, Gray 46-14-83-3, M.D. Crowe 4-0-13-0, Bracewell 23.4-7-57-2, Rutherford 3-0-8-0.

NEW ZEALAND

J.G. Wright	b Dilley	0	(2) c Gower b Dilley	0
B.A. Edgar	c Gatting b Gooch	83	(1) c Gower b Foster	0
K.R. Rutherford	c Gooch b Dilley	0	not out	24
M.D. Crowe	c and b Edmonds	106	not out	11
J.J. Crowe	c Gatting b Edmonds	18		
* J.V. Coney	c Gooch b Radford	51		
E.J. Gray	c Gower b Edmonds	11		
R.J. Hadlee	b Edmonds	19		
† I.D.S. Smith	c Edmonds b Dilley	18		
J.G. Bracewell	not out	1		
W. Watson	lbw b Dilley	1		
Extras	(b4, lb9, w6, nb15)	34	(lb4, nb2)	6
	(140.1 overs)	342	(2 wkts) (15 overs)	41

Fall: 2,5,215,218,274,292,310,340,340.   0,8.

Bowling: Dilley 35.1-9-82-4, Foster 25-6-56-0, Radford 25-4-71-1, Edmonds 42-10-97-4, Gooch 13-6-23-1.

Second innings: Foster 3-1-13-1, Dilley 6-3-5-1, Edmonds 5-0-18-0, Gower 1-0-1-0.

Toss: England   Umpires: H.D. Bird and A.G.T. Whitehead

Close of play: (1) E. 248 for 5 (Willey 27, Edmonds 6)
(2) N.Z. 127 for 2 (Edgar 52, M.D. Crowe 52)
(3) N.Z. 342 for 9 (Bracewell 1, Watson 1)
(4) E. 110 for 3 (Gooch 64, Gatting 21)
French retired hurt at 259 for 6

MATCH DRAWN

New Zealand won the second Test, at Trent Bridge, by eight wickets, with Bracewell, batting at No. 8, hitting 110; Hadlee took 10 wickets on his adopted home ground. The tourists clinched their first series win in England when the final Test, at The Oval, was drawn. Much of the playing time was lost to rain, the later stages being enlivened by a whirlwind 59 from the restored Botham. Earlier, Wright, Gower and Lamb had all scored centuries.

1987

According to the script, MCC's Bicentenary was to be celebrated by a year of enjoyment and harmony at various gala events. However, the reality was somewhat different. The year began with the club's secretary Jack Bailey and treasurer David Clark resigning over a point of principle; this inauspicious start was followed by unseasonal gales which blew down the huge marquee erected for the club's prestigious Bicentenary ball. The showpiece event of the celebrations, a special match between MCC and the Rest of the World, played at the end of the season, was indeed a great occasion for four days – but rain, which had blighted much of the summer, returned, spoiling the climax by washing out the whole of the final day's play.

The Lord's Test, earlier in the year, was even worse-hit. The visitors, Pakistan, under their charismatic captain Imran Khan, came to Lord's all-square, over half the playing time in the first Test at Old Trafford having been washed out. The tourists hoped for better things in London, especially as their brilliant legspinner Abdul Qadir had joined the tour after being delayed at home, but the special curse which seems to haunt England-Pakistan Tests at Lord's returned with a vengeance: the 84 Lord's Tests have seen 16 days where no play at all has been possible, and nine of these days have come in eight matches against Pakistan.

Even before the match, Lord's was flooded, but great efforts from the groundstaff produced a playable, comfortable pitch for the first day, and England, after winning the toss, progressed to 231 for 4 before bad light brought an early close. The feature of the day was Athey's only Test century, which he reached in 256 minutes. The Yorkshire-born Gloucestershire batsman shared a stand of 89 with Broad, with whom he had forged a successful opening partnership in Australia the previous winter (when Gatting's side retained the Ashes). The innocent-looking bowling of Mudassar accounted for Broad and, as in his famous 'Golden Arm' spell in 1982, for Gower. Athey and Gatting then added 102, the stand ending just before stumps when Gatting took on Salim Malik's arm from long leg.

Persistent rain prevented any play on the second day, bringing the TCCB's ticket-refund scheme (instituted in 1985) into play for the first time: the insurers were kept busy when the fourth and fifth days were also washed out.

According to *Wisden*, some 3000 gallons of water were removed from the outfield to enable play to start at 2.45 on the third day. Athey took his score to 123 (315 minutes, 14 fours), and nightwatchman French played a pleasant innings of 42. Botham disappointed in his 13th Lord's Test – his last to date – falling to Akram for 6.

The innings ended at 368, and there was no time for Pakistan to begin their reply: for the next two days they waited in vain to start as the rain pelted down. Only seven hours 10 minutes' actual play was possible in one of the more forgettable Lord's Tests. The watery final days were enlivened by the pronouncements of the excitable Pakistani manager Haseeb Ahsan, who took every opportunity to complain about the tour itinerary, the administration of cricket in England and, most vehemently, the standard of English umpires in general – in particular, the performance of David Constant, whose rejection of a confident lbw appeal by Akram against Gatting had upset the tourists.

Gloucestershire's Yorkshire exile Bill Athey, who scored the only Test century of his career in the truncated Lord's Test of 1987

ENGLAND v PAKISTAN
June 18, 19 (no play), 20, 22 (no play), 23 (no play), 1987

ENGLAND

B.C. Broad	b Mudassar	55	Bowling:
R.T. Robinson	c Yousuf b Kamal	7	Imran 34.5-7-90-2,
C.W.J. Athey	b Imran	123	Akram 28-1-98-2,
D.I. Gower	c Yousuf b Mudassar	8	Kamal 9-2-42-1,
* M.W. Gatting	run out	43	Qadir 25-1-100-1,
† B.N. French	b Akram	42	Mudassar 16-6-26-2.
I.T. Botham	c Miandad b Akram	6	
J.E. Emburey	run out	12	
N.A. Foster	b Qadir	21	
P.H. Edmonds	not out	17	
G.R. Dilley	c Yousuf b Imran	17	
Extras	(lb12, w1, nb4)	17	
	(112.5 overs)	368	

Fall: 29,118,128,230,272,294,305,329,340.

PAKISTAN
Mudassar Nazar, Shoaib Mohammad, Mansoor Akhtar, Javed Miandad, Salim Malik, *Imran Khan, Ijaz Ahmed, Abdul Qadir, †Salim Yousuf, Wasim Akram, Mohsin Kamal.

Toss: England
Close of play: (1) E. 231 for 4 (Athey 107, French 1)
(3) E. 368 all out

Umpires: D.J. Constant and A.G.T. Whitehead

MATCH DRAWN

Pakistan won the third Test, at Headingley, by an innings, Imran taking 10 wickets, including his 300th in Tests. England missed their chance at Edgbaston, failing to reach a victory target of 124 in the last 18 overs of the match, and at The Oval Pakistan clinched their first-ever series victory in England, Miandad (260) being the main contributor to the tourists' massive total of 708. Salim Malik (who made 99 at Leeds) and Imran also scored centuries, and later a marathon innings from Gatting forced a draw after England had followed on.

1988i

England went into the 1988 Test series confident that their recent record against West Indies (played 10, lost 10) could be improved. After success in the one-day internationals, two fine innings from Gooch at Trent Bridge brought the draw which ended the losing streak. From then on, however, it was all downhill. Newspaper allegations about a late-night drink with a hotel barmaid cost Gatting the captaincy, and he dropped out of the side for the Lord's Test, his replacement at the helm being his county deputy, Emburey. England were also without Botham, who missed most of the season with a back problem which needed an operation.

West Indies had no such worries, but the pace of Dilley posed problems enough on the first morning of the Lord's Test. Richards, who had assumed the captaincy when Clive Lloyd retired, had deliberated long and hard after winning the toss in the sunshine, but eventually decided to bat on what soon became an overcast morning.

Dilley made the most of the conditions in perhaps his finest spell for England. Steaming in from the Nursery end, the blond paceman was consistently hostile in a 2½-hour spell, his accurate awayswingers being supported for a time by five slips and a gully. A sharp catch by Moxon at short leg disposed of Haynes, and three more wickets came Dilley's way, including the prize scalp of Richards, caught behind for 6. Small chipped in with Hooper's wicket, leaving West Indies rocking at 54 for 5, but a saving stand of 130 between Logie and Dujon rectified matters. It might have been different, though, Pringle at first slip dropping the diminutive Logie when he had made only 10.

Logie's half-century included 12 fours, but he hit only two more in reaching 81 before Small removed him after three hours at the crease. The elegant Dujon, dropped by Gooch at slip off Jarvis at 42, went on to 53 before playing on to Emburey – the offspinner's first first-class wicket of the season at his home ground. Small polished off the innings for 209 by bowling Patterson three balls after Lamb had dropped an enormous skyer from Walsh.

England had to face only 6.4 overs before bad light brought an early end to proceedings, but lost a wicket in that time, Broad being less than pleased with the decision that saw him lbw to Marshall.

A disappointing batting display by England on the second day surrendered the initiative. Moxon, often beaten, looked far from secure during his 26, and eventually fell to the gangling Ambrose. Gower hit seven fours in his breezy 46, dominating a stand of 54 with Gooch, who had become almost becalmed (he spent 100 minutes in the 30s). After Gower chipped Walsh to deep midwicket and Marshall breached Gooch's defence, no-one could exceed Downton's 11. The last eight wickets crashed for 53, Marshall taking five of them to finish with 6 for 32, the best figures by a West Indian in a Lord's Test. Marshall had greeted Emburey with a helmet-thumping bouncer, and mopped up the innings with the wickets of Jarvis and Dilley with successive balls, leaving him on a hat-trick when England batted again.

West Indies reached 16 without loss by the close, the brief innings being interrupted three times by bad light.

Allan Lamb hits out during his 113 in 1988, his third Test century at Lord's. The short-leg fielder is Gus Logie, whose success with the bat – 81 and 95 not out – did much to ensure another West Indian victory

The sun shone on an exciting batting display in the third day, as West Indies built on their lead. Haynes was soon gone, and Richardson was dropped twice before falling for 26, but their departures brought together two master batsmen in fine form. Greenidge, the great opener, stayed for four hours, reaching his century with his 14th four, a textbook straight-drive; he passed 6000 Test runs when 49 (he had reached the 4000-run landmark during his epic 1984 Lord's Test double-century). He was overshadowed, though, by a marvellous display from Richards, who ran to 72 in 112 minutes. He struck his eighth ball, from his rival captain, for a huge six, and also hit 12 fours, four of them in succession off Small.

Richards finally played on to Pringle, and the quick departure of Hooper left the tourists at 240 for 5, but Logie and Dujon combined for their second century partnership of the match, lifting the score to 354 by the close.

The sixth-wicket pair extended their stand to 131 on the fourth morning before Dujon fell to Jarvis for 52; as in the first innings, he hit eight fours. Jarvis and Dilley (who took nine wickets in the match) polished off the innings without further ado, Ambrose collecting a 'pair' as the unfortunate Logie was stranded on 95, his 200-minute innings containing 12 fours and a five.

England were left with 172 overs to score the little matter of 442, a target which soon became academic as Marshall removed both openers and the pacey Patterson disposed of Gower. Moxon defended for more than two hours for 14, while Lamb, on his 34th birthday, salvaged his Test career after a disappointing run. He had progressed to 99 when Test cricket's longest day ended at 7.40, West Indies having dawdled through their overs at the rate of 11.2 an hour. Downton played a brave 75-minute innings of 27, while Emburey's defiant 30, which contained six fours, came to an end shortly before the close when a high full-toss from Ambrose hit the stumps, via the batsman's hand. At the close England were 214 for 7, still 227 behind.

On the final morning Lamb took 25 minutes to complete his eighth Test century and join the ranks of those with three hundreds at Lord's (Boycott, Compton, John Edrich, Gooch, Hobbs, Hutton and Vengsarkar are the others), but he was eventually run out for 113, Hooper's good throw thwarting Lamb's attempts to farm the strike. Marshall claimed his 10th wicket of the match by having Small caught, but Jarvis and Dilley hit out merrily, adding 53 for the last wicket in even time. The return of Patterson was too much for Dilley, however, and West Indies clinched victory by 134 runs at two o'clock. It was their fourth victory at Lord's, England having also won four of the 13 matches, with five drawn. England's last success, however, came in 1957.

One consolation for English cricket came in the match receipts which, for the first time, exceeded £1,000,000.

ENGLAND v WEST INDIES
June 16, 17, 18, 20, 21, 1988

WEST INDIES

C.G. Greenidge	c Downton b Dilley	22	c Emburey b Dilley	103
D.L. Haynes	c Moxon b Dilley	12	c Downton b Dilley	5
R.B. Richardson	c Emburey b Dilley	5	lbw b Pringle	26
* I.V.A. Richards	c Downton b Dilley	6	b Pringle	72
C.L. Hooper	c Downton b Small	3	c Downton b Jarvis	11
A.L. Logie	c Emburey b Small	81	not out	95
† P.J.L. Dujon	b Emburey	53	b Jarvis	52
M.D. Marshall	c Gooch b Dilley	11	b Jarvis	6
C.E.L. Ambrose	c Gower b Small	0	b Dilley	0
C.A. Walsh	not out	9	b Dilley	0
B.P. Patterson	b Small	0	c Downton b Jarvis	2
Extras	(lb6, nb1)	7	(lb19, w1, nb5)	25
	(67.5 overs)	209	(108 overs)	397

Fall: 21,40,47,50,54,184,199,199,199.   32,115,198,226,240,371,379,380,384.

Bowling: Dilley 23-6-55-5, Jarvis 13-2-47-0, Small 18.5-5-64-4, Pringle 7-3-20-0,
Emburey 6-2-17-1.

Second innings: Dilley 27-6-73-4, Small 19-1-76-0, Jarvis 26-3-107-4, Emburey 15-1-62-0,
Pringle 21-4-60-2.

ENGLAND

G.A. Gooch	b Marshall	44	lbw b Marshall	16
B.C. Broad	lbw b Marshall	0	c Dujon b Marshall	1
M.D. Moxon	c Richards b Ambrose	26	run out	14
D.I. Gower	c sub (K.L.T. Arthurton) b Walsh	46	c Richardson b Patterson	1
A.J. Lamb	lbw b Marshall	10	run out	113
D.R. Pringle	c Dujon b Walsh	1	lbw b Walsh	0
† P.R. Downton	lbw b Marshall	11	lbw b Marshall	27
* J.E. Emburey	b Patterson	7	b Ambrose	30
G.C. Small	not out	5	c Richards b Marshall	7
P.W. Jarvis	c Haynes b Marshall	7	not out	29
G.R. Dilley	b Marshall	0	c Richardson b Patterson	28
Extras	(lb6, nb2)	8	(b5, lb20, w2, nb14)	41
	(59 overs)	165	(86.5 overs)	307

Fall: 13,58,112,129,134,140,153,157,165.   27,29,31,104,105,161,212,232,254.

Bowling: Marshall 18-5-32-6, Patterson 13-3-52-1, Ambrose 12-1-39-1,
Walsh 16-6-36-2.

Second innings: Marshall 25-5-60-4, Patterson 21.5-2-100-2, Walsh 20-1-75-1,
Ambrose 20-4-47-1.

Toss: West Indies   Umpires: K.E. Palmer and D.R. Shepherd
Close of play: (1) E. 20 for 1 (Gooch 17, Moxon 3)
                 (2) W.I. 16 for 0 (Greenidge 12, Haynes 4)
                 (3) W.I. 354 for 5 (Logie 69, Dujon 45)
                 (4) E. 214 for 7 (Lamb 99, Small 0)

WEST INDIES WON BY 134 RUNS

Facing an increasingly disorganised England side, West Indies took the remaining three Tests by wide margins. At Old Trafford England, who could muster only 135 and 93 (Marshall 7 for 22), lost by an innings. At Headingley, with Chris Cowdrey replacing Emburey as captain, West Indies won by 10 wickets, and although England performed better at The Oval (Gooch now having replaced Cowdrey), the final result was similar.

1988ii

After the embarrassments of 1984, England were unlikely to underestimate the Sri Lankans, who returned at the end of the 1988 season for another one-off Test at Lord's. Sri Lanka had played little Test cricket in the interim, however – only one Test (a crushing defeat by Australia) since a massive bomb in Colombo brought a sudden end to New Zealand's tour in early 1987: to date Sri Lanka have not staged another home Test match.

Two of Sri Lanka's centurymakers from Lord's 1984 returned, in Mendis (now replaced as captain by Madugalle) and wicketkeeper Silva. The visitors were without Wettimuny, however, who had retired. England, at the end of a disastrous season, introduced four new caps in Barnett, Lawrence, Newport and wicketkeeper Russell: Sri Lanka had two debutants, Madurasinghe and Samarasekera, the former having made his first-class debut – also at Lord's – less than a month previously.

Gooch, England's fourth captain of the summer, won the toss and chose to bowl first, a decision vindicated by his bowlers' immediate success. The Sri Lankans, perhaps overawed, slipped to 63 for 6 shortly before lunch, with only Kuruppu reaching double figures: he hit six fours in his attacking 46, but the next five batsmen in the order could muster only 12 between them. Mendis and Ratnayeke almost doubled the score before the tubby Mendis sent an extravagant cut spiralling down to third man, giving the impressive Lawrence his first Test wicket. Two more quick wickets saw Sri Lanka struggling at 130 for 9, but a sensible last-wicket stand saw the total reach a more respectable 194. Ratnayeke finished with 59 not out, hitting nine fours in 175 minutes at the crease, but the revelation was the No. 11, Labrooy, who produced some pedigree strokes in his 42, a textbook straight-drive off Lawrence being the pick of his six fours.

England lost Robinson shortly before bad light brought an early close, but captain Gooch and nightwatchman Russell (dropped behind the wicket when 10) shared a stand of 131 on the second morning, Gooch going for 75 (eight fours) after looking set for another century. England moved into the lead with only two wickets down, Russell producing strokes unsuspected of a man who, for some time, had been kept out of the Test side by inferior keepers thought to be better batsmen. Russell had moved within sight of his maiden first-class century when he spooned a simple catch into the covers. His 94, which contained 11 fours, took 276 minutes.

Barnett reached a half-century in his first Test innings before the close, which found England comfortably placed at 278 for 3, 84 ahead. Barnett fell early on Day 3 for 66, but Lamb continued his good Lord's form with 63, and useful contributions from the lower order took England to 429. Labrooy, whose batting had already impressed, was the most successful bowler, finishing with 4 for 119.

Kuruppu was undaunted by England's big lead, and again blazed away for 25 before falling to Foster. Silva also went before the close, which again was hastened by bad light. 'Big Sam' Samarasekera had made light of the murky conditions, however, hitting two fours and a six in four balls when Foster decided to try some bouncers.

Samarasekera continued to a bright 57 on the fourth morning before he missed

Graham Gooch, another of the select band who have scored three Test centuries at Lord's, hits out during his 75 against Sri Lanka in 1988. Gooch led England to their first win for 18 Tests in this match

a sweep at Emburey and was lbw. At 147 for 5 a four-day England win seemed likely, but a stand of 104 between the well-built pair of Ranatunga and Mendis rendered that unlikely. Ranatunga carved his way to 78: he hit 10 fours, and thrice was unlucky when powerful straight-drives broke the stumps at the bowler's end. Mendis's 52 came in typical style, and he hit eight fours before Pringle removed him. Another sensible innings from Ratnayeke ended England's hopes of a day off, a luxury sought especially by Gooch and Emburey, who were hoping to play in their county's matches which, by a quirk of the fixture-list, started on the final day of this match.

Newport rounded off a highly satisfactory debut match by taking his seventh wicket to end Sri Lanka's innings at 331, leaving England 97 to win: they reduced their target by eight in three overs on the fourth evening.

England made heavy weather of the last rites on the final day, Gooch lasting 96 minutes for 36 before falling to the gentle pace of Samarasekera, who immmediately removed Barnett for a duck. The equally friendly bowling of Ranatunga accounted for Lamb, and when the last over before lunch began, England needed eight to win. Smith hit the first ball for three, and Robinson found the boundary with the third ball . . . but the remaining three balls were scoreless, and the teams had to reconvene for four balls after lunch, whereupon Smith hit the winning four. Gooch and Emburey eventually left for their county games, becoming the first players this century to appear in two different first-class matches on the same day, but their departure, already postponed by England's inability to manage that winning run before lunch, was further held up when the BBC persuaded the authorities to delay the after-match presentation ceremony until the popular Australian TV soap-opera *Neighbours* had finished its daily screening.

England's win was their first for 18 Tests and, of course, their first over Sri Lanka at Lord's, the only previous match having been drawn. It was the home side's first Lord's Test victory since 1983, and only their third in the last 15 matches at HQ.

ENGLAND v SRI LANKA
August 25, 26, 27, 29, 30, 1988

SRI LANKA

D.S.B.P. Kuruppu	c Gooch b Newport	46	c Barnett b Foster	25
† S.A.R. Silva	c Russell b Foster	1	c Russell b Newport	16
M.A.R. Samarasekera	c Russell b Foster	0	lbw b Emburey	57
P.A. de Silva	c Gooch b Newport	3	lbw b Lawrence	18
* R.S. Madugalle	lbw b Foster	3	b Foster	20
A. Ranatunga	lbw b Newport	5	b Newport	78
L.R.D. Mendis	c Smith b Lawrence	21	lbw b Pringle	56
J.R. Ratnayeke	not out	59	c Lamb b Lawrence	32
A.W.R. Madurasinghe	run out	4	b Newport	2
C.P.H. Ramanayake	lbw b Pringle	0	(11) c Gooch b Newport	2
G.F. Labrooy	lbw b Pringle	42	(10) not out	9
Extras	(b1, lb7, nb2)	10	(lb8, nb8)	16
	(65.5 overs)	194	(109.3 overs)	331

Fall: 7,44,52,53,61,63,122,127,130. 43,51,96,145,147,251,309,311,323.

Bowling: Foster 21-5-51-3, Lawrence 15-4-37-1, Newport 21-4-77-3, Pringle 6.5-1-17-2, Emburey 2-1-4-0.
Second innings: Foster 33-10-98-2, Lawrence 21-5-74-2, Newport 26.3-7-87-4, Pringle 11-2-30-1, Emburey 18-9-34-1.

ENGLAND

* G.A. Gooch	lbw b Ratnayeke	75	c Silva b Samarasekera	36
R.T. Robinson	c Samarasekera b Ratnayeke	19	not out	34
† R.C. Russell	c Samarasekera b Labrooy	94		
K.J. Barnett	c Ranatunga b Labrooy	66	(3) c Silva b Samarasekera	0
A.J. Lamb	b Labrooy	63	(4) c de Silva b Ranatunga	8
R.A. Smith	b Ranatunga	31	(5) not out	8
D.R. Pringle	c Silva b Labrooy	14		
J.E. Emburey	c de Silva b Samarasekera	0		
P.J. Newport	c de Silva b Ramanayake	26		
N.A. Foster	not out	14		
D.V. Lawrence	c Mendis b Ramanayake	4		
Extras	(b1, lb3, w2, nb17)	23	(lb8, w2, nb4)	14
	(143.2 overs)	429	(3 wkts) (34.4 overs)	100

Fall: 40,171,233,320,358,373,378,383,420. 73,73,82.

Bowling: Ratnayeke 32-3-107-2, Labrooy 40-7-119-4, Ramanayake 27.2-3-86-2, Madurasinghe 16-4-41-0, Samarasekera 22-5-66-1, Ranatunga 6-3-6-1.
Second innings: Labrooy 9-0-24-0, Ratnayeke 7-1-16-0, Samarasekera 10-0-38-2, Ranatunga 8.4-4-14-1.

Toss: England   Umpires: D.J. Constant and J.W. Holder
Close of play: (1) E. 47 for 1 (Gooch 24, Russell 2)
(2) E. 278 for 3 (Barnett 55, Lamb 20)
(3) S.L. 92 for 2 (Samarasekera 30, de Silva 15)
(4) E. 8 for 0 (Gooch 1, Robinson 4)

ENGLAND WON BY 7 WICKETS

1989

The cancellation of the scheduled 1988-89 tour (hosts India refused visas to eight England players with South African connections) gave England time to regroup after the disappointing summer of 1988. Chairman of selectors Peter May stood down, and was replaced by a new supremo in Ted Dexter. His first act was to restore David Gower as captain (it later emerged that Dexter's original choice of Gatting had been vetoed by the TCCB), and the 'new era' was ushered in with a narrow victory in the one-day internationals against the touring Australians.

Things were different, though, in the first Test: a dramatic last-day collapse saw England defeated by 210 runs, Australia having earlier run up 601 for 7, with Waugh making 177 not out.

At Lord's, as in 1985, Gower tossed up with Border: this time Gower won and chose to bat. Gooch made a solid 60, but after a promising start three quick wickets went down, two of them in successive balls from Hughes, who removed Barnett and Gatting (first ball) thanks to similar short-leg catches from Boon. Gower made the most of a let-off to Jones at long leg, scoring an attractive 57: he hit eight fours, one fewer than Gooch. Eventually, though, the captain played on to Lawson, who also removed the dangerous Smith (who hit six fours, five of them in the space of two overs from Waugh) for 32. Foster defended for nearly an hour, once being hit on the helmet visor by Hughes. Russell took his Lord's Test average to 158 with a plucky undefeated 64, but England were all out shortly before the close for a disappointing 286, too many of the batsmen having played innings more appropriate to one-day cricket.

Australia's openers negotiated the solitary over remaining on Day 1 without fuss, but Marsh soon fell to a good catch from Russell on the second morning. Left-hander Taylor, who had marked his first Test against England with 136 at Headingley, impressed again, scoring 62 in a stand of 145 with Boon, who hit 12 fours in his 94. Border and Jones threatened to dominate, but England worked their way through the order to reduce Australia to 276 for 6 – still 10 behind – by the close.

Honours were therefore even at the start of the third day, but Australia now took a firm hold, Gower's handling of his bowlers being difficult to understand at times. Waugh, 35 overnight, added 66 with Hughes (30), then 50 with Hohns (21): the placid New South Welshman, who preferred the Australian cap to the anonymous helmet, again showed the virtue of orthodox strokeplay and a straight bat. Then came the final straw for England as Lawson enjoyed himself with a career-best 74, slamming 11 fours in his 107 minutes at the crease. He and Waugh, who by now had reached his second Test century, added 130 to see the score past 500. The innings eventually closed at 528 with Waugh still there with 152 after 329 minutes: he faced 249 balls and hit 17 fours.

England stumbled to 58 for 3 by stumps, losing Gooch for 0 and Barnett for 3, both out to Alderman, who had taken 10 wickets at Leeds and was to add nine more here on his way to 41 victims in the series. Broad, too, was gone before the close, after which some pointed questions at the mid-match Press conference caused Gower to lose his temper and storm out . . . providing some even more lurid headlines for the Sunday newspapers.

A concerted appeal by the Australians, and Mike Gatting, in what seems likely to be his final Test, is caught by the helmeted Boon off Hughes for a duck.
Between bowler and catcher is Steve Waugh, whose 152 not out guided his side to their imposing total of 528; the other fielders are (l-r) skipper Border, Alderman, Taylor and wicketkeeper Healy. During this match, non-striker Gooch became the third player (after Boycott and Gower) to reach 1000 runs in Tests at Lord's

Gower therefore was under a lot of pressure when he resumed his innings on the fourth day, and he answered his critics in fine style, hitting his 15th Test century. Playing in his 16th Lord's Test – equalling Boycott's overall record – the Leicestershire left-hander, reprieved by Marsh in the gully when 26, hit 16 fours in his 106, which lasted 268 minutes before he fended a Hughes lifter straight to Border. Gower's main support came from Smith, who combined watchful defence with the occasional vicious cut or drive, reaching 96 before a fine ball from Alderman bowled him after 269 minutes. Earlier, what seems likely to have been Gatting's final Test innings was ended in the same way as rather too many of his others, when he played no stroke at Alderman and was lbw.

Another useful innings from Russell and defence from Emburey took the score to 322 for 9 by the close, a slender lead of 80: England's hopes of survival were kept alive by the miserable weather forecast for the next day.

The weather, though, did not save England: the promised storms skirted the ground, one 50-minute hold-up being the best the gods could provide for the home side. Emburey and Dilley prolonged the innings for an hour, their stand eventually raising 45 in 81 minutes. Australia needed 118 to win, but soon lost Marsh cheaply for the second time in the match. Taylor made 27 before three quick wickets from Foster upset Australia's equilibrium: after the opener gave a slip catch to Gooch, Border hooked a bouncer straight to long leg, where the substitute, Robin Sims of the MCC cricket staff, judged the catch well. Border may have been unsettled by Foster's previous ball, a freak 'double-bouncer' which the startled batsman swiped at in vain as it bobbled down the pitch.

Foster's third wicket came when Jones fell for a duck, but that was the extent of the panic. Boon, with his second responsible innings of the match, saw his side to safety; appropriately enough Waugh made the winning hit just before five o'clock. Waugh's 21 not out took his series aggregate to 350 without being dismissed.

Australia's success was their 11th in 29 Lord's Test against England, who have won five, four of those victories coming in the 19th century and the fifth and last in 1934. There have been 13 draws: Australia also won their 1912 Lord's Test against South Africa. Gower emerged from the match with an unwanted record: this was his eighth successive Test defeat as captain.

ENGLAND v AUSTRALIA
June 22, 23, 24, 26, 27, 1989

ENGLAND

G.A. Gooch	c Healy b Waugh	60	lbw b Alderman	0
B.C. Broad	lbw b Alderman	18	b Lawson	20
K.J. Barnett	c Boon b Hughes	14	c Jones b Alderman	3
M.W. Gatting	c Boon b Hughes	0	lbw b Alderman	22
* D.I. Gower	b Lawson	57	c Border b Hughes	106
R.A. Smith	c Hohns b Lawson	32	b Alderman	96
J.E. Emburey	b Alderman	0	(8) not out	36
† R.C. Russell	not out	64	(7) c Boon b Lawson	29
N.A. Foster	c Jones b Hughes	16	lbw b Alderman	4
P.W. Jarvis	c Marsh b Hughes	6	lbw b Alderman	5
G.R. Dilley	c Border b Alderman	7	c Boon b Hughes	24
Extras	(lb9, nb3)	12	(b6, lb6, nb2)	14
	(86.5 overs)	286	(130 overs)	359

Fall: 31,52,58,131,180,185,191,237,253.   0,18,28,84,223,274,300,304,314.

Bowling: Alderman 20.5-4-60-3, Lawson 27-8-88-2, Hughes 23-6-71-4, Waugh 9-3-49-1, Hohns 7-3-9-0.

Second innings: Alderman 38-6-128-6, Lawson 39-10-99-2, Hughes 24-8-44-2, Border 9-3-23-0, Hohns 13-6-33-0, Waugh 7-2-20-0.

AUSTRALIA

G.R. Marsh	c Russell b Dilley	3	(2) b Dilley	1
M.A. Taylor	lbw b Foster	62	(1) c Gooch b Foster	27
D.C. Boon	c Gooch b Dilley	94	not out	58
* A.R. Border	c Smith b Emburey	35	c sub (R.J. Sims) b Foster	1
D.M. Jones	lbw b Foster	27	c Russell b Foster	0
S.R. Waugh	not out	152	not out	21
† I.A. Healy	c Russell b Jarvis	3		
M.G. Hughes	c Gooch b Foster	30		
T.V. Hohns	b Emburey	21		
G.F. Lawson	c Broad b Emburey	74		
T.M. Alderman	lbw b Emburey	8		
Extras	(lb11, nb8)	19	(b3, lb4, nb4)	11
	(158 overs)	528	(4 wkts) (40.2 overs)	119

Fall: 6,151,192,221,235,265,331,381,511.   9,51,61,67.

Bowling: Dilley 34-3-141-2, Foster 45-7-129-3, Jarvis 31-3-150-1, Emburey 42-12-88-4, Gooch 6-2-9-0.

Second innings: Dilley 10-2-27-1, Foster 18-3-39-3, Emburey 3-0-8-0, Jarvis 9.2-0-38-0.

Toss: England   Umpires: H.D. Bird and N.T. Plews
Close of play: (1) A. 4 for 0 (Marsh 3, Taylor 1)
                 (2) A. 276 for 6 (Waugh 35, Hughes 2)
                 (3) E. 58 for 3 (Gatting 16, Gower 15)
                 (4) E. 322 for 9 (Emburey 21, Dilley 4)

AUSTRALIA WON BY 6 WICKETS

Rain prevented a result in the third Test, at Edgbaston, after Jones's 157 had put Australia on top, but the visitors took the series 4-0 (and regained the Ashes) with convincing wins at Old Trafford and Trent Bridge, where Australia's openers Marsh (138) and Taylor (219) batted throughout the first day on their way to a record stand of 329. Smith made centuries in vain for England in both these matches. Another century from Jones gave Australia the upper hand at The Oval, but bad weather and Gower's elegant 79 meant that England escaped with a draw.

Records

*All records refer **only** to Test matches at Lord's*

RESULTS

England v Australia	Played 29	England 5	Australia 11	Drawn 13
England v South Africa	Played 10	England 6	South Africa 1	Drawn 3
England v West Indies	Played 13	England 4	West Indies 4	Drawn 5
England v New Zealand	Played 10	England 5	New Zealand 0	Drawn 5
England v India	Played 11	England 8	India 1	Drawn 2
England v Pakistan	Played 8	England 2	Pakistan 1	Drawn 5
England v Sri Lanka	Played 2	England 1	Sri Lanka 0	Drawn 1
Australia v South Africa	Played 1	Australia 1	South Africa 0	Drawn 0

HIGHEST TOTALS

729 for 6 dec	Australia v England	1930
652 for 8 dec	West Indies v England	1973
629	England v India	1974
554 for 8 dec	England v South Africa	1947
551 for 9 dec	New Zealand v England	1973
537	England v India	1952
531 for 2 dec	England v South Africa	1947
528	Australia v England	1989
518	West Indies v England	1980

The highest totals recorded by the other countries are:

491 for 7 dec	Sri Lanka v England	1984
428 for 8 dec	Pakistan v England	1982
378	India v England	1952
327	South Africa v England	1947

LOWEST TOTALS

* one player absent hurt   ** one player retired hurt

42*	India v England	1974
47	New Zealand v England	1958
53	England v Australia	1888
53	Australia v England	1896
58	South Africa v England	1912
60	Australia v England	1888
62	England v Australia	1888
67	New Zealand v England	1978

74	New Zealand v England	1958
78**	Australia v England	1968
87	Pakistan v England	1954
93	India v England	1936
96	India v England	1979
97	West Indies v England	1933

Sri Lanka's lowest all-out total was 194 in 1988

LARGEST MARGINS OF VICTORY

Innings & 285 runs	England v India	1974
Innings & 226 runs	West Indies v England	1973
Innings & 148 runs	England v New Zealand	1958
Innings & 124 runs	England v India	1967
Innings & 120 runs	England v Pakistan	1978
Innings & 106 runs	England v Australia	1886

409 runs	Australia v England	1948
326 runs	West Indies v England	1950
230 runs	England v New Zealand	1969

10 wkts	Australia v England	1899
10 wkts	Australia v South Africa	1912
10 wkts	England v India	1946
10 wkts	England v South Africa	1947
10 wkts	England v South Africa	1951
10 wkts	Pakistan v England	1982

England lost only 2 wickets in defeating South Africa in 1924

NARROWEST MARGINS OF VICTORY

4 wkts	Australia v England	1985
5 wkts	Australia v England	1961
5 wkts	India v England	1986

61 runs	Australia v England	1888
71 runs	England v South Africa	1955

MOST RUNS IN A DAY

522	England (503-2) and South Africa (19-0)	1924 (2nd day)

FEWEST RUNS IN A DAY

151	England (114-8) and New Zealand (37-7)	1978 (3rd day)

MOST APPEARANCES

England			Australia		
	16	G. Boycott		9	S.E. Gregory
		D.I. Gower		5	W. Bardsley
	14	A.P.E. Knott			J.M. Blackham
	13	I.T. Botham			C.G. Macartney
		M.C. Cowdrey			R.W. Marsh
		J.H. Edrich		4	W.W. Armstrong
		T.G. Evans			A.R. Border
		G.A. Gooch			D.G. Bradman
	12	K.F. Barrington			G.S. Chappell
		W.R. Hammond			J. Darling
		L. Hutton			G. Giffen
		F.S. Trueman			C. Hill
	11	D.C.S. Compton			J.J. Kelly
		M.W. Gatting			D.K. Lillee
		T.W. Graveney			M.A. Noble
		R. Illingworth			G.H.S. Trott
	10	J.A. Snow			H. Trumble
					V.T. Trumper
South Africa	4	G.A. Faulkner			K.D. Walters
		A.W. Nourse			
	3	D.J. McGlew	West Indies	5	C.H. Lloyd
		B. Mitchell			G.S. Sobers
		A.D. Nourse		4	L.R. Gibbs
		S.J. Pegler			C.G. Greenidge
		R.O. Schwarz			R.B. Kanhai
		H.W. Taylor			D.L. Murray
		J.H.B. Waite		3	B.F. Butcher
					R.C. Fredericks
New Zealand	4	B.E. Congdon			D.L. Haynes
	3	M.G. Burgess			V.A. Holder
		R.O. Collinge			A.I. Kallicharran
		B.A. Edgar			I.V.A. Richards
		R.J. Hadlee			F.M.M. Worrell
		V. Pollard			
		B.R. Taylor	India	5	S.M. Gavaskar
		J.G. Wright		4	B.S. Bedi
					G.R. Viswanath
Pakistan	5	Wasim Bari		3	B.S. Chandrasekhar
	4	Mushtaq Mohammad			F.M. Engineer
	3	Asif Iqbal			Kapil Dev
		Hanif Mohammad			D.B. Vengsarkar
		Imran Khan			A.L. Wadekar
		Javed Miandad			
		Majid Jahangir Khan	Sri Lanka	2	P.A. de Silva
		Mudassar Nazar			R.S. Madugalle
		Sadiq Mohammad			L.R.D. Mendis
		Zaheer Abbas			A. Ranatunga
					J.R. Ratnayeke
					S.A.R. Silva

A.H. Kardar (India 1946, Pakistan 1954) is the only player to appear for two different countries in Tests at Lord's

MOST RUNS IN A CAREER

ENGLAND	M	I	NO	Runs	HS	Av	100	50
G. Boycott	16	29	3	1189	128*	45.73	3	6
D.I. Gower	16	28	1	1169	108	43.30	2	8
G.A. Gooch	13	24	1	1004	183*	43.65	3	3
D.C.S. Compton	11	17	2	882	208	58.80	3	5
T.W. Graveney	11	16	1	843	153	56.20	2	5
K.F. Barrington	12	18	–	838	148	46.56	1	7
L. Hutton	12	23	4	812	196	42.74	3	1
W.R. Hammond	12	19	1	772	240	42.89	2	–
J.H. Edrich	13	20	1	746	175	39.26	3	2
M.C. Cowdrey	13	21	3	733	152	40.72	2	2
F.E. Woolley	8	12	1	690	134*	62.73	1	5
A.J. Lamb	9	17	1	635	113	39.69	3	1
I.T. Botham	13	18	–	622	108	34.56	1	5
A.W. Greig	8	14	–	563	106	40.21	1	4
L.E.G. Ames	7	12	2	555	137	55.50	2	3
M.W. Gatting	11	20	3	543	81	31.94	–	4
A.P.E. Knott	14	22	1	533	83	25.38	–	4

AUSTRALIA	M	I	NO	Runs	HS	Av	100	50
W. Bardsley	5	7	2	575	193*	115.00	2	2
D.G. Bradman	4	8	1	551	254	78.71	2	1
A.R. Border	4	8	4	426	196	106.50	1	2
G.S. Chappell	4	8	2	411	131	68.50	1	3
W.A. Brown	3	6	1	379	206*	75.80	2	–
C.G. Macartney	5	7	1	324	133*	54.00	1	1
A.R. Morris	2	4	–	286	105	71.50	1	2
K.R. Miller	3	6	–	270	109	45.00	1	1
W.M. Woodfull	3	6	1	259	155	51.80	1	–
A.L. Hassett	3	6	–	252	104	42.00	1	1
S.E. Gregory	9	11	1	250	103	25.00	1	1
K.J. Hughes	2	4	–	247	117	61.75	1	1
G.M. Wood	3	6	1	240	112	48.00	1	1

SOUTH AFRICA	M	I	NO	Runs	HS	Av	100	50
B. Mitchell	3	6	1	371	164*	74.20	1	1

WEST INDIES	M	I	NO	Runs	HS	Av	100	50
G.S. Sobers	5	9	3	571	163*	95.17	2	2
C G. Greenidge	4	7	1	471	214*	78.50	2	1
R.B. Kanhai	4	7	–	350	157	50.00	1	1
C.H. Lloyd	5	7	–	329	70	47.00	–	4
R.C. Fredericks	3	5	–	312	138	62.40	1	3
I.V.A. Richards	3	4	–	295	145	73.75	1	2
G.A. Headley	2	4	–	276	107	69.00	2	1
B.F. Butcher	3	6	–	232	133	38.67	1	–
D.L. Haynes	3	5	–	230	184	46.00	1	–
E.D. Weekes	2	4	–	229	90	57.25	–	3
C.L. Walcott	2	4	1	217	168*	72.33	1	–

NEW ZEALAND

B.E. Congdon	4	7	–	264	175	37.71	1	–
M.P. Donnelly	2	3	–	227	206	75.67	1	–
B.A. Edgar	3	6	–	223	83	37.17	–	2
V. Pollard	3	5	1	223	105*	55.75	1	2
M.G. Burgess	3	5	–	203	105	40.60	1	1

INDIA

D.B. Vengsarkar	3	6	1	421	157	84.20	3	–
S.M. Gavaskar	5	10	–	340	59	34.00	–	2
M.H. Mankad	2	4	–	333	184	83.25	1	2
G.R. Viswanath	4	8	–	272	113	34.00	1	2

PAKISTAN

Mohsin Khan	2	4	1	316	200	105.33	1	–
Hanif Mohammad	3	5	1	283	187*	70.75	1	–

SRI LANKA

L.R.D. Mendis	2	4	–	282	111	70.50	1	2
S. Wettimuny	1	2	–	203	190	101.50	1	–

HIGHEST INDIVIDUAL SCORES

254	D.G. Bradman	Australia v England	1930
240	W.R. Hammond	England v Australia	1938
214*	C.G. Greenidge	West Indies v England	1984
211	J.B. Hobbs	England v South Africa	1924
208	D.C.S. Compton	England v South Africa	1947
206*	W.A. Brown	Australia v England	1938
206	M.P. Donnelly	New Zealand v England	1949
205*	J. Hardstaff jnr	England v India	1945
200	Mohsin Khan	Pakistan v England	1982

The highest scores for the other countries are:

190	S. Wettimuny	Sri Lanka v England	1984
184	M.H. Mankad	India v England	1952
164*	B. Mitchell	South Africa v England	1935

CARRYING BAT THROUGH COMPLETED INNINGS

J.E. Barrett (67*/176)	Australia v England	1890
W. Bardsley (193*/383)	Australia v England	1926
W.A. Brown (206*/422)	Australia v England	1938
G.M. Turner (43*/131)	New Zealand v England	1969

CENTURIES

ENGLAND (68)

G.O.B. Allen	122	v New Zealand	1931
L.E.G. Ames (2)	137	v New Zealand	1931
	120	v Australia	1934
D.L. Amiss	188	v India	1974
C.W.J. Athey	123	v Pakistan	1987
K.F. Barrington	148	v Pakistan	1967
I.T. Botham	108	v Pakistan	1978
G. Boycott (3)	106	v West Indies	1969
	121*	v Pakistan	1971
	128*	v Australia	1980
L.C. Braund	104	v South Africa	1907
A.P.F. Chapman	121	v Australia	1930
D.C.S. Compton (3)	120	v West Indies	1939
	208	v South Africa	1947
	116	v New Zealand	1949
M.C. Cowdrey (2)	152	v West Indies	1957
	119	v New Zealand	1965
M.H. Denness	118	v India	1974
K.S. Duleepsinhji	173	v Australia	1930
J.H. Edrich (3)	120	v Australia	1964
	115	v New Zealand	1969
	175	v Australia	1975
W.J. Edrich	189	v South Africa	1947
T.G. Evans	104	v India	1952
K.W.R. Fletcher	178	v New Zealand	1973
G. Fowler	106	v West Indies	1984
G.A. Gooch (3)	123	v West Indies	1980
	114	v India	1986
	183	v New Zealand	1986
D.I. Gower (2)	108	v New Zealand	1983
	106	v Australia	1989
T.W. Graveney (2)	153	v Pakistan	1962
	151	v India	1967
A.W. Greig	106	v India	1974
W.R. Hammond (2)	140	v New Zealand	1937
	240	v Australia	1938
J.H. Hampshire	107	v West Indies	1969
J. Hardstaff jnr (2)	114	v New Zealand	1937
	205*	v India	1946
E.H. Hendren	127*	v Australia	1926
J.B. Hobbs (3)	107	v Australia	1912
	211	v South Africa	1924
	119	v Australia	1926
L. Hutton (3)	196	v West Indies	1939
	150	v India	1952
	145	v Australia	1953
R. Illingworth	113	v West Indies	1969
A.J. Lamb (3)	110	v West Indies	1984
	107	v Sri Lanka	1984
	113	v West Indies	1988

M. Leyland (2)	102	v South Africa	1929
	109	v Australia	1934
P.B.H. May	112	v South Africa	1955
C. Milburn	126*	v West Indies	1966
D.W. Randall	126	v India	1982
J.D.B. Robertson	121	v New Zealand	1949
A. Shrewsbury (2)	164	v Australia	1886
	106	v Australia	1893
R.H. Spooner	119	v South Africa	1912
A.G. Steel	148	v Australia	1884
H. Sutcliffe (2)	122	v South Africa	1924
	100	v South Africa	1929
M.W. Tate	100*	v South Africa	1929
G.E. Tyldesley	122	v West Indies	1928
C. Washbrook	114	v West Indies	1950
W. Watson	109	v Australia	1953
F.E. Woolley	134*	v South Africa	1924
R.A. Woolmer	120	v Australia	1977

AUSTRALIA (25)

W. Bardsley (2)	164	v South Africa	1912
	193*	v England	1926
S.G. Barnes	141	v England	1948
A.R. Border	196	v England	1985
D.G. Bradman (2)	254	v England	1930
	102*	v England	1938
W.A. Brown (2)	105	v England	1934
	206*	v England	1938
G.S. Chappell	131	v England	1972
H. Graham	107	v England	1893
S.E. Gregory	103	v England	1896
A.L. Hassett	104	v England	1953
C. Hill	135	v England	1899
K.J. Hughes	117	v England	1980
C. Kelleway	102	v South Africa	1912
W.M. Lawry	130	v England	1961
C.G. Macartney	133*	v England	1926
K.R. Miller	109	v England	1953
A.R. Morris	105	v England	1948
V.S. Ransford	143	v England	1909
G.H.S. Trott	143	v England	1896
V.T. Trumper	135*	v England	1899
S.R. Waugh	152*	v England	1989
G.M. Wood	112	v England	1980
W.M. Woodfull	155	v England	1930

SOUTH AFRICA (5)

R.H. Catterall	120	v England	1924
R.A. McLean	142	v England	1955
A. Melville	117	v England	1947
B. Mitchell	164*	v England	1935
P.W. Sherwell	115	v England	1907

WEST INDIES (16)

B.F. Butcher	133	v England	1963
C.A. Davis	103	v England	1969
R.C. Fredericks	138	v England	1976
C.G. Greenidge (2)	214*	v England	1984
	103	v England	1988
D.L. Haynes	184	v England	1980
G.A. Headley (2)	106	v England	1939
	107	v England	1939
D.A.J. Holford	105*	v England	1966
R.B. Kanhai	157	v England	1973
B.D. Julien	121	v England	1973
A.F. Rae	106	v England	1950
I.V.A. Richards	145	v England	1980
G.S. Sobers (2)	163*	v England	1966
	150*	v England	1973
C.L. Walcott	168*	v England	1950

G.A. Headley is the only player to score a century in each innings of a Lord's Test

NEW ZEALAND (8)

M.G. Burgess	105	v England	1973
B.E. Congdon	175	v England	1973
M.D. Crowe	106	v England	1986
C.S. Dempster	120	v England	1931
M.P. Donnelly	206	v England	1949
G.P. Howarth	123	v England	1978
M.L. Page	104	v England	1931
V. Pollard	105*	v England	1973

INDIA (5)

M.H. Mankad	184	v England	1952
D.B. Vengsarkar (3)	103	v England	1979
	157	v England	1982
	126*	v England	1986
G.R. Viswanath	113	v England	1979

PAKISTAN (4)

Hanif Mohammad	187*	v England	1967
Javed Burki	101	v England	1962
Mohsin Khan	200	v England	1982
Nasim-ul-Ghani	101	v England	1962

SRI LANKA (3)

L.R.D. Mendis	111	v England	1984
S.A.R. Silva	102*	v England	1984
S. Wettimuny	190	v England	1984

CENTURY BEFORE LUNCH

W. Bardsley (32*–150*)	Australia v South Africa	1912 (2nd day)
J.B. Hobbs (12*–114*)	England v South Africa	1924 (2nd day)

BATSMEN DISMISSED FOR 99

R. Edwards	Australia v England	1975
C.G. Macartney	Australia v England	1912
E. Paynter	England v Australia	1938
M.J.K. Smith	England v South Africa	1960

BATSMEN DISMISSED FOR A 'PAIR'

C.E.L. Ambrose	West Indies v England	1988
C.L. Badcock	Australia v England	1938
A.C. Bannerman	Australia v England	1888
I.T. Botham	England v Australia	1981
E. Evans	Australia v England	1886
Iqbal Qasim	Pakistan v England	1978
A.P.E. Knott	England v New Zealand	1973
D.J. McGlew	South Africa v England	1955
J.T. Murray	England v Pakistan	1967
S. Ramadhin	West Indies v England	1957
C.A. Roach	West Indies v England	1933
R. Surendranath	India v England	1959
J.H. Wardle	England v Australia	1956
J.G. Wright	New Zealand v England	1986

RECORD WICKET PARTNERSHIPS

† *denotes record partnership in all Tests at Lord's*

ENGLAND v AUSTRALIA

1st	182	J.B. Hobbs (119) and H. Sutcliffe (182)	1926
2nd	168	L. Hutton (145) and T.W. Graveney (78)	1953
3rd	140	F.E. Woolley (87) and E.H. Hendren (127*)	1926
4th	222	W.R. Hammond (240) and E. Paynter (99)	1938
5th	163	W. Watson (109) and T.E. Bailey (71)	1953
6th	186	W.R. Hammond (240) and L.E.G. Ames (83)	1938
7th	131	M.W. Gatting (75*) and I.T. Botham (85)	1985
8th	76	A.G. Steel (148) and Hon. A. Lyttelton (31)	1884
9th	53	A.E. Relf (17) and A.F.A. Lilley (47)	1909
10th	45	J.E. Emburey (36*) and G.R. Dilley (24)	1989

AUSTRALIA v ENGLAND

1st	162	W.M. Woodfull (155) and W.H. Ponsford (81)	1930
2nd	231	W.M. Woodfull (155) and D.G. Bradman (254)	1930
3rd	192‡	D.G. Bradman (254) and A.F. Kippax (83)	1930
4th	221	G.H.S. Trott (143) and S.E. Gregory (103)	1896
5th	216†	A.R. Border (196) and G.M. Ritchie (94)	1985
6th	142	S.E. Gregory (57) and H. Graham (107)	1893
7th	117	K.D. Mackay (31) and R. Benaud (97)	1956

8th	85	W.A. Brown (206*) and W.J. O'Reilly (42)	1938
9th	130†	S.R. Waugh (152*) and G.F. Lawson (74)	1989
10th	69	{ H.J.H. Scott (75) and H.F. Boyle (26*)	1884
		{ D.K. Lillee (73*) and A.A. Mallett (14*)	1975

‡ *C. Kelleway (102) and W. Bardsley (164) shared a higher 3rd-wicket partnership of 242 against South Africa in 1912*

ENGLAND v SOUTH AFRICA

1st	268†	J.B. Hobbs (211) and H. Sutcliffe (122)	1924
2nd	142	J.B. Hobbs (211) and F.E. Woolley (134*)	1924
3rd	370†	W.J. Edrich (189) and D.C.S. Compton (208)	1947
4th	122	D.C.S. Compton (79) and W. Watson (79)	1951
5th	113	P.F. Warner (39) and F.E. Woolley (73)	1912
6th	145	L.C. Braund (104) and G.L. Jessop (93)	1907
7th	54	J.M. Parks (32) and F.J. Titmus (59)	1965
8th	34	J.H. Wardle (18) and A.V. Bedser (26*)	1951
9th	54	L.C. Braund (104) and A.F.A. Lilley (48)	1907
10th	27	A.F.A. Lilley (48) and C. Blythe (4*)	1907

SOUTH AFRICA v ENGLAND

1st	95	B. Mitchell (46) and A. Melville (117)	1947
2nd	139	P.W. Sherwell (115) and C.M.H. Hathorn (30)	1907
3rd	118	A. Melville (117) and A.D. Nourse (61)	1947
4th	112	M.J. Susskind (64) and R.H. Catterall (120)	1924
5th	94	J.E. Cheetham (54) and G.M. Fullerton (60)	1951
6th	109	R.A. McLean (142) and H.J. Keith (57)	1955
7th	101	B. Mitchell (164*) and A.B.C. Langton (44)	1935
8th	43	H.J. Keith (57) and H.J. Tayfield (21)	1955
9th	29‡	J.T. Botten (33) and P.M. Pollock (34)	1965
10th	43	H.G. Owen-Smith (52*) and A.J. Bell (13)	1929

‡ *H.W. Taylor (93) and S.J. Pegler (25) shared a higher 9th-wicket partnership of 37 against Australia in 1912*

ENGLAND v WEST INDIES

1st	101	G. Fowler (106) and B.C. Broad (55)	1984
2nd	145	G.A. Gooch (123) and C.J. Tavaré (42)	1980
3rd	84	J.M. Brearley (40) and D.B. Close (60)	1976
4th	248†	L. Hutton (196) and D.C.S. Compton (120)	1939
5th	130*	C. Milburn (126*) and T.W. Graveney (30*)	1966
6th	128	J.H. Hampshire (107) and A.P.E. Knott (53)	1969
7th	174†	M.C. Cowdrey (152) and T.G. Evans (82)	1957
8th	36	F.J. Titmus (52*) and F.S. Trueman (10)	1963
9th	59	J.M. Parks (91) and K. Higgs (13)	1966
10th	83†	R. Illingworth (113) and J.A. Snow (9*)	1969

WEST INDIES v ENGLAND

1st	106	R.C. Fredericks (63) and G.S. Camacho (67)	1969
2nd	287*†	C.G. Greenidge (214*) and H.A. Gomes (92*)	1984
3rd	138	R.B. Kanhai (157) and C.H. Lloyd (63)	1973

4th	103	I.V.A. Richards (72) and C.H. Lloyd (39)	1984
5th	100	G.S. Sobers (66) and E.D. Weekes (90)	1957
6th	274*†	G.S. Sobers (163*) and D.A.J. Holford (105*)	1966
7th	155*§	G.S. Sobers (150*) and B.D. Julien (121)	1973
8th	47	J.A. Small (52) and C.R. Browne (44)	1928
9th	42*	G.S. Sobers (150*) and V.A. Holder (23*)	1973
10th	26	G.N. Francis (11*) and H.C. Griffith (18)	1933

§ 231 runs were added for the 7th wicket in 1973, G.S. Sobers retiring ill and being replaced by K.D. Boyce (36) after 155 had been added

ENGLAND v NEW ZEALAND

1st	143	L. Hutton (66) and J.D.B. Robertson (121)	1949
2nd	149	C.J. Tavaré (51) and D.I. Gower (108)	1983
3rd	245	J. Hardstaff jnr (114) and W.R. Hammond (140)	1937
4th	64	G.A. Gooch (183) and M.W. Gatting (26)	1986
5th	126	G.A. Gooch (183) and P. Willey (42)	1986
6th	189	D.C.S. Compton (116) and T.E. Bailey (93)	1949
7th	45	R. Illingworth (53) and B.R. Knight (29)	1969
8th	246†	L.E.G. Ames (137) and G.O.B. Allen (122)	1931
9th	92	K.W.R. Fletcher (178) and G.G. Arnold (23*)	1973
10th	40	B.R. Knight (49) and A. Ward (19*)	1969

NEW ZEALAND v ENGLAND

1st	89	B. Sutcliffe (57) and V.J. Scott (42)	1949
2nd	99	C.S. Dempster (120) and G.L. Weir (40)	1931
3rd	210	B.A. Edgar (83) and M.D. Crowe (106)	1986
4th	142	M.L. Page (104) and R.C. Blunt (96)	1931
5th	81	B.E. Congdon (175) and M.G. Burgess (105)	1973
6th	117	M.G. Burgess (105) and V. Pollard (105*)	1973
7th	92	V. Pollard (55) and B.R. Taylor (51)	1965
8th	104	D.A.R. Moloney (64) and A.W. Roberts (66*)	1937
9th	63	T.C. Lowry (34) and C.F.W. Allcott (20*)	1931
10th	44	V. Pollard (55) and F.J. Cameron (9*)	1965

ENGLAND v INDIA

1st	116	D.L. Amiss (188) and D. Lloyd (46)	1974
2nd	221	D.L. Amiss (188) and J.H. Edrich (96)	1974
3rd	96*	M.C. Cowdrey (63*) and P.B.H. May (33*)	1959
4th	122	T.W. Graveney (151) and B.L. D'Oliveira (33)	1967
5th	202	M.H. Denness (118) and A.W. Greig (106)	1974
6th	159	T.W. Graveney (73) and T.G. Evans (104)	1952
7th	125	D.W. Randall (126) and P.H. Edmonds (64)	1982
8th	103	G. Miller (62) and R.W. Taylor (64)	1979
9th	71	J.A. Snow (73) and N. Gifford (17)	1971
10th	70	P.J.W. Allott (41*) and R.G.D. Willis (28)	1982

INDIA v ENGLAND

1st	131	S.M. Gavaskar (49) and F.M. Engineer (86)	1974
2nd	59	S.M. Gavaskar (34) and M.B. Amarnath (69)	1986
3rd	211	M.H. Mankad (184) and V.S. Hazare (49)	1952

4th	83	N.J. Contractor (81) and J.M. Ghorpade (41)	1959
5th	142	D.B. Vengsarkar (157) and Yashpal Sharma (37)	1982
6th	92	G.R. Viswanath (68) and E.D. Solkar (67)	1971
7th	57	R.S. Modi (57*) and A.H. Kardar (43)	1946
8th	74	Lall Singh (29) and L.Amar Singh (51)	1932
9th	66	Kapil Dev (89) and S. Madan Lal (15)	1982
10th	43	R.S. Modi (57*) and S.G. Shinde (10)	1946

ENGLAND v PAKISTAN

1st	124	G. Boycott (121*) and B.W. Luckhurst (46)	1971
2nd	89	B.C. Broad (55) and C.W.J. Athey (123)	1987
3rd	201	K.F. Barrington (148) and T.W. Graveney (81)	1967
4th	112	C.J. Tavaré (82) and I.T. Botham (69)	1982
5th	104	B.L. D'Oliveira (81*) and D.B. Close (36)	1967
6th	118	G.R.J. Roope (69) and I.T. Botham (108)	1978
7th	69	A.P.E. Knott (83) and C.M. Old (41)	1974
8th	60	B.L. D'Oliveira (59) and K. Higgs (14)	1967
9th	76	T.W. Graveney (153) and F.S. Trueman (29)	1962
10th	41	R.W. Taylor (24*) and R.D. Jackman (17)	1982

PAKISTAN v ENGLAND

1st	77*	Mohsin Khan (39*) and Javed Miandad (26*)	1982
2nd	144	Mohsin Khan (200) and Mansoor Akhtar (57)	1982
3rd	55	Mohsin Khan (46) and Talaat Ali (40)	1978
4th	153	Mohsin Khan (200) and Zaheer Abbas (75)	1982
5th	197	Javed Burki (101) and Nasim-ul-Ghani (101)	1962
6th	27	Majid Jahangir Khan (9) and Intikhab Alam (18)	1971
7th	40	Hanif Mohammad (187*) and Intikhab Alam (17)	1967
8th	130	Hanif Mohammad (187*) and Asif Iqbal (76)	1967
9th	41	Hanif Mohammad (187*) and Wasim Bari (13)	1967
10th	44	Hanif Mohammad (187*) and Salim Altaf (2)	1967

ENGLAND v SRI LANKA

1st	73	G.A. Gooch (36) and R.T. Robinson (34*)	1988
2nd	131	G.A. Gooch (75) and R.C. Russell (94)	1988
3rd	85	B.C. Broad (86) and D.I. Gower (55)	1984
4th	87	K.J. Barnett (66) and A.J. Lamb (63)	1988
5th	38	A.J. Lamb (63) and R.A. Smith (31)	1988
6th	87	A.J. Lamb (107) and R.M. Ellison (41)	1984
7th	49	A.J. Lamb (107) and P.R. Downton (10)	1984
8th	5	D.R. Pringle (14) and P.J. Newport (26)	1988
9th	37	P.J. Newport (26) and N.A. Foster (14*)	1988
10th	9	N.A. Foster (14*) and D.V. Lawrence (4)	1988

SRI LANKA v ENGLAND

1st	43	D.S.B.P. Kuruppu (25) and S.A.R. Silva (16)	1988
2nd	37	D.S.B.P. Kuruppu (46) and M.A.R. Samarasekera (0)	1988
3rd	101	S. Wettimuny (190) and R.L. Dias (32)	1984
4th	148	S. Wettimuny (190) and A. Ranatunga (84)	1984
5th	150	S. Wettimuny (190) and L.R.D. Mendis (111)	1984

6th	138	S.A.R. Silva (102*) and L.R.D. Mendis (94)	1984
7th	59	L.R.D. Mendis (21) and J.R. Ratnayeke (59*)	1988
8th	27*	A.L.F. de Mel (20*) and J.R. Ratnayeke (5*)	1984
9th	12	J.R. Ratnayeke (32) and G.F. Labrooy (9*)	1988
10th	64	J.R. Ratnayeke (59*) and G.F. Labrooy (42)	1988

MOST WICKETS IN A CAREER

ENGLAND	M	Balls	Runs	Wkts	Av	BB	5i	10m
I.T. Botham	13	3068	1643	68	24.16	8–34	8	1
F.S. Trueman	12	3087	1394	63	22.13	6–31	5	1
R.G.D. Willis	9	1901	882	47	18.77	7–78	3	–
J.B. Statham	9	2268	786	45	17.47	7–39	3	1
H. Verity	7	1923	613	42	14.60	8–43	2	1
J.A. Snow	10	2267	1000	38	26.32	5–57	2	–
D.L. Underwood	9	1967	643	38	16.92	8–51	4	2
A.V. Bedser	7	2627	957	34	28.14	7–49	2	1
R.W.V. Robins	7	1523	789	31	25.45	6–32	1	–
G.R. Dilley	6	1302	681	28	24.32	5–55	1	–
C.M. Old	7	1457	677	27	25.07	5–21	2	–
J.H. Wardle	7	1748	616	23	26.78	4–33	–	–
D.V.P. Wright	5	1277	675	23	29.35	5–80	2	1
R. Illingworth	11	1750	560	22	25.45	6–29	1	–
T.E. Bailey	7	1151	530	20	26.50	7–44	1	1

AUSTRALIA	M	Balls	Runs	Wkts	Av	BB	5i	10m
C.T.B. Turner	3	821	278	19	14.63	6–67	3	1
G.F. Lawson	3	1057	496	18	27.56	7–81	1	–
D.K. Lillee	4	1190	584	17	34.35	4–43	–	–
R.A.L. Massie	1	361	137	16	8.56	8–53	2	1
R.R. Lindwall	2	556	223	15	14.87	5–66	2	–
E. Jones	3	672	301	13	23.15	7–88	1	1
W.W. Armstrong	4	719	185	12	15.42	6–35	1	–
J.J. Ferris	2	501	142	12	11.83	5–26	1	–
G.D. McKenzie	3	756	298	12	24.83	5–37	1	–

SOUTH AFRICA	M	Balls	Runs	Wkts	Av	BB	5i	10m
S.J. Pegler	3	575	279	11	25.36	7–65	1	–
X.C. Balaskas	1	354	103	9	11.44	5–49	1	–

WEST INDIES	M	Balls	Runs	Wkts	Av	BB	5i	10m
M.D. Marshall	2	611	262	18	14.56	6–32	2	1
V.A. Holder	3	694	278	12	23.17	4–56	–	–
S. Ramadhin	2	822	235	12	19.58	6–86	2	1
L.R. Gibbs	4	1168	414	11	37.64	3–26	–	–
C.C. Griffith	2	570	272	11	24.73	5–91	1	–
W.W. Hall	2	648	329	11	29.91	4–93	–	–
J. Garner	2	612	215	10	21.50	4–36	–	–
A.M.E. Roberts	2	503	197	10	19.70	5–60	2	1

NEW ZEALAND

R.J. Hadlee	3	1060	408	22	18.55	6–80	3	–
H.J. Howarth	2	978	312	12	26.00	4–144	–	–
R.O. Collinge	3	776	322	10	32.20	4–85	–	–
B.R. Taylor	3	761	360	10	36.00	3–35	–	–

INDIA

B.S. Bedi	4	1224	492	17	28.94	6–226	1	–
Kapil Dev	3	864	380	16	23.75	5–125	1	–
L. Amar Singh	2	683	230	10	23.00	6–35	1	–
B.S. Chandrasekhar	3	807	330	10	33.00	5–127	1	–
Mahomed Nissar	2	402	197	10	19.70	5–93	1	–

PAKISTAN

Mudassar Nazar	3	260	80	9	8.89	6–32	1	–
Imran Khan	3	707	277	8	34.63	2–48	–	–

SRI LANKA

A.L.F. de Mel	1	222	110	4	27.50	4–110	–	–
V.B. John	1	235	98	4	24.50	4–98	–	–
G.F. Labrooy	1	294	143	4	35.75	4–119	–	–

MOST WICKETS IN A MATCH

16-137	R.A.L. Massie	Australia v England	1972
15-104	H. Verity	England v Australia	1934
13-71	D.L. Underwood	England v Pakistan	1974
12-101	R. Tattersall	England v South Africa	1951
11-70	D.L. Underwood	England v New Zealand	1969
11-74	J. Briggs	England v Australia	1886
11-97	J.B. Statham	England v South Africa	1960
11-98	T.E. Bailey	England v West Indies	1957
11-110	S.F. Barnes	England v South Africa	1912
11-140	I.T. Botham	England v New Zealand	1978
11-145	A.V. Bedser	England v India	1946
11-152	S. Ramadhin	West Indies v England	1950
11-152	F.S. Trueman	England v West Indies	1963
11-173	T. Richardson	England v Australia	1896
10-63	C.T.B. Turner	Australia v England	1888
10-78	G.O.B. Allen	England v India	1936
10-92	M.D. Marshall	West Indies v England	1988
10-123	A.M.E. Roberts	West Indies v England	1976
10-152	K.R. Miller	Australia v England	1953
10-164	E. Jones	Australia v England	1899
10-175	D.V.P. Wright	England v South Africa	1947

The best match analyses for the other countries are:

9-103	X.C. Balaskas	South Africa v England	1935
8-135	R.J. Hadlee	New Zealand v England	1983

8-168	Kapil Dev	India v England	1982
6-38	Mudassar Nazar	Pakistan v England	1982
4-98	V.B. John	Sri Lanka v England	1984

MOST WICKETS IN AN INNINGS

8-34	I.T. Botham	England v Pakistan	1978
8-43	H. Verity	England v Australia	1934
8-51	D.L. Underwood	England v Pakistan	1974
8-53	R.A.L. Massie	Australia v England	1972
8-84	R.A.L. Massie	Australia v England	1972
8-103	I.T. Botham	England v West Indies	1984
7-32	D.L. Underwood	England v New Zealand	1969
7-36	G. Ulyett	England v Australia	1884
7-39	J.B. Statham	England v South Africa	1955
7-44	T.E. Bailey	England v West Indies	1957
7-49	A.V. Bedser	England v India	1946
7-52	R. Tattersall	England v South Africa	1951
7-61	H. Verity	England v Australia	1934
7-65	S.J. Pegler	South Africa v England	1912
7-78	R.G.D. Willis	England v Australia	1977
7-81	G.F. Lawson	Australia v England	1981
7-88	E. Jones	Australia v England	1899
7-128	A.E.E. Vogler	South Africa v England	1907

The best innings analyses for the other countries are:

6-32	Mudassar Nazar	Pakistan v England	1982
6-32	M.D. Marshall	West Indies v England	1988
6-35	L. Amar Singh	India v England	1936
6-80	R.J. Hadlee	New Zealand v England	1986
4-98	V.B. John	Sri Lanka v England	1984

I.T. Botham has taken five or more wickets in an innings eight times; F.S. Trueman achieved the feat on five occasions, D.L. Underwood four times. The record by an overseas bowler is three times, by C.T.B. Turner (Australia) and R.J. Hadlee (New Zealand)

HAT-TRICK

| G.M. Griffin | South Africa v England | 1960 |

Griffin dismissed M.J.K. Smith, P.M. Walker and F.S. Trueman with successive balls. Earlier in the innings he had been no-balled 11 times for throwing, becoming the only bowler to be 'called' in a Lord's Test.

D. Shackleton (England) took three wickets in four balls in 1963, dismissing J.S. Solomon, C.C. Griffith and L.R. Gibbs to end the West Indian innings

276

WICKETKEEPING

MOST DISMISSALS IN A MATCH

9	(8ct, 1st)	G.R.A. Langley	Australia v England	1956
8	(8ct)	A.T.W. Grout	Australia v England	1961
7	(6ct, 1st)	T.G. Evans	England v South Africa	1955
7	(6ct, 1st)	T.G. Evans	England v Australia	1956
6	(6ct)	W.A.S. Oldfield	Australia v England	1930
6	(6ct)	J.M. Parks	England v South Africa	1960
6	(6ct)	D.L. Murray	West Indies v England	1963
6	(6ct)	J.T. Murray	England v India	1967
6	(6ct)	P.R. Downton	England v West Indies	1988
5	(1ct, 4st)	J.M. Blackham	Australia v England	1888
5	(5ct)	A.E. Dick	New Zealand v England	1965
5	(5ct)	J.M. Parks	England v New Zealand	1965
5	(5ct)	J.M. Parks	England v West Indies	1966
5	(5ct)	K.J. Wadsworth	New Zealand v England	1969
5	(5ct)	R.W. Marsh	Australia v England	1972
5	(5ct)	A.P.E. Knott	England v India	1974
5	(4ct, 1st)	R.W. Taylor	England v New Zealand	1978
5	(5ct)	K.S. Moré	India v England	1986

MOST DISMISSALS IN AN INNINGS

6	(6ct)	J.T. Murray	England v India	1967
5	(5ct)	G.R.A. Langley	Australia v England	1956
5	(5ct)	A.T.W. Grout	Australia v England	1961
4	(4ct)	A.F.A. Lilley	England v Australia	1899
4	(4ct)	W.A.S. Oldfield	Australia v England	1930
4	(2ct, 2st)	C.L. Walcott	West Indies v England	1950
4	(3ct, 1st)	M.K. Mantri	India v England	1952
4	(3ct, 1st)	T.G. Evans	England v South Africa	1955
4	(4ct)	T.G. Evans	England v Australia	1956
4	(3ct, 1st)	G.R.A. Langley	Australia v England	1956
4	(4ct)	E.C. Petrie	New Zealand v England	1958
4	(4ct)	D.L. Murray	West Indies v England	1963
4	(4ct)	A.E. Dick	New Zealand v England	1965
4	(4ct)	K.J. Wadsworth	New Zealand v England	1969
4	(4ct)	A.P.E. Knott	England v Pakistan	1971

MOST DISMISSALS IN A CAREER

ENGLAND

37	(25ct, 12st)	T.G. Evans	13 matches
33	(32ct, 1st)	A.P.E. Knott	14 matches
23	(22ct, 1st)	R.W. Taylor	7 matches
22	(21ct, 1st)	J.M. Parks	6 matches
15	(15ct)	A.F.A. Lilley	6 matches
13	(13ct)	P.R. Downton	5 matches
11	(11ct)	J.T. Murray	3 matches

AUSTRALIA

14	(14ct)	R.W. Marsh	5 matches
12	(10ct, 2st)	G.R.A. Langley	2 matches

SOUTH AFRICA

6	(5ct, 1st)	H.B. Cameron	2 matches

WEST INDIES

15	(15ct)	D.L. Murray	4 matches

NEW ZEALAND

7	(7ct)	K.J. Wadsworth	2 matches

INDIA

5	(4ct, 1st)	F.M. Engineer	3 matches
5	(5ct)	K.S. Moré	1 match

PAKISTAN

10	(9ct, 1st)	Wasim Bari	5 matches

SRI LANKA

6	(6ct)	S.A.R. Silva	2 matches

FIELDERS

MOST CATCHES IN A MATCH

6	M.C. Cowdrey	England v West Indies	1963
6	G.S. Sobers	West Indies v England	1973
6	A.J. Lamb	England v New Zealand	1983
5	H. Sutcliffe	England v Australia	1926
5	G.B. Hole	Australia v England	1953
4	G.A. Lohmann	England v Australia	1888
4	H. Trumble	Australia v England	1899
4	W.J. Edrich	England v South Africa	1947
4	J.T. Ikin	England v South Africa	1951
4	P.H. Parfitt	England v Australia	1964
4	A.L. Wadekar	India v England	1971
4	H.J. Howarth	New Zealand v England	1973
4	A.W. Greig	England v Pakistan	1974
4	G. Cook	England v India	1982
4	A.R. Border	Australia v England	1985
4	D.C. Boon	Australia v England	1989

MOST CATCHES IN AN INNINGS

4	G.S. Sobers	West Indies v England	1973
4	A.J. Lamb	England v New Zealand	1983

On 26 occasions a fielder has taken three catches in an innings; M.C. Cowdrey did it four times, in 1962, 1963 (twice) and 1968

MOST CATCHES IN A CAREER

ENGLAND

20	M.C. Cowdrey	13 matches
20	W.R. Hammond	12 matches
15	G.A. Gooch	13 matches
14	A.J. Lamb	9 matches
12	T.W. Graveney	11 matches
12	R. Illingworth	11 matches
11	A.W. Greig	8 matches
11	L. Hutton	12 matches
10	H. Sutcliffe	8 matches
10	H. Verity	7 matches

AUSTRALIA

8	A.R. Border	4 matches
6	D.C. Boon	2 matches
6	G.S. Chappell	4 matches
6	S.J. McCabe	3 matches
6	H. Trumble	4 matches
6	K.D. Walters	4 matches

SOUTH AFRICA

4	R.A. McLean	2 matches
4	B. Mitchell	3 matches

WEST INDIES

8	G.S. Sobers	5 matches
5	R.C. Fredericks	3 matches
5	R.B. Kanhai	4 matches

Kanhai's total includes two catches taken while keeping wicket

NEW ZEALAND

6	B.E. Congdon	4 matches
5	M.D. Crowe	2 matches

INDIA

5	E.D. Solkar	2 matches
4	M. Jahangir Khan	2 matches
4	A.L. Wadekar	3 matches

PAKISTAN

4	Javed Miandad	3 matches
4	Mohsin Khan	2 matches

SRI LANKA

3	P.A. de Silva	2 matches

INDEX

The index contains only those mentioned in the match accounts.
Page numbers in *italics* refer to illustrations.

282

286

287

The publishers regret that some late changes to page design mean that certain of the numbers in the above index are incorrect. In these cases the reference to the player concerned will be found within one page of that stated.